VOICING
CREATION'S
PRAISE

VOICING CREATION'S PRAISE

TOWARDS A THEOLOGY
OF THE ARTS

JEREMY BEGBIE

continuum
T&T CLARK

T&T Clark
A Continuum imprint

Continuum

The Tower Building
11 York Road
London SE1 7NX

80 Maiden Lane
Suite 704
New York, NY 10038

www.continuumbooks.com

First published 1991
Latest impression 1998, 2006

British Library Cataloguing-in-Publication Data
A catalogue record for this book is available from the British Library

ISBN 0 567 29188 X

Typeset by Trinity Typesetting, Edinburgh
Printed and bound in Great Britain by MPG Digital Solutions, Bodmin, Cornwall

To R. C. J. B.

Contents

Preface

My grateful thanks are due first of all to Professor James B. Torrance who acted as my supervisor for the research out of which this book grew. I shall always be profoundly appreciative of his consistent depth of insight, patience, warm encouragement, and the gentleness with which he deals with his fellow theologians. Professor Colin Gunton of King's College, London has read the manuscript and offered valuable and penetrating comments as well as writing a generous foreword. Pages of out-dated Dutch were skilfully translated by Nelleke Scherff. I have also benefited greatly from conversations with Dr Alan Lewis, Dr Stephen May, Professor Alan Torrance and the Rev Malcolm Guite. To these and the many others who have helped me in so many ways, I should like to express my immense gratitude. Needless to say, I take full responsibility for any inadequacies in the text.

This project would not have seen its present form if it were not for the Principal, Hugo de Waal, and the staff and students of Ridley Hall, Cambridge who have graciously tolerated a Director of Studies who chooses to write as well as teach. My parents also deserve special mention for their unstinting practical support without which this endeavour would have been quite impossible. Above all, I owe an incalculable debt to my wife Rachel and my children Helen, Mark and Heather, who, without complaint, have revealed to me an entirely new dimension of Paul's words: 'waiting in eager expectation'.

Jeremy Begbie
Ridley Hall, Cambridge
Pentecost, 1990

Foreword

The word 'fragmentation' is often used to characterise the apparent disorder that marks modern culture, whose complexity is in so many ways not enriching, but a scene of sterile self-assertion, self-expression and conflict. At the heart of the disorder is a fragmentation of experience, so that our worlds of thought, action and expression appear to exist independently of, or in conflict with one another. The causes of the development are many, but the intellectual shape of the fragmentation can be expressed quite simply. The three great transcendentals of traditional philosophical enquiry — truth, goodness and beauty — are no longer seen to be all truly universal features of our world existing in harmonious interrelationship. The outcome is that truth — if objective truth is believed to exist at all — is widely thought to be the province solely of the scientist, whose work accordingly appears either to be unrelated to the deeper meaning of things or, worse, to impose a view of an empty and meaningless universe.

It is part of the paradox of the modern age that science's discoveries of the sheer beauty, unity and rationality of the universe co-exist with assertions of its essential meaninglessness or indifference to moral values. In face of such a world, human morality appears simply an exercise in self-assertion, in tilting against windmills of unmeaning. Similarly it may be believed that the indifference of the universe to human value entails that there is no true beauty to be discerned and expressed by the artist, whose task becomes accordingly the expression of subjective 'creativity' or experience, and who thus effects the compounding rather than the healing of fragmentation.

Christian theology is part of culture, being one of the forms which human rational and symbolic activity takes. As such, it shares in the fragmentation which we experience. It does so in two senses. In the first place, it is itself fragmented, both within and between its various sub-disciplines. It has always been diverse, of course, but it is doubtful if there has been, except perhaps in its earliest days, so widespread disagreement about what it is and what it ought to be doing. Second, and in parallel with this, it has developed an insularity and self-preoccupation which have prevented its engagement with other disciplines which have in previous times been in more fruitful interaction with it.

There is even a sense in which theology is the cause of modern intellectual fragmentation, particularly in relation to the arts. As Dr Begbie notes in his preface, Christianity has tended to be ambivalent about the arts, at once fostering and developing them and yet always ready to doubt their true value. And yet if theology has a responsibility to give some account of human culture, it can scarcely ignore so universal a feature of our experience. The importance of *Voicing Creation's Praise* is that by engaging with the strengths and weaknesses of recent theological treatment of aesthetics, it engages with the very root of cultural fragmentation.

Readers of this book will find much of relevance both to the problems of modern culture and life and to the responsibility of theology in assisting a healing of our fragmentation. It is interesting that Paul Tillich, the first major figure to be treated, made the overcoming of fragmentation one of his major concerns from the very beginning of his theological career. According to Dr Begbie, he has much to say to us, particularly in respect to theology's responsibility to culture and its need to take seriously — as, for example, some revivalist hymns do not — modern alienation and loss of faith. There are, however, some sharp criticisms of Tillich, both as an interpreter of art and more particularly concerning what can be called the docetic or idealising aspects of his aesthetics and theology.

Tillich's aesthetics have been much discussed in recent scholarship. Counterposed to him are a group of Dutch Neo-Calvinists of the school of Abraham Kuyper who are less celebrated figures. Not being familiar with the work of these writers, which continues to this day, I was excited by the account. Here are interesting contributions from the Calvinist tradition to a theology of art and meaning. At the very least, this section should lay to rest the slander that the tradition of Calvin and Jonathan Ewards has no contribution to make to aesthetics. But the Neo-Calvinists, too, are found by the author to be wanting in certain important respects. In particular, their tendency to separate the order of creation from the order of redemption—one of the features of their thought which has, apparently, been used by some to aid the development of *apartheid* doctrine—vitiates their otherwise promising theology.

The third section of the book develops a theology in which creation and redemption are held together with the help of Christological and trinitarian conceptuality. In this light, and with the help of other recent authors who have probed the weaknesses of modernity — a growing band, one could almost say galaxy, from Polanyi and Gadamer to the much lamented

Peter Fuller — the roots of modern fragmentation are exposed. Many sides of developments up to and since Kant are explored, but two of them are of particular importance: the loss of a due appreciation of the place of the material world and the isolation of art from everyday life and affairs. We come to realise as we read how simply *odd* is the modern world: pictures simply for contemplation, not for painting; music simply for listening, rather than for playing. The alienation of art is one fact of the social alienation, the fragmentation of social life, that is such a feature of our time.

One of the most interesting features of the book is its treatment of the concept of beauty. Dr Begbie shows that too great a stress on it leads to a platonizing denial not only of the material world, but of its fallenness. A theological account of aesthetics may not forget the fact that redemption is achieved only through the death of him who had 'no beauty that we should desire him'. Beauty is a part of the matter, but not the whole. That elusive reality is sought with the help of metaphor, which Dr Begbie claims to be the key to the nature of art. Here he explores not only the rather fragmentary thought of Polanyi on the topic, but Leonard Bernstein's theory of music as metaphor — one instance of the richness and diversity of the material which has been drawn on. Metaphor, like art, is irreducible to other features of our world and experience, and yet in essential relation to them. The end product of the book's argument is a cognitive view of art, one which relates both to other features of our experience and to our embodied and social reality.

The heart of modern fragmentation derives in the final analysis from the attempt to locate the unity of the cosmos in human thought or agency. Cultural fragmentation is in the last analysis to be diagnosed theologically, for it is only through the concept of a reality giving unity — albeit a unity in diversity — to the world that the interrelatedness of things can be maintained. The Christian theological contribution to a healing of our sickness will derive, as this book shows, from a renewal first of Christology, where we witness God's involvement with and redemption of the material world; and second of trinitarian theology, where we may find the heart of our social being. It is as the one who became incarnate that the eternal Son enables us to encompass at once the sovereignty of God over the world and the goodness of the human culture which takes place on the soil of the material creation. To that process of renewal and healing, this book makes a real contribution.

Professor Colin E. Gunton
King's College, London

Prologue

For many years I have been fascinated by the relationship between the arts and the Christian faith. From an early age, I intended to pursue a career in music. When I sensed a call to ordination, it was natural that many urged me not to let my interest in music wane. Before long I was plunged into the exhilarating world of theology. My eyes were opened to the immensity of God's purposes. I was assured that nothing need be excluded from the transforming influence of Jesus Christ — the arts included. Yet I soon discovered that there was little written to assist me in making the links between the world of the arts and the new-found world of the Christian Gospel. When I stumbled across these words of Dorothy Sayers, I could only concur.

> "In such a thing as politics, finance, sociology, and so on, there really is a philosophy and a Christian tradition; we do know more or less what the church has said and thought about them, how they are related to Christian dogma, and what they are supposed to do in a Christian country.
>
> But oddly enough, we have no Christian aesthetic — no Christian philosophy of the Arts. The Church as a body has never made up her mind about the Arts, and it is hardly too much to say that she has never tried. She has, of course, from time to time puritanically denounced the Arts as irreligious and mischievous, or tried to exploit the Arts as a means to the teaching of religion and morals...............And there have, of course, been plenty of writers on aesthetics who happened to be Christians, but they seldom made any consistent attempt to relate their aesthetic to the central Christian dogmas."[1]

Of course, Sayers is overstating her case. Though the philosophy of art has never played a major part in theology, some of our illustrious forebears — Augustine and Aquinas among them — have explored the field at length and attempted to relate what they have found to their systematic theology. But as far as the last two centuries of Protestant theology are concerned, Sayers' remarks are distinctly apt: scant attention has been paid to the connections between art and the 'central Christian dogmas'.

Nevertheless, in modern Protestantism, there are two significant exceptions amidst this rather bleak state of affairs. One is the German theologian Paul Tillich, the other is the Dutch Neo-Calvinist tradition stemming from the nineteenth-century scholar Abraham Kuyper. Both Tillich and the Dutch Neo-Calvinists make a serious and rigorous attempt to come to terms with the arts theologically. In Parts I and II of this book, I propose to elucidate and assess their views on art in the light of the theology they assume. In Part III, I shall attempt to outline a third way forward for a Christian perspective on the arts, based on rather different theological foundations.

An important question needs to be addressed at the outset, one which it would be all too easy to evade, namely: why should the theologian spend any time on this topic at all? Is there anything particularly reprehensible about modern theologians showing so little interest in the arts? Is art not simply a luxurious ornament to our lives, a distraction for those who have spare time on their hands? After all, in any given society, the number of people who care deeply about the arts is relatively small. Compared to the other pressing issues of our day — the population explosion, the ecological crisis, mass starvation — the arts seem a somewhat trivial concern.

Space forbids a lengthy reply, but a number of brief points should be made. First of all, we know of no people or race at any time which has not practised art in some form. The anthropologist Raymond Firth writes:

> "It is commonly held that economic activity is a necessity, but that art is a luxury. Yet we can assert empirically the universality of art in man's social history........Even in the hardest natural environments, art has been produced........It is easy, then, to refute the idea that at the primitive stages of man's existence the theme of subsistence dominated his life to the exclusion of the arts."[2]

Considering this widespread prevalence of art in the past, it would seem odd if theologians did not in some manner make an effort to engage with the arts at depth. To extend the same point, second, art is an unavoidable phenomenon in the everyday life of contemporary Western culture. Scarcely a day passes when a person is not confronted with or surrounded by objects which are generally agreed to be 'works of art'. Would it not be strange, to say the least, if there were no theological comment to be made about so omnipresent a feature of our lives? Third, rarely has there been a period when the Church has ceased altogether to employ at least one type of art in its worship and mission. To examine art theologically will not only suggest some reasons for this persistent partnership, it might also indicate ways in which the arts could be contributing more effectively to the realisation of the Church's calling in the world. Fourth, as a host of recent scholars have impressed upon us, many issues in biblical hermeneutics are significantly illuminated by a careful study of the arts, not least the way in which meaning is realised in myth, narrative, parable and allegory. Fifth, it is generally agreed that at their greatest, the arts are capable of reflecting the character of a culture or age in a unique and profound way. This would suggest that, as a recent writer puts it, "if theologians did not attend at all to what is taking place in the contemporary arts, their understanding of man's being in the world would undoubtedly become even less pertinent to our needs and hopes than it now seems to be."[3] Sixth, and finally, a somewhat less obvious consideration needs to be brought to the fore, highlighted in George Steiner's remarkable book *Real Presences*.[4] Steiner is convinced that works of art enact "a root-impulse of the human spirit to explore possibilities of meaning and of truth that lie outside empirical seizure or proof.......Serious music, art, literature, in their own wager on survivance, are refusals of analytic-empirical criteria of constraint." He continues: "it is, I believe, poetry, art and music which relate us most directly to that in being which is not ours."[5] The subtleties of Steiner's reflective argument cannot be explored here, but the fact that many have endorsed his conviction that "there is some fundamental encounter with transcendence in the creation of art and in its experiencing"[6] should at least begin to prompt the theologian into a careful estimation of art and its possible links with the divine.

A number of further preliminary comments need to be made before we begin. First, with regard to the section on Paul Tillich, I should acknowledge my indebtedness to the fine work of Michael Palmer, *Paul Tillich's Philosophy of Art*. It is a book of enormous erudition and thoroughness, and my criticisms of Tillich in chapter 6 of Part I overlap and concur with much of what Palmer says. My own approach to Tillich, however, is significantly different. Palmer proceeds thematically, whereas I have adopted a chronological approach which charts the growth of Tillich's philosophy of art alongside the development of his philosophy and theology. This, I believe, helps us to see more clearly the interplay between his views on art and the basic convictions which undergird them. Moreover, I hope that something extra will be gained by comparing and contrasting

Tillich with other theological traditions, especially Dutch Neo-Calvinism.

Second, the terms 'art', 'aesthetic' and 'aesthetics' need clarifying. I am using the word 'art' in a very wide sense to refer to what most most people would understand by 'the arts' - painting, music, poetry, dance, drama, etc. (This of course begs many questions about what we are to include and exclude under the heading 'art', some of which I shall tackle later but which need not detain us here.) As far as 'aesthetic' is concerned, the word is sometimes taken to refer to a particular type of experience or attitude — typically one of detached contemplation with a view to the apprehension of form — which may or may not be directed towards a work of art.[7] On this basis a distinction is often made between 'aesthetics' or 'a theory of the aesthetic' which seeks to give an account of the aesthetic attitude and aesthetic objects in general, and 'the philosophy of art' which is devoted to the study of the concept of art and works of art. This seems to me a helpful distinction and will govern my use of the terms 'aesthetic', 'aesthetics' and 'philosophy of art' throughout (unless stated otherwise). Although questions about aesthetic apprehension in general will inevitably arise, my primary interest in this book is in the philosophy of art.

Third, due primarily to lack of space, I have had to confine myself to the bearing of theology on the arts. No doubt there will be many who are more interested in the reverse question — what can the arts offer to theology? Of course the two are interrelated, and in Tillich's case they are so inseparable that I have to deal with both. Nevertheless, even with Tillich, and certainly for the remainder of the book, my major concern is with what theology can bring to the task of understanding and enhancing the arts, not what the arts can bring to theology.

Fourth, I have limited the field mainly to Protestant theology. This is not to suggest that other contributions in this area are insignificant, only that to do them justice would make the length of this study unmanageable. This in part explains why I have not given the work of Hans Urs von Balthasar more attention, despite his magnificent multi-volume work on theological aesthetics, *The Glory of the Lord*. Furthermore, while acknowledging the wealth of insight into the arts which he offers, von Balthasar's main interest is in exploring the bearing of aesthetics on theology. He bids us look at theology as showing forth a certain form whose inner radiance is beauty and whose various manifestations are mediations of this original form of beauty. While not denying the legitimacy of this enterprise, my own work, as I have just indicated, moves in the other direction.

Fifth, Christian discussions about the arts have a habit of gravitating quickly around ethical questions. How should we react to a piece of art which includes scenes of blatant pornography? How are we to assess works like Verdi's *Requiem*, written by a man who made no claim to religious faith? Is rock music intrinsically evil? Should a Christian support censorship in the arts? Such questions are very much alive and express proper concerns. But it is my belief that they can only be tackled if we set them against a broader, theological canvas. Though we cannot exclude moral issues, one of the main aims of this study is to maintain a theological (rather than ethical) focus in our dicsussion, to enquire as to how the arts might relate to the character and purposes of God for his world.

Finally, for economy of style, I have used masculine terms when referring to an artist or theologian in general; such terms should of course, be understood inclusively.

With these points in mind, let us now turn to the first of our 'theologians of art', Paul Tillich.

Notes

1 "Towards a Christian Aesthetic," as quoted in Nicholas Wolterstorff, *Art in Action*, Grand Rapids, Michigan: Eerdmans, 1980, p. ix.
2 "The Social Framework of Primitive Art," in *The Many Faces of Primitive Art*, ed. Douglas Fraser, Englewood Cliffs, New Jersey: Prentice-Hall, 1966, p. 12. Cp. Paul S. Wingert: "There were no primitive peoples, however meagre their cultural achievements, who offered no patronage to the artist." *Primitive Art*, New York: Meridian Books, 1965, p. 18.
3 Roger Hazelton, *A Theological Approach to Art*, Nashville and New York: Abingdon Press, 1967, p. 14.
4 London: Faber & Faber, 1989.
5 *Ibid.*, pp. 225, 226.
6 *Ibid.*, p. 228.
7 For a summary of these approaches, cf. George Dickie, *Aesthetics: An Introduction*, Indianapolis, Indiana: Bobbs-Merrill Educational Publishing, 1979, pp. 43ff.

Part I

Paul Tillich —
Art and Ultimate Reality

1. Introduction

There must be few theologians of this century for whom art has been more important than Paul Tillich (1886-1965). In addition to being a valuable means of recreation, it also served as a source of immense intellectual stimulation. As enthusiasts of Tillich will know well, nearly every one of his major works refers to art at some stage, often at considerable length. He seems to have been constantly excited by the implications of art for his work as a philosopher and theologian. His friends tell us that he was "a delightful companion in an art gallery or museum; he talked little but was visibly absorbed and markedly relaxed. Throughout his life he made pilgrimages to great art collections all over the world, returning to them again and again, often in the company of friends."[1] Certainly, Tillich never claimed to be a connoisseur of art, nor an expert aesthetician. His tastes were somewhat eccentric and limited, his knowledge of the history of art patchy and at times superficial. He had little interest in the philosophy of art as such and never tried to devise an aesthetic system in the manner of some of his great German predecessors. Nevertheless, if we collate carefully his reflections on the arts - scattered over many books, articles, essays and lectures - the outline of a consistent and fascinating art-philosophy emerges, with its own distinctive shape and emphases, worthy of serious attention by both theologians and aestheticians. It will be our task here to elucidate this latent philosophy of art and expose it to critical assessment.

We shall quickly discover that Tillich's understanding of art was profoundly affected by his philosophy and theology. This is hardly surprising: he had a passionate desire to relate the whole of culture to an all-embracing theory of meaning and being. But we shall also find that the influence worked both ways: not only did philosophy and theology bear on his philosophy of art, but his encounter with art to a significant extent moulded his central philosophical and theological ideas. It is this two-way influence which makes Tillich so intriguing and enriching to study. In order to bring out this mutual penetration as clearly as possible, the method I propose to adopt below is chronological: to trace the gradual development of Tillich's theory of art in parallel with the evolution of his metaphysics and ontology. This is best tackled in three parts: first, by examining his works up to and including those of 1925, second, those which date from the period from 1925 to 1933, and lastly, those written after 1933.

Notes
[1] Wilhelm and Marion Pauck, *Paul Tillich: His Life & Thought*, 1, London: Collins, 1977, p. 79.

2. Foundations (1919-1925)

"The truth of science is correctness; the truth of art is power of expression."

Tillich, *The System of Sciences*

In the spring of 1919, Tillich, by this time a university graduate and minister of the German Evangelical Lutheran Church, became a *Privatdozent* or free-lance instructor at Berlin University. A post of this kind was normally seen as an opportunity for promising young teachers to establish themselves through articles and books with a view to an academic career. By 1924, it seems that Tillich had sufficiently impressed his contemporaries to be granted an associate professorship of theology at Marburg University, and there he remained for three semesters. Commentators are generally agreed that it was in Berlin and Marburg that the foundations of his thought were firmly laid. Certainly, as far as his thinking on the arts is concerned, there is virtually nothing he writes later which cannot be traced to themes he expounded in these early years. It will therefore be worth our while to consider at some length this seminal period.

(1) The Philosophy of Meaning

Speaking of his book of 1923, *The System of Sciences*, in which he lays out the theoretical basis of his early metaphysics, Tillich tells us that the keystone of the whole edifice is the philosophy of meaning (*Sinnphilosophie*).[1] This, then, is where we must begin. Two preliminary comments need to be made to set the stage. First, amidst the complex terminology and tangled arguments which are so typical of the early Tillich, it would be easy to forget that his motivation was primarily practical. Everything he wrote flowed out of a longing to counteract what he felt to be a sense of meaninglessness and futility in his own culture. The first World War effectively marked the breakdown of an old order, the end of a great historical epoch, the collapse of traditional conceptions of God and religion. Tillich was acutely sensitive to these social, political and religious uncertainties, and believed that philosophers and theologians would be foolish

3

to ignore them. He later recalled:

> "The political problems [of this period] determined our whole
> existence; even after revolution and inflation they were
> matters of life and death. The social structure was in a state
> of dissolution, the human relations with respect to authority,
> education, family, sex, friendship and pleasure were in a
> creative chaos. Revolutionary art came into the foreground,
> supported by the Republic, attacked by the majority of people.
> Psychoanalytic ideas spread and produced a consciousness of
> realities which had been carefully repressed in previous
> generations. The participation in these movements created
> manifold problems, conflicts, fears, expectations, ecstasies and
> despairs, practically as well as theoretically. All this was at
> the same time material for an apologetic theology."[2]

Tillich's deeply felt concern for the struggles of his age is obvious
here. It would have been unthinkable for Tillich to have turned
his back on the complex issues they posed. And the way he
chose to tackle them was to offer a comprehensive account of
the meaning of existence at every possible level. The second
point to bear in mind is that Tillich belonged to a long line of
mainly German thinkers — such as Hegel, Fichte, Schelling,
Kant, Dilthey, Troeltsch — who saw the question of meaning
as crucial for both philosophy and theology. In developing a
philosophy of meaning, Tillich did not see himself as initiating
something radically novel. Rather he was consciously drawing
on a rich philosophical and theological heritage, one which he
knew intimately and believed had the potential to be fruitful
for his own era.

The Creation of Meaning

Now to the content of Tillich's philosophy of meaning. The
three basic components are pure thinking (*Denken*), pure being
(*Sein*), and spirit (*Geist*); or, to put it differently, the act of
thinking, that to which thought is directed, and the power of
human creativity which relates and fuses thought and being.[3]
In the case of logic and mathematics (the sciences of thinking),
universal concepts or laws of thought are formulated *a priori*,
apart from any particular facts or experiences. In the natural
sciences, thought is determined by being, by the network of
cause and effect in which objects are observed. In the activity
of *Geist*, thought frees itself both from the attitude of
subservience to reality (as in the natural sciences), and from
the attitude of abstraction from reality (as in logic and
mathematics). When this happens, there is an interaction

between thought and being, resulting in something which is not deducible from pure thought, nor from pure being, but which reaches beyond both.[4] Such is the inner dynamic of human creativity. Something new and unique is brought into existence which does not derive simply from our thought, nor simply from what is given in the physical world, but from an engagement between both. The power which makes this possible is *Geist* or spirit. Spirit enables and propels the dynamic process of creativity in humankind. The act of creating something, the cultural act, can therefore be spoken of as a 'spiritual act'.

Another way in which Tillich expresses this coalescence of thought and being is in terms of the realisation of meaning (*Sinn*). When thinking and being are interrelated in human culture through the power of *Geist*, meaning is achieved, a new form of the meaning of life is created — a 'Spirit-bearing form' (*Gestalt*).[5] *Geist* is thus the medium for "the actualisation of meaning (*Sinnvollzug*)".[6]   Luther Adams paraphrases Tillich thus:

> "Spirit is.........creative in the realm of meaning.......it is characteristically oriented to the realm of meaning; where individuality expresses itself by living in and beyond reality, by accommodating itself to the realm of being but also giving to being a novel expression."[7]

Tillich enlarges on this by distinguishing three elements in the awareness of meaning:

> "First, an awareness of the context of meaning in which every separate meaning stands out and without which it would be meaningless. Second, an awareness of the ultimate meaning of the context of meaning and through that, of every particular meaning, i.e. the consciousness of an unconditioned meaning which is present in every particular meaning. Third, an awareness of the demand under which a particular meaning stands, to fulfil the unconditioned meaning."[8]

The underlying 'unconditioned meaning' is not one meaning among others, but is itself the ground of all meaningfulness and all particular forms of meaning: the meaningfulness that gives to every particular meaning its reality and significance. It is — to introduce another of Tillich's key terms — the 'import (*Gehalt*)' of meaning. *Gehalt* is the *prius* and goal of every individual apprehension of meaning.[9]

Form, Gehalt and Inhalt

We are now in a position to approach one of the most crucial conceptual models of Tillich's early metaphysics. Every spiritual act, he claims, has three aspects to it: form (*Form*), import (*Gehalt*), and content (*Inhalt*).[10] "By *Inhalt* we mean something objective in its simple existence which is taken up through form (*Form*) into the spiritual-cultural sphere." By *Gehalt* "one is to understand the meaning (*der Sinn*), the spiritual substantiality, which alone gives significance to form. *Gehalt* is grasped in an *Inhalt* by means of a *Form* and brought to expression."[11] Tillich proceeds to assimilate *Inhalt* into *Form* and to reduce the former's significance considerably:

> "*Inhalt* is the contingent element, *Gehalt* the essential one and form the mediating agent. The *Form* must be appropriate to the *Inhalt*, so that no antithesis occurs between cultivation of *Form* and cultivation of *Inhalt*. Rather, they stand together on one side, whereas the cultivation of *Gehalt* stands on the other. The shattering of *Form* by *Gehalt* is identical with *Inhalt's* becoming insignificant and unessential. *Form* loses its necessary connection with *Inhalt*, because *Inhalt* is lost sight of in comparison with the overwhelming intensity of *Gehalt*. Thereby *Form* becomes somewhat detached, or free-floating, so that it is related directly to *Gehalt* and loses its natural and necessary relationship to *Inhalt*. In this way it becomes *Form* in a paradoxical sense in that it allows its own natural connection to be shattered by *Gehalt*."[12]

The relationship between the three elements is made somewhat clearer by means of an illustration:

> "If we imagine the import (or ultimate meaning) (*Gehalt*) to be the sun, and form the orbit of the planet, then for every form of culture there is proximity to and distance from the sun or the import. If on the one hand it is the power of the sun which is revealed in the nearness to the sun it is on the other hand the peculiar power in the movement of the planets which is expressed in the distance from the sun; and yet, it is the sun itself which supports both nearness and distance."[13]

This passage would suggest that Tillich sees the primary tension in the spiritual act not between *Inhalt* and *Form*, but between *Gehalt* and *Form*, between unconditioned meaning and the conditioned forms through which that meaning is made explicit.

(2) Religion and Culture

The dialectic between *Form* and *Gehalt* equips Tillich with his major tool for understanding the relationship between religion and culture. He claims that "If consciousness is directed toward the particular forms of meaning and their unity, we have to do with *culture*; if it is directed toward the unconditional meaning, toward the import of meaning, we have *religion*."[14] And because form and import belong together — we cannot posit one without the other — every cultural act is ultimately based on, contains and receives its power from, the import of meaning. Every cultural act is therefore implicitly religious, even if not by intention. It is necessarily rooted in the unconditioned meaning or ground of all meaning. "Culture as culture is.......substantially, but not intentionally, religious."[15] Any act which deliberately attempts to free itself from unconditioned meaning cannot be a meaning-fulfilling act, for meaning is only realised when form and import, the conditioned and the unconditioned, are brought together.[16] By the same token, a religious act can only direct itself toward the unconditioned *through* particular forms of meaning. Every religious act is, from the point of view of form, cultural. So, Tillich concludes, in the case of the cultural act, "the religious is substantial; in the religious act the cultural is formal."[17] Or, in his famous dictum, *"As religion is the substance of culture, so culture is the form of religion."*[18]

Tillich's overriding concern here was to overcome the damaging and destructive dualism between religion and culture which he believed was painfully evident in Europe during the aftermath of the first World War. On returning from that horrendous conflict, he spoke of "a deep gap between the cultural revolution and the religious tradition in central and eastern Europe". It was obvious for "those of us with spiritual ties with both sides that this situation was intolerable".[19] This "double existence" had to "be abolished at all costs".[20] By means of his theology of culture, Tillich sought to provide a theoretical framework which would help to heal the rift. A mood of vibrant optimism drove Tillich and his associates: "we believed that a new beginning, a period of radical transformation..........had come upon us".[21] "We believed it was possible to close the gap [between religion and culture] partly by creating movements such as religious socialism, partly by a fresh interpretation of the mutual immanence of religion and culture within each other."[22]

Vital to this 'fresh interpretation' was the spurning any view of religion which relegated it to a separate sphere or department of life. Repeatedly Tillich launches swingeing attacks on any such notion. Religion, he declares,

> "cannot allow itself to become a special area within culture,
> or to take a position beside culture..........In either case, religion

becomes superfluous and must disappear because the structure of culture is completed and self-contained without
religion."[23]

Or again,

"Religion..........is not one meaning-function alongside others
..........That which is the basis of all functions of meaning
cannot itself be one of those functions."[24]

In Tillich's view, we cannot assign religion to the theoretical
sphere (as in Hegel) or to morality (Kant) or to the realm of
feeling (Schleiermacher). Religion is a dimension of the spirit
which combines and relates all three in a complex whole. It is
not "one function alongside others" but "an attitude in all the
other functions."[25] Religion needs to be constantly rediscovered
as that which undergirds all human activity, including those
parts of life normally dissociated from it. The transparency of
culture to the religious dimension must be brought to bear on
all cultural activities if culture is ever to attain a genuine unity.

(3) Autonomy, Heteronomy and Theonomy

At this point, a further conceptual triad needs to be introduced,
one which pervades nearly all of Tillich's writings throughout
his life: autonomy, heteronomy and theonomy.[26] If, as we have
seen, religion is directedness toward the unconditioned, and
culture is directedness toward the conditioned, the fulfilment of
culture is only possible when culture gives expression to the
unconditioned meaning through its forms. If, however, culture
relates to conditioned forms without giving due attention to the
unconditioned, the result is autonomy (*Autonomie*). Autonomous
culture pays heed to *Form* — thought-forms, social forms etc.,
but tries to free itself from obedience to unconditioned meaning.
Hence, "left to its own devices [it] leads to increasing
emptiness."[27] As examples of an autonomous attitude, Tillich
cites those who take refuge in traditional religious symbols and
rites without ever questioning their validity, and those who
attempt to drive religion and culture apart and confine religion
to a kind of spiritual ghetto.[28] Autonomy is also seen in
'naturalism', that world-view which effectively denies the reality
of anything beyond what we sense directly, and which thus
eliminates the unconditional entirely.[29] Heteronomy (*Heter-*

onomie) stands at the opposite end of the spectrum, arising out of a desire to reaffirm the unconditioned against autonomy. The failing of heteronomy is that it attempts to grasp import apart from form, or, more commonly, tries to limit unconditioned import to certain particular, conditioned forms. One type of heteronomous culture, for example, tends to invest the Church with ultimacy and infallibility. But in so elevating one conditioned form in this way, heteronomy forgets that the infinite cannot be swallowed up by a portion of the finite, and that religion cannot be restricted to a particular area of cultural life. In other words, heteronomy repeatedly loses sight of the autonomy of *Form*.[30] A heteronomous world-view is seen best in 'supranaturalism' (the opposite of naturalism) where God is treated as some kind of object or entity utterly beyond the realm of nature. As we would expect, supranaturalist theology was one of Tillich's lifelong bête noires.[31]

As Tillich sees the matter, autonomy and heteronomy tend to topple over into each other. For instance, heteronomous political and religious ideologies have commonly arisen, so Tillich believes, in protest against the naturalistic and autonomous character of modern secular culture. But neither autonomy nor heteronomy can adequately relate the absolute and the relative, the unconditioned and the conditioned. This is why Tillich introduces a third concept, that of theonomy (*Theonomie*).[32] Theonomy is seen when the unconditioned demand for meaning is conjoined with the autonomous consciousness of form. In theonomy, import shatters, without destroying, autonomous forms, breaking through them, revealing their inadequacy, while at the same time pointing to the ultimate meaning-reality they contain.[33] A theonomous culture neither ignores the unconditioned nor idolises a finite form, but allows the unconditioned to break into and through conditioned forms of meaning.

(4) The System of Sciences

Classifying the Sciences

In order to complete our sketch of Tillich's early philosophy and theology, something needs to be said about the way in which he sets out and relates the various disciplines of human enquiry in *The System of Sciences*.[34] The triad of thought, being and spirit leads to Tillich distinguishing between the sciences of thinking (*die Denkwissenschaften*), the empirical sciences (*die*

Seinswissenschaften), and the cultural sciences or 'sciences of the spirit (*die Geisteswissenschaften*)'. The first group comprises logic and mathematics; the second, the descriptive sciences (including physics, chemistry, biology, sociology, psychology, history, anthropology, ethnology etc.), and the third, epistemology, aesthetics, metaphysics, political science and ethics. The sciences of thought possess a certainty lacking in other kinds of knowledge for they are concerned with the universal laws of meaning (what Tillich calls the 'valid'). In the empirical sciences, thought is directed towards things with a view to correct description. In the cultural sciences, however, the object of thought is not *a priori*, nor pre-given, but is created, born in the dynamic process of *Geist*.[35]

The unique character of the spiritual or cultural act requires a special method to investigate it and understand it correctly. Above all, we must take into account the commitment of the individual who performs the act: *"the standpoint of the systematic thinker belongs to the heart of the matter itself"*.[36] An approach is needed which transcends both formal logic (the analysis of universal thought-forms) and the empirical method of investigating particular entities. Somehow we need to move with *Geist* beyond thought and being. This can be achieved, so Tillich believes, using a 'metalogical' method — logical "because of the forms of thought, metalogical because of the import of being."[37] Logical forms are penetrated to see that which transcends all particular forms of thought, and being is approached as 'living import', not simply as 'object'. From the point of view of metalogic, being can be defined as 'the principle of the unconditionally real', and thought as 'the principle of the unconditionally valid'. In the spiritual act, both principles are operative. The metalogical method, with regard to being, seeks to apprehend import; with regard to thought (which is now seen as the unconditionally valid), it sets up norms 'in an individual-creative way', that is, in a manner which recognises that we are both the subject and object of the investigation.[38]

Tillich goes on to argue that the product of a cultural act, the spirit-bearing *Gestalt*, can relate itself either to thought or to being. This gives Tillich the means to distinguish between the 'theoretical' and 'practical' cultural sciences.[39] Examples of the former are metaphysics and epistemology; of the latter, ethics and political science. Further, the spiritual act may be directed either towards the individual form and the individual existence (the 'supporting function'), or it may be directed toward the unconditioned (the 'supported function'). Supported functions themselves can be directed toward either forms, or toward the

unconditioned which these forms express.[40] I have attempted
to summarise this diagrammatically:

Fig. 1

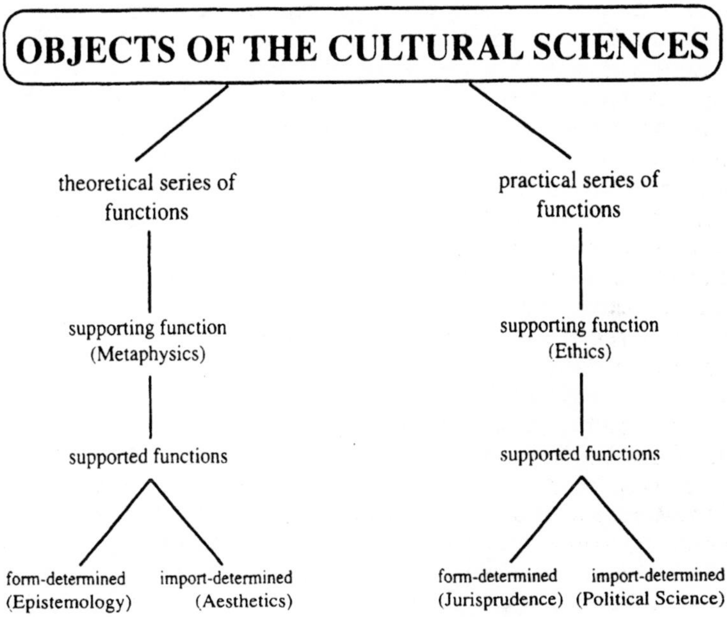

OBJECTS OF THE CULTURAL SCIENCES

theoretical series of functions	practical series of functions
supporting function (Metaphysics)	supporting function (Ethics)
supported functions	supported functions
form-determined (Epistemology)　import-determined (Aesthetics)	form-determined (Jurisprudence)　import-determined (Political Science)

Every cultural science is given a tripartite classification. First,
each must make clear its principles of meaning (the *a priori*
universal forms appropriate to it); second, each must outline
the material of meaning (a history of the particular realisations
of meaning within that sphere); and third, each must address
itself to the task of setting up norms of meaning.[41] For example,
in ethics, we have, first, the philosophy of ethics (which
addresses questions about the nature of ethics in general),
second, the history of ethics, and third, the normative science
of ethics (which deals with the norms of right and wrong, good
and bad). A theology of culture is subject to the same three-
fold division appropriate to all the cultural sciences. It consists
of, first, the philosophy of culture "which is concerned with the
universal forms, the *a priori* of all culture"; second, the
philosophy of the history of cultural values; and third, setting
up cultural norms.[42]

What are these norms of culture, the laws, so to speak, which are to govern cultural life? It comes as no surprise to find Tillich urging that they are not be regarded as standards imposed from some completely external source, for instance, by a supernatural God. It is also folly to attempt to distil universal norms for the cultural sciences by means of pure thought.[43] We cannot, as it were, 'work them out' rationally and then simply apply them to the world. Nor can we merely 'read them off' the finite world as if we were engaging in natural science. Rather, cultural norms arise and are known only in the realisation of meaning in culture, through human cultural activity. They are not so much found as created in the creative process of spirit. This is presumably part of what Tillich means by saying that they are to be set up in an 'individual-creative' way. However, he also stresses that such norms are not purely relative to the individual, for they are always striving in the direction of the unconditionally valid and the unconditionally real. They are constantly directing our attention to what is eternally and universally true rather than merely to what is true for an individual or group.[44]

Fundamental here is Tillich's conviction that only theology can provide a basis for an adequate account of culture seen as the form of religion. Theology, Tillich pleads, is not the study of some 'object' or separate 'being' called 'God'; its brief is much wider and profounder. It is concerned with theonomy, with the manifold ways in which the unconditioned is revealed through the conditioned, *Gehalt* through *Form*. It is the third, normative element in the 'science of religion', the first two being the philosophy of religion (the descriptive discipline dealing with the universal forms of all reality), and the cultural history of religion. Hence Tillich can speak of theology as "the theonomous doctrine of the norms of meaning."[45]

Aesthetics

Now we need to turn to the tightly argued section of *The System of Sciences* in which Tillich examines the science of aesthetics.[46] He begins by insisting that the aesthetic function in a person cannot be considered apart from its characteristic product — art. Every aesthetic intuition of reality depends on the "creative fulfilment this intuition has found in the work of art."[47] Therefore, the distinction between a function and its product (basic to the empirical sciences) does not hold here. More importantly, in drawing out this contrast between aesthetics and empirical science, Tillich speaks of a bias towards the unconditioned in the arts. While the empirical sciences study the form (*Form*) of things, aesthetics is orientated toward the import (*Gehalt*) of things through form. Aesthetics is thus an 'import-determined' function. Art has a unique ability to disclose the unconditioned, for it "seeks to grasp things from the perspective of being, of pure import, without relinquishing thought, or form."[48] The name Tillich gives to the disclosure of the unconditioned through form is 'expression'. "The truth of science is correctness," he writes, whereas "the truth of art is power of expression (*Ausdrucksmächtige*)."[49]

Aesthetics, as well as being 'import-determined', is also a *theoretical* science. The root idea behind this is the Greek *theoria*, which Tillich describes as the "meaning-fulfilling absorption of reality", the "pure intuition of objects."[50] (We shall have occasion to examine this concept more extensively in due course, for it is central to Tillich's understanding of art.) Tillich sees it as quite erroneous to set art over against the theoretical so that it comes to be seen as a matter only of 'feeling (*Gefühl*)'. Although feeling and emotion play an important part in creating and enjoying art, every meaning-fulfilling act involves some degree of emotion. Moreover, to see art purely in terms of the feelings of the individual is to lose sight of the power of *Gehalt* in all things which it is the task of art to disclose.[51] It is also misleading to construe art as a synthesis of the theoretical and the practical, for this implies that art is essentially concerned with embodying moral ideals, whereas the effectiveness of art turns on the extent to which *Gehalt* is revealed through *Form*. Both of these mistaken views fail to take account of the 'supporting' role of metaphysics in aesthetics. For metaphysics demonstrates that

> "the prius of every individual comprehension of meaning is the unconditioned meaning itself, that the prius of every form of meaning is direction toward the unconditioned form, and that the prius of every import of meaning is the unconditioned import.........Metaphysics is the will to grasp the Unconditioned."[52]

Furthermore, it is only when we allow metaphysics its proper place in aesthetics will we appreciate why there are different styles in art. For it is the various ways in which the form/import tension shows itself in art that give us the key to classifying artistic style.[53]

Like any other cultural science, Tillich divides aesthetics into three subsidiary disciplines. First, there is the philosophy of art which examines the nature of the aesthetic function and aesthetic categories. Second, there is the examination of the ways in which import has been expressed in specific works of art and the consequent arrangement of styles. And third, through indicating the character of truly religious styles, there is the task of discovering and making explicit aesthetic norms.[54]

If we had only *The System of Sciences* to guide us, it would be very hard to know what the practical implications of these highly abstract reflections might be for the art-critic or art-historian, not to mention the artist of the 1990's. Indeed, despite his keen awareness of contemporary social and political life during this formative period of his thought, Tillich tends to ignore the down-to-earth questions about culture which might be asked by those unacquainted with the complexities of German Idealism. Tillich appears to be far more interested in the wide metaphysical horizons which lie behind culture than in the particular concerns of ordinary people. Fortunately, however, in the case of art, more specific issues are dealt with in other writings which clarify the somewhat turgid prose of *The System of Sciences*. It is to these we now turn.

(5) Tillich's Encounter with Expressionism

Tillich's father was a keen musician but had little interest in architecture or the visual arts. By contrast, Tillich himself had a passion for architecture and at one stage even considered it as a career.[55] But it was painting which had the most decisive influence on him. "The discovery of painting was a crucial experience for me. It happened during World War I, as a reaction to the horror, the ugliness, and destructiveness of war."[56] While serving as an army chaplain, much of Tillich's spare time was spent educating himself in the history of painting, even though he had to rely on the poor reproductions available in the military bookstores. He tells us that on his last furlough, during a visit to an exhibition in the Kaiser Friedrich Museum in Berlin, Boticelli's 'Madonna with Singing Angels' had an enormous impact — "almost a revelation."[57]

An even greater breakthrough came when his close friend, the art-historian Eckart von Sydow, introduced him to Expressionism.[58] Strictly speaking, 'Expressionism' refers to a movement in German painting (and literature) covering a period roughly from 1905 to 1919.[59] It began with the formation of the *Brücke* group in 1905 in Dresden — an anti-authoritarian, left-wing movement, which reacted against German Impressionism and the romanticism of artists such as Böcklin, Klinger and

Marées. Among its members were Ernst Ludwig Kirchner, Erick Heckel, Max Pechstein, Karl Schmidt-Rottluff, Fritz Bleyl and Emil Nolde. Following an exhibition in 1912, a second group arose, the *Blaue Reiter*, which included Kandinsky, Macke, Jawlensky, Klee, Marc, Felauny, and Münter. The element of protest in much of the Expressionists' art often led to a disruption of structure and form in their paintings. Some of the Expressionists invested this form-destruction with metaphysical significance. Pechstein wrote: "Most important for us........was the inner experience of the cosmos and the burning ambition to transmute this in its many parts in the artist's soul and then to recreate it in its greatness and simplicity."[60] "We no longer cling to reproduction of nature," Franz Marc claimed, "but destroy it, so as to reveal the right laws which hold sway behind the beautiful exterior".[61] In similar way, the historian Bernard Myers claims that Expressionist art "destroys the appearance of things to arrive at nonrational and spiritual values", and in so doing, "constantly tries to voice or formulate a cosmic feeling." The artist attempts to "cut through temporary naturalistic appearances in pursuit of the inner truth, by means of intensified colour and twisted form".[62] On this account, Expressionism was not trying to copy the natural world, or record momentary effect, or analyse the forms of reality; it was concerned with the revelation of transcendent and eternal truth through the dissolution of natural form.

Whether or not this is an accurate interpretation of the movement as a whole, it is certainly the one which Tillich favoured and which he was eager to use in his 'theonomous metaphysics'. In his essay of 1919 on the theology of culture, he writes:

> "To start with, it is clear that in Expressionism content (*Inhalt*) has to a very great extent lost its significance, namely content in the sense of the external factuality of objects and events.......Nature has been robbed of her external appearance; her uttermost depth is visible. But, according to Schelling, horror dwells in the depths of every living creature; and this horror seizes us from the work of Expressionist painters, who aim at more than the mere destruction of form (*Form*) in favour of the fullest, most vital and flourishing life within...........In their work a form-shattering religious import (*formzerersprengender religiöser Gehalt*) is struggling to find form, a paradox that most people find incomprehensible and annoying".[63]

So we find Tillich applying the terms *Form*, *Inhalt* and *Gehalt* to art.[64] *Form* is that which transforms the content into a work of art. It is the result of the artist's skill in mastering a particular artistic medium. To speak of a piece of art as a 'painting' is to speak about its form. (Tillich also uses the term to refer to the structure of that which is represented in a painting.) *Inhalt* (content) denotes subject-matter. *Gehalt* (import) is the unconditioned meaning presupposed (even if not intentionally) in the work of art, which gives the painting its ultimate meaning or significance. It is, so to speak, the 'religious' element in art.

> "The unconditioned significance pulsates in and through every aesthetic experience, and every aesthetic feeling is a transcendent feeling, that is, one in which the empirical emotional agitation includes a kernel of experience pointing to the unconditional."[65]

For Tillich, then, all three elements — *Form, Inhalt* and *Gehalt* constitute a work of art. However, they are not of equal importance. The subject-matter (*Inhalt*) is irrelevant in determining the extent to which import is revealed. A work of art can be religious irrespective of its *Inhalt*. Specifically religious themes or motifs (e.g. the cross, scenes in the life of Jesus) do not guarantee the disclosure of import. Further, *Form, Inhalt* and *Gehalt* vary in strength from one work of art to another. Indeed, it is their relative prominence which enables us to distinguish different artistic styles. Within the visual arts there are 'naturalistic' styles in which the primary concern is to represent the objectively real, 'impressionistic' styles in which *Inhalt* and *Gehalt* are subservient to formal properties such as shape and colour, and 'expressionistic' styles where the artist seeks to unveil the inner universal significance or *Gehalt* of his subject-matter.[66] As we might expect, it is the expressionistic style, seen supremely in German Expressionism, which Tillich believes is *Gehalt*-predominant. Here subject-matter is relatively unimportant: "*Inhalt* is lost sight of in comparison with the overwhelming intensity of *Gehalt*."[67] And although Tillich could detect both a form-affirming and a form-denying element in Expressionism, he thought that the latter element was uppermost. *Form* is burst or shattered, the natural forms of reality deliberately distorted in order that *Gehalt* may be expressed.[68]

This account of Expressionism has strong links with the way in which Tillich interpreted the prevailing social conditions of his time. Indeed, it is impossible to divorce Tillich's approach to art from broader socio-cultural issues. He saw the Expressionists' form-disruption as symptomatic of a widespread revolt against self-sufficient, autonomous, capitalist society.[69] He links Marc's 'Yellow Horses' with a fierce riot he witnessed between the intelligentsia and the 'lower petty bourgeoisie'.[70] This desire to relate art to its social setting can also be seen in Tillich's study of paintings which depict masses or large crowds, *Masse und Geist* (1922).[71] In early Gothic paintings, he maintains, the crowd is entirely dominated by the idea it represents.   Everything individual is suppressed.   Three-dimensional space, which highlights the individuality of persons, is absent.   This Tillich calls the 'mystical conception of the masses'.[72]   Later, when the fabric of medieval society was breaking apart, there is a discovery of the uniqueness of the individual, and the new use of three-dimensional space. The mystical mass has been replaced by the 'realistic mass'.[73] In Baroque art we notice a shift towards the inner personal conviction of faith characteristic of an urban, aristocratic society. In the nineteenth century, with the rise of Impressionism, form has become dominant.   Nature is viewed in its external appearance and everything is a study in light, colour, and movement. This is the age of the 'technological mass'.[74] Later, towards the end of the nineteenth century, and particularly in the first decade of the twentieth, a new spirit of protest and revolt emerges, finding its acme in the 'new mysticism' of Expressionist painting. Here a disintegration of outward shape is combined with a new perception of the depth or 'essentiality' of visible forms. Two-dimensional space deprives people of their individuality, and yet they are also raised above humanity to new ecstatic and visionary heights. A mystical element breaks out of the depths of the soul while remaining in the reality of the world. The masses have become the subject again. We see here the 'masses of the immanent mysticism'.[75]

From *Masse und Geist* and the other essays we have examined, it is clear that Tillich's account of art is shaped at every turn by his metaphysics. But now we need to ask: to what extent is this reversed? Did Tillich's encounter with art (particularly Expressionist art) play a significant part in determining the development of his metaphysics? It appears that this is precisely what happened. We need only read Tillich's own testimony. "My love for the arts" he tells us, "has been of great importance to my theological and philosophical work."[76] Writing of his first experience of painting in Berlin during the war, he recalls:

"Out of the philosophical and theological reflection that followed these experiences, I developed some fundamental

categories of philosophy of religion and culture, viz., form
and substance [i.e. import]."[77]

He continues:

"It was the expressionist style emerging in Germany during
the first decade of this century and winning public recognition
following the war and the bitter struggle with an
uncomprehending lower middle-class taste that opened my
eyes to how the substance [i.e. import] of a work of art could
destroy form and to the creative ecstasy implied in this
process."[78]

Further evidence is supplied in his essay on the theology of
culture of 1919. When looking for an effective example of the
relationship between form and import, Tillich turns directly to
Expressionist art; firstly, he says, "because it seems to.......offer
a particularly impressive example of the....relation between form
and import"; and secondly, because "these definitions [viz. of
form and import] were worked out partly under its influence."[79]
Many years later, Tillich claimed that some of his writings took
their cue from Nolde's painting 'Pentecost', adding: "I always
learned more from pictures than from theological books."[80]
Furthermore, he explicitly states that the notion of
'breakthrough (*durchbrechen*)' in his theory of revelation (the
unconditioned breaking through the conditioned forms) arose
directly from his experience of expressionist art.[81] It is also
worth noting that the *Form/Inhalt/Gehalt* triad plays no part
in Tillich's seventy-two theses on systematic theology of 1913,
nor in any published or unpublished writings which have been
discovered before the first World War, which suggests that it
was only after encountering Renaissance and (more importantly)
Expressionist art that he was led to develop these metaphysical
concepts. There seems, then, good reason to endorse Wilhelm
and Marion Pauck's assessment: "Tillich was led from his study
of painting to the insight that became the major theme of his
philosophy of religion.......religion "is the substance of culture,"
while culture is the form through which religion expresses
itself."[82] Ian Thompson goes as far as saying that, having
developed his theory of the way meaning is created, expressed
and fulfilled in art, Tillich "then applies this, *mutatis mutandis*
to philosophy, ethics and politics."[83]

Clearly it would be foolish to press the point too far. There
were a number of different factors bearing on his theology and
philosophy during this period. Many of his central philosophical
convictions had developed prior to his experience of
Expressionism.[84] Nevertheless, at the very least, we can say

that for Tillich, art, particularly of the Expressionistic variety, had a crucial part to play in shaping and refining the main categories of his metaphysics of theonomy.

It would be a courageous person who claimed to grasp and comprehend every detail of Tillich's early metaphysics and philosophy of art. Quite apart from the considerable difficulties of translation and Tillich's tortuous style, the ethereal atmosphere of German Idealism presents formidable problems to any who are not familiar with its leading ideas and distinctive emphases. Nevertheless, the broad lines of Tillich's thinking are clear enough. Fundamental to his entire project is the desire to view religion as a dimension of the whole of existence rather than a special zone in which specifically religious things are said and done. For Tillich, everything and everyone that is, exists by participation in the unconditioned or the import of being. On this basis, employing an elaborate philosophy of meaning, he aims to construct a synthesis of religion and culture in the form of a theology of culture. In all human culture, thought is fused with being in such a way that some new entity is created which displays form, content and import. The main dialectic here is between form and import. Culture is to be seen as the form of religion and religion as the substance of culture. When the unconditioned is forgotten or suppressed, autonomy arises; when particular finite realities are exalted as infinite and substituted for the authentic import of being, the result is heteronomy. In theonomy, however, there is a disclosure of the unconditioned in and through finite form; the import of being which supports all things breaks through, without destroying, the conditioned forms of meaning.

We have seen something of the important role which Expressionist art came to exercise in Tillich's thought. Not only did his metaphysics determine his interpretation of Expressionism, but his understanding of Expressionism to a large extent determined his metaphysics. Because of the universal, spiritual interpretation of reality which Expressionism seemed to offer, it became the most powerful example of the mutual immanence of religion and culture, of the revelation of the unconditioned through *Form*. In Expressionism, the surface of reality is broken, not only to shake the complacency of human autonomy, but to reveal the infinite depth of reality which gives meaning to finite reality (as well as depriving it of absolute independence). Tillich found here not merely an artistic barometer of the age: Expressionism was not only *illustrative* of the authentic spiritual act, it was also *paradigmatic*. Here was a style which reached a level unmatched by any other. As Michael Palmer puts it, Expressionism came to be "arrayed in the robes of a prophet."[85] It provided Tillich with nothing less than the criterion for distinguishing between religious and non-religious art. Art is truly religious not when it employs traditional religious subjects, still less when it seeks a photographic depiction of reality, but when it probes beneath the surface of the finite and brings to light the ultimate meaning which lies beyond and beneath all things.

Notes

1. *On the Boundary* (henceforth *OB*), London: Collins, 1967, p. 55. James Luther Adams writes: "meaning is the characteristic concern of the human spirit, and hence it is, for Tillich, the foundation of his whole system." *Paul Tillich's Philosophy of Culture, Science and Religion* (henceforth *PCSR*), New York: Harper & Row, 1965, p. 56.

2. *The Theology of Paul Tillich* (henceforth *TPT*), ed. Charles Kegley and Robert W. Bretall, London: Macmillan, 1956, pp. 13f. Luther Adams comments: "Tillich was confronted with the necessity of coming to terms with the intellectual struggle of his generation for a new *Weltanschauung*." *PCSR*, p. 122.

3. *The System of Sciences according to Objects and Methods* (henceforth *SS*), trans. Paul Wiebe, London and Toronto: Associated University Press, 1981, pp. 34-37. (For *The System of Sciences* in German, cf. Paul Tillich, *Gesammelte Werke* (henceforth *GW*), I, Stuttgart: Evangelisches Verlagswerk, 1959, pp. 109-293.)

4. *SS*, pp. 35-41.

5. *Ibid.*, pp. 137ff.

6. *What is Religion?* (henceforth *WR*), ed. James Luther Adams, New York: Harper & Row 1969, p. 56. These words are from his seminal address of 1919, "Über die Idee einer Theologie der Kultur," to be found in its original German in *GW*, IX, 1967, pp. 13-31.

7. *PCSR*, p. 58.

8. *WR*, p. 57. The full essay from which this quotation is taken (entitled "Religionsphilosophie") can be found in *GW*, I, pp. 295-364.

9. *WR*, p. 58. In fact, *Gehalt* is used in a number of diverse ways by Tillich: most commentators recognise the confusion over the use of this term. Cf. *GW*, I, pp. 116ff.; IX, pp. 35, 318, 321, 323. It has also been translated in a variety of ways; we shall render it 'import' throughout.

10. *WR*, pp. 165ff.

11. *Ibid.*, p. 165.

12. *GW*, IX, p. 22. We follow here the translation by John P. Clayton in *The Concept of Correlation: Paul Tillich and the Possibility of a*

Mediating Theology, Berlin and New York: de Gruyter, 1980, p. 197.
[13] "Religiöser Stil und religiöser Stoff in der bildenden Kunst," in *GW*, IX, p. 319.
[14] *WR*, p. 59.
[15] *Ibid.*
[16] *Ibid.*, p. 60.
[17] *Ibid.*
[18] *OB*, pp. 69f. My italics. Cf. *WR*, pp. 72-76 for further elucidation of this relationship.
[19] "Religion and Secular Culture," *The Journal of Religion*, 26, 2 (April 1946), p. 79.
[20] *WR*, p. 162.
[21] "Religion and Secular Culture," p. 80.
[22] *The Protestant Era* (henceforth *PE*), London: Nisbet, 1951, p. 61.
[23] *OB*, p. 69.
[24] *WR*, p. 73. Tillich rejected Ernst Troeltsch's view of the religious *a priori* because he felt it made man's religious life one among many of his functions. Troeltsch had developed Kant's insight that something unconditional breaks into the realm of temporal and causal existence in man's moral experience, by suggesting that there is a theoretical *a priori*, a moral *a priori*, an aesthetic *a priori*, and a religious *a priori*, each of which reveals itself as the unconditioned and unconditional ground of meaning. In Tillich's eyes, this relativises religion by making the religious *a priori* another cultural function alongside the theoretical, moral and aesthetic. *GW*, I, p. 370. For Tillich, "the meaning-functions come to fulfilment in meaning only in relatedness to the unconditioned meaning, and..........therefore the religious intention is the presupposition for successful meaning-fulfilment in all functions." *WR*, p. 73.
[25] *WR*, p. 34.
[26] The concepts of autonomy and heteronomy have a rich history in German thought. Cf. James Luther Adams, "What Kind of Religion has a Place in Higher Education?," *Journal of Bible and Religion*, 13 (1945), pp. 185-192.
[27] *WR*, p. 75.
[28] *Ibid.*, pp. 74f.
[29] *Ibid.*, p. 144.
[30] *Ibid.*, pp. 75, 77f.
[31] For his scathing attacks on supranaturalism, cf. e.g. *ibid.*, pp. 37, 83f., 131, 158, 177. Cp. the much later passage in *Systematic Theology* (henceforth *ST*), 2, London: Nisbet, 1964, pp. 5-11.
[32] *WR*, p. 74.
[33] *Ibid.*, p. 108.
[34] We should keep in mind that here the word translated 'science (*Wissenschaft*)' has a much wider meaning than in English; broadly, 'cognitive discipline', or 'discipline of knowing'. The implication is that there are other legitimate modes of knowledge than what we call the 'natural' and 'social' sciences.
[35] *SS*, pp. 37ff.

³⁶ *WR*, p. 155.
³⁷ *SS*, 39.
³⁸ *WR*, pp. 50ff; *SS*, pp. 39ff., 146f., 228f.
³⁹ *SS*, p. 157. Behind 'theoretical', here lies the notion of *theoria* — the "meaning-fulfilling absorption of reality", the "pure intuition of objects." *Ibid.* Much later, in *ST*, 3, 1963, *theoria* reappears in the context of his distinction between the theoretical and the practical (p. 66).
⁴⁰ *SS*, pp. 157f.
⁴¹ *Ibid.*, pp. 151f.; *WR*, p. 32. This was the same classification proposed by Troeltsch (*Der Historismus und seine Überwindung*, Berlin: Rolf Heise, 1924, p. 28). It is significant that Tillich dedicated *The System of Sciences* to Troeltsch.
⁴² *WR*, p. 165ff.
⁴³ *SS*, p. 156.
⁴⁴ *SS*, pp. 147ff.
⁴⁵ *SS*, pp. 207f.
⁴⁶ *Ibid.*, pp. 178-181.
⁴⁷ *Ibid.*, p. 178.
⁴⁸ *Ibid.*
⁴⁹ *Ibid.*, p. 179.
⁵⁰ *Ibid.*
⁵¹ *Ibid.*, pp. 179f.
⁵² *Ibid.*, p. 183.
⁵³ *Ibid.*, pp. 180f. "Whether it be the art of a period, a group, an individual, or even a particular work of art, style is the universal determination of aesthetic forms by the way import in general is grasped............the dependence of art on metaphysics is evident in the tension between form and import, that is, in style." *SS*, p. 181.
⁵⁴ Later on, Tillich points out that theology can show what artistic attitudes are closest to the metaphysical attitude of theonomy, but it cannot of itself create the material — separate and identifiable as religious subject-matter — which will guarantee a theonomous attitude. In this sense a 'theological aesthetic' is impossible. *SS*, pp. 211ff.
⁵⁵ "Honesty and Consecration," in *Protestant Church Buildings and Equipment*, 13, 3 (September 1965), p. 15.
⁵⁶ *OB*, p. 27.
⁵⁷ *Ibid.*, p. 28. "He felt he was looking not merely at angels but at the holy itself." Pauck, *op. cit.*, p. 76. Tillich refers to the 'Madonna' again in "I'll always Remember........One Moment of Beauty," *Parade*, (25 September 1955), p. 2. Cf. also "Zur Theologie der bildenden Kunst und der Architektur," in *GW*, IX, p. 345.
⁵⁸ *OB*, p. 28.
⁵⁹ In fact Tillich includes many artists under the heading 'expressionist' — e.g. Van Gogh, Cézanne, Gaugin, Chagall, Rouault, Sutherland. The expressionist style interested Tillich more than any particular historical period. Nevertheless, it was the German Expressionism of the early 1900's which Tillich regarded as the most potent example of the expressionist style.

⁶⁰ As quoted and translated by Frank Whitford in his book *Expressionism*, London, New York, Sydney and Toronto: Hamlyn, 1970, p. 185.

⁶¹ As translated by Wolf-Dieter Dube, *The Expressionists*, London: Thames and Hudson, 1972, p. 132.

⁶² *Expressionism: A Generation in Revolt*, London: Thames and Hudson, 1963, pp. 11, 40, 41.

⁶³ *WR*, p. 169. The reference to the Idealist philosopher, F. W. J. von Schelling (1775-1854) is significant. Tillich wrote two very early dissertations on Schelling (1910 and 1912). Schelling's exalted view of art as a medium for the disclosure of ultimate truth undoubtedly influenced Tillich. More than this, Schelling's philosophical system provided Tillich with ontological categories which became essential to his whole theology of culture. (Cf. Raymond F. Bulman, *A Blueprint for Humanity. Paul Tillich's Theology of Culture*, London and Toronto: Associated University Presses, 1981, pp. 56-67; G. F. Sommer, "The Significance of the Late Philosophy of Schelling for the Formation and Interpretation of the Thought of Paul Tillich," PhD Thesis, Duke University, 1961; S. T. Crary, "Idealistic Elements in Tillich's Thought," PhD Thesis, Yale University, 1955.)

⁶⁴ Although Tillich did not use the terms *Form, Inhalt*, and *Gehalt* until after the first World War, similar concepts had been employed in aesthetics by Fichte, Schelling, and Hegel. We do not know the extent of the direct influence of these writers on Tillich's philosophy of art.

⁶⁵ *WR*, p. 67.

⁶⁶ *Ibid.*, pp. 169f. Cf. "Religiöser Stil und Religiöser Stoff in der bildenden Kunst," pp. 319f.

⁶⁷ *GW*, IX, p. 22.

⁶⁸ *WR*, p. 169. Cp. his lecture of 1921 delivered at Berlin University, where he speaks of Franz Marc's 'Tower of the Blue Horses' as destroying natural forms and colours in order to gain an insight into the inner truth of things. "Zur Theologie der bildenden Kunst und der Architektur," *GW*, IX, pp. 345f. The University buildings stood immediately opposite the art gallery.

⁶⁹ *The Religious Situation* (henceforth *RS*), trans. H. Richard Niebuhr, London: Thames and Hudson, 1956, pp. 87ff.

⁷⁰ Cf. "Art and Ultimate Reality," (henceforth AUR), *Cross Currents*, 10 (Winter 1960), p. 10.

⁷¹ *GW*, II, 1962, pp. 35-90.

⁷² *Ibid.*, p. 37.

⁷³ *Ibid.*, p. 38.

⁷⁴ *Ibid.*, pp. 38f.

⁷⁵ *Ibid.*, p. 40.

⁷⁶ *OB*, p. 26.

⁷⁷ *Ibid.*, p. 28.

⁷⁸ *Ibid.* It may be asked why a picture such as Boticelli's 'Madonna with Singing Angels', with its Christian subject-matter and impeccable formal organisation, should have been such a 'revelation' to Tillich during the war. This can be explained if we assume Tillich's

reaction to the Boticelli picture was triggered by the *contrast* between its peaceful sublimity and the horror of war which Tillich had experienced. Cf. Michael Palmer, *Paul Tillich's Philosophy of Art*, Berlin and New York: de Gruyter, 1984, pp. 7f.

[79] *WR*, p. 169.

[80] "*AUR*," p. 10.

[81] *OB*, 28. Cf. *My Travel Diary:1936*, London: SCM, 1970, p. 104, where Tillich speaks of the powerful effect on him of Cézanne's painting 'The Breakthrough'. Franz Marc spoke in the same terms of Expressionistic painting, claiming that we see "a breakthrough (*Durchbruch*) of import (*Gehalt*) in form (*Form*) and colour". *Briefe aus dem Feld*, Berlin: Helmut Rauschenbusch Verlag, 1948, p. 75.

[82] *Op. cit.*, p. 78.

[83] Ian E. Thompson, *Being and Meaning. Paul Tillich's Theory of Meaning, Truth and Logic*, Edinburgh: Edinburgh University Press, 1981, p. 88. Cf. also Jean-Paul Gabus, *Introduction à la Théologie de la Culture de Paul Tillich*, Paris: Presses Universitaires de France, 1969, p. 17; Bulman, *op. cit.*, pp. 99ff.

[84] Cf. Clayton, *op. cit.*, pp. 204ff.

[85] *Op. cit.*, p. 12. Cf. Pauck, *op. cit.*, p. 78: "the world of art was a prophetic instrument for Tillich as well as an inspiration."

3. Belief-ful Realism (1926-1933)

"The new realism tries to point to the spiritual meaning of
the real by using its given forms. In these movements art is
driving toward a self-transcending realism."

Tillich, *The Protestant Era*

(1) The New Realism

By the mid-1920's, along with many of his contemporaries,
Tillich realised that there could be no fundamental social reform
in Germany under the Weimar government, still less (as was
his earlier hope) a theonomous unification of cultural beliefs
and values. He began to lose confidence in religious socialism.
The spirit of capitalist society had been too resilient, his own
theonomous vision over-optimistic. And so from the mid-1920's,
without relinquishing his primary convictions, Tillich set out
on a fresh path, advocating what he called 'belief-ful realism
(*gläubiger Realismus*)', or, following a suggestion of James
Luther Adams, 'self-transcending' realism. Two elements mark
out belief-ful realism: on the one hand, a stress on the real and
the concrete, a refusal to ignore things as they appear to us; on
the other, a recognition that finite forms point beyond themselves
to an ultimate meaning, the infinite power and depth of reality.
In Richard Niebuhr's words, belief-ful realism "sees the world
with the sober eyes of the scientist or realistic artist, accepting
it at the same time as symbolic of the eternal and unconditioned
source of all meaning and ground of all being."[1] Tillich insists
that we should not confuse belief-ful realism with other forms
of realism. In positivism, pragmatism, and empiricism, we see
'self-limiting', 'self-sufficient' realism, which restricts its vision
to what is merely finite. 'Historical realism', associated with
writers like Troeltsch, Rickert and Dilthey, focuses on the
realities of the present, and mistakenly tries to grasp the
unconditioned in a particular historical situation. 'Mystical
realism', which attempts a direct union of conditioned and
unconditioned through contemplation, effectively denies the
tension between finite and infinite. Idealism is also deficient
because it seeks to break free from the finite altogether:

"Idealism does not see the gap between the unconditional and the unconditioned which no ontological or ethical self-elevation can bridge........The limitation and tragedy of idealism lie in the fact that it idealises the real instead of transcending it in the power of the transcendent, i.e. in faith."[2]

What Tillich was looking for, and what he believed he had found in belief-ful realism, was an attitude which gave due attention to the realities of the contingent, finite world, but which at the same time acknowledged that finite things have a metaphysical reference beyond their contingency to that which transcends the finite in power and meaning.[3]

It had, of course, always been axiomatic for Tillich that the finite and infinite could never simply be resolved into each other; he was fully aware that his theonomous vision for culture could only be achieved in a piecemeal and fragmentary way. But from 1925 we notice a re-affirmation of the distinctiveness and irreducibility of finite form. Increasingly, the emphasis falls on the separation of *Form* and *Gehalt* rather than on their interpenetration. If Tillich detects even so much as a sniff of idolatry, any careless exaltation of some finite reality, he is quick to attack. Repeatedly he affirms the 'Protestant principle': that nothing which is less than ultimate should be allowed to usurp the supremacy which belongs to God alone. Indeed, he can even speak of belief-ful realism as having a 'genuinely Protestant character'.[4] As we shall see, when he later came to expound his *Systematic Theology*, he introduced a method of 'correlation' which was designed to relate autonomous cultural forms and theonomous religious import in a way which would not risk compromising the limitations of the finite. John Clayton comments: "Whereas Tillich had earlier sought to establish within his philosophy of religion the mutual immanence of cultural form and religious content, after 1933 he sought to define their differences and to mediate between them within the context of his theological system. If the symbol of the one approach is *theonomy*, the symbol of the other is *correlation*; and 1933 marks in some sense the divide between the two."[5]

Various factors contributed to this shift in Tillich's outlook. Among them were his increasing pessimism about the future of the Weimar regime and his disappointment that some of his key ideas had been sorely misused by religious socialists to endorse utopianism.[6] In addition, he became acutely aware of what he called the 'experience of the abyss', evinced above all in the dreadful suffering and chaos of 1914-18. He even began to speak of a polarity between two opposing ontological principles within God, the divine and the demonic, one positive and meaningful and the other negative and destructive.[7] But for our own purposes, the question we need to address here is to what extent these new philosophical and theological interests were bound up with his encounter with contemporary art.

(2) Belief-ful Realism in Art

By the mid-1920's, German Expressionism in art had developed in two main directions. On the one hand, Kandinsky, Klee, Albers and others moved towards increasingly abstract and non-representational styles, wedded to a disciplined use of colours and composition. On the other hand, a number of artists sought to combine the basic aims of Expressionism with a fresh recognition of the finite, physical, and tangible nature of things. The main representatives of this latter group were George Grosz, Otto Dix and Max Beckmann, and their outlook came to be spoken of as *die neue Sachlichkeit* ('the new realism').[8] In their eyes, the earlier Expressionists had failed to come to terms with the formidable challenges of post-war Germany.

> "[The new realism] was related to the general contemporary feeling in Germany of resignation and cynicism after a period of exuberant hopes (which had found an outlet in Expressionism). Cynicism and resignation are the negative side of the 'Neue Sachlichkeit'; the positive side expresses itself in the enthusiasm for immediate reality as a result of the desire to take things entirely objectively on a natural basis without immediately investing them with ideal implications."[9]

Thus, the new realist, so to speak, brings us down to earth; we are made to "examine at close range — under the microscope — the various aspects of present-day reality."[10] There is a clarity of form, a concern for precision, exactness and accuracy, not in order to achieve point-by-point reproduction but to convey "an emotionally heightened interpretation of the clearly observed fact."[11]

On moving to Dresden in 1925, and later to Frankfurt to become a professor there in 1929, Tillich maintained his keen interest in the arts, and was fully alert to the stirrings of *die neue Sachlichkeit*: He later wrote:

> "At this time [from c. 1925] works of art appeared which kept *much closer to the natural forms of things* than the expressionists did. They could, however, not be considered as a relapse to the nineteenth-century naturalism. They

represented a post-expressionistic style. They repudiated the
elements of subjectivism and romanticism in the preceding
period without giving up the depth and cosmic symbolism of
their predecessors........the new realism was not interested in
the natural forms of things for their own sake but for their
power of expressing the profounder levels and universal
significance of things. Nineteenth-century realism had
deprived reality of its symbolic power; expressionism had
tried to re-establish this power by shattering the surface of
reality. *The new realism tries to point to the spiritual meaning
of the real by using its given forms.* In these movements art
is driving toward a self-transcending realism."[12]

This assessment of the new realism is carried through most
thoroughly in Tillich's book of 1926, *The Religious Situation*.[13]
Here he speaks of a widespread revolt against the 'capitalist
spirit' in the West, against the emptiness of modern, secular,
industrial society, against the belief that the world is self-
sufficient, tightly closed against 'invasions of the eternal'. He
traces the various forms of this protest in the natural sciences,
philosophy, art, economics, sociology, and theology. A new
outlook is emerging — belief-ful realism. Although conceding
individuality to observable phenomena, belief-ful realism is not
interested in the conditioned forms of reality for their own sake,
but primarily for their power to express the unconditioned
significance of things. It is in painting, Tillich says, that the
anti-capitalist rebellion is seen at its most intense. Impressionism belongs to the bourgeois spirit, with its concentration on
finite forms perceived in a fleeting moment. Naturalism is
similar, except that its tendency is towards an over-emphasis
on the object represented.[14] In the expressionist style, there is
a move beyond finite form to the unconditioned. Here the self-
contained finitude of capitalist civilisation is pierced. Cézanne,
for example, restores to things their 'metaphysical meaning';
Van Gogh reveals the 'creative dynamic in light and colour';
Munch shows the 'cosmic dread present in nature and mankind'.
Expressionism arose

> "with a revolutionary consciousness and revolutionary force.
> The individual forms of things were dissolved, not in favour
> of subjective impressions [as in impressionist art] but in
> favour of objective metaphysical expression..........the
> transcendent reference in things to that which lies beyond
> them is expressed."[15]

These basic expressionist insights, Tillich continues, have been
extended in futurism, cubism and constructivism. He readily
admits that the dissolution of natural form often provokes a

hostile and vehement reaction from the public, but this only confirms that the nerve centre of the capitalist mentality has been touched. Once again, Tillich mounts a vehement assault on so-called 'religious' art. Religious subject-matter is not the measure of sacred art. "It is not an exaggeration to ascribe more of the quality of sacredness to a still-life by Cézanne or a tree by Van Gogh than to a picture of Jesus by Uhde."[16] (The German painter Fritz von Uhde (1848-1911) was best known for his religious pictures, particularly 'Sermon on the Mount' (1887).) Tillich also argues that traditional religious symbols cannot be wedded to the expressionistic style because "the continuity of the religious tradition has been broken by capitalist culture." Only through a "pure, mystic immediacy" will modern religious consciousness find itself again.[17]

At this point, the *neue Sachlichkeit* movement enters to take pride of place.[18] Even though it penetrates beyond the finite, it shares with capitalism an element of realism, and is thus carrying "the battle into the very camp of the enemy and employing his own best weapons against him."[19] We can see it in a number of art genres. In sculpture and architecture, Tillich discerns a new 'spiritualised realism'. Dance too has undergone a renaissance and has moved in the direction of 'ritual dance'. In literature, Strindberg, von Hauptmann, Hugo von Hoffmannsthal and Dehmel disclose 'metaphysical' meaning. In Rilke, 'poetry is given a directly religious turn', and Stefan George is the most important poet of the time because of his effort to 'find the pure form which is superior to subject and object' and so express a metaphysical view of reality.[20] Tillich also mentions a 'demonic transcendence' in the writings of Dehmel, Edschmid and Heinrich Mann, and Wedekind. Dostoievsky's writings, he claims, display a 'mystical realism', giving vent to a protest against the capitalist ethos.[21] Tillich concludes:

> "the realism and impressionism of the capitalist period have been destroyed in the development of symbolism, mysticism and expressionism but..........a new realism is about to gain ascendancy; with emotional zeal at first, then with objective and metaphysical intuition it has uncovered the demonism present in the social world and, perhaps, as in the case of metaphysics and painting, it may be at the point of developing into a *belief-ful realism.*"[22]

Similar concerns, although tackled from a different angle, can be seen in Tillich's address given at the opening of an exhibition in Berlin in 1930, "Kult und Form."[23] This lecture is of particular interest as it contains Tillich's first extended thoughts on the use of the arts in worship. Characteristically, he opens by stating that religion is "the experience of being grasped unconditionally and inescapably by that which is the supporting ground and the consuming abyss of our existence". The whole of life is the service and worship of God: forms of art for worship are simply those which express the ultimate foundation of our lives. Religious art (in this case, liturgical art) must satisfy three conditions. First, it must be determined by everyday life, by daily routine. It cannot be divorced from what we experience from day to day. Second, it should be determined by our own religious situation. We cannot uncritically adopt the styles of some past age; we must express our own contemporary awareness of ultimate meaning. Third, it must be determined by the depth of reality in individual things:

> "Everything has its own powerfulness, a radiance, an abundance of reality (*Realitätsfülle*)...........Whoever attempts to create new art forms for religion should know that a cross is no opportunity for decorative embellishment, that a chalice is a drinking vessel whose meaning and power is its use as such, that we no longer see the power of writing in its magical radiance but rather in its clarity, in its inner appropriateness to that which it expresses, in its capacity to communicate ideas."[24]

It is a stinging indictment on 'religious art', Tillich points out, that those who take no active part in any religious worship are often most sensitive to the ultimate depths of reality. Most of the 'religious' items in the exhibition betray, according to Tillich, a false notion of worship as a special 'sphere' alongside other spheres, separate from everyday life, and consequently lack both depth and contemporaneity. He declares: "It is at the same time both characteristic and disgraceful for our religious situation that in this exhibition the secular objects alone are entirely penetrating and impressive, the things that are presented as expressly not for liturgical use."[25]

(3) The Place of Belief-ful Realism in Tillich's Thought

We have seen enough to suggest a close parallel between Tillich's exposition of *die neue Sachlichkeit* in art and the concurrent change of direction in his philosophy and theology. But can we go further? To what extent did belief-ful realism in the arts actually affect the advancement of his philosophical and theological thinking? According to Tillich himself, the answer is clear. When "expressionism gave way to a new realism," he writes, "I developed my concept of 'belief-ful realism' from a study of the new style [in art]. The idea of 'belief-ful realism' is the central concept of my book, *The Religious Situation*, which for that reason is dedicated to an artist friend."[26] It seems, as with Expressionism, that *die neue Sachlichkeit* furnished Tillich with a vital tool for developing his metaphysical convictions. John Clayton comments: "the visual arts played a unique role not only in the formation and extension of Tillich's conception of the relationship between *Form* and *Gehalt*, but also in the modification of that conception from around 1925."[27]

Does this mean that for Tillich the 'new realism' replaced Expressionism as the supremely religious style? Was Expressionism supplanted by *die neue Sachlichkeit* as the exemplary model of 'form-breaking import'? Not at all. We would do better to speak of a transfer of emphasis rather than a radical innovation. Only in the writings of the 1920's, when Tillich's exposure to the new artistic movement was at its greatest, does he make a distinction between Expressionism and the 'new realism'. No mention is made of *die neue Sachlichkeit* in his later surveys of art: expressionism is presented as the paradigmatic religious style, and moreover, it is spoken of in the same terms as he used during the 1920's for belief-ful realism.[28] It would appear that Tillich saw in the new realist movement not so much a reversal but an extension of the Expressionists' aims. This is the only way to make sense of Tillich's assertion that in both Expressionism and the New Realism "art is driving toward a self-transcending realism."[29] As Michael Palmer helpfully explains,

> "both styles can be called 'realistic' because they seek to reveal the spiritual meaning of reality by using its given forms, asserting that it is possible to seek for the ultimate power of reality *within the concreteness of its structures*; and both can be called 'belief-ful' because they claim that the ultimate meaning and power sought cannot be derived from the whole of reality and cannot be apprehended by the scientific or conceptual processes *belonging to the whole of reality*."[30]

Notes
[1] Preface to *RS*, p. 13.
[2] *Ibid.*, p. 76.
[3] *Ibid.*, pp. 75-88.

[4] *PE*, p. 75.

[5] *Op. cit.*, p. 218. (Cp. Bulman, pp. 82ff.) Clayton rightly adds that we cannot speak of an absolute division between the two, nor be so precise about the date. After all, theonomy continues to play an important part in the *Systematic Theology* (*ST*, 1, 1953, pp. 202-210; *ST*, 3, pp. 157f., 250). And although the first volume of the *Systematic Theology* - in which the principle of correlation is given its fullest treatment - did not appear until 1951, he was working on it from as early as 1925.

[6] Cf. Clayton, pp. 209ff.

[7] *The Interpretation of History* (henceforth *IH*), trans. N. A. Rasetzki and Elsa L. Talmey, New York and London: Charles Scribner's Sons, 1936, pp. 80f.

[8] The term was first used by Gustav Friedrich Hartlaub, the director of the Kunsthalle in Mannheim, to refer to the work of Grosz, Dix and Beckmann in the 1920's.

[9] Hartlaub, as quoted in Myers, *op. cit.*, p. 224.

[10] *Ibid.*, pp. 229f.

[11] *Ibid.*, p. 229.

[12] *PE*, pp. 74f. My italics. Cp. *RS*, pp. 90f.

[13] *RS*, pp. 85-101.

[14] *Ibid.*, pp. 86f.

[15] *Ibid.*, p. 87. Tillich wrote in 1919: "Many of the remarks made by these artists confirm the existence of a strong religious passion struggling for expression........The religious meaning of this art is to a large extent consciously affirmed by its representatives." *WR*, pp. 169f.

[16] *Ibid.*, p. 89. Later, Tillich tempered his judgement, conceding that "Basically [Uhde] too, is religious." *My Travel Diary: 1936*, p. 104.

[17] *RS*, p. 89.

[18] *Ibid.*, pp. 90f.

[19] *Ibid.*, p. 91.

[20] *Ibid.*, pp. 96ff. Writing later of Rilke in *On the Boundary*, Tillich says: "Its profound psychoanalytical realism, the mystical richness, and a prophetic form charged with metaphysical content made this poetry a vehicle for insights that I could elaborate only abstractly through the concepts of my philosophy of religion. For myself and my wife, who introduced me to poetry, these poems became a book of devotions that I read again and again." *OB*, pp. 29f.

[21] *RS*, pp. 98f.

[22] *Ibid.*, p. 101.

[23] *GW*, IX, pp. 324-327.

[24] *Ibid.*, pp. 326f.

[25] *Ibid.*, p. 327.

[26] *OB*, p. 28.

[27] *Op. cit.*, p. 224.

[28] Cf. e.g. *Theology of Culture* (henceforth *TC*), ed. Robert C. Kimball, New York: Oxford University Press, 1959, pp. 74f.

[29] *PE*, p. 75.

[30] *Op. cit.*, p. 19.

4. Correlation, Ontological Reason and Art (After 1933)

> The expressionist style "is most able to express the self-transcendence of life........It......shows the Spiritual Presence in symbols of broken finitude."
>
> Tillich, *Systematic Theology*

In the last chapter, we observed how Tillich began to lose confidence in some aspects of his early and somewhat optimistic vision of the unity of religion and culture. From the mid-1920's, he came to be increasingly conscious of the danger of losing sight of the empirical reality and concreteness of things and the hazards of treating finite entities as ultimate. The new realist movement in painting not only provided Tillich with a means of illustrating these emphases in his thinking, but also to some extent actually initiated them in the first place.

In 1933, the turbulent events in Germany after Hitler's rise to power led to Tillich's dismissal from his chair at Frankfurt. He emigrated to the United States and was appointed Professor of Philosophical Theology at Union Seminary in New York, a position he held until 1955. The main lines of thought set out in the late 1920's were followed through, and, together with a number of fresh philosophical ingredients, gave rise to his most sustained theological treatise, the three-volume *Systematic Theology*. During this period too, Tillich drew voraciously on his love of the arts. In order to trace the close correspondence between his theology and his philosophy of art, I shall begin by looking at the key concept undergirding the structure of the *Systematic Theology* — 'correlation', and then at the main philosophical category which informs his ontology — 'ontological reason'. From this perspective, we can examine what Tillich means by the 'aesthetic function', and compare what he has to say about art in the *Systematic Theology* with his comments in other writings. In the next chapter, we shall discuss some of the key areas where his philosophy of art and ontology meet most directly, and glance briefly at his view of the place of the arts in the Church.

(1) Correlation

As is well known, the concept of correlation came to hold a central place in Tillich's thinking. It rested on the assumption that there is a direct correspondence between the revelation of Jesus as the Christ and the profound experiences of ultimate reality which are common to all human beings. The method of correlation was an attempt to bring together the most urgent, pressing and deep-rooted questions of modern human existence with the theological answers given in revelation so that the Christian message might engage effectively with our contemporary world. In Tillich's words, theology aims to answer "the questions implied in the [human] 'situation' in the power of the eternal message and with the means provided by the situation whose questions it answers."[1] Accordingly, the structure of the *Systematic Theology* displays a dialectical pattern. Each of its five parts analyses the existential state of humankind and the questions which arise from this analysis, and seeks to show that "the symbols used in the Christian message are the answers to these very questions."[2] One side deals with humanity in its existential situation (with what we are in existence), while the other deals with our essential nature (what we ought to be). The analysis of the present state of humanity is the task of the philosopher, and because theology always responds to the analysis of our existential situation, theology is first and foremost concerned with the nature of human being, our experience of 'non-being', ontological 'anxiety' and what Tillich calls the 'ambiguities' of life. Philosophy and theology he sees as quite inseparable.[3]

In his analysis of the human situation, Tillich drew extensively on the philosophy of existentialism, notably that of Martin Heidegger. An examination of the human condition shows that 'estrangement' is its primary and universal characteristic. There is a split between our essential nature and our actual existence, between what we are meant to be and what we actually are. "Man as he exists is not what he essentially is and ought to be. He is estranged from his true being".[4] He is at odds with himself, the world and God. Each of us is subject to the ambiguities, fractures, distortions and destructive influences of the world in which we live. We turn away from God as the ground of our being and treat ourselves as the absolute centre of our world.[5] By estrangement Tillich also refers to our experience of living under the limitations of finitude: death, suffering, doubt, meaninglessness, temptation, despair and condemnation.[6] Tillich is quite emphatic that we are quite unable to save ourselves from this predicament of estrangement; we cannot move from existence to essence in our own power.[7]

However, three inseparable elements make up Tillich's anthropology: essential being, existential being, and the longing and hope for salvation in which the estrangement between essence and existence is overcome. Religion is, as it were, the place where the question of salvation is asked and the answer given in revelation. Yet again, Tillich insists that religion is not a discrete area of life, the preserve of those who would call themselves 'religious', but rather a universal, ontological dimension of humankind. To be religious is a matter of being orientated towards that reality through which salvation can take place.[8] More specifically, our longing for salvation has found its fulfilment in Jesus of Nazareth. Here the answer to our appalling crisis is given in revelation; in him the tragic conditions of human estrangement are overcome. This one life actualised without existential disruption the eternal God-man unity which characterises our essential nature. Thus in the biblical portrayal of Jesus as the Christ, we are presented with a picture of the one who is himself the bearer of the New Being. Faith in him is the recognition and reception of this New Being mediated by him, experienced as transforming, healing power. In the midst of estrangement, we discover unity with the unconditioned mystery which is the ground of being and meaning. Outside of Christ, an authentic encounter with divine grace is certainly possible, but the New Being in Jesus as the Christ stands as the prime criterion of all saving and healing processes.[9]

(2) Ontological Reason and the Aesthetic Function

We now need to explore more fully the ontology which underlies this account of our state in the world.[10] Central here is his adaptation of the ancient doctrine of a universal *Logos* permeating and supporting all things. Modern thought has been plagued, so Tillich argues, by too narrow an understanding of reason — 'technical reason', the human ability to calculate, predict and match means to ends. This lacks depth, and when allowed to dominate a culture, leads to an alienation of humanity from ultimate reality. So Tillich chooses to revive the concept of the *Logos*, an intelligible order common to the structure of the mind and the structure of the world.[11] He speaks of 'ontological reason', which he defines as "the structure of the mind which enables it to grasp and shape reality."[12] Within ontological reason, Tillich makes a distinction between 'subjective reason' — "the structure of the mind which enables it to grasp and shape reality on the basis of a corresponding structure of reality", and 'objective reason' — "the rational structure of reality which the mind can grasp and according to which it can shape reality."[13] Reason in its objective and subjective structure points to something that appears in these structures but which transcends them in power and meaning, namely, the unconditioned ground and abyss of reason, the 'ground of being', 'being-itself', the 'infinite potentiality of being and meaning', or simply 'God'.[14]

Through subjective reason, Tillich maintains, we can relate to the world in one of two ways: either by 'grasping' or 'shaping' reality, that is, either theoretically or practically. Grasping is a 'receptive' function which involves "penetrating into the depth, into the essential nature of a thing or an event, understanding and expressing it."[15] In the third volume of *Systematic Theology*, Tillich speaks of this as *theoria*, "the act of looking at the encountered world in order to take something of it into the centred self as a meaningful, structured whole."[16] When this happens, we are in touch with the 'power of being', with that level of reality which transcends the particular and the finite: "*theoria* is union with the really real, with that level of a thing in which the 'power of being' (*ousia*, 'Seinsmächtigkeit') is situated."[17] Shaping, in contrast, involves ordering reality, through disciplines such as economics, medicine, administration and education. This 'reactive' activity Tillich calls *praxis*. "*Praxis* is the whole of cultural acts of centred personalities who as members of social groups act upon each other and themselves. *Praxis* in this sense is the self-creation of life in the personal-communal realm."[18]

Because of the emotional element in every human act, there is a basic polarity in both grasping and shaping. On the receptive (or grasping) side, there is a cognitive/aesthetic polarity, and on the reactive (or shaping) side, an organisational/organic polarity[19] (Fig. 2):

These polarities each encompass a continuum, along which various human activities may be placed. For example,

> "Music is further removed from the cognitive function than the novel, and technical science is further removed from the aesthetic realm than biography or ontology. Personal communion is further removed from organisation than national community, and commercial law is further removed from the organic realm than government."[20]

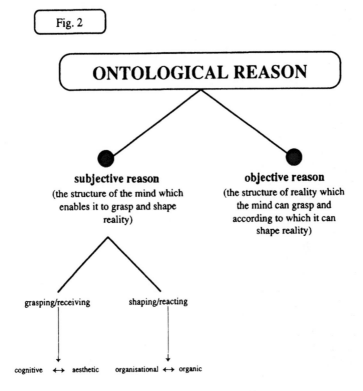

Fig. 2

ONTOLOGICAL REASON

subjective reason
(the structure of the mind which
enables it to grasp and shape
reality)

objective reason
(the structure of reality which
the mind can grasp and
according to which it can
shape reality)

grasping/receiving   shaping/reacting

cognitive ⟷ aesthetic   organisational ⟷ organic

Structural Elements in Ontological Reason

Tillich goes on to speak of various 'structural elements' of
ontological reason in its essential nature which, in the realm of
existence, lead to various conflicts and tensions. Through these
conflicts, we are driven towards the quest for revelation and
salvation (Fig. 3):

It is worth considering each of these elements and conflicts
in turn since they throw much light on Tillich's understanding
of art.[21] Firstly, there is the polarity between *structure and
depth*, which, under the conditions of existence, results in a
conflict between autonomous reason and heteronomous reason.
Out of this tension comes the quest for theonomy.[22] Here we
meet again the categories of autonomy, heteronomy and
theonomy. Autonomy, which closes itself to the infinite, is
ultimately superficial, for it lacks any dimension of depth. In
autonomous culture, the attempt is made to create forms of

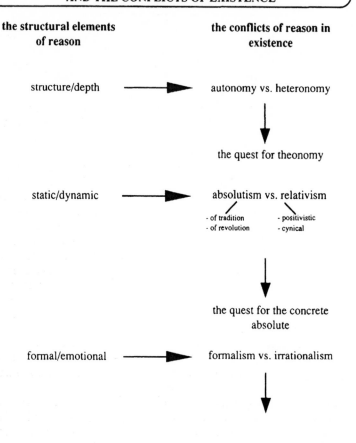

Fig. 3

THE STRUCTURAL ELEMENTS OF ONTOLOGICAL REASON
AND THE CONFLICTS OF EXISTENCE

the structural elements
of reason

the conflicts of reason in
existence

structure/depth ⟶ autonomy vs. heteronomy

↓

the quest for theonomy

static/dynamic ⟶ absolutism vs. relativism

- of tradition   - positivistic
- of revolution   - cynical

↓

the quest for the concrete
absolute

formal/emotional ⟶ formalism vs. irrationalism

↓

the quest for the union of
form and mystery

personal and social life "without any reference to something
ultimate and unconditional, following only the demands of
theoretical and practical rationality".[23] Heteronomy tries to fill
the void created by autonomy, for we cannot exist for long
without recognising ultimate meaning. Heteronomy demands
that we come under the power of other beings or of supra-
personal forces and structures. It "issues commands from

'outside' on how reason should grasp and shape reality...........The basis of a genuine heteronomy is the claim to speak in the name of the ground of being and therefore in an unconditional and ultimate way."[24] In a heteronomous culture, people are subjected to the "authoritative criteria of an ecclesiastical religion or a political quasi-religion, even at the price of destroying the structures of rationality".[25] But nothing short of the infinite can satisfy our inner longing for ultimacy in meaning and being.   Thus the antithesis between autonomy and heteronomy gives rise to the desire for theonomy. Theonomy occurs when the dimension of ultimate depth, implicit in all reality, is revealed in and through finite forms. A theonomous attitude denies both that we ourselves are the source and measure of religion (autonomy), and that we should be subjected to some alien or supposedly superior law (heteronomy).[26]

What might autonomy, heteronomy and theonomy look like in art?   Surprisingly, this is not something which Tillich explicitly addresses. But, following Palmer, it would seem quite in keeping with what we have found to propose the following. 'Autonomous art' would be that art which deals only with the surface of things, reality in its immediacy. This is the way in which Tillich interprets Impressionism.   'Heteronomous art' would arise from the imposition of particular stylistic norms by authoritarian religious or secular powers. (Tillich cites Greek Orthodox iconography as an example of what happens when the Church prescribes definite rules "according to which a sacred picture must be made."[27]) 'Theonomous art' would transcend the divisive tendencies of autonomous and heteronomous art, and reveal the dimension of depth of reality. This would occur when the expressionist style was predominant: in one place Tillich claims that "expressionism is the genuinely theonomous element."[28]

Secondly, Tillich speaks of a polarity between the *static and dynamic*. Under the conditions of existence, this polarity gives rise to a conflict between between absolutism and relativism. In the arts, there can be an absolutism of tradition (where a particular artistic tradition is revered and clung to at all costs) and an absolutism of revolution (where all forms of past tradition are disparaged). There is also positivistic relativism and cynical relativism; in the former, all previous styles are treated as of equal value, in the latter, any hope of finding universal standards in art is abandoned.[29]

Thirdly, a polarity holds between the *formal and emotional*. In its essential structure, reason unites formal and emotional elements, with a predominance of the formal element in the cognitive and legal functions, and a predominance of the emotional element in the aesthetic and communal functions. But under the conditions of existence this polarity leads to an antithesis between formalism and irrationalism. Little is said by Tillich about irrationalism in the arts. But formalism involves "the exclusive emphasis on the formal side of every rational function" and "the separation of the functions from each other."[30] In the cognitive realm, it shows itself as 'intellectualism'. In the field of the arts, we see it in 'aestheticism', where all the interest is in form and structure, and where detached judgements of taste and connoisseurship are substituted for committed, emotional encounter.[31]

(3) Art and Knowledge

We can now inquire into what kind of relation holds between the aesthetic and cognitive functions. It is basic for Tillich that we cannot drive a wedge between art and knowledge. Both art and knowing are concerned with grasping, rather than shaping reality. Both are functions of the activity of *theoria* which 'looks at the encountered world in order to take something of it into the centred self as a meaningful, structured whole'. Both involve the perception of universals, for every product of *theoria* (cognitive and aesthetic) is

> "a mirror of encountered reality, a fragment of a universe of meaning.........if Van Gogh paints a tree, it becomes an image of his dynamic vision of the world. He contributes to the creation of the universe of meanings by creating an image both of treehood and of the universe as reflected in the particular mirror of a tree."[32]

Further, both attempt to bridge the gap between the self and the world.[33] Although self and world are estranged under the conditions of existence, in knowledge and the arts there is a real striving towards union, initiated by the ambiguities of life in its mixture of essence and existence.[34] In all knowledge, knower and known are united: "The subject 'grasps' the object, adapts it to itself, and, at the same time, adapts itself to the object."[35] A similar union can take place in aesthetic activity: "there are degrees of depth and authenticity of this union, depending on the creative power of the artists, but there is always some kind of union."[36]

However, despite the similarities between the cognitive and aesthetic, the way in which Tillich speaks about them reveals four important differences. In the first place, emotion is more pronounced in the aesthetic function.[37] As we saw above, it is emotion which determines the cognitive/aesthetic polarity. All knowing contains an element of emotion, and a particular type of knowledge — 'receiving knowledge' — includes a very high degree of emotional involvement.[38] But the *content* of knowledge is never itself emotional: "it is rational, something to be verified, to be looked at with critical caution."[39] This contrasts with the content of aesthetic experience which, on Tillich's reckoning, is emotional through and through.

Secondly, the cognitive and aesthetic functions differ with respect to their main aims. The activity of knowing is directed primarily towards truth, through the union of subject and object by means of the creation of concepts.[40] In every aesthetic act, on the other hand, even though the artist is not unconcerned with truth, the chief aim is to express ultimate qualities of being by means of the creation of 'images'.[41] ('Image' here is used in a very wide sense, to cover all aesthetic creations.) At times, the aim of art has been described in terms of beauty. Tillich is uneasy about the term because of its associations with perfect proportion and balance; for him these have little to do with the potency of art. He prefers 'expressive power' or 'expressiveness', the disclosure of an infinite meaning and ultimate significance.[42] The aesthetic function, then, unlike the cognitive function, is by its very nature geared towards the disclosure of ultimate reality, irrespective of an artist's conscious intention.

Thirdly, the cognitive and aesthetic functions unite self and world in different ways. Art may involve an encounter between finite subject and finite object(s), but it is orientated chiefly towards expressing the unconditional, which by definition transcends subject and object. Art at its greatest, truly religious art, exhibits that level of reality in which the contrast between subject and object no longer exists, where the distinction between knowing subject and known object is no longer actual. This means that the experience gained in such art is of a very different kind from that gained in ordinary cognition. In the latter case, we are primarily conscious of recognising and grasping a finite object as something distinct from us. In art, especially that in which the expressive style holds sway, we are made aware of that which transcends the subject-object division.

It is thus not surprising to find a strong link between Tillich's account of expressionist art and his account of revelation. For he repeatedly insists that what is received in revelation is not an awareness of some object alongside other objects, but of being-itself which is the *prius* of subject and object. God is not 'one being' among others, but the "power inherent in everything............the power......above everything, the infinite power of being".[43] (It is worth bearing in mind that, for Tillich, both the reality which the artist encounters and the work of art itself are, potentially at least, revelations of ultimate depth. As we shall discover, this is vital for understanding Tillich's Christology.)

Fourthly, the aesthetic and cognitive differ with respect to the characteristic tension which pertains to each. In the cognitive function, under the conditions of existence, a tension arises between the knowing subject and the known object.[44] However, in the aesthetic function, the main tension is that between the expression and that which is expressed, between finite reality and the ultimate reality which supports and breaks through it.[45] It is on this basis that Tillich distinguishes between 'authentic' and 'inauthentic' art. Art can be inauthentic for two reasons, "either because it copies the surface instead of expressing the depth or because it expresses the subjectivity of the creating artist instead of his artistic encounter with reality." Authentic art, on the other hand, results when "an otherwise hidden quality of a piece of the universe (and implicitly of the universe itself) is united with an otherwise hidden receptive power of the mind (and implicitly of the person as a whole)".[46]

This tension between the expression and the expressed provides Tillich with a valuable tool to elaborate a typology of stylistic elements which he believes characterise every work of art, at least to some extent. In the third volume of his *Systematic Theology* they appear as the 'naturalistic', the 'idealistic' and the 'expressionistic'.[47] Naturalism involves an over-emphasis on subject-matter and the "impulse to present the object as ordinarily known or scientifically sharpened or drastically sharpened or drastically exaggerated."[48] In its extreme form it is seen in the simple imitation of nature: finitude is accepted in its finitude.[49] In his article "Art and Ultimate Reality," Tillich speaks of this as 'descriptive realism', citing as examples Courbet's 'Wave', Corinth's 'Self-Portrait with Death', and works by the American artists Hopper and Sheeler. Here ultimate reality is revealed to us when our eyes are opened to a truth which is lost in our everyday lives. "It is the humility of accepting the given which provides it with religious power."[50] Idealism, so Tillich believes, moves beyond ordinarily encountered reality to things in their essence, things as they ought to have been or ought yet to be. It shows "the potentialities in the depths of a being or event, and brings them into existence as artistic images".[51] "It is the anticipation of a fulfilment that cannot be found in an actual encounter and that is, theologically speaking, eschatological".[52]   Much Renaissance art has this quality — for example, the works of Francesca, Perugino — but it can also be seen in Poussin and Ingres. It corresponds to 'religious humanism', which looks for a full realisation of the unity of God and humankind within history. But it carries with it a significant drawback: instead of showing the depth of reality, ingredients are added to objects represented in order to falsify them. This is 'dishonest beautification' and 'idealised naturalism'. Tillich is convinced that this tendency has been evident in much of what passes as 'religious' art.[53] Expressionism has arisen to counteract both idealism and naturalism. Tillich links it with the 'ecstatic-spiritual' type of religious experience, "realistic and at the same time mystical," restless and yet also pointing to eternal rest. In his *Theology of Culture*, Tillich describes this in terms which are by now very familiar:

> "The expressive element in a style implies a radical transformation of ordinarily encountered reality by using elements of it in a way which does not exist in the ordinarily encountered reality. Expressionism disrupts the naturally given appearance of things...........That which is expressed is the 'dimension of depth' in the encountered reality, the ground and abyss in which everything is rooted."[54]

Van Gogh's 'Hills at St. Remy', Munch's 'The Scream', Derain's 'London Bridge', Marc's 'Yellow Horses', and works by Schmidt-Rottluff, Heckel and Nolde are all mentioned in this connection.[55] This style is supremely religious. It is "essentially adequate to express religious meaning directly, both through the medium of secular and through the medium of traditional religious subject matter."[56] It is the decisive feature of the great religious art of the past, though it is frequently displayed in works which are not created specifically for church use. This style has made religious art possible again in our time.[57] So Tillich can assert bluntly: "Religious art is Expressionistic".[58]

Notes

[1] *ST*, 1, p. 6.

[2] *Ibid.*, p. 70.

[3] *Ibid.*, pp. 21ff. In Tillich's early works, 'ontology' is described as that discipline concerned with Being (*Sein*), and is subordinate to metaphysics whose object of inquiry is Meaning (*Sinn*). After encountering the 'fundamental ontology' of Heidegger, Tillich replaced metaphysics with ontology as the fundamental philosophical

discipline; Being now becomes the philosophical absolute. Moreover, the word 'ontology' came to have an important existential nuance for Tillich ("participating in a situation......with the whole of one's existence"); cf. *The Courage to Be*, London: Nisbet, 1952, p. 124. Ontology deals with human existence, particularly the human encounter with 'non-being'. Cf. Adrian Thatcher, *The Ontology of Paul Tillich*, Oxford: Oxford University Press, 1978, pp. 10-24.

4 *ST*, 2, p. 51.
5 *Ibid.*, pp. 53-63.
6 *Ibid.*, pp. 77-90.
7 *Ibid.*, pp. 92-100.
8 *Ibid.*, p. 99.
9 *Ibid.*, chs. 16-21.
10 The ontology of the *Systematic Theology* is an extension of thoughts which were germinating in Tillich in the late 1920's. The chapter on 'The Structure of Reason' is virtually a re-working of "Über gläubigen Realismus," published in 1928.
11 *ST*, 1, pp. 81ff. Cp. *IH*, pp. 123-175.
12 *ST*, 1, p. 83.
13 *Ibid.*, pp. 84, 86.
14 *Ibid.*, pp. 88, 172f.
15 *Ibid.*, p. 85.
16 *ST*, 3, p. 66.
17 *PE*, pp. 76f.
18 *ST*, 1, pp. 69f. This distinction between *theoria* and *praxis* corresponds to Tillich's earlier distinction between the theoretical and practical in *The System of Sciences*.
19 *Ibid.*, p. 85.
20 *Ibid.*, pp. 85f.
21 Strangely, Palmer, in his study of Tillich's philosophy of art, only seems to recognise the structure/depth conflict as being relevant to art. *Op. cit.*, pp. 100ff.
22 *ST*, 1, pp. 92-96.
23 *PE*, p. 63.
24 *ST*, 1, pp. 93, 94.
25 *PE*, p. 63.
26 It is important to note that Tillich does not set up theonomy in total opposition to autonomy. Theonomy is a type of autonomy, an authentic autonomy which avoids pure secularism by recognising and affirming ultimate reality within finite reality. "Theonomy," he writes, "does not stand against autonomy as heteronomy does. Theonomy is the answer to the question implied in autonomy, the question concerning a religious substance and an ultimate meaning of life and culture." *PE*, p. 53; cp. *ST*, 1, p. 85.
27 "Theology, Architecture, and Art," *Church Management*, 33, 1, (1956), p. 7.
28 *ST*, 3, p. 274. Cf. Palmer *op. cit.*, pp. 100ff. See also *The World Situation*, Philadelphia: Fortress Press, 1965, where Tillich writes of a gradual replacement of theonomy by autonomy as we move through Giotto and Titian to Rembrandt. In Giotto's portraits of St. Francis,

we find the theonomous ideal: "every individual participates in a communal movement created by loyalty to a transcendent reality." In Titian however "the transcendental reality to which Giotto subjects all individuals........has disappeared." And in Rembrandt there emerges the truly 'unique individual', the personality of the 'early bourgeois spirit'. By the time we reach the late nineteenth century we witness the climax of the autonomous attitude. Remarkably, Tillich claims that from Rembrandt to the Expressionists, there was "no important religious art". *Ibid.*, pp. 11, 14, 33.

[29] *ST*, 1, pp. 96ff.

[30] *Ibid.*, p. 99.

[31] *Ibid.*, p. 100.

[32] *ST*, 3, p. 66.

[33] In Tillich's system, the self-world polarity is the most basic articulation of being. It is the basis of the subject-object structure of reason: both self and world are bearers of ontological reason and are thus interdependent. *ST*, 1, p. 183.

[34] *ST*, 3, pp. 68f.

[35] *ST*, 1, p. 105.

[36] *ST*, 3, p. 69.

[37] *ST*, 1, p. 99. When considering the contrast between music and mathematics, for example, Tillich comments: "The emotional element in music opens up a dimension of reality which is closed to mathematics." *Ibid.*, p. 86.

[38] According to Tillich, knowledge in any form is characterised by detachment as well as union: "the union of knowledge is a peculiar one; it is a union through separation. Detachment is the condition of cognitive union. In order to know, one must 'look' at a thing, and, in order to look at a thing, one must be 'at a distance'." *Ibid.*, p. 105. Knowledge characterised primarily by detachment Tillich calls 'controlling knowledge', and that characterised predominantly by emotional union 'receiving knowledge'.

[39] *Ibid.*, p. 109.

[40] *Ibid.*, p. 112. Cf. *ST*, 3, pp. 66f.

[41] *ST*, 3, pp. 66f.; 68. Tillich justifies this use of the term 'image' for a musical composition because one often transfers a visual term to the sonic sphere (e.g. 'musical figures') and *vice versa*. Cp. "Art and Ultimate Reality," (henceforth "AUR") *Cross Currents*, 10 (Winter 1960), p. 3.

[42] *ST*, 3, p. 68. Cp. *ST*, 1, p. 88: "In the aesthetic realm the depth of reason is its quality of pointing to 'beauty-itself,' namely, to an infinite meaning and ultimate significance, through the creations in every field of aesthetic inutition."

[43] *ST*, 1, p. 261.

[44] *ST*, 3, pp. 69f.

[45] *Ibid.*, pp. 68f.

[46] *Ibid.*

[47] *Ibid.*, pp. 76f.

[48] *Ibid.*, p. 76.

[49] *Ibid.*, p. 274.

50 "AUR," p. 7.
51 *Ibid.*, p. 8.
52 *ST*, 3, pp. 76f.
53 "AUR," p. 8; cp. *CTB*, p. 145; *ST*, 3, p. 77. Tillich admits that there was a time when he believed that this style was quite unable to mediate ultimate reality, but changed his mind when he realised it involved the anticipation of the highest possibilities of being. "AUR", p. 8.
54 *TC*, p. 74.
55 "AUR," p. 10.
56 *TC*, p. 73.
57 *Ibid.*, pp. 74f. Cp. *ST*, 3, p. 274.
58 "Theology, Architecture and Art," p. 55. Tillich is willing to concede the potential danger of this style, namely that the artist merely expresses his own subjectivity. "AUR," p. 10. We should note that in "Art and Ultimate Reality" Tillich distinguishes two further stylistic elements in addition to those mentioned above. There is 'magical' or 'numinous' realism which depicts ordinary things, persons and events in such a way that they are laden with mysterious power (p. 4); this runs the risk of idolatry. And there is the 'mystical' style - the attempt to reach ultimate reality without the mediation of individual things at all. (In *ST*, 2, Tillich calls this 'the non-historical expectation' of the New Being.) As examples, he cites Japanese and Chinese landscapes, and the backgrounds of many Asiatic and Western paintings. This can very easily lead to the expression of nothing at all: the sacred emptiness "can become mere emptiness, and the spatial emptiness of some pictures indicate merely artistic emptiness." ("AUR," p. 6.) It is not at all clear how these two styles fit into the naturalism/idealism/expressionism scheme which seems so basic in Tillich's other surveys.

5. Meeting Points (After 1933)

> "Art indicates what the character of a spiritual situation is;
> it does this more immediately and directly than do science
> and philosophy for it is less burdened by objective
> considerations. Its symbols have something of a revelatory
> character while scientific conceptualisation must suppress
> the symbolical in favour of objective adequacy."
>
> Tillich, *The Religious Situation*

Having sketched the general shape of Tillich's systematic
theology after 1933 and seen something of how Tillich
understands our aesthetic awareness, we can now go on to
examine three specific areas where Tillich's philosophy of art
and his philosophical theology interweave very closely during
this period: his concept of ultimate concern, his theory of symbol,
and his treatment of the New Testament portrayal of Jesus as
the Christ. I shall conclude the chapter with a short look at
Tillich's comments on the place of the arts in the Church.

(1) Art and Ultimate Concern

Tillich's desire to restore the existential dimension to theology
and philosophy, so characteristic of his mature thought, meant
that the notion of 'ultimate concern' came to hold a crucial
place for him. It provided the key to integrating his account of
religious commitment and his understanding of God as the
ultimate ground of meaning and being. For Tillich, God is that
which ultimately or unconditionally concerns us.[1] Hence he
writes:

> "This then is the first formal criterion of theology: *The object
> of theology is what concerns us ultimately. Only those
> propositions are theological which deal with their object so
> far as it can become a matter of ultimate concern for us.*"[2]

The second criterion Tillich states thus:

> "Our ultimate concern is that which determines our being or
> non-being. Only those statements are theological which deal
> with their object in so far as it can become a matter of being

47

or non-being for us. This is the second formal criterion of theology."[3]

It comes as no surprise to find Tillich's critics accusing him here of unacceptable ambiguity. Does ultimate concern refer to an attitude of ultimate concern or to the object of concern? In fact, the equivocation is quite deliberate. To press the distinction between the attitude and the content of faith is to run the risk of construing our knowledge of God according to the traditional subject/object pattern, which, as we have seen, Tillich is at pains to avoid. Indeed, in at least one place he explicitly identifies the attitude of ultimate concern with its object: "The ultimate of the act of faith and the ultimate that is meant in the act of faith are one and the same".[4] In other words, ultimate concern is not a matter of the human subject adopting a certain attitude to a divine Object, but rather a form of human participation in the infinite ground of being.

Four Levels of Relation between Religion and Art

How, then, does this notion of ultimate concern relate to art? As we might have anticipated, Tillich maintains that every artist's work will to some degree display his ultimate concern and that of his culture: the artist "cannot help but betray by his style his own ultimate concern, as well as that of his group, and his period........in every style the ultimate concern of a human group is manifest."[5] Tillich expands on this in his article of 1955, "Existentialist Aspects of Modern Art", where he identifies four levels of relation between religion and art.[6]

The first is where a non-religious style (one in which ultimate concern is not directly expressed) is combined with non-religious content (subject-matter which is not specifically religious or ecclesiastical).[7] This combination is to be seen in 'secular art' where the power of being is indirectly visible, for example in Jan Steen's 'The World Upside Down' and Rubens' 'The Return of the Prodigal'.[8]

At the second level, non-religious content is combined with religious style. In art of this type, our existential predicament is revealed, the "large scale displacement of our existence" portrayed.[9] Such art is existentialist because it poses sharply the 'religious question', what Tillich elsewhere calls the 'ontological' or 'Protestant' question, namely 'why is there something; why not nothing?' This is not a straightforward logical question: it does not seek some kind of explanation for the origin or purpose of the universe. Tillich has in mind the profounder question about what concerns us ultimately, the intuitive cry arising from our awareness of existential estrangement, from experiences such as pointless suffering, a sense of meaninglessness, a consciousness of being finite and limited. Art of this second level faces us squarely with our universal predicament and the burning questioning which emerges from it.[10] Here Tillich forges a strong link between his existentialist concept of ultimate concern and the expressionistic motif of 'breaking through from the depth to the surface'. Existentialism, which reveals human estrangement, and the expressionist style, in which the power of ultimate reality is disclosed through finite forms, are seen to be inseparable. The depth of reality is "present in those experiences of reality in which its negative, ugly and destructive side is encountered. It is present as the divine-demonic and judging background of everything that is."[11] Tillich's comments on the painter Munch confirm the connection.

> "He has painted pictures........of horror, crime, shock, that which is uncanny, that which you cannot grasp. In this way, this Nordic man also became one of the existentialists, at the same time in which Strindberg wrote his great existentialist dramas with all the terrible tensions, sufferings, and anxieties."[12]

Essentially the same point is made in "Art and Ultimate Reality" and *The Courage to Be*, where Tillich speaks of expressionism as unveiling humanity's estrangement.[13] We could also highlight the way in which his history of existentialism in *Theology of Culture* follows the same pattern as his earlier accounts of the expressionist style.[14] In short, as Tillich sees it, expressionism is existentialist through and through; it is *the* existentialist style of art.

Of course he is not claiming that existentialist art can be confined to German Expressionism, or even to twentieth-century art. He mentions paintings by artists as varied as Bosch, Breughel, Callot, Dix, Goya, Daumier and Ensor; in *The Courage to Be*, he lists Dante, Baudelaire, Eliot, Auden, Flaubert, Kafka, Camus, Ibsen, Grünewald and Cézanne.[15] He reserves special adulation for Picasso's 'Guernica', acclaiming it as the supreme example of a 'Protestant' picture. 'Guernica' exemplifies *par excellence* the 'Protestant principle' — that the finite cannot contain the infinite: "Protestantism means that, first of all, we do not have to cover up anything, but have to look at the human situation in its depths of estrangement and despair".[16]

> "['Guernica'] shows what very soon followed in most European countries in terms of the second World War, and it shows

what is now in the souls of many Americans as disruptiveness, existential doubt, emptiness and meaninglessness."[17]

We can compare these remarks with his estimation of American theatre in the 1950's:

> "The American playwrights Arthur Miller, Tennessee Williams and Eugene O'Neill are not tragedians. They simply show the desperate situation of man. Here is the pure negativity of man who has lost an ultimate principle of meaning, of man who has become a thing, and who fights desperately to remain a man."[18]

Tillich also includes in this category historical styles which do not pose the ontological question but which still attempt to uncover the fundamental structures of reality and thereby reveal the power of being — futurism, Chirico's surrealism, the cubism of Cézanne and Braque, and Chagall's symbolism.[19]

True to his method of correlation, Tillich is emphatic that works in this second class do not furnish us with an answer to the ontological question; they only unveil the human dilemma in all its starkness. In 'Guernica' we see only the 'radicalism of the Protestant question', not the answer.[20] It is for the Christian to offer the answer.[21] And yet, existentialist art is not wholly pessimistic. We recall that the three elements in Tillich's theological anthropology — essential being, existential being and salvation — belong together and presuppose each other. To give an account of human estrangement assumes at least some idea of what we essentially are; "even the most radical existentialist, if he wants to say something, necessarily falls back to some essentialist statements because without them he cannot speak".[22] We recall too that in Tillich's schema, existential analysis provides the material for, and thus also determines the shape of, the answer given in revelation. This is why he believes that it is so important for the Church to open its eyes and ears to existentialist art. For the 'answer' given in revelation will only be received if it is framed in a cultural vocabulary which is appropriate to its hearers.

We must move on now to Tillich's third level, where non-religious style is combined with religious content — in other words, where we have religious subject-matter treated irreligiously. Here Tillich is at his most derogatory. Raphael's 'Madonna and Child' is dismissed as thoroughly non-religious since there is no hint of the 'disruptiveness of reality'. Other examples are adduced: Fouquet's 'Madonna' and Rubens' 'Madonna and Child'. Worse still are the 'dangerously irreligious' pictures of religious *Kitsch*, a style against which "everybody who understands the situation of our time has to fight."[23]

Lastly, Tillich speaks of a fourth level, where religious style is allied to religious content, the level of 'sacred art'. Here a surface-breaking expressionist element coalesces with the depiction of traditional religious symbols. This is religious art in the profoundest sense. As examples, Tillich cites pictures of the crucifixion by Grünewald, El Greco, Nolde and Graham Sutherland, commenting that in his view the most successful portraits of Jesus have arisen within the modern expressionist tradition.[24]

(2) Art and Symbol

We shall return in due course to Tillich's treatment of sacred art. For the moment, we turn to another sphere where art and theology converge in his thinking, his theory of symbol. Amidst the plethora of secondary literature on this topic[25] it is easy to lose sight of Tillich's purpose in tackling the theme and its place in his theological system. He never had any intention of constructing a comprehensive account of symbol. His chief aim was much more modest, namely, to give an account of religious and mythological symbols, the symbols of our ultimate concern. As Ian Thompson rightly points out:

"If we are to do justice to this theory [of symbolism] we must understand it as an attempt to provide concrete theological and cultural applications for his general metaphysics of meaning..........His specific interest is in religious symbols."[26]

Nevertheless, Tillich is firmly convinced that all symbols of whatever kind share common features. Like signs, they point beyond themselves. Unlike signs, they participate in the reality, power and meaning of that to which they point. (For example, letters — which are signs — do not not participate in the sound which they indicate; a flag — a symbol — participates in the power of the nation for which it stands.) Although symbols live and grow, and can be discarded and die, they cannot be replaced arbitrarily or according to expediency. Symbols also open up levels of reality and of ourselves which are otherwise closed to us. And they have a unique and irreplaceable role in human communication.[27]

The distinctive features of *religious* symbols are conveniently summarised by Tillich as follows:

"A religious symbol uses the material of ordinary experience in speaking of God, but in such a way that the ordinary meaning of the material used is both affirmed and denied.

> Every religious symbol negates itself in its literal meaning,
> but it affirms itself in its self-transcending meaning. It is
> not a sign pointing to something with which it has no inner
> relationship. It represents the power and meaning of what
> is symbolised through participation. The symbol participates
> in the reality which is symbolised. Therefore, one should
> never say 'only a symbol'. This is to confuse symbol with
> sign. Thus it follows that everything religion has to say
> about God, including his qualities, actions and manifestations,
> has a symbolic character and that the meaning of 'God' is
> completely missed if one takes the symbolic language
> literally."[28]

Therefore, the three criteria which religious symbols must satisfy
are that they should dialectically negate their literal meaning
but affirm their self-transcending meaning, be transparent
towards their ultimate ground, and participate in the unconditioned which they symbolise.

The dialectic of affirmation and negation should not surprise
us. For God, as Tillich puts it, is both the 'ground' and the
'abyss' of being. He is the power inherent in all things and
undergirding all things, but he is not conditioned by finite reality
as an object among others. Thus, for a religious symbol to work
effectively, it must possess a two-sided quality. It must affirm
the necessity of using material taken from finite reality and
simultaneously negate the normal cognitive use of those finite
materials by expressing that which transcends the structure of
being to which those materials belong. It must never take the
material it uses in its literal meaning. The truth of a religious
symbol "has nothing to do with the validity of factual statements
concerning the symbolic material."[29] For no element of the
finite world can serve as the medium of revelation unless it
becomes transparent to the ultimate ground of being and
meaning. Hence, paradoxically, the religious symbol is "negated
by that to which it points."[30]

It is on these grounds that Tillich insists that all language
and every statement about God is symbolic. It is impossible to
speak about God literally, for God transcends the subject-object
distinction implicit in literal discourse. Symbols are not a
substitute for direct, literal expression; they are the only fitting
language to articulate religious experience, for they deal with
that reality which by its very nature transcends all objective,
finite categories. Thus Tillich declares: "To speak unsymbolically
about being-itself is untrue".[31] The only exception is the
assertion that 'God is being-itself'; this is the only non-symbolic
affirmation about God we can make. This statement "means

what it says directly and properly; if we speak of the actuality of God we first assert that he is not God if he is not being-itself."[32]

Tillich goes on to distinguish between two different types of religious symbol — the 'primary' and the 'secondary'. The former points directly to being-itself, the latter supports or 're-symbolises' the primary symbol.[33] Primary religious symbols operate at two levels: the 'transcendent' level — "the level which goes *beyond* the empirical reality we encounter", and the 'immanent' level — "the level which we find *within* the encounter with reality".[34] As examples of primary-transcendent religious symbols, Tillich cites, among others, personality, power, love, justice, and all those symbols characterising divine actions, such as creation, providence, judgement etc.   Primary-immanent religious symbols on the other hand, live in the realm of "appearances of the divine in time and space", and so include all events, things or people through which the unconditioned has been manifested".[35]   Even so, they do not mediate any literal truth from which their meaning as symbols may be deduced.

Religious Symbols and Art

It is intriguing to see how closely this theory of religious symbol mirrors Tillich's account of expressionist or religious art. For, as we have discovered, expressionist works of art also 'point beyond themselves'; they participate in the power and meaning of the reality which they symbolise; they are not invented or abolished but grow and die in a cultural setting; and they open levels of reality and ourselves which cannot be disclosed in any other way.[36] Furthermore, all three requirements of the religious symbol are met in expressionist works of art. They dialectically negate their literal meaning and affirm their self-transcending meaning. They are part of the finite world and yet witness to and reveal that which transcends the merely finite: "It is the riddle and the depth of all expression that it both reveals and hides at the same time."[37] Expressionist art is also transparent towards its ultimate ground.   Moreover, through participating in the unconditioned, it participates in that which it expresses.

More precisely, we can say that expressionist works of art are examples of primary-immanent religious symbols. That is, they are media in which ultimate reality appears *within* the finite, natural order.   Just as primary-immanent religious symbols do not convey literal truth, so in the same way, the meaning or value of a work of art cannot be measured by the extent to which it corresponds to some finite entity. This concurs with Tillich's repeated assault on the notion that objective accuracy can be used to judge the validity of art. We cannot assess the effectiveness of the revelation of ultimate reality on the basis of the kind of critical assessment which we would apply to a finite thing. For a work of art is not making an ordinary 'statement' about an object or objects in the world in the manner of a scientific assertion. Its power hinges on the expression of the ultimate *in its unconditionedness*.[38] We are back to *The System of Sciences*: the truth of science is 'correctness'; the truth of art is 'power of expression'.

One final comment ought to be made before we leave Tillich's account of religious symbols. The fact that in nearly every paper on religious symbolism Tillich uses illustrations taken from art as his primary examples[39] suggests that religious, expressionist art is seen by Tillich as the exemplary model of religious symbolism. More than this, it would not be fanciful to suppose that his interpretation of the way in which religious symbols operate owes a good deal to his experience of expressionist art.[40] Certainly, whatever the precise origins of Tillich's symbolic theory, the relation between it and expressionist art is extremely close. (The intimate link is further confirmed by the correspondence between his theory of symbol and his account of revelation. The latter, as Tillich himself tells us, was formed partly under the impact of his encounter with art.[41]) It would seem that once again Tillich's understanding of art has significantly affected one of the key categories of his philosophical theology.

However, it is when we turn to Tillich's Christology that we see most clearly the interconnections between his theological ontology and his art-theory. Here more than anywhere else, his philosophy of meaning, ontology, existentialism, symbolic theory and the philosophy of art are fused firmly together.

(3) Art and the Biblical Picture of Christ

We noted above that the culminating element in Tillich's anthropology is the hope for salvation, a hope shared by all human beings. The New Testament picture of Jesus incorporates the fulfilment of this expectation by presenting us with an image of a life which overcomes the finite conditions of estrangement. In Jesus, the finite is surrendered (but not annihilated) in order to manifest the infinite ground of all finite reality. The life of Jesus pictured in the Gospels reveals under the conditions of existence what humanity essentially is and ought to be. In and through this human life, the universal quest for New Being is fulfilled.[42]

A double-sided event lies behind the biblical portrait of Jesus. One side of this event is concerned with historical occurrence, the other with Jesus' reception as the Christ. These two facets are inseparable. The biblical picture is a confessional portrait. We encounter Jesus as the Christ only through the biblical picture's witness to the original encounter between Jesus and his followers. Tillich has no time for a 'quest for the historical Jesus'. He is not interested in probing 'behind' the portrait of Jesus in the New Testament to get at the 'real facts'.[43] This witness to Jesus as the Christ is the only perceptible 'fact' we know about Jesus. None the less, Tillich wants to maintain that the New Testament presents us with a 'real picture' of an actual event in which Jesus the Christ is "both an historical *fact* and a *subject* of believing reception".[44]

A further point follows from this. Both the appearance of the New Being in Jesus and the portrait of Jesus as the Christ are revelations. Tillich backs this up with a distinction between 'original' and 'dependent' revelation. Peter's confession at Caeserea Philippi was an original revelation; here, the manifestation of the New Being in Jesus was received for the first time. The many receptions of Jesus as the Christ by subsequent generations of Christians are dependent revelations.[45] Tillich also speaks of a subjective (or 'ecstatic'/ 'receiving') side of revelation and an objective ('miracle'/'giving') side. A revelation needs to be both given and received.[46] The biblical picture of Jesus as the Christ operates as the objective side of a dependent revelation. It includes the biblical writers' witness to, and their response to, the original revelation of the New Being in Jesus of Nazareth.

Expressionism and the Biblical Portrait

How might this relate to Tillich's philosophy of art? Significantly, he believes that the biblical picture of Jesus as the Christ displays all the characteristics of an expressionistic painting. Indeed, he describes it as an expressionist portrait.[47] It is not 'naturalistic': there is no attempt to offer a photographic account of the life of Jesus. Nor is it 'idealistic' — a "projection of the experiences and ideals of the most religiously profound minds in the period of the Emperor Augustus". Rather, the painter has tried to enter into "the deepest levels of the person with whom he deals," so that

"his surface traits are neither reproduced as in photography
(or naturalistically imitated) nor idealised according to the
painter's ideal of beauty but are used to express what the
painter has experienced through his participation in the being
of his subject. This third way is meant when we use the
term 'real picture' with reference to the Gospel records of
Jesus as the Christ."[48]

Therefore, like the expressionist painting, the impact of the
biblical portrait does not hinge on its factual accuracy or
reliability, but on its mediation of that power the first disciples
experienced in their encounter with Jesus. No amount of
historical research can falsify or validate the biblical portrait of
Jesus as the Christ. To pick up Tillich's earlier terminology, if
the *Form* of the biblical picture is 'the life of a person', the
Inhalt is 'information about Jesus of Nazareth', and *Gehalt* is
'the power of the New Being', the effectiveness of the New
Testament picture of Christ is not determined by *Inhalt* but
derives from the way in which we are grasped by *Gehalt*.[49]
Furthermore, as with the biblical portrait, religious or
expressionist works of art both point to a revelation and are
themselves finite media of revelation. They are the objective/
giving side of a dependent revelation. The original revelation
— the artist's encounter with reality — is only received by us
through the artist's representation of that encounter.[50]
   What emerges, then, is a close correspondence between the
biblical portrait of Jesus as the Christ and an expressionist
painting (Fig. 4).

History and Faith

A fairly obvious weakness in Tillich's Christology is immediately
apparent, which, as we shall see later, has serious consequences
for his view of art. If we can never demonstrate a
correspondence between the historical information in the biblical
picture and the actual life of the man it interprets as the Christ,
how can we ever claim with any confidence that Jesus of
Nazareth actually was the manifestation of the New Being,
and that the title 'Christ' was an apt title for him? In the first
instance, Tillich's reply is that the experience of faith itself
gives us the necessary confidence that, in history, someone has
appeared who mediates the New Being. Faith, Tillich writes,
can guarantee

"only its own foundation, namely, the appearance of that
reality which has created the faith.......This alone faith is
able to guarantee — and that because its own existence is
identical with the presence of the New Being".[51]

Fig. 4

The Portrait of Jesus as the Christ

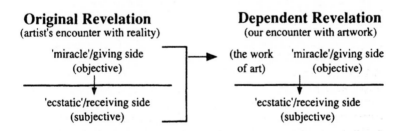

Original Revelation   **Dependent Revelation**

'miracle'/giving side   →   (the biblical   'miracle'/giving side
(objective)   portrait)   (objective)

'ecstatic'/receiving side   'ecstatic'/receiving side
(subjective)   (subjective)

The Work of (Expressionist) Art

Original Revelation   **Dependent Revelation**
(artist's encounter with reality)   (our encounter with artwork)

'miracle'/giving side   →   (the work   'miracle'/giving side
(objective)   of art)   (objective)

'ecstatic'/receiving side   'ecstatic'/receiving side
(subjective)   (subjective)

Thus, it is only faithful participation and not historical argument which "guarantees the reality of the event upon which Christianity is based".[52] It makes little sense to say that faith can provide certainty about the historical grounds of Christianity because by definition, faith speaks of 'someone' overcoming existence *in* existence, but cannot, and need not, affirm that this 'someone' was Jesus of Nazareth. Likewise, for someone today to have faith entails only that he has received that which *has* overcome existence *in* existence.[53] Nevertheless, Tillich assures us that faith does involve certainty about the meaning of the event on which it is based and to which its responds — it can affirm the reality of a personal life in the past which conquered the estranged condition of old being.

> "Faith can say that the reality which is manifest in the New Testament picture of Jesus as the Christ has saving power for those who are grasped by it, no matter how much or how little can be traced to the historical figure who is called Jesus of Nazareth."[54]

But there still remains the problem of establishing some continuity between a figure of the past in which the New Being allegedly appeared and the biblical portrait of that person. With this objection in mind, Tillich introduces a new element in his argument: the *analogia imaginis*. He claims that there is an analogy between the biblical picture of Jesus as the Christ and the concrete, personal life which gave rise to that picture.[55] This analogy is not based on historical correspondence. Its significance lies rather in the continuity of transforming power between the portrait and the event. The biblical portrait of Jesus as the Christ is analogous to its subject because the power of the New Being (received in the original revelation) is similarly encountered by present faith through the portrait (in a dependent revelation). The *analogia imaginis* is quite independent of historical enquiry because it is confirmed by each individual's participation (by faith) in the power of the New Being in Jesus as the Christ. Christians today know that ultimate meaning is rightly ascribed to Jesus: they believe that Jesus as the Christ lives in the biblical picture because the power of New Being bursts through that portrait, and that the figure therein called 'the Christ' lived apart from his portrait because the power they now experience must correspond to the real life of the one whose power it was to overcome existence.

This will hardly satisfy the hard-nosed theological sceptic, particularly if he finds Tillich's general philosophical outlook less than congenial. Moreover, the problems we encounter here all have their counterpart in his philosophy of art, and are just as intractable there. But before we move on to assessment and criticism, one final topic needs to be tackled briefly, namely Tillich's treatment of the role of the arts in the life and witness of the Church.

(4) The Church and the Arts

In the third volume of his *Systematic Theology*, Tillich deals at some length with the Church's aesthetic task, in a section on the 'constructing functions of the churches'.[56] The constructing functions are those which attempt to correlate the Church's experience of the New Being with all the cultural dimensions of life. The Church is called to use materials taken from every area of culture in order to express its encounter with the New Being. The aesthetic realm

"is used by the church for the sake of the religious arts. In them the church expresses the meaning of its life in artistic symbols. The content of the artistic symbols (poetic, musical, visual) is the religious symbols given by the original revelatory experiences and by the traditions based on them."[57]

Tillich believes that in all the constructing functions there is an inescapable tension between 'form-transcendence' — the Spirit must break into finite cultural forms giving them an 'ecstatic, form-transcending quality', and 'form-affirmation' — there must be no violation of the inherent nature of the cultural form which is used.[58] (This corresponds to the tension — often mentioned in Tillich's mature works — between the medium of revelation and that which is revealed.) Applied to the artist, this means, first, that he must observe the 'principle of consecration'. That is, he must be able to work within a specific religious tradition, with accepted religious symbols (the cross, for example), and with styles which reflect a genuinely religious encounter with reality.[59] But, second, the church artist is also limited by the 'principle of honesty'. Stylistic forms are not changeless, sacrosanct absolutes. When the styles of the past lose their expressive power, their adequacy for contemporary Church art must be called into question. Tillich highlights the modern imitation of Gothic architecture as an example of a particularly ineffective revival of a dead style.[60]

As far as artistic styles are concerned, Tillich believes that some have no place in the Church at all. For example, some brands of naturalism are quite unable to penetrate the surface level of reality. Tillich also rejects what he calls the 'contemporary non-objective style' (no examples are given) because "it excludes the organic figure and the human face".[61] Here again it is expressionism which is extolled as superlative. Even though an expressionist element is never entirely absent from any style, it is those styles "in which the expressionistic quality is predominant which lend themselves most readily to an artistic expression of the Spiritual Presence."[62]

How does Tillich envisage the future partnership between the churches and the arts? We can distinguish, I think, two main convictions. First, he believes passionately that the

Church, the Protestant Church in particular, is being called to renew its efforts in the arts, most of all in the visual sphere, and to counteract its obsessive fear of idolatry. In music and hymnical poetry, Protestantism has often surpassed the achievements of the early and medieval churches, but in the visual arts, and in those which combine seeing and hearing (religious dance and theatre), it has a lamentable record. Acknowledging the ever-present danger of worshipping the finite, we must not forget that the dimension of the Spirit includes all dimensions of life, including the visible. Religious art cannot confine itself to the spoken word. "The lack of the arts of the eye in the context of Protestant life is, though historically understandable, systematically untenable and practically regrettable."[63] Second, Tillich is convinced that expressionism has a unique part to play in the rebirth of religious art through its compelling evocation of our true condition. This highlights again the very close bond in Tillich's thinking between expressionism and existentialism. The Church has all too easily disregarded contemporary art, but we cannot afford to forget that those who have attempted to re-create religious art in this century have been led to a rediscovery of the symbols "in which the negativity of man's predicament is expressed."[64] Tillich seems to long for a new marriage of the expressionistic style with the traditional religious symbols of Christianity, but he believes this will only be possible if the Church learns to look and listen to the art of its own era. Thus,

> "[existentialist] art has a tremendous religious function, in visual art as well as in all other realms of art, namely, to rediscover the basic questions to which the Christian symbols are the answers in a way which is understandable to our time."[65]

Elsewhere, he writes: "The predominance of the expressive style in contemporary art is a chance for the rebirth of religious art", but adds: "whether, and to what degree, the artists (and the churches) will use this opportunity cannot be anticipated."[66] The matter cannot be forced, for the principle of honesty requires that we cannot simply impose styles at will. A new historical style "is created not only by the autonomous act of an individual but also by historical destiny."[67]

In the last two chapters, I have tried to uncover something of the striking interplay which developed after 1933 between

Tillich's philosophical theology and his philosophy of art.

The method of correlation is expounded as the way in which religion and culture are to be related. The systematic theologian must be faithful both to the demands of the contents of his faith as given in revelation, and the demand of his culture that he interpret this revelation intelligibly to those without any overt religious commitment. It is systematic theology which brings together an analysis of humanity's existential questioning with the answers provided in revelation. Revelation centres on the biblical portrayal of Jesus as the one in whom the hiatus between essence and existence is overcome. Through his concept of ontological reason, Tillich propounded a vision of the oneness of reality which would avoid the domination of technical reason so characteristic of our age. We examined Tillich's account of the dynamics of reason in essence and existence, and observed how these tensions and conflicts applied to art. For Tillich, art cannot be divorced from knowledge, but differs from ordinary cognition substantially — emotion plays a larger part in art; art is by its very nature specifically directed towards the disclosure of ultimate reality; art concerns the revelation of that which transcends the polarity between subject and object; and the crucial tension which needs to be maintained in order for it to be effective is that between the expression and the expressed, between finite and infinite reality. I went on to trace the very close connection between Tillich's existential doctrine of ultimate concern and his understanding of expressionist art, between the way in which he sees religious symbols operating and the way he believes expressionist art manifests the depth of reality, and between his account of the biblical picture of Jesus as the Christ and his account of expressionist painting. We found that Tillich's theory of revelation runs parallel to his interpretation of the disclosure of ultimate meaning in expressionist art. And all his major convictions about art are confirmed in his reflections on the role of the arts in the Church's life and worship.

We cannot fail to be impressed by how consonant all this is with Tillich's earlier thought. The main features of his theology of culture outlined in that seminal speech on theology and culture of 1919 ("Über die Idee einer Theologie der Kultur") are all extended and re-affirmed. No-one attending that address would have been surprised by the main thrust of the *Systematic Theology*. Most of his mature work is a refinement, fine-tuning, and adaptation of earlier insights in response to the intellectual demands which contemporary culture thrust before him. The same can be said of his philosophy of art. True enough, he had to come to terms with a wider range of art than he had known earlier, and weave it all into his system, but the principal emphases are the same as before, and the keystone stands as firm as ever: expressionism is the supremely religious style, and all else is judged in the light of it.

Notes

1 *ST*, 1, p. 14.
2 *Ibid.*, p. 15.
3 *Ibid.*, p. 17.
4 *Dynamics of Faith* (henceforth DF), London: Allen & Unwin, 1957, p. 11. On this point, cf. Anthony C. Thiselton, "The Theology of Paul Tillich," *The Churchman*, 88, 2 (1974), p. 92.
5 *TC*, p. 70. Tillich continues: "there is no style which excludes the artistic expression of ultimate concern, for the ultimate is not bound to any special form of things or experiences." *Ibid.*, p. 72.
6 (Henceforth *EAMA*), in *Christianity and the Existentialists*, ed. Carl Michalson, New York: Charles Scribner's Sons, 1956, pp. 128-147.
7 The word 'content' is equivalent to his earlier word *Inhalt*. In *TC*, p. 69, he describes 'content' as "potentially identical with everything which can be received by the human mind in sensory images."
8 "EAMA," pp. 133ff.
9 *Ibid.*, p. 141.
10 "EAMA," p. 140. It is the failure to appreciate the existential character of the ontological question which has led to a number of shallow criticisms of Tillich. See Thatcher's discussion, *op. cit.*, pp. 16-24; John Macquarrie, *20th Century Religious Thought*, London: SCM, 1971, pp. 367f.
11 *TC*, p. 73.
12 "EAMA," p. 137; cp. *RS*, p. 87
13 "AUR," p. 11; *CTB*, pp. 140f; 144f.
14 *TC*, pp. 93ff.
15 *CTB*, pp. 128f., 136, 141ff.
16 "EAMA," p. 138; cp. *TC*, pp. 68f.
17 "EAMA," p. 138.
18 "Art and Literature," from a series of lectures delivered at King's Chapel, Boston in 1958, entitled "The Self-Understanding of Man in Contemporary Thought."
19 His treatment of these historical styles and pictures follows very much the same lines as "Art and Ultimate Reality". Braque's 'Table' shows the dissolution of organic realities into "planes, lines, colours, elements of reality.......the essence of reality is contained in these original forms." "EAMA," pp. 138f. Of Chagall's works, Tillich mentions 'River without Edges' (in which "the artist tries to use some elements of the encountered world to go beyond the surface into the depths of the phenomenon of time"), and 'Lovers' (in which "the forms are taken out of the possibility of natural relationships"). *Ibid.*, pp. 139f.
20 *TC*, p. 68.

[21] "EAMA," p. 141.

[22] *TC*, p. 121; cp. *CTB*, p. 139.

[23] "EAMA," pp. 142f. In "Art and Ultimate reality" (1959), Tillich tempers his judgements on Renaissance art, but by 1961 he is on the attack again: "Zur Theologie der bildenden Kunst und der Architektur," (1961) *GW*, IX, p. 349.

[24] "EAMA," pp. 143f.

[25] Cf. e.g. Lewis S. Ford, "The Three Strands of Tillich's Theory of Religious Symbols," *The Journal of Religion*, 46, 2 (1 January 1966), pp. 104-130; H. D. McDonald, "The Symbolic Theology of Paul Tillich," *Scottish Journal of Theology*, 17 (1964), pp. 414-430; Paul L. Holmer, "Paul Tillich and the Language about God," *Journal of Religious Thought*, 22, 1 (1 January, 1965-66), pp. 35-50; W. L. Rowe, *Religious Symbols and God*, Chicago and London: University of Chicago Press, 1968.

[26] *Op. cit.*, p. 98. Battista Mondin underscores the point when he writes "it is a theological and not a philosophical doctrine, i.e. it is the doctrine of a theologian, not of a philosopher; it is a doctrine asserted in the circle of faith and not the product of philosophical reason". *The Principle of Analogy in Protestant and Catholic Thought*, The Hague: Martinus Nijhof, 1963, p. 133.

[27] "The Word of God," in *Language: An Enquiry into its Meaning and Function*, ed. Ruth N. Anshen, New York: Harper Bros., 1957, pp. 122-133.

[28] *ST*, 2, p. 10.

[29] "The Meaning and Justification of Religious Symbols," in *Religious Experience and Truth*, ed. S. Hook, New York: New York University Press, 1961, p. 11.

[30] *ST*, 1, p. 239.

[31] *CTB*, p. 175.

[32] *ST*, 1, p. 265.

[33] "The Meaning and Justification of Religious Symbols," p. 8.

[34] *TC*, p. 61.

[35] *Ibid.*, pp. 64f.

[36] Cp. "EAMA," pp. 135f.: in symbols taken from ordinary experience, "a level of reality [is revealed] *which cannot be grasped in any other way. If this were not the case, art would be unnecessary from the very beginning and would be abolished.*" My italics.

[37] "AUR," p. 2.

[38] Cf. Palmer, *op. cit.*, pp. 151ff.

[39] Cf. e.g., "The Word of God," p. 132; "Theology and Symbolism," in *Religious Symbolism*, ed. F. Ernest Johnson, New York: Harper & Bros., 1955, p. 109; "The Nature of Religious Language," in *TC*, pp. 56f.

[40] This is Thompson's conclusion in his masterly discussion of symbolism in Tillich (*op. cit.*, pp. 99ff.), although Thompson points out that politics and depth psychology also had a significant part to play.

[41] *OB*, 28. David Kelsey notes that Tillich's theory of symbol matches up almost point for point with his account of 'miracle' in revelation.

The Fabric of Paul Tillich's Theology, New Haven: Yale University Press, 1967, p. 40.

42 *ST*, 2, pp. 112-208.

43 *Ibid.*, pp. 116-123.

44 *Ibid.*, p. 113.

45 *ST*, 1, p. 140.

46 *Ibid.*, pp. 124-131.

47 *ST*, 2, p. 133.

48 *Ibid.*

49 Cf. John P. Clayton, "Is Jesus Necessary for Christology?," in *Christ, Faith and History*, ed. S. W. Sykes and J. P. Clayton, Cambridge: Cambridge University Press, 1972, pp. 153f.

50 This can also be approached from the perspective of Tillich's theory of symbolism: the biblical picture of Jesus as the Christ is the supreme example of a religious symbol. Admittedly, Tillich does not speak precisely in these terms. He writes of 'Christological symbols' (e.g. 'Son of Man', 'Son of God', etc., *ibid.*, pp. 125-130) and of the 'central symbols' of the cross and resurrection (*ibid.*, pp. 176-190). Nevertheless, to construe the biblical portrait in this way is quite justified in the light of everything he says both about the way in which a religious symbol functions and about the New Testament portrait of Jesus.

51 *ST*, 2, p. 131.

52 *Ibid.*

53 *Ibid.*, pp. 138f.

54 *DF*, pp. 88f.

55 *ST*, 2, p. 132.

56 *ST*, 3, pp. 209ff.

57 *Ibid.*, p. 210.

58 *Ibid.*, pp. 200f.

59 *Ibid.*, p. 211.

60 *Ibid.*, p. 212. This runs parallel to Tillich's conviction that religious symbols live and grow, but can also be discarded and die.

61 This concurs with Tillich's comments in "Art and Ultimate Reality," where he claims that "Non-objective art like its mystical background is the elevation above the world of concrete symbols," and that the "mystical-panentheistic element of artistic styles resists radically the attempt to use it for the representation of concrete religious symbols." (p. 11.)

62 *ST*, 3, p. 213.

63 *Ibid.*, p. 214.

64 *TC*, p. 75.

65 "EAMA," pp. 46f. Cp. *CB*, p. 145.

66 *TC*, p 75.

67 *ST*, 3, p. 214.

6. Tillich, Christ and Art

I have attempted to chart the development of Tillich's philosophy of art against the background of the evolution of his metaphysics and ontology. The time has now come to offer a critical appraisal of what we have found. Two preliminary remarks ought to be made. The first reiterates a point made earlier — that it was never Tillich's intention to formulate a complete and all-encompassing philosophy of art. He was interested in art chiefly as a means of exemplifying the central theme of his theology of culture — that religion is the substance of culture, and culture the form of religion. Expressionist art in particular gave him "a tailor-made example of a theory of the relation of culture to religion as form to substance."[1] Hence we need not be puzzled to find that numerous artistic styles and genres are either passed by or receive only scant attention. Nor should it surprise us that many of the conundrums which have engaged the ablest philosophers of art in the past are of little interest to Tillich. His paramount concerns were theological and apologetic. Second, our study has shown clearly that Tillich's ontology and his philosophy of art are intimately intertwined. Palmer underscores the point:

> "so crucial is the theological-philosophical element to Tillich's aesthetics that its rejection entails a rejection of that aesthetics...........Invariably we find that an aesthetic judgement can be explained only by reference to the theological or philosophical concept that stands behind it."[2]

Further, we have seen that not only does Tillich's account of art reflect his ontology, but that his determining ontological categories bear the impact of his encounter with art. We are not trying to claim that Tillich's metaphysics had its primary source in his experience of art; it would be nearer the mark to say that he inherited general philosophical and theological convictions from a number of sources, and that his engagement with art, especially expressionist art, provided the impetus for their articulation and systematic development.

With these observations in mind, what can be said by way of assessment?

On the positive side, we should note first the impressive way in which, as a systematic theologian, Tillich is at such great pains to come to terms with art, particularly that of his own era. With considerable passion, he seeks to penetrate into what he believes to be the spiritual significance of contemporary art, to listen attentively to its implicit meanings, to relate what he finds to other streams of cultural life, and to integrate all this with his larger theological and metaphysical interests. Time and time again, he challenges us to look at a familiar work of art or artistic tradition from the perspective of ultimate reality, so that we begin to discern dimensions of depth which might easily have gone unnoticed. Particularly laudable also is his regard for art beyond the Church's walls. Frequently, Tillich spoke of himself as a theologian 'on the boundary' — on the boundary between the community of faith and modern culture. Most of his comments on art apply to works which come from outside the sphere of explicitly Christian or 'religious' activity. In this respect, Tillich is virtually unique amongst contemporary theologians. As Thomas Matthews points out:

> "no other modern theologian has written so often on the sub-ject [of modern art], nor has any other had so high a regard for the accomplishment of modern art. If one intends to dis-cuss modern art and religion Tillich is the most important figure to be reckoned with."[3]

Another of Tillich's merits lies in his highlighting the generally feeble state of religious art in modern Protestant church life. His voice, comments Brian Halsey, was "one of the few significant ones raised against this situation in the early part of our century."[4] For Tillich, neither the presence of particular religious symbols, nor the use of traditional religious subject-matter guarantees religious art. His remarks need to be taken to heart today, especially when so often what passes as 'Christian' art fails to take with any seriousness the apathy, despair and fearfulness so widespread in our society. To take one example, few of the songs of the contemporary renewal movement deal at any depth with such themes as rebellion against God, anger, social injustice, alienation: the implied message is frequently one of joy without tears. Whatever the reservations we may have about Tillich, it is hard to deny that his remarks on religious art are often painfully apt.

Furthermore, although Tillich may have been inexpert as an aesthetician, he shows himself adept at handling at least some of the notorious and thorny issues of philosophical aesthetics — for example, self-expression vs. representation, the place of emotion in art, the relation between truth and art. Once again, in this respect he has no parallel amongst twentieth-century

Protestant theologians, who have largely absented themselves from aesthetic debate.

However, whilst acknowledging Tillich's substantial contribution to the dialogue between theology and the arts, there are several areas of weakness which deserve attention.

History of Art

The first and most obvious concerns Tillich's reading of the history of art. Stimulating he may be, but he is prone to extreme generalisations and bizarre judgements. A good case in point is his approach to Expressionism. If the majority of art-historians are to be believed, German Expressionism was in fact never one co-ordinated movement in the way Tillich suggests. Indeed, at the beginning of the century, German visual art seems to have been fragmented and highly diverse, lacking a common manifesto or set of sharply defined principles.[5] Schmidt-Rottluff believed that Expressionism had no one programme or stylistic classification, and, like Marc, was unhappy with the term 'Expressionism'. Further, Tillich was very fond of characterising Expressionism as an anti-bourgeois protest movement, yet social comment and criticism are notably absent from the Expressionists' early art. Moreover, not all German Expressionists of that period were 'anti-naturalistic': Schmidt-Rottluff's paintings can hardly be said to fall into this category. And it is stretching a point to say that all German Expressionist painters saw themselves as attempting to disclose the universal significance of reality. Some undoubtedly had broadly religious concerns, but many did not. Marc, for instance, believed that the Expressionists' aims were summed up in Willhelm Worringer's *Abstraction and Empathy* (1907), a book which has little mention of religious matters. If the Expressionists did have one conviction in common, it was probably that their art should be regarded principally as an expression of the artist's own emotional state, and that it was this emotional eruption which might issue in a destruction of form. As Myers puts it, the artist "often subordinates considerations of structure to the furious necessities of his outpourings".[6] But even here, such outpourings were not always interpreted as disclosing infinite meaning in the way Tillich supposes. Therefore, even though Expressionist art may have substantially moulded Tillich's method, it was a highly distinctive interpretation of Expressionism he chose to employ, and one which tended to gloss over a considerable variety of persuasion amongst the painters themselves.

Similar comments can be made about Tillich's handling of other traditions. His suggestion that belief-ful realism marked a return to naturalism assumes that Expressionism was essentially *anti*-naturalistic, a view which, as we have just seen, cannot be taken for granted. Or, to cite another example, in *The Religious Situation*, he describes Impressionism as a "genuine product of the capitalist temper" with its "forms of self-sufficient finitude" and its "metaphysics of a finitude which postulates its own absoluteness."[7] Yet he fails to mention that most of the leading Impressionists were politically left-wing (Pissarro was actually committed to revolution), and that their work generated a large measure of hostility in contemporary French society.[8] In short, while granting that Tillich made no claim to be an art-historian, a greater sensitivity to the character and nuances of particular movements in art would have made him less open to the charge that he was forcing artistic traditions on to a metaphysical Procrustean bed.[9]

Ultimate Reality and the Shattering of Form

Second, there is Tillich's questionable assumption that in order for reality to be portrayed in any depth, and for ultimate meaning to be apprehended, the natural forms of reality have to be shattered or broken. The evidence to support this is far from conclusive. Halsey points out that "there are numerous examples of styles that disrupt natural appearances and yet are not 'expressionistic' in the sense in which Tillich uses the term (viz. as uncovering the depths of reality)."[10] Indeed, there is no compelling reason why we should dismiss a close formal correspondence between picture and reality as a legitimate means of communicating ultimate reality.[11] Along similar lines, Matthews remarks:

> "Tillich's theory.......holding for an essentially expressionistic style in all religious art, has little justification in the actual history of art as we know it. Not only is it inadequate to cover some of the most important movements in religious art, but it would also positively exclude some of the most important figures in the history of religious art".[12]

Symbolism

Third, a host of difficulties arise in connection with Tillich's theory of religious symbolism. To begin with, he fails to come to terms with the distinction between discursive symbolism (appropriate to language) and presentational symbolism (appropriate to, for example, visual art). In the former case, meaning is grasped by means of a string of units (e.g. words), in the latter, as a single *Gestalt*.[13] Tillich uses the latter to interpret the former: he expounds the nature of religious language in terms which properly belong to presentational symbolism. But it is misleading to speak of language about God as symbolic in the same way as a painting is symbolic, since meaning is apprehended in such different ways in each case. His understanding of signs is likewise limited. Sign and symbol are distinguished, but no distinction is made between, on the one hand, natural signs, which include indices (indicating what they represent) and images (imitating what they represent), and on the other hand, conventional signs, which include archetypes, paradigmatic individuals, words and artificial symbolic notation.[14] For Tillich, all symbols are presentational and all signs are conventional.

This double restriction of sign and symbol leads to a number of weaknesses in Tillich's account of religious language. We are told that all language about God is necessarily symbolic; to treat it literally is to fasten upon its surface meaning and so to miss its real point. The only non-symbolic statement about being-itself is 'God is being-itself'. Every subsequent statement about being-itself (made on the basis of this non-symbolic statement) must be symbolic. Literal definition belongs to cognition, and cognition turns on the subject/object distinction which has no place when speaking of God. However, all this bristles with problems, as Tillich's critics have been quick to point out. There seems to be no connection between symbolic statements about God and ordinary statements about finite realities. How are we to relate the allegedly non-symbolic statement 'God is being-itself' to any other theological statement? If the statement 'God is being-itself' is a literal statement, it must have literal consequences and implications. Otherwise we evacuate it of all meaning.[15] Furthermore, if all statements about being-itself are symbolic then it seems impossible to sort out the more appropriate statements from the less appropriate, the true from the false. If we cannot say what it is that is literally affirmed and negated in any statement about being-itself, then how can statements about being-itself be validated or assessed? In other words, a meaningful symbolic statement must have some non-symbolic criterion or criteria of truth. As Anthony Thiselton observes pointedly, to say that symbols participate in the reality they symbolise "is to say something about their *power* but not about their *truth*."[16]

A major cause of Tillich being led into these linguistic cul-desacs is his failure to find a proper place for metaphor or analogy in his account of religious language. Never do we find a distinction between ordinary literal discourse and ordinary figurative discourse: all factual statements define literal meaning and all non-factual statements are to be construed as symbolic. One wonders whether the influence of Immanuel Kant here has been too pervasive. Thompson writes:

> "A less uncritically Kantian view of ordinary language might have allowed Tillich to explore more sensitively the nuances of ordinary language in its literal and figurative modes, and to realise that within scientific language itself there is both factual and metaphorical symbolism."[17]

The root difficulty here, I would suggest, is Tillich's horror of any kind of conceptualisation in theological knowledge and discourse, together with an extreme suspicion of the subject/object framework as applicable to our knowledge of God. In this he stands firmly in a long line of German philosophical and theological thought, according to which we cannot speak in conceptual terms 'about' God, or know him conceptually, because this would presuppose the very gulf between subject and object which God transcends. However, it is doubtful whether there is a form of language which avoids all conceptualisation and which does not at the same time fall into subjectivism, a flood of ambiguity, or sheer meaninglessness. And, as will be apparent later in our study, it is certainly not obvious that a biblical doctrine of God — more specifically, a trinitarian doctrine of God — together with an ontology which does justice to the particularity of God's interaction with the finite world, necessarily precludes the use of subject/object language in theological epistemology.[18]

I have dwelt on what I think are the deficiencies in Tillich's theory of symbolism because, as we might expect, they have their counterparts in his philosophy of art. Just as he construes all religious symbols as presentational, he tends to treat all works of art as presentational, with the result that he can do little justice to those forms of art which communicate by means of a sequence of units over a period of time. This is doubtless related to a deep 'contemplative' current in Tillich's philosophy and theology, his sympathy for a meditative, gentle openness to the mysterious divine dimension which supports the whole of reality. Early in his intellectual development, he had drunk deeply from the well of Neo-Platonism, especially through the writings of Schelling and Jakob Boehme. Throughout his life, he was strongly attracted to the quiet contemplation of the permanent, unchanging, eternal reality embracing and upholding all things.[19] Of course, this was only one side of Tillich. There was also Tillich the cultural activist, immersed in the vicissitudes of history, intensely involved in social and political affairs. But it is the contemplative model — encapsulated in the concept of *theoria* — which largely governs his philosophy of art and his theory of symbol. According to this model, which is primarily a visual one, meaning is grasped by the mind as a single whole. When we look at a painting, although our eyes may roam over it as we enjoy it, we endeavour to appreciate its meaning as an instantaneous unity. The movement of time is not intrinsic to the apprehension of its meaning. It is not insignificant that Tillich wants to describe all works of art as 'images'. And it is not surprising that he makes virtually no mention of music in his writings, and very little of poetry and literature. In any of his surveys of artistic styles, visual art invariably dominates the discussion. In Part III, we shall explore the problems inherent in adopting a visual model of perception as paradigmatic for the arts, and the need for an epistemology which takes our engagement with the temporal and material much more seriously. At this stage, we need only note that a better grasp of the diversity of types of symbol might have led Tillich to a more adequate understanding of the variety of the arts, and, conversely, a broader account of the arts might have made him appreciate better the different forms of symbol.

We have drawn attention to Tillich's inability to say in non-symbolic terms just what it is that is affirmed and negated in a religious symbol. The same applies to art. Deprived of any literal correlates to the statement 'God is being-itself', it is very hard to know how we can talk meaningfully at all about the disclosure of ultimate reality in art. How can we maintain at one and the same time that art discloses ultimate reality and that there are no non-symbolic means for assessing the effectiveness of this supposed disclosure? The trouble with expressionism, as John Clayton observes, is that it cannot produce "a criterion by which its product can be checked against that which allegedly brings it to expression".[20] Charles Kegley, in the course of a penetrating article on Tillich's philosophy of art, speaks of a dangerous subjectivism in Tillich, and asks:

"By what standard(s) can we judge whether and to what extent it is ultimate reality that is rendered transparent? ....By what tests can we judge whether, as Tillich aptly says, 'the work of art is merely the expression of subjectivity, 'over-excitement,' or a person who didn't learn his job'?......

[Tillich's] absence of criteria........poses a very serious difficulty.[21]

To echo Thiselton, claiming that a work of art has *power* is not necessarily saying anything about its *truth*. I would contend, with Clayton, that the weight Tillich puts on *Gehalt* needs to be counterbalanced by a greater stress on *Inhalt* or subject-matter.[22]

Art and Christology

Fourth, these problems are seen in an even clearer form when we turn to Tillich's Christology. For, on the one hand, Tillich wants to affirm that there was a human being called 'Jesus of Nazareth' who would support the Christological claim in the biblical portrait.[23] On the other hand, he insists that the truth of the biblical portrait does not depend on its factual accuracy. How can these two claims be maintained at one and the same time? Put crudely, might not the biblical portrait be complete fiction? Tillich's introduction of the *analogia imaginis*, far from resolving the difficulties, only leads to a circularity in his argument. To respond in faith to a work of art, claims Tillich, is to identify that work as arising from an objective revelation. But faith consists in being transformed by the power generated in the revelation of God as the ground of being and meaning. It seems that faith at one and the same time both presupposes and guarantees objective revelation. Can Tillich have it both ways?

Ruth Page offers a defence of Tillich on this matter.[24] She admits that Tillich's language is 'repeatedly obscure' but contends, *pace* commentators like Van Harvey, David Kelsey and John Clayton, that Tillich is impregnable given his basic intentions and ontological presuppositions: "Tillich's is certainly a very convenient philosophy and his definitions may appear stipulative, but within his own terms he is consistent."[25] For Tillich "it is the *Gehalt* of New Being that counts........the New Being is there in the picture constituting its import and confirmed by the power it has to mediate this experience to others."[26] When Tillich speaks of 'events' and 'facts' he is talking about "events and facts of experience, either the act of experiencing or that which is experienced........The biblical picture is connected with past and present experience, not past history."[27] The claim that the New Being has appeared in a personal life is thus a necessary, not a contingent, proposition. The structural requirements of the biblical picture are logically independent of its contingent ingredients.

Page's argument needs to be taken seriously, especially by those who would hastily dismiss Tillich's Christology. Even so, an important and very obvious question remains: is Tillich's ontology fundamentally congruous with that presupposed in the New Testament? As Page herself observes, if the material world is taken to be the arena for our encounter with God, then Tillich's system discounts "the contingent too readily in an evasion of matters which rightly belong to theology, including the history of Jesus of Nazareth and the composition of the biblical picture."[28] The incarnation is interpreted, as in the manner of so much German Idealism, not as a decisive intersection of eternity and time, of God and the world, but as an instance of a more general openness to ultimate reality which characterises the world as a whole. (This is symptomatic of a frequent tendency in Tillich's writings, noted earlier, to jump too quickly from the level of particularity to the level of metaphysics.) With regard to the 'bearer of New Being', this marked lack of contingency and specificity seems to make faith possible without recourse to any particular figure beyond the biblical picture of Jesus as the Christ.[29] We cannot, so Tillich insists, specify any *particular* individual and identify him as the bearer of the New Being in history, for the concept of New Being is a universal that can never be fully and exclusively identified with any particular event. Therefore, in spite of Tillich's claim that philosophical questions only determine the 'form' of the answers given in revelation (and not their 'content', which is supposedly derived from revelation), his notion of New Being seems to have determined both the form and content of revelation. The particular historical existence of Jesus has been substituted for a highly idealistic notion of what salvation must be like in order to bring about the transformation of reality. As R. A. Killen points out, this means that there is a "real danger......that some of [Tillich's] successors may find some other religion just as compatible with his ontology while rejecting the Christ whom he represents".[30] The centre of gravity appears to lie less in Jesus himself than in something which he merely exemplifies or embodies: it is not the *actualisation* of the New Being in Jesus which is decisive, but its *manifestation* to us.[31]

What bearing does this have on Tillich's philosophy of art? As with his discussion of religious symbols, the question repeatedly arises of how we are to confirm the validity of pictures which are said to convey ultimate reality. How can a relationship be established between the artist's response to a revelation of ultimate reality (embodied in his art) and the revelation of ultimate reality itself? Tillich's fundamental theological and ontological convictions prevent him from providing a satisfactory answer.[32] His reply that the experience of faith itself guarantees the connection is hardly cogent. For it is clearly not the case that a historical judgement is true simply because someone believes it to be true. Tillich seems to have no means of showing how the experience of transformation which comes from an encounter with the biblical picture differs from that which results from viewing any other picture. To take the point further, if we were to try to use Tillich's theory of art as a basis for making any theological evaluation of works of art, we are faced with the real danger that we may find some other religion which fully supports all our assessments while completely rejecting the Christ proclaimed as Lord. Certainly, in art-criticism, the Christian may frequently find himself agreeing with a non-Christian art-critic. This is not at issue. But the Christian theologian working in the arena of the arts will surely be keen to discover and elucidate criteria for assessment which are distinctive to his faith, which are finally rooted in the historical particularity of Jesus Christ, especially if he believes that some kind of unique interaction between God and his creation has taken place in the life, death and resurrection of Jesus of Nazareth. Tillich can offer little help in this direction because his Christology is so deeply coloured by his ontology.

To conclude, in Tillich's philosophy of art we are offered a valuable and rich resource which theologians working in this area would be very foolish to pass over. Nevertheless, those who wish in some fashion to follow Tillich in his courageous attempt to relate the world of the arts and the world of theology will need to pay serious attention to the weaknesses which vitiate his approach. Ironically, although Tillich is often classified as a radical, perhaps it is nearer the heart of the matter to say that he is not radical enough. To put it at its sharpest: in his scheme, Christology tends to be swallowed up in an idealist ontology; the penetrating sounds of the Gospel muffled by the 'system'. One senses that Tillich has not driven far enough into the heart of the New Testament witness to Christ in order to grasp the immense implications of Christology for the ontology of God and his relationship to the finite world. Some of these implications we shall attempt to unfold in due course. As we leave Tillich, we would do well to heed an acute observation by Alasdair Heron: "It is the almost inevitable fate of those who seek to work 'on the boundary' to find that they do not satisfy those on *either* side."[33]

Notes
[1] John Heywood Thomas, "The Problem of Defining a Theology of

Culture," in *Creation, Christ and Culture*, ed. Richard W. A. McKinney, Edinburgh: T. &.T. Clark, 1976, p. 282.

2 Palmer, *op. cit.*, pp. 176f.

3 Thomas F. Matthews, "Tillich on Religious Content in Modern Art," *College Art Journal*, 27 (1967), p. 16.

4 Brian Halsey, "Paul Tillich on Religion and Art," *Lexington Theological Quarterly*, 9 (1974), p. 111.

5 Myers, *op. cit.*, pp. 15-19; Norbert Lynton, *Concepts of Modern Art*, London: Penguin Books, 1974, p. 38.

6 Myers, *op. cit.*, pp. 40f. This is how Myers accounts for the importance of Van Gogh for the Expressionists: his "ability to represent the essentials of a given mood through the distortions of forms, local colour, and space." *Ibid.*, p. 92. Roger Cardinal has recently challenged the notion that painters such as Van Gogh, Marc and Kandinsky were concerned only with expressing purely private emotion. (*Expressionism*, London: Paladin, 1984, pp. 68ff.) Yet Cardinal adds that it is unusual for the typically expressionist artist to rise above the level of ego-bound feelings (p. 77).

7 *RS*, pp. 86f.

8 Mark Powell-Jones, *Impressionist Painting*, Oxford: Phaidon Press, 1979, pp. 41ff.

9 Matthews finds in Tillich a "blurring of all lines that differentiate artists and movements in this century, in the interests of a superimposed religious meaning", and claims that "the first task of the critic is submission to the art work." *Loc. cit.*, p. 18.

10 E.g. 'Art Nouveau' and Greek art of the sixth and seventh centuries B. C. *Loc. cit.*, pp. 109f.

11 Palmer, *op. cit.*, pp. 192f.

12 *Loc. cit.*, p. 17.

13 Cf. Susanne Langer, *Philosophy in a New Key*, Cambridge, Massachusetts: Harvard University Press, 1957, ch. IV.

14 Mathematicians and logicians, in using conventional signs, regularly speak of them as 'symbols'.

15 Cf. Lewis S. Ford, "Tillich's One Non-Symbolic Statement: A Propos of a Recent Study by Rowe," *Journal of the American Academy of Religion*, 38, 2 (1970), pp. 176-182.

16 "The Theology of Paul Tillich," p. 100. Thiselton goes on to point out that the mentally ill will turn anything and everything into symbolism, but this does not guarantee that they are justified in doing so (p. 102).

17 Thompson, *op. cit.*, p. 105.

18 Cf. Anthony C. Thiselton, *The Two Horizons: New Testament Hermeneutics and Philosophical Description with Special Reference to Heidegger, Bultmann, Gadamer, and Wittgenstein*, Exeter: Paternoster Press, 1980, pp. 154-161, 187-194; 209-217, 229-234, 245-251, 255-257, 332-336; "The Theology of Paul Tillich," pp. 99-102; and Thomas F. Torrance, *Theological Science*, Oxford, London and New York: Oxford University Press, 1978, pp. 14ff.

19 Cf. e.g., Bulman, *op. cit.*, pp. 106ff.

20 "Is Jesus Necessary for Christology?," p. 163.

[21] "Paul Tillich on the Philosophy of Art," *Journal of Aesthetics and Art Criticism*, 19 (1960), p. 182.

[22] *Loc. cit.*, pp. 162f. Cf. Palmer, *op. cit.*, pp. 210f.

[23] Cf. e.g., *ST*, 2, pp. 55f., 113f., 123, 175.

[24] "The Consistent Christology of Paul Tillich," *Scottish Journal of Theology*, 36 (1983), pp. 195-212.

[25] *Ibid.*, pp. 207f.

[26] *Ibid.*, p. 205.

[27] *Ibid.*, pp. 205f.

[28] *Ibid.*, p. 209.

[29] Cf. e.g. George Tavard, *Paul Tillich and the Christian Message*, New York: Charles Scribner's Sons, 1962, p. 172; Thomas E. McCollough, "The Ontology of Tillich and Biblical Personalism," *Scottish Journal of Theology*, 15 (1962), pp. 266-281.

[30] *Op. cit.*, p. 256.

[31] This is Alister McGrath's verdict (shared by many) in *The Making of Modern German Christology*, Oxford: Blackwell, 1986, pp. 143-146. Particularly influential on Tillich was his professor at Halle, Martin Kähler (1835-1912). Kähler argued that the historical (*historisch*) study of Jesus which attempts to reconstruct the 'real' Jesus as he existed in the past has no relevance to faith. The object of faith is the Christ of *Geschichte*, the Christ who is preached. The biblical picture of Jesus is neither an idealised collective portrait, nor "the loftiest poem of mankind." *The So-called Historical Jesus and the Historic, Biblical Christ*, trans. and ed. Carl E. Braaten, Philadelphia: Fortress Press, 1964, pp. 53, 78f. Propounding his own version of the *analogia imaginis*, Kähler believed that we encounter Christ within a tradition which possesses the power to convince us of its divine authenticity. *Ibid.*, pp. 121f.

[32] David Kelsey argues that there are two aesthetics at work in Tillich's Christology. The first understands the meaning of a picture in terms of the power and effect it has on the observer. The second understands the meaning of a work of art in terms of its formal or structural correspondence with the original revelation, without reference to its effect on the beholder. The second is used by Tillich to demonstrate the formal parallel between the biblical picture (particularly its central symbols — the cross and the resurrection) and the original revelation (*ST*, 2, pp. 152-160). The problem is, as Kelsey sees it, that nowhere does Tillich attempt to show the relationship between these two approaches. The biblical picture's formal features "are theologically important only if it can be shown that they somehow explain its ability to mediate power, and no such thing is ever shown." *Op. cit.*, p. 153; see pp. 105-153.

However, we have not detected this secondary aesthetic in our study. We would concur with Ruth Page. Kelsey wrongly assumes that for Tillich, "the warrants for judgements about the symbol are produced by analyses of revelatory events and not by ontology". Page, *loc. cit.*, p. 206. Cf. Kelsey, *op. cit.*, p. 88. (We might add that Kelsey uses 'form' to refer only to the internal structural properties of an art work, whereas Tillich understands the word in a wider sense. Moreover, Kelsey employs the word 'content' to denote 'meaning' or 'significance', not Tillich's *Inhalt*.)

[33] *Op. cit.*, p. 143.

Part II

The Dutch Neo-Calvinists —
Art, Creation and Beauty

1. Introduction

In recent years, as the world witnesses the increasing precariousness of the political regime in South Africa, much attention has been focused on the theological factors which have contributed to that country's social identity. Sooner or later, any student of South African affairs will encounter 'Dutch Neo-Calvinism' or 'Kuyperianism' (after its founder, Abraham Kuyper). Few would deny that this brand of theology — albeit in a grossly distorted form — has had a key part to play in shaping the ideology of *apartheid*.[1] Yet the impact of Kuyperianism on modern South Africa should not blind us to its considerable influence elsewhere, and to its long and rich history. Its roots lie in the sixteenth century in the Netherlands, where the Calvinist wing of the Reformation held sway. The Synod of Dort (1618-1619), which sought to defend the doctrine of God's sovereign grace against the encroachment of Arminianism, provided the Dutch Reformed Church with its most famous confession and doctrinal standard.[2] In the late nineteenth century, faced with the intellectual upheaval of the Enlightenment, the Dort tradition seemed to be increasingly under threat from a number of quarters, and there were signs in the Reformed Church of a disenchantment with Calvinism as traditionally stated. It was only a matter of time before a number of able Christian leaders, among them Groen Van Prinsterer, tried to arrest the drift away from historic orthodoxy.[3] The eventual result was a secession from the Reformed Church and the formation of the *Christelijke Gereformeerde Kerk*. By 1854, this fast-growing body had set up its own theological school in Kampen, and later helped to establish the Free University of Amsterdam, an institution dedicated to higher education according to the principles of conservative Calvinism. The mantle of Groen van Prinsterer was assumed by Abraham Kuyper, the founder and first rector of the Free University. It is the tradition flowing from Kuyper which is usually referred to as 'Dutch Neo-Calvinism'. By 1920 it had written much of the social and cultural agenda of the Netherlands. Today, though hardly a powerful force in its home country, it is still a productive school of thought elsewhere, not least in the United States and Canada.[4]

At first sight, it would be hard to imagine a greater theological contrast than that between Tillich and the Dutch Neo-Calvinists. Glaring dissimilarities are immediately apparent. On the one side stands Tillich, a Lutheran by background, deeply immersed in nineteenth-century German thought, intensely suspicious of any language about God as 'a Being', relatively unconcerned about the historical accuracy of the New Testament, and with no qualms about employing a wide range of non-Christian thought. On the other side stand the Calvinists, with little time for Kant or Idealism, happily speaking about God as a distinct Being and about Scripture as inerrant in all matters of history and doctrine, and wary of any philosophy not bearing a Christian label. Despite these differences, however, they do in fact hold much in common. Both are considerably motivated by practical concerns — analysing the world is not enough, it needs to be changed and transformed; both are passionately devoted to relating the Christian faith to every sphere of cultural life and quite opposed to the idea that religion belongs to some private, timeless realm; and — most important for our purposes — both give sustained attention to the arts.

To keep the discussion within reasonable limits, I shall restrict myself largely to those Neo-Calvinists who have made a serious effort to come to terms with the arts, namely Abraham Kuyper, Herman Bavinck, Herman Dooyeweerd, Hans Rookmaaker and Calvin Seerveld.[5] Clearly it is far beyond my scope to present a detailed account of the theology of each of these men, or of the subtle matters of dispute between them. My aim is rather, first, to try to make clear the theological currents which underlie their work, and second, to trace the connections between these currents and the philosophy of art which they espouse. In so doing, I hope to show that the issues raised by these writers are still very much with us, and that, whatever their failings, they have an invaluable contribution to make to the interaction between theology and the arts.

Before we begin, it is worth bearing in mind that Dutch Neo-Calvinism is largely driven by two closely related convictions, both of which originate in Kuyper himself. First, there is the consuming desire to activate the Church into a thorough engagement with every field of culture. Kuyper's theology was a clarion call to awaken the devout from their pietistic slumbers and remind them of the universal kingship of Christ. There must be no withdrawl into the refuge of a religious ghetto, but instead a longing to spread the aroma of Christ into every corner of culture, not least the arts. (Indeed, the Neo-Calvinists are especially keen to counteract the popular idea that Calvinism is inherently anti-artistic.[6]) Second, there is the belief that the only adequate theological backing for this cultural involvement will be found in what they see as a 'Calvinist' world-view. These, I would suggest, are the two major forces which propel Dutch Neo-Calvinism. There are, as we shall discover, many other factors at work, and the prominence given to Calvinism as a system varies from writer to writer. But these two convictions — the necessity for Christian involvement in culture, and the supremacy of Calvinism — do, I believe, motivate at a deep level virtually all that is written and argued within this tradition. With this in mind, let us turn to Kuyper and Bavinck.

Notes

1. T. Dunbar Moodie, *The Rise of Afrikanerdom*, Berkeley, Los Angeles, London: University of California Press, 1975, pp. 52-72; John W. de Gruchy, *The Church Struggle in South Africa*, London: Collins, 1986, pp. 5-10, 21, 32, 81, 90, 201; Jaap Durand, "Church and State in South Africa: Karl Barth vs. Abraham Kuyper," in *On Reading Karl Barth in South Africa*, ed. Charles Villa-Vicencio, Grand Rapids, Michigan: Eerdmans, 1988, pp. 121-137.

2. The five main sections of the Articles of the Synod of Dort became the basis of the 'five points' of Calvinism: (1) unconditional election, (2) limited atonement, (3) the total depravity of man, (4) irresistible grace, and (5) the final perseverance of the saints. Cf. *The Articles of the Synod of Dort and the Rejection of Errors*, London: Sovereign Grace Union, 1932. All this was thought to be in line with both the Belgic Confession (1561) and the Heidelberg Catechism (1562).

3. The statesman, historian, journalist, and essayist Guillaume Groen van Prinsterer (1801-1876) devoted a large part of his life to arguing that Calvinist Christianity was the most powerful agent of cultural renewal.

4. Cf. James D. Bratt, "The Dutch Schools," and C. T. McIntyre, "Herman Dooyeweerd in North America," both in D. F. Wells, ed., *Reformed Theology in America*, Grand Rapids, Michigan: Eerdmans, 1985, pp. 135-152 and 172-185 respectively; James D. Bratt, *Dutch Calvinism in Modern America: A History of a Conservative Subculture*, Grand Rapids, Michigan: Eerdmans, 1984, particularly Part IV.

5. I have decided not to deal with Nicholas Wolterstorff's *Art in Action*, (Grand Rapids, Michigan: Eerdmans, 1980) in this part of the book, apart from a few passing references. His theology is broadly Calvinist, and he clearly has sympathy for Dutch Neo-Calvinism, but his philosophy of art strays far from the Kuyperian path.

6. For the same sentiment, cf. e.g. M. P. Ramsay, *Calvin and Art*, London: Moray Press, 1938; Howard A. Redmond, "The Sense for Beauty in Calvinism," PhD Thesis, University of Southern California, 1953, especially pp. 2-59; Leon Wencelius, *L'aesthétique de Calvin*, Paris: Belles Lettres, 1938; Percy Scholes, *The Puritans and Music*, London: Oxford University Press, 1934.

2. Kuyper and Bavinck: Art, Beauty and the Sovereignty of God

"There is not a single inch of the whole terrain of our human existence over which Christ.....does not exclaim, 'Mine!'"

Abraham Kuyper

In modern times, for a major head of state to make a substantial contribution to theology would be a rare occurrence. Yet such was one of the many achievements of Abraham Kuyper (1837-1920). By any standards, Kuyper was a man of astounding gifts. A politician, churchman, journalist and author, he not only defined the ideology of Neo-Calvinism but also personified it. During a period of over fifty years, he produced a steady stream of articles, pamphlets, brochures and books, linking all areas of human knowledge to the Calvinism of the Synod of Dort. As the principal architect of the *Gereformeerde Kerken* (Reformed Church),[1] and through the foundation of the Free University of Amsterdam in 1880, he exercised a lasting influence on countless Christians in the Netherlands, who, as he saw it, were in danger of accommodating their thought to the dominant premises of liberal humanist philosophy. Possessing considerable acumen as a politician, he led the Anti-Revolutionary Party for some forty years, a body which was to play a crucial role in Dutch politics until the second World War. His career culminated in his being made prime minister of Holland from 1901-1905.[2]

Kuyper's successor at the Free University was Herman Bavinck (1854-1921), another polymath, adept in theology, philosophy, education, psychology and political theory. Very different in temperament from Kuyper — more eirenic, less passionate — Bavinck nevertheless shared Kuyper's ideals and followed through the broad lines of his predecessor's thought. He too was a prolific writer, his *magnum opus* being the four-volume *Reformed Dogmatics* (*Gereformeerde Dogmatiek*).[3] Without seeking to blur the differences between them, it makes sense to consider Kuyper and Bavinck together in this chapter, for each presupposes a very similar theological framework.

(1) God's Sovereignty and Sphere Sovereignty

The first major theme of Kuyperian theology is formed by the twin ideas of the sovereignty of God over creation and 'sphere sovereignty' within creation. Kuyper describes Calvinism as a 'life-system', providing an all-embracing, comprehensive view of our place in the world and our calling before God.[4] At the centre of this vision stands the indomitable sovereignty of God. This is the heart of true Calvinism. To quote Kuyper:

> "First stands the confession of the absolute Sovereignty of the Triune God; for of Him, through Him, and unto Him are all things.........This is the fundamental conception of religion as maintained by Calvinism, and hitherto, no one has ever found a higher conception. For no higher conception *can* be found."[5]

This universal rule of God consists in the "authority that contains all right within itself......and exercises power to.......destroy every resistance to [God's] will." God "is absolute sovereign, the only planner, creator, ordainer, and determiner of all things."[6] All things were created for God's own glory. And as sovereign Lord, He has set a plan for all things in his counsel in eternity. Creation, writes Bavinck, "cannot be deduced from [God's] goodness or love, even though both of these, too, are manifested in the world.......the cause of the creation is simply and solely the free power of God, his eternal good pleasure, his absolute sovereignty".[7]

Kuyper follows this through by arguing that God has created the world in such a way that it is impregnated with unalterable laws which provide the framework within which we live. These laws do not arise from *within* nature but are imposed *upon* nature by God. Moreover, each area or sphere of life has its own appropriate ordinances: "all created life necessarily bears in itself a law for its own existence, instituted by God Himself."[8] So, Kuyper writes,

> "there are ordinances of God for our bodies, for the blood that courses through our arteries and veins, and for our lungs as organs of respiration. And even so there are ordinances of God in logic, to regulate our thoughts; ordinances of God for our imagination, in the domain of aesthetics; and so, also, strict ordinances of God for the whole of human life in the domain of morals."[9]

In similar terms, Bavinck states: "Everything was created with its own nature and is based upon ordinances appointed by God for it. Sun and moon and stars have their own peculiar tasks;

plants and animals and man have their own distinct natures."[10]
He continues:

> "As the moral law was created in Adam's heart as the rule of
> his life, so all creatures carried in their own nature the
> principles and laws of their own development...........The whole
> creation is a system of divine ordinances.......God gave to all
> creatures a certain order, a law which they do not violate".[11]

Thus we can discern a magnificent diversity in the created
order:

> "As creatures were given their own peculiar natures along
> with differences among them, so there are also differences in
> the law by which they act and in the relationships which
> they sustain to each other."[12]

But, Bavinck adds,

> "in this diversity there is also a supreme unity......It is [God]
> who created all things according to his incomparable wisdom,
> who continually sustains them in their distinct natures, who
> guides and governs them according to the potentials and
> laws created in them.......Here is a unity which does not
> destroy, but maintains diversity, and a diversity which does
> not depreciate unity, but unfolds it in its richness."[13]

When he comes to speak of the uniqueness of each zone or
aspect of creation, Kuyper's favourite expression is 'sphere
sovereignty'.[14] In human culture, he says, three major spheres
of sovereignty can be distinguished: the sovereignty of the state,
the sovereignty of society, and the sovereignty of the Church.[15]
But within each of these there are a myriad of further spheres.
In the address he delivered at the opening of the Free University,
Kuyper declared that

> "Human life.....appears to be neither simple nor uniform but
> represents an infinitely complex composite organism. It is so
> constituted that........there are all kinds of spheres in life, as
> many as the starry hosts in the firmament, whose boundaries
> are drawn with firm lines, each having its own principle as a
> focal point.........And because each has its own domain, within
> the boundaries of that domain each has its own sovereignty."[16]

Thus each sphere of creation has its own distinctive character,
preserved by its God-given laws. The integrity of a sphere must
not be damaged or infringed. There must be no attempt to
impose the principles of one sphere on another. Kuyper was
adamant that no one sphere could be made pre-eminent and
exercise an authority over all others. In this regard Kuyper

was particularly wary of allowing the state to play too dominant a role in culture; only God possesses absolute sovereignty. As Cornelius Veenhof puts it, summarising Kuyper,

> "[The spheres] lie in this world *next* to one another and may not supplant or take advantage of one another. And thus lying *next* to one another, they all stand *under* the sovereignty of God."[17]

(2) Common Grace

Kuyper and Common Grace

The theory of creation as a law-ordered system under the overall governance of God, with its innate, irreducible realms, is one that we shall meet in all the Dutch Neo-Calvinists. The second theme which we need to highlight is more distinctive of Kuyper and Bavinck, namely 'common grace'.[18] To be sure, there is much in Kuyper's account of common grace which is opaque and confusing, but the broad lines are clear enough. The main purpose of God's common grace is the preservation of creation. Common grace is rooted in Christ as Mediator of creation, and ultimately in the eternal decrees of God.[19] Although it operated immediately after the fall of Adam, it found its 'solid historical starting-point (*vaste geschiedkundige uitsgangspunt*)' in God's covenant with Noah.[20] It has both a negative and positive aspect. Negatively, and most importantly, it refers to the restraint of the destructive effects of sin in creation. This Kuyper calls the 'constant' operation of common grace. We can see this in the natural world, but also in

> "[God's restraint] of the power of sin in the heart of man, to make possible the appearance of civil righteousness on earth among sinners and heathen.............This is the common grace that leads to the maintenance and control of our human life."[21]

Indeed, so powerful is sin, if it were not for common grace holding back the spread of evil, mankind and the world as a whole would fall apart and disintegrate. Creation could not run its assigned courses nor fulfil its purposes.[22] Positively, there is the 'progressive' aspect of common grace, through which God brings the latent potential in creation to fruition.

> "[Common] grace could not stop at [the] first and constant operation. Mere maintenance and control afford no answer to the question as to what end the world is to be preserved

and why it has passed through a history of ages. If things remain the same why should they remain at all?....... Accordingly there is added to the first constant operation of grace............another, wholly different, operation.......... calculated to make human life and the life of the whole world pass through a process and develop itself more fully and richly".[23]

The key difference between the constant and progressive aspects is that in the former, God acts independently of human effort, whereas in the latter, humankind acts as "instrument and co-labourer with God".[24]

It is important to recognise the crucial place which this doctrine of common grace occupies in Kuyper's theology of culture. For Kuyper, it is only because of common grace that human culture can flourish and the original powers implicit in creation be developed to God's glory. Without common grace, there simply would be no culture, whether Christian or non-Christian.[25] In Kuyper's hands, therefore, the concept of common grace became a key tool for spurring Christians into cultural involvement. As James Bratt explains,

"It encouraged the redeemed to respect the good remaining in the world and to strive to augment it. Even more, it made many elements of human culture......not just products but *means* of grace, instruments whereby God restrained sin and enabled men to try to develop creation as he had originally designed. Finally, it legitimised a certain amount of cooperation between the redeemed and unbelievers on the grounds that to some extent they shared a sense of good and therefore a common purpose."[26]

Nevertheless, Kuyper never lost sight of the limitations of common grace. Common grace is unable to remove or cleanse sin. In order to be restored and renewed, we need special or redeeming grace, which is far more radical than common grace. Common grace, as it were, lays the ground for special grace, but special grace, which flows from the Mediator of salvation, the God-man Jesus Christ, heals and renews creation and those sinners chosen for salvation. In the natural world, it is not geared towards conservation (as with common grace), but re-creation. Moreover, common grace is restricted to this earthly, temporal life whereas special grace is supernatural and extends into eternity.[27]

It is important for Kuyper that the redemptive work of special grace is aimed not simply at restoring the fallen world to its original state, but creating a richer and fuller world than would have been possible had the fall never occurred. Kuyper is prepared to say that the world was created in such a way that it would have gone through a general development and progression according to God's will, whether or not there had been a fall. God deposited germs and possibilities in the creation which were intended to grow and unfold to the praise of his glory. Yet this process has been arrested by sin, and the redemption of sin in Jesus Christ sets in motion a re-creative activity which will issue in a greater glory than creation would have attained had there been no sin and no incarnation.[28]

Bavinck and Common Grace

Bavinck too was happy to espouse a doctrine of common grace. Indeed, he stressed its importance long before Kuyper published a word on the subject.[29] Common grace, for Bavinck, has its ultimate origin in God's plan for the world.[30] Nevertheless, it was first manifest only after the fall:

> "When God, in spite of man's trespass, again calls and visits him and establishes enmity instead of the concluded friendship, *an entirely new element appears in the revelation, viz., that of pity and the mercy of God*. From now on, everything flows towards man out of grace".[31]

Prior to the fall, humankind stood under God as to a law-giver; man and woman were created to obey God and the divine laws established in creation. On this basis, God made a covenant with Adam, a 'covenant of works' (*foedus operum*), which guaranteed him eternal life on condition that he kept the divine laws.[32] Through his disobedience, Adam brought a curse upon himself and the whole of humankind. Subsequently a new relationship with God was made possible through the 'covenant of grace' made with the elect and sealed in Christ. (Kuyper employed the same distinction between the covenant of works and the covenant of grace.[33] It belongs to the core of scholastic Calvinism.) Thus,

> "There is a big difference...........between the way in which man before the fall was to share in the eternal life, and the way in which alone he can obtain it after the fall.........Before the fall the rule was: through works to eternal life. Now, after the fall, in the covenant of grace, the eternal life comes first, and out of that life the good works follow as fruits of faith."[34]

So, in Bavinck's scheme, in the period preceding the fall, God was related to man and woman as one who commands and demands, the relationship being maintained only insofar as the divine laws were obeyed. But after the fall, by virtue of the covenant of grace, God relates to the elect as the loving Father who bestows eternal life.

It is at this point that grace enters the scene. For Bavinck, God's grace is of two types: 'general' or 'common' on the one hand and 'special' on the other. Common grace is directed towards creation and humankind as a whole, restraining the pernicious consequences of sin and making culture possible. Its effects are seen in that the world does not degenerate into oblivion; the human race continues to flourish; man and woman remain rational beings, with natural gifts, a moral sense, etc.[35] Like Kuyper, Bavinck also holds that common grace was affirmed and re-established in the covenant with Noah — a 'covenant of nature' made with all creation, arresting sin's influence on the world.[36] At this point the ordinances governing humanity and the world were firmly fixed:

> "The tremendous natural forces which formerly operated, and which were also at work in the flood itself, were curbed............
> By this covenant bans and restrictions were laid upon nature and man. Laws and ordinances appeared everywhere...........
> Order, measure and number came to be the characterising earmark of creation."[37]

Even though there is less emphasis in Bavinck on what Kuyper called 'progressive' common grace, Bavinck shares with Kuyper the belief that it would be quite impossible to account for culture without speaking of common grace.[38] But although culture may be advanced and sustained by common grace, its source is not to be found there. Its origin is rather in God's mandate, given before the fall, to man and woman to cultivate and subdue the earth (Gen. 1:28).[39] Man was made "that [he] should have dominion over all living creatures and that he should multiply and spread out over the world, subduing it."[40] Therefore,

> "[culture] exists because God gave us the power to rule the earth. It is the communal calling of humanity to possess the earth, to form it for ownership and as an organ of personality, to turn the whole riches of created life, spiritual, moral, and natural into a pure organism, and to rule it."[41]

In another place, he expands on the same point:

> "Adam had to subdue the earth and have dominion over it, and this he must do in a two-fold sense: he must cultivate it, open it up, and so cause to come up out of it all the treasures which God has stored there for man's use; and he must also

watch over it, safeguard it, protect it against all evil that
may threaten it, must, in short, secure it against the service
of corruption in which the whole of creation now groans."[42]

For Bavinck, these tasks cannot be separated from our obligation
to submit to the will of God. The command to cultivate the
earth must be held together with the command to obey our
maker.[43] Moreover, although Adam violated the covenant of
works, the cultural mandate was not thereby abolished. Indeed,
it still stands today as a duty binding on all humankind: no
man or woman is exempt.[44]

What then of special grace? In line with Kuyper, Bavinck
bids us remember the essential difference between common
and special grace. Common grace cannot of itself bring eternal
life; at best it can only prepare the way for special grace.[45]
Special grace is revealed in God's work of redemption,
regeneration and conversion, making its first appearance in
the covenant of grace. It finds its culmination in the life, death
and resurrection of Christ. In Christ, the demands of the
covenant of works have been met, and salvation won for the
elect.

> "Christ.........takes upon Himself, the fulfilment not only of
> what the first man has done amiss but also of what he should
> have done and did not do; He satisfied for us the demands
> made by the moral law; and He now gathers together into
> one unit His whole church in the form of a renewed humanity
> under Himself as Head."[46]

A crucial point emerges at this juncture. For Bavinck, the
headship of Christ as man extends only to the community of
the elect. Under the covenant of works, prior to sin, Adam was
the head of the whole human race, but in the post-fall era,
Christ is head only of the redeemed. Citing passages like Col.
1:15, 2:10 and Eph. 1:10, Bavinck concedes that there is a
sense in which Christ is head over all humankind and all
creation. However,

> "the name of head has a different significance in these
> contexts than it has when Christ is called the head of his
> church. In the second instance Paul is thinking especially of
> the organic relationship, the unifying principle of life, of Christ
> and his church. But when Christ is called the head of man,
> or of angels, or of the world, the figure of a sovereign and
> king is being stressed. All creatures without exception are
> subordinate to Christ, even as He Himself as Mediator is
> subordinated to the Father (1 Cor. 11:13)."[47]

Earlier in the same passage, Bavinck brings out the contrast even more succinctly: "There is a kingship of Christ over Zion, over His people, the Church, and there is also a kingship which He exercises over his enemies. *The first is a kingship of grace, and the other is a kingship of power*."[48] As we shall see, this sharp distinction between grace and power is highly significant, and is characteristic not only of Bavinck but of Dutch Neo-Calvinism in general.

Corresponding to the difference between common and special grace is a further distinction between God's 'general' (or 'material') calling and his 'special' calling. Through his common grace, God issues to all humankind a general summons, a call which can be discerned in the natural world, in human history and in our inner moral sense.

> "God speaks to [the Gentiles] in nature (Rom. 1:20), in history (Acts 17:26), in the reason (Jn. 1:9), and through the conscience (Rom. 2:14-15). True, this calling is inadequate for salvation, for it does not know of Christ, who is the only way to the Father, and the only name given under heaven to salvation (Jn. 14:6 and Acts 4:12), but it is nevertheless of great value and may not be underestimated in its significance."[49]

The substance of this general calling is the moral law given to Adam under the covenant of works: this law is "the content and the proclamation, the rule and the norm, of the original covenantal relationship which God established with the newly created man."[50] The general calling, then,

> "may not be a proclamation of the gospel, but it is certainly a preaching of the law..........it has........the same moral law as its content, materially and essentially, as the one which God originally gave man and wrote upon his heart. That calling, therefore, no matter how corrupted and denatured...........still lays down the requirement that man must love God above all things and his neighbour as himself."[51]

The general calling also includes the cultural mandate: "human society and civic righteousness is made possible by [the general calling], and these in turn open up the way for a higher civilization, a richer culture, and a flowering of arts and sciences."[52]

By contrast, God's special calling is specific, historically mediated, and comes to us supremely in Christ. It is the call of the Gospel, the Holy Spirit's summons to faith and repentance. This call does not annul the general calling, but fulfils it, empowering us to obey the laws of God. This means that, although a cultural involvement is obligatory for all humankind, it is those who have been made one with Christ who will be closest to discharging their cultural duty in the way God intends. For Christ is the one who flawlessly obeyed the cultural mandate — those united to Him will be best enabled to obey the divine charge to cultivate the earth.[53]

Common and Special Grace

As we have seen, both Kuyper and Bavinck sharply distinguish common and special grace. Yet neither want to let this deepen into a dichotomy. As Kuyper put it, common and special grace are not each

> "enclosed within the walls of its own terrain. They work together in the same terrain. They, therefore, come in touch with each other. They meet each other in every plain of life. They often are mutually interwoven. Involuntarily they work upon each other. You find both in the human heart, in the same life, in the same family, in the same generation, in the same people"[54]

Amplifying this, Kuyper writes of an indirect and direct influence of special grace on common grace within culture. Indirectly, Christian faith curbs the harmful effects of sin.[55] Directly, there is the immediate impact made by Christians when they commit themselves to a rigorous engagement with contemporary culture.[56] Bavinck too makes every effort not to drive a wedge between the two graces. "Grace [in its saving sense] restores nature and leads it to the highest heights, but it does not add to it a new heterogenous element."[57] Just as special revelation does not destroy but fulfils general revelation, so the special calling does not destroy the general calling but rather absorbs and strengthens it.[58] It has always been God's purpose to renew creation rather than destroy it: "God does not negate, but respects and unfolds everything which He called into being through creation."[59] Bavinck declares:

> "Grace is something other and higher than nature, but it nevertheless joins up with nature, does not destroy it but restores it rather. Grace........[flows] on in the river-bed which has been dug out in the natural relationships of the human race."[60]

(3) The Antithesis

The third theme to highlight in Kuyperian thought is the 'antithesis', a concept especially prominent in Kuyper and adopted by a number of his followers. The word refers to that profound difference between the Christian and the non-Christian which arises from the distinctive orientation of the human 'heart'. It is from the heart, the centre and focus of our personality, that our life flows:

> "it is our repeated experience that in the depths of our hearts, at the point where we disclose ourselves to the Eternal One, all the rays of our life converge as in one focus, and there alone regain that harmony, which we so often and so painfully lose in the stress of daily duty."[61]
>
> "The heart..........is to be understood not as an organ of feeling but as the point from which God acts and from which He acts on the understanding."[62]

It is not precisely clear what 'heart' denotes here. At any rate, Kuyper urges that the state of our heart determines our 'faith', our ultimate commitments and certainties. A person's 'faith' is the *a priori* of all his or her activity. In this sense, all people exercise faith, whatever their precise religious affiliations.[63]

> "In every expression of his personality, as well as in the acquisition of scientific conviction, every man starts out from *faith*. In every realm *faith* is, and always will be, the last link by which the object of our knowledge is placed in connection with our knowing *ego*.......*faith* is the element in our mind by which we obtain certainty, not only in the spiritual, but equally in the material sciences."[64]

Because sin is chiefly a turning of the heart away from God, and because regeneration is only possible through God's Spirit, Kuyper insists unequivocally that there are two classes of people in the world, regenerate and unregenerate. There is no middle way, no 'neutral' humanity. Regeneration "breaks humanity in two, and repeals the unity of the human consciousness."[65] Of the two groups, Kuyper says that "one is inwardly different from the other, and consequently feels a different content arising from his consciousness; thus they face the cosmos from different points of view, and are impelled by different impulses."[66] Kuyper is unrelenting in pointing out the consequences of the antithesis for every field of human activity. For example, he asserts bluntly that there are two kinds of science. The intellect is not immune to the antithesis; reason is the servant of the heart, not its master. To claim that science is essentially one unified activity, "taken in its absolute sense........leads to the rejection of the Christian religion."[67] Hence the putative conflict between 'faith' and 'science' is a fiction: since all science is rooted in faith, the real battle is between two types of faith and thus two types of science. "Not faith and science, therefore, but *two scientific systems*, or if you choose, two scientific elaborations, are opposed to each other, *each having its own faith*."[68]

On this theme Bavinck is (characteristically) more muted. Certainly, a deep gulf divides regenerate and unregenerate but general revelation continues to illuminate all people, even those estranged from God. Bavinck is prepared to give a much more positive assessment of non-Christian philosophy and science than Kuyper, and is especially keen to recognise and appreciate important 'elements of truth' in other religions.[69]

Needless to say, today Kuyper's approach would strike many as hopelessly harsh. Such a rigid stress on the distinction between the Christian and non-Christian would hardly seem the most promising way ahead for a positive theology of culture. But we need to remember that for Kuyper, the antithesis was not so much a means of denigrating the non-Christian but of activating the Christian, a way of generating confidence in the uniqueness and power of the Christian faith as a transformer of culture. His burning desire for the Netherlands was that the Church would address the issues of its time in a *distinctively Christian* fashion, and not lose sight of the radical difference between Christian and non-Christian outlooks. This was the only path to national renewal, so he believed. And for a significant period, this indeed was the route the Netherlands followed: the Neo-Calvinists established a Calvinistic university, Calvinist elementary schools, political parties, newspapers, hospitals, welfare agencies and trade associations. This whole programme was not undermined by an emphasis on the antithesis; on the contrary, for Kuyper it was one of the key assumptions on which it rested.

(4) Art

"Understand that art is no fringe that is attached to the garment, and no amusement that is added to life, but a most serious power in our present existence."[70]

So Kuyper affirms in the fifth of his famous Stone lectures on Calvinism, revealing the importance he ascribes to the arts. In this address, fully aware that his own tradition has frequently held art in contempt, he sets himself a three-fold task: first, to explain why Calvinism was not allowed to develop a religious art-style of its own; second, to discover the place of art in a Calvinist world-view; and third, to show what Calvinism has done for the advancement of art. Here we shall begin with the first and third of these issues, and then move on to the second.

As far as the first question is concerned, it is not any inflexibility in Calvinism which accounts for the absence of a distinctive style but rather its suspicion of state-religion. In cultures which have evolved a uniform style of architecture for worship, for example, one form of state-religion has been imposed upon a whole nation. Calvinism, in contrast,

> "has led to a multiformity of life-tendencies, it has broken the power of the State within the domain of religion......it abandoned the symbolical form of worship, and refused, at the demand of art, to embody its religious spirit in monuments of splendour."[71]

This explains why the only biblical references to specific architectural forms for worship are in the Old Testament. And there they are regarded as provisional.

> "In Israel we find a state-religion.........[which] makes its appearance in symbols, and is consequently embodied in the splendid temple of Solomon. But.......Christ comes to prophesy the hour when God shall no longer be worshipped in the monumental temple in Jerusalem, but shall rather be worshipped in spirit and in truth."[72]

In addition, Kuyper points out that Calvinism has traditionally held that religion and art are essentially of a different order: "[Calvinism's] effort must be to release religion and divine worship more and more from its sensual form and to encourage its vigorous spirituality."[73] Thus Calvinism could not develop a particular symbolic expression of its own religion, for this would be to deny its very character. And in reply to those who say that Calvinism ought to have developed a purely secular style of its own (without any reference to God), Kuyper insists that this would be impossible for a faith which knows of no sphere of life which is not under the sovereignty of God.[74] In tackling the third question — the contribution of Calvinism to the historical development of art — as we might expect, Kuyper launches a spirited defence. It belongs to the greatness of Calvinism that it emancipates art from the tutelage of the 'Church State'. Calvinism can proudly claim credit for some of the finest art the world has ever seen, not least in the field of music.[75] Here, even the most ardent supporter of Kuyper would have to concede that he is lightweight and unconvincing. His desperation to paint Calvinism in glowing colours means he never seriously addresses the problem of Calvinism's frequent disparagement of the arts. However, when he moves away from history and tackles the second question of the Stone lecture — the place of art in a Calvinist world-view — the argument becomes more substantial.

Here everything centres around the concept of beauty, which "is not the product of our own fantasy, nor of our subjective perception, but has an objective existence, being itself the expression of a Divine perfection."[76] The 'divine perfection' is 'glory (*Heerlijkheid*)' — God's radiance, splendour, divinity (*theotēs*). Strictly speaking we should use this only when speaking of God and heaven. Indeed, glory is the highest form of beauty.[77] However, even if the fulness of glory is denied to us in this life, we can see it mirrored in the beauty of the created world, primarily in the qualities of harmony: balance, rhythm, symmetry, proportion, etc. "Creating harmony (*harmonisch*) in our character, our surroundings is beautiful art." Or again: "where there remains any harmony (*harmonie*) in our inner struggle......there bodily beauty remains beauty".[78] Created beauty is not there simply for our benefit.

> "One should not.........humanise beauty, as if beauty existed for our human perception and could only be enjoyed by us.........the calling of creation is to radiate back to [God] the θειοτης that God showered over us and dropped as divine dew."[79]

In its original state, Kuyper believes, the world possessed a perfect beauty. But through human sin, disfigurement and ugliness marred the world, and, despite the restraining influence of common grace, it remains spoiled.[80] In Jesus Christ, however, we see our human nature climb "from the depths of scorn to the most beautiful harmony of glory. Christ.......is the canon and ideal of all beauty."[81] In his earthly life, the beauty of Jesus was inward and hidden, but in his risen life, it is displayed in all its splendour, and is now revealed through those who follow him. Beauty therefore must now be understood in the light of Jesus Christ, through whom all things were created, and in whom creation is restored to its intended beauty.

> "Our being cannot be satisfied unless the thirst for beauty is quenched. That is why the child of God fights for beauty and holiness, because at the creation man was absolutely beautiful. The beautiful and the good for which Plato was searching will come when the Lord returns."[82]

How does this relate to art? An artist, so Kuyper believes, should more than anything else be concerned with making something that is beautiful. Art "can work no enchantment except in keeping with the ordinances which God ordained for the beautiful".[83] And in this, it is God himself, the source of all beauty, who works in and through the artist: "God is the Creator of everything; the power of really producing new things is his alone, and therefore he always continues to be the creative artist."[84] God is the one who inspires the artist by a "stirring of the Holy Spirit".[85] So it is that "Art is born from God; practice and effort only diminish the obstacles to the kindling of the divine spark (*goddelijke vonk*) in the artist."[86]

It appears then that art has to do first and foremost with God's activity in and through the artist which enables him to create works which display beauty. This does not, however, mean that all art issues from special grace. Authentic artistic creativity is evident outside the Church, promoted and carried forward through God's common grace.[87]

What then is the link between the beauty of art and the beauty of creation? We recall that, for Kuyper, creation cannot offer the highest form of beauty; this belongs to the glory of God and heaven. Therefore, the artist should not be concerned simply with imitating the created world: "Nature is our example for form and colours, but the real artist augments those earthly lines and tints with deeper, richer beauty."[88] Although the artist must do full justice to the "forms and relations of all actual reality", he must also "discover in those natural forms the order of the beautiful, and, enriched by this higher knowledge..............produce a beautiful world that transcends the beauty of nature."[89] Thus, sustained by his knowledge of the beauty of pre-fallen creation and the beauty of the Kingdom to come, it is the artist's role to fashion a new beauty which reaches beyond that of the natural world. In this way, art can both hark back to the beauty of the world's pre-fallen state and anticipate the perfect beauty of the new creation:

> "art points out to the Calvinist both the still visible lines of the original plan, and what is even more, the splendid restoration by which the Supreme Artist and Master-Builder will one day renew and enhance even the beauty of his original creation."[90]

As we might expect, commentators have been quick to detect Platonic influences here. Kuyper seems to believe that beauty (or glory) is one of a system of spiritual and timeless universals. Hence beauty appears to be a quality which the created world only points to and indicates, rather than actually contains or embodies. This strain of Platonism is by no means absent elsewhere in Kuyper's theology, and, paradoxically, weakens his huge emphasis on the inherent orderliness of creation.[91]

Bavinck also breathes much of the spirit of Plato in his theory of art.[92] Once again, beauty is central. The sense for beauty, we are told, is universal in humankind, though it is found in varying degrees.[93] Its power is immense:

"[Beauty] deepens, broadens, and enrichens our inner life, raises us momentarily above the horizontal, sinful, and sad actuality, and in a purifying, liberating, and saving manner affects our bowed and disconsolate hearts."[94]

The aesthetic side of human nature must be understood alongside the intellect and will. Truth, goodness and beauty form an inseparable triad, as the Greeks realised. And all three are essentially other-worldly qualities:

"If truth, goodness, and beauty originally belong to God, they possess first of all, from the very nature of the case, an immaterial, a spiritual character and cannot inwardly be opposed to one another. Neither of the three can be equated with the empirical reality perceived by the senses; they raise themselves above it as norms above the laws of nature, as ideas above the reality of the senses. They cannot be observed by the sense organs, as animals possess these, but only by the higher faculty of the perception of man, by the spirit that dwells in him. Even as truth stands far above actuality, the good raises itself above the useful, and the beautiful above the pleasing. All three belong to the realm of intelligible things".[95]

Bavinck also clearly shares Kuyper's notion of beauty as harmony with a particular resplendence:

"Beauty exists in the agreement between content and form, idea and appearance; in harmony, proportion, unity in differentiation, organisation; in splendour, glory, radiant perfection, *perfectio phaenomenon.*"[96]

As such, earthly beauty participates in that higher, absolute beauty which rests in God alone. It is God's perfect beauty which sends its rays into our hearts through nature and art.[97] This lends a uniquely prophetic character to creaturely beauty, momentarily lifting us above life's conflicts, reaching out for something not yet revealed; earthly beauty is a "prophecy and pledge that this world is not meant for destruction, but for glory, the nostalgic longing for which dwells in every heart."[98] It is the calling of the artist, more than anything else, to give expression to beauty. In this way, art, provided it is not divorced

from what is good and true, can be "one of the many triumphs
of the soul which together are prophecy and pledge of a future
in which the good will triumph over evil, and grace over all
unrighteousness."[99] Even so, Bavinck eloquently pleads, art can
never win us salvation:

> "it is only in the imagination that we can enjoy the beauty
> which [art] discloses. Art cannot close the gulf between the
> ideal and the real. It cannot make the *yonder* of its vision the
> *here* of our present world. It shows us the glory of Canaan
> from a distance, but it does not usher us into the better
> country nor make us citizens of it. Art is much, but it is not
> everything........Art cannot reconcile sin. It cannot cleanse us
> of our pollution. And it is not able even to dry our tears in
> the griefs of life."[100]

(5) Summary

In the first part of this chapter we looked at the primary axes
on which the theology of Kuyper and Bavinck turn. At the very
heart of their thinking lies the theme of the absolute sovereignty
of God as Creator and law-giver. God orders the world through
a system of unalterable ordinances. From this derives the theory
of sphere sovereignty: each domain within creation has its own
characteristic principles which must not be overruled by those
of other spheres. Out of a concern to do justice to human culture
at large, Kuyper elaborates his doctrine of common grace.
Directed towards creation as a whole, common grace curbs the
effects of sin and promotes the development of the world through
human culture. Special grace, by contrast, is aimed at saving
the elect and renewing the created world. These leading ideas
of Kuyper were extended and developed by Bavinck. Sharp
contrasts are made between God's attitude to humankind before
and after the fall, the covenant of works and the covenant of
grace, and (in Bavinck) a general calling and a special calling.
Culture is rooted very firmly in the cultural mandate; it is part
of God's general law imposed on Adam and Eve prior to the
fall. Both Kuyper and Bavinck insist on a sharp demarcation
between the regenerate and unregenerate, Kuyper being the
more extreme of the two.

As far as the arts are concerned, neither Kuyper nor Bavinck
would have much time for the modern aesthetician's fascination
in the artist's inner state. For them, however much the artist's
individual creativity may play a part, the centre of gravity is on
an objective reality to which he has to be faithful — namely

beauty — which is grounded ultimately in the being and nature of God. It is the main task of art to strive for beauty. For Kuyper, earthy beauty is a reflection in creation of the glory and splendour of God — through it, God radiates his glory. It is seen supremely in Jesus Christ and is manifest those qualities relating to harmony. Through art a fresh beauty is born, echoing the original beauty of creation and anticipating the final consummation. Bavinck too sees beauty in terms of proportion, unity-in-diversity, and traces its origin to God, but even more than Kuyper, construes it in markedly Platonic terms as a trans-worldly universal. Curiously, this strand of Platonism in Bavinck and Kuyper detracts from their repeated stress on the intrinsic orderliness of creation. In the last resort, beauty seems to be something which creation simply reflects and mirrors rather than possesses. The weaknesses of this way of interpreting beauty and art I shall explore in due course. For the moment, we need to turn to our next writer, Herman Dooyeweerd, who, whatever else we say about him, could never be described as Platonic.

Notes

[1] This was founded in 1892 to unite the *Gereformeerde Doleerende Kerk* (a breakaway church of the 1880's) and the majority of the old *Christelijke Gereformeerde Kerk*.

[2] On Kuyper's life, cf. J. M. Van der Kroef, "Abraham Kuyper and the Rise of Neo-Calvinism in the Netherlands," *Church History*, 17 (1948), pp. 316-334; Frank Vanden Berg, *Abraham Kuyper*, St. Catherine's, Ontario: Paideia Press, 1978.

[3] (Henceforth *GD*), 4 Vols., 2nd ed., Kampen: Bos, 1908. The translations below from the *Gereformeerde Dogmatiek*, unless otherwise stated, are those of B. Kruithof in "The Relation of Christianity and Culture in the Teaching of Herman Bavinck," PhD Thesis, Edinburgh University, 1955. Bavinck's own synopsis of the substance of the *Gereformeerde Dogmatiek* appears in English as *Our Reasonable Faith* (henceforth *RF*), Grand Rapids, Michigan: Eerdmans, 1956.

[4] *Calvinism*, London: Sovereign Grace Union, 1932, pp. 27-42. These are the Stone Lectures delivered at Princeton Theological Seminary in 1898.

[5] *Ibid.*, p. 81.

[6] As translated by G. C. Berkouwer in *A Half Century of Theology*, Grand Rapids, Michigan: Eerdmans, 1977, p. 90.

[7] *RF*, p. 168.

[8] *Encyclopaedia of Sacred Theology*, trans. Hendrik de Vries, London: Hodder & Stoughton, 1899, pp. 113f.

[9] *Calvinism*, p. 114.

[10] As translated (from *GD*, II) by Gordon Spykman in "Sphere-sovereignty in Calvin and the Calvinist Tradition," in *Exploring the*

Heritage of John Calvin, ed. David E. Holwerda, Grand Rapids, Michigan: Baker Book House, 1976, p. 180.

[11] *Ibid.*

[12] *Ibid.*

[13] *Ibid.*

[14] In fact, Groen van Prinsterer was the first to use the concept of 'sovereignty within its own sphere (*Souvereiniteit in eigen sfeer*)'. Cf. Herman Dooyeweerd, *Roots of Western Culture*, Toronto: Wedge Publishing Foundation, 1979, p. 53.

[15] *Ibid.*, p. 126.

[16] "Souvereiniteit in Eigen Kring," (1880) as translated by Spykman, *op. cit.*, pp. 182f.

[17] *Souvereiniteit in Eigen Kring*, Goes: Oosterbaan & Le-Cointre, 1939, pp. 50f. On this issue, Kuyper has frequently been misunderstood. Cf. Veenhof, *op. cit.*, pp. 91f.; John de Gruchy, *Bonhoeffer and South Africa*, Grand Rapids, Michigan: 1984, pp. 110-114; *The Church Struggle in South Africa*, pp. 6f.; Moodie, *op. cit.*, pp. 65ff.

[18] For a discussion of this issue and a brief survey of the proponents of the doctrine prior to Kuyper, cf. Herman Kuiper, *Calvin on Common Grace*, Grand Rapids, Michigan: Smitter Book Co., 1928. For many years Kuyper wrote on the subject in the journal *Heraut*, and developed his insights into a vast three-volume work entitled *De Gemeene Gratie* (henceforth DGG), 3 Vols., Kampen: Kok, 4th ed., no date.

[19] *DGG*, II, pp. 645, 609, 611.

[20] *DGG*, I, pp. 11ff.

[21] *DGG*, II, p. 605. Kuyper's treatment of this negative aspect of common grace predominates in Volume I of *DGG*.

[22] *DGG*, I, pp. 213, 220.

[23] *DGG*, II, p. 605. Kuyper's treatment of the progressive aspect predominates in Volume II of *DGG*.

[24] *Ibid.*, p. 606.

[25] *Ibid.*, p. 118; III, 435.

[26] *Op. cit.*, p. 20.

[27] *DGG*, II, pp. 245ff., cp. pp. 613ff., 682ff. *et passim*.

[28] *De Vleeschwording des Woords*, Amsterdam: J. A. Wormser, 1887, pp. 247ff.

[29] Cf. his lecture of 1894, *De Algemeene Genade* (henceforth *DAG*), Grand Rapids, Michigan: Eerdmans, no date. Bavinck was convinced that common grace was crucial to Calvin. Cf. Kruithof, *op. cit.*, pp.129-135.

[30] *GD*, II, pp. 409f.

[31] *DAG*, pp. 4f. My italics. He speaks often of common grace beginning to operate straight after the fall (e.g. in *Handleiding bij het Onderwijs in den Christelijken Godsdienst*, Kampen: Kok, 1913, p. 109). In *De Offerande des Lofs*, 'S-Gravenhage: Verschoor, 1903, Bavinck describes grace as a 'stream' which had its beginning subsequent to the fall (p. 16).

[32] *RF*, p. 218. Cf. the helpful summary of Bavinck's teaching on this covenantal relationship in Chul Won Suh, *The Creator-Mediatorship*

of Jesus Christ, Amsterdam: Rodopi, 1982, pp. 201f.
³³ *DGG*, I, p. 163.
³⁴ *RF*, pp. 271, 272. Bavinck adds that the term 'covenant of grace' should not be used to speak about God's relationship with humankind immediately after the fall, but should be reserved for God's pledge to Abraham. *Ibid.*, p. 275. Nevertheless, in what Bavinck calls the 'mother-promise' (Gen. 3:14-15), "there is all that constitutes the meaning of the covenant of grace." *Ibid.*, p. 271.
³⁵ *Beginselen der Psychologie*, Kampen: Kok, 1897, p. 200.
³⁶ *GD*, III, pp. 226f; *RF*, pp. 48f.; *Handleiding*, p. 109.
³⁷ *RF*, p. 50.
³⁸ *GD*, III, pp. 226f., 661.
³⁹ *RF*, p. 204.
⁴⁰ *Ibid.*, p. 206.
⁴¹ "Het Rijk Gods Het Hoogste Goed," in *Kennis en Leven*, Kampen: Kok, 1922, pp. 49f. Cf. *RF*, p. 207, 215.
⁴² *RF*, p. 187.
⁴³ *Ibid.*
⁴⁴ *GD*, III, p. 7; IV, 477.
⁴⁵ *GD*, III, p. 152; IV, p. 47; *DAG*, pp. 27f.
⁴⁶ *RF*, p. 277. Cf. p. 410: "Christ fulfils the requirements which God by reason of the covenant of works can bring to bear on us." On the work of Christ, cf. pp. 308-356.
⁴⁷ *Ibid.*, p. 384.
⁴⁸ *Ibid.*, p. 382. My italics.
⁴⁹ *Ibid.*, p. 408.
⁵⁰ *Ibid.*, p. 407.
⁵¹ *Ibid.*, p. 408.
⁵² *Ibid.*, p. 409.
⁵³ Ibid., pp. 409ff.; *GD*, II, pp. 616, 763.
⁵⁴ *DGG*, II, p. 634.
⁵⁵ *Ibid.*, pp. 246, 260, 275, 457, 670-674; III, 105.
⁵⁶ *DGG*, I, 644, 684; II, pp. 350; *Pro Rege*, I, Kampen: Kok, 1911, pp. 370, 526, 567; III, Kampen: Kok, 1912, pp. 188ff.
⁵⁷ *GD*, III, p. 666; cf. *GD*, IV, p. 657.
⁵⁸ *RF*, p. 409.
⁵⁹ As quoted and translated by Spykman, *loc. cit.*, p. 181. Cf. *GD*, II, p. 343; III, p. 666; *De Offerande des Lofs*, p. 75.
⁶⁰ *RF*, p. 277.
⁶¹ *Calvinism*, p. 45.
⁶² *Ibid.*, p. 80.
⁶³ *Encyclopedia of Sacred Theology*, pp.131ff.
⁶⁴ *Ibid.*, pp. 143f.
⁶⁵ *Ibid.*, p. 152.
⁶⁶ *Ibid.*, p. 154.
⁶⁷ *Ibid.*
⁶⁸ *Calvinism*, p. 203. We should bear in mind, however, that Kuyper allows for a certain 'common ground' (or 'common terrain') between believer and unbeliever. Regeneration does not affect our sense of touch, seeing, hearing, etc., nor does it change the appearance of

the external world. The whole field of basic observation — measuring, weighing and counting — is common to both believer and unbeliever. *Encyclopaedia of Sacred Theology*, 157ff.

[69] *GD*, I, pp. 292ff.

[70] *Calvinism*, p. 229. His other main passages on art can be found in *DGG*, III, pp. 529-572; *Het Calvinisme en de Kunst*, Amsterdam: J. A. Wormser, 1888; and *Pro Rege*, III, pp. 470-580.

[71] *Calvinism*, p. 223.

[72] *Ibid.*, p. 224.

[73] *Ibid.*, p. 226.

[74] *Ibid.*, pp. 224ff.

[75] *Ibid.*, pp. 238-257.

[76] *Ibid.*, p. 237. Cf. *DGG*, III, pp. 538ff.

[77] *Het Calvinisme*, p. 15: "Even when beauty of a very low order seem to allow analysis, it withdraws proudly from being understood as soon as it rises in dignity, until at last beauty, transposed into glory, denies all access to analysis and only permits admiration."

[78] *Ibid.*, pp. 14, 17; *Pro Rege*, III, pp. 505ff. Kuyper warns us that the attempt to analyse precisely just what it is that makes something beautiful is doomed to failure. *Het Calvinisme*, pp. 14f; *Pro Rege*, III, pp. 509ff.

[79] *Het Calvinisme*, p. 13.

[80] *Ibid.*, pp. 11f.; *Pro Rege*, III, p. 499, 520f.; *DGG*, III, pp. 546ff.

[81] *Het Calvinisme*, p. 12.

[82] As translated by Hans R. Rookmaaker in *Art and the Public Today*, Huémoz-sur-Ollon, Switzerland: L'Abri Fellowship Foundation, 1969, p. 51. Cp. *DGG*, III, pp. 546-557.

[83] *Calvinism*, p. 237.

[84] *Ibid.*, p. 236. Cp. *Het Calvinisme*, pp. 52f.

[85] *Pro Rege*, III, pp. 531f. Cp. *Het Calvinisme*, p. 15.

[86] *Ibid.*, p. 16. Cf. p. 15 where he speaks of the 'spark (*vonk*)' of genius. Inspiration, in Kuyper's view, is certainly not limited to artists. Cf. *Het Werk den Heiligen Geest*, Amsterdam: J. A. Wormser, 1888, pp. 48, 53.

[87] *Calvinism*, pp. 243-247.

[88] *Het Calvinisme.*, p. 16.

[89] *Calvinism*, p. 234. Cf. *DGG*, pp. 550ff.

[90] *Calvinism*, p. 235. Cp. *Pro Rege*, III, p. 533; *DGG*, III, pp. 543ff., 547.

[91] Cf. Cornelius Van Til's discussion and attack on Kuyper's Platonism in *Common Grace and the Gospel*, Philadelphia: Presbyterian and Reformed Publishing Co., 1974, pp. 35ff.

[92] *Ibid.*, pp. 44-58. Bavinck's reflections on art are to be found principally in "Van Schoonheid en Schoonheidsleer" (henceforth "VSS"), in *Verzamelde Opstellen*, Kampen: Kok, 1921, pp. 262ff.

[93] "VSS," p. 278.

[94] *Ibid.*, p. 279.

[95] *Ibid.*, p. 275.

[96] *Ibid.*, p. 276.

[97] *GD*, II, pp. 258f.; pp. 457ff.; "VSS," pp. 279f. However, Bavinck

attacks the notion that art is merely a copy of the beauty of nature. The originality and imagination of the artist play as important a part. *Ibid.*, p. 268; cp. *Beginselen der Psychologie*, p. 96.

[98] "VSS," p. 280; *De Overwinning der Ziel*, Kampen: Kok, 1916, p. 33

[99] *De Overwinning der Ziel*, p. 34. Cp. *Beginselen der Psychologie*, p. 115.

[100] *RF*, p. 21.

3. Dooyeweerd: Christian Philosophy, Art and Beauty

"The scriptural ground motive of the Christian religion — creation, fall and redemption through Christ Jesus - operates through God's Spirit as a driving force.......As soon as it grips a person completely, it brings about a radical conversion of his life's stance and of his whole view of temporal life."

Herman Dooyeweerd

Some fifteen years after Kuyper's death, Herman Dooyeweerd (1894-1977), professor of jurisprudence at the Free University of Amsterdam, was putting the finishing touches to his magisterial work *A New Critique of Theoretical Thought* (1935-6).[1] Even if he had written nothing else, the *New Critique* alone would have been enough to establish Dooyeweerd as a major figure in continental philosophy. In addition, he published more than two hundred books and articles spanning a very broad range of topics, from sociology to the philosophy of science. Although virtually unknown in Britain, Dooyeweerd has captured the imaginations of many elsewhere, notably in Canada and the United States. His comprehensive interests and astonishing intellectual versatility have endeared him to numerous Christians who seek an all-embracing view of our lives in relation to God. In recent years, hundreds of students and scholars have flocked to the most vibrant centre of Dooyeweerdianism today, the Institute for Christian Studies in Toronto.[2]

Dooyeweerd never hid his allegiance to Kuyper. He speaks of five main themes adopted from the father of Neo-Calvinism: the sovereignty of God, the grounding of all human thought and science in the 'heart', common grace as the basis of human culture, the antithesis between regenerate and unregenerate, and sphere sovereignty.[3] But Dooyeweerd believed that Kuyper had not gone far enough. Most important, Kuyper had failed to see the need for a 'Christian philosophy', an account of the foundations of human thought which would clear the ground for a genuinely biblical world-view. Only a careful reconstruction of theoretical thinking on a solid Christian platform could answer the challenges of twentieth-century culture.[4] This was the task which Dooyeweerd set himself.

The sheer scale and labyrinthine complexity of Dooyeweerd's programme makes him by far the most formidable of the Dutch Neo-Calvinists. His style does nothing to help. To read Dooyeweerd is to enter a strange new world of unfamiliar terminology. What we might think of as relatively straightforward words acquire new and delicate nuances. It is little wonder that Dooyeweerd is not more widely read — such is the fate of scholars who surround themselves with idiosyncratic language-systems. Nevertheless, behind the linguistic twists and turns, the principal thrusts of Dooyeweerd's thinking are usually clear, and his thought repays careful attention, not least from those pursuing a Christian account of the arts. As with Kuyper and Bavinck, my aim here is to outline Dooyeweerd's chief philosophical and theological assumptions, and then go on to consider how these relate to his understanding of art.

(1) Christian Philosophy

At first glance, the most striking feature of Dooyeweerd is the prominent place he gives to philosophy. For him, philosophy is the most fundamental science, for it is concerned with created reality as a whole in contrast to the special sciences which focus on only one aspect of creation. It provides the theoretical foundation for all other sciences by uncovering the bedrock, the *a priori* of all human experience.[5] As such, it must find a proper starting-point for its investigation. This Dooyeweerd calls the 'Archimedean point': "The fixed point from which alone, in the course of philosophical thought, we are able to form the idea of the totality of meaning, we call the *Archimedean point* of philosophy."[6] Influenced by Kuyper, Dooyeweerd locates this point in the human 'heart', the religious root, the 'concentration point' of our lives. The heart is deeper than any particular function (such as feeling or the intellect) and transcends the diversity of the created world. Out of the heart arise all our deeds, our thoughts and feelings. "The great turning point in my thought," Dooyeweerd tells us,

> "was marked by the discovery of the religious root of thought itself whereby a new light was shed on the failure of all attempts, including my own, to bring about an inner synthesis between the Christian faith and a philosophy which is rooted in the self-sufficiency of human reason. I came to understand the central significance of the 'heart', repeatedly proclaimed by Holy Scripture to be the religious root of human existence."[7]

The heart, Dooyeweerd urges, is never neutral; it is either turned against God or towards him. For the philosopher even to strive for absolute neutrality is completely fallacious. Every discipline of thought and enquiry operates, consciously or unconsciously, with deep-seated religious presuppositions.[8] The so-called 'autonomy of philosophical thought', so beloved of the Enlightenment, needs to be exposed as thoroughly misleading. Philosophy either proceeds from a Christian or an apostate basis, depending on the orientation of the heart; there is no third way. Non-Christian philosophy has no option but to deify something in the created world. Cut off from the creator, the heart can only worship something *within* creation. The result is what Dooyeweerd calls 'immanence-philosophy' — for example, rationalism, empiricism, materialism.[9] Christian philosophy, on the other hand, finds its starting-point in the converted heart of the Christian believer. It issues from a heart humbled before God in obedience and faithfulness, and is thus set on course to discover truth and reality.

Here the Kuyperian tones are unmistakable. The absolute antithesis between Christian and non-Christian thought is emphasised time and time again by Dooyeweerd.[10] But he is careful to add a caveat. The antithesis is only a way of highlighting the dichotomy between two different motivating forces in humanity; it is not a tool for making clear-cut divisions between specific groups of people.

> "The antithesis is not........a dividing line between a Christian and a non-Christian group. It is the unrelenting battle between two spiritual principles that cut through the nation, through all mankind, and that fail to respect the safe retreat in Christian patterns and ghettos."[11]

> "An act of passing judgement on the personal religious condition of an adversary would be a kind of human pride which supposes it can exalt itself to God's judgement seat."[12]

Further, Dooyeweerd claims no infallibility for his own 'Christian philosophy' simply because it attempts to proceed from the correct starting-point: "our thinking is constantly exposed to the influence of apostate motives. For this reason a Christian philosophy can only be a fallible and faulty human effort."[13]

Clearly, Christian philosophy — in Dooyeweerd's sense — cannot be separated from theological assumptions about God, sin, regeneration etc. Dooyeweerd is happy to admit this, yet he is adamant that theology and philosophy should never be confused. Enormous problems arise when theology tries to set itself up as a kind of authoritarian adjudicator over all other disciplines. Theology's role is relatively modest compared to philosophy. Its focus of attention is on the particular dogmas, doctrines and articles of the Christian faith. It does not, and should not even try to give us a comprehensive picture of the general structure of the world and human existence. Nor should it seek to overhaul all theoretical thought in order to set it on a proper basis. These tasks belong to philosophy. Christian philosophy thus forms the matrix *within which* theology functions.[14]

One more important feature of Dooyeweerd's conception of Christian philosophy needs to be mentioned at this stage: its dependence on 'naive' (or 'pre-theoretical') experience. By this Dooyeweerd means something very close to what we might call 'everyday' experience, a way of looking at reality which does not analyse and dissect but which apprehends the numerous aspects of reality in their unity. When we look at a tree, for instance, we do not normally consider each aspect of it separately, as we would in theoretical thought — that it occupies space, that it grows by means of photosynthesis, that it has a certain beauty, and so on. In naive experience, we simply see it as one entity, a tree. Philosophy, Dooyeweerd believes, cannot ignore this integral vision which belongs to naive experience. For, although philosophy does distinguish multiple aspects of reality, it does so in such a way that their interrelationship, their essential oneness, is always kept in view.[15]

(2) The Diversity and Unity of Creation

Christian philosophy, then, is concerned with elaborating a faithful account of created reality as a whole. What kind of picture of creation emerges when the philosopher gets to work? One of Dooyeweerd's most basic premises is that nothing exists by itself or for itself. Every aspect of reality points beyond itself to other aspects, and the universe as a whole is utterly dependent for its being and sustenance on God. Dooyeweerd calls this the 'meaning character' of reality.[16] Approached from a different angle, we can say that all creation is under 'law' — that is, it is subject to the ordinances and norms which God has instilled in it. Law, in this sense, constitutes the 'boundary' between God and his world. It is what distinguishes God from creation. God is 'above' law: he is not subject to his own laws (though he is faithful to them). The created order, on the other hand, is 'under' law; that is to say, it is subject to a multitude of divinely bestowed precepts.[17]

Law-Spheres

The multiplicity of God's laws established in creation can be arranged in a hierarchy of categories or 'modal law-spheres'.[18] The spheres are not Kantian 'categories of the understanding' nor inventions of the human consciousness, but are objective, structural principles embedded in creation.[19] Nor are they, so to speak, pigeon-holes into which we can slot individual things. They are not categories of things but modes of being, the different *ways* in which things exist. As such, they are unchangeable, though not eternal. Dooyeweerd lists fifteen law-spheres:[20]

> sphere of faith (faith)
> moral sphere (love)
> juridical sphere (retribution)
> aesthetic sphere (harmony)
> economic sphere (economy)
> social sphere (social intercourse)
> lingual sphere (symbolical signification)
> historical sphere (control/mastery)
> logical sphere (analytical mode of distinction)
> psychic sphere (feeling)
> biotic sphere (organic life)
> physical sphere (energy)
> kinematic sphere (motion)
> spatial sphere (space)
> numerical sphere (number)[21]

Corresponding to each law-sphere is the 'meaning aspect' (or 'modality', or simply 'aspect') of a thing. An individual thing has various meaning-aspects because it belongs to a number of law-spheres.[22] Dooyeweerd also points out that any one sphere can be examined from the point of view of the spheres which form its foundation — the 'foundational direction', or from the point of view of the modalities of which it forms a foundation — the 'transcendental direction'. A sphere's preceding modalities form its 'substratum' and its succeeding spheres its 'superstratum'.[23]

The numerical sphere is the first and simplest, and thus has no substratum. If we attempt to think away some thing's number, nothing remains. There is no thing in the world in which numbers do not play a role. The physical modality is based on the previous three modalities — a stone, for example, can move, it takes up space, and it has a numerical function. At the top of the list, we notice that the sphere of faith has no superstratum. Faith is not directed to some higher aspect of creation: it finds its proper focus in Jesus Christ.[24]

Echoing Kuyper, Dooyeweerd argues that each sphere has its own distinctive character, or 'sovereignty'. Because this rich cosmic law-order has been ordained by God, a contradiction of laws within the law-order is *a priori* impossible. Failure to recognise this leads to insurmountable contradictions or 'antinomies'.[25]

> "Each modal aspect of temporal reality has its proper sphere
> of laws, irreducible to those of other modal aspects, and in
> this sense it is sovereign in its own orbit, because of its
> irreducible modality of meaning."[26]

This irreducibility is upheld through each aspect possessing a 'nucleus' or 'nuclear moment' — the prime, distinguishing and qualifying feature of that aspect of reality. (In the list above, the nuclear moment of each sphere appears in brackets.)

On the other hand, it is equally important for Dooyeweerd that the spheres are bound together in an unbreakable coherence. As we have noted, in our day to day 'naive' experience, we do not experience the different aspects of reality as discrete, fragmented units, but as inseparably related. Thus, in addition to sphere sovereignty we must also speak of the 'universality' of each sphere.[27] Every sphere has links with every other sphere. Applied to things we encounter in the world, this means that every entity is related to every law-sphere either as subject, or partly as a subject and partly as an object. A plant, for instance, occupies space, and thus functions as a subject in the spatial sphere. Yet it cannot feel, so in the psychical sphere it functions as an object (of our perception and enjoyment). Only human beings function as subjects in all modalities. The highest modality in which a thing functions as subject determines its 'qualifying function'. The qualifying function of a plant is the biotic function; the qualifying function of the state is its juridical function. The qualifying function of a thing gives us a way of classifying it: a stone we would call a physical thing, a plant we would call a living thing, and so on. But, we should note, when it comes to the products of culture, like works of art, we refer to them not by their qualifying function but by their object-function. A painting, to take one example, is an object of aesthetic enjoyment, not simply a physical object (unless of course it happens to be an appalling painting!).[28]

The links between the spheres is further explained by Dooyeweerd in terms of 'analogies' (or resemblances). Within the structure of each modality, Dooyeweerd believes, many 'modal moments' are grouped around the nuclear moment, and these relate to other modalities. Some of these moments reach ahead to later superstratum modalities — anticipatory moments; some point back to earlier substratum modalities — retrocipatory moments. For example, a feeling for logic and a sense of justice are meaning moments in the sensitive aspect which point ahead to the logical and juridical spheres. 'Harmonisation of interests' in the juridical sphere points back to the meaning nucleus of the aesthetic aspect. The sphere of faith has no anticipatory moments, and the numerical sphere has no retrocipatory moments.[29]

Another factor to note, of particular relevance to art, is the difference between 'normative' and 'non-normative' spheres. Things which function as subjects in the first six spheres, the non-normative spheres, have no option but to obey their own appropriate laws. A stone, for instance, must conform to the law of gravity. There is no choice about the matter. But from the analytical sphere upwards, in the anormative spheres, the laws become norms. That is, they need to be discovered, chosen and applied; they can either be followed or disobeyed.[30] Clearly this is important in the case of art, for the principles which God has laid down for the artist are strictly speaking only norms, not laws. They do not compel obedience, but can be discounted and ignored at will.

In his presentation of this highly intricate network of modal law-spheres, Dooyeweerd is of course taking up Kuyper's double emphasis on the unity of the world under God and the irreducibility of its various realms. Yet Kuyper's ideas have been extended and followed through with a thoroughness far beyond anything Kuyper himself would have attempted. Dooyeweerd presents us with a comprehensive system of universal scope, designed to take account, quite literally, of every aspect of created existence.

Individuality Structures

But, Dooyeweerd avers, the Christian philosopher not only considers modal law-spheres, the way things exist. He must also attend to individual things themselves, pointing out what it is about various objects which make them distinct from other objects. That is to say, he must consider 'individuality structures'.[31] Whether we are thinking of the family, the state, the church, or whatever, each entity in creation has its own internal constitution or pattern by which we can contrast it with other entities. Individuality structures, so Dooyeweerd believes, can be schematised into various types. There are 'radical types' which are distinguished according to the aspect to which their qualifying functions belong. For example, 'plant' is a radical type, biotically qualified; 'animal' is a radical type, psychically qualified. Members of a radical type we can call collectively a 'kingdom'. Within each kingdom there are various 'geno-types'. Within the radical type animal, we find the geno-types 'bird', 'mammal', 'insect', etc. If the structure of a thing is affected by factors external to it (for instance, in the case of a plant by its environment), we may speak of a further typological category: that of 'pheno-type' or 'variability-type'.[32]

(3) Culture

I have attempted to sketch the principal features of Dooyeweerd's account of the structure of the created world. And it is against this wide horizon that his reflections on art need to be set. But there is, as it were, a closer horizon which forms the immediate background to his aesthetics: his understanding of culture.

The Opening Process

The created world, Dooyeweerd argues, is marked by an inner movement of progressive development, in which its hidden potential is gradually opened up. In this 'opening process', the latent modal anticipations in each aspect/sphere are disclosed and made explicit.[33] For example, cultural feeling arises as an opened anticipation of the historical modality, and religious feeling as an opened anticipation of the faith aspect. Here, latent meaning-moments in the psychical/sensitive modality anticipate the superstratum spheres. New terms are introduced by Dooyeweerd at this point. When the anticipatory spheres of a modality are still closed, the modality reveals itself in a rigid, 'restrictive' form. For example, animals give no anticipations of aspects higher than the biotic — they do not feel, or think analytically. But in the opening process, a modality is enriched, appearing in a 'deepened' or 'expansive' form. Men and women, for example, express the physical modality in an expansive form: we find chemical compounds in organic life which are absent in inorganic things. In this case, the physical aspect of reality is revealed in a profounder and richer way. It is the biotic aspect which is the agent of this opening process in the animal — the physical aspect cannot engineer its own opening.

It is, to use Dooyeweerd's words, a 'guiding' function, and the physical aspect the 'guided' function.[34]

The particular part of the opening process in which humanity is actively involved we call 'culture'. Culture consists in drawing out what is implicit in creation, unfolding the various aspects of reality by reacting to and shaping our environment. Culture is to be interpreted in its original sense of 'formative control' or 'formgiving'.[35] This, we recall, is the nuclear moment of the historical sphere; hence Dooyeweerd can say that culture "is the way that reality reveals itself in the historical aspect."[36] The history of human culture is the story of the myriad of ways in which men and women have sought to open up creation through interacting with the natural world and with each other. In true Kuyperian style, Dooyeweerd traces culture back ultimately to God's law: it "is grounded in God's creation order. God...........gave man the great cultural mandate: subdue the earth and have dominion over it. God placed this cultural command in the midst of the other creational ordinances."[37]

Today this cultural directive comes to us in a world racked by human sin and evil. If the opening process took place in a perfect world, culture would advance in complete harmony according to God's laws. But human beings are marred by an ingrained distortion of the heart which inevitably affects their cultural vocation. Dooyeweerd is insistent here that sin cannot be understood solely in individual terms. Whole communities can be set on paths which are thoroughly un-Christian, and the way in which an individual engages in the cultural task will very likely be influenced by the underlying orientation of the community in which he or she lives.   This brings us to Dooyeweerd's classification of religious 'ground-motives'.

The Ground-Motives of Western Thought

In his early writings, Dooyeweerd often speaks of people being informed by a 'cosmonomic idea (*Wetsidee*)', a pre-scientific conception of the origin, purpose and structure of creation.[38] In his later works, he wants to say that behind cosmonomic ideas lie deeper directive forces — ground-motives — which take hold of the human heart and can extend to entire cultures. Scanning the history of the West, Dooyeweerd believes he can distinguish four such motives.

To begin with, he speaks of the 'form-matter' motive, the driving power behind ancient Greek philosophy. The origin of this lies in the conflict between two religious traditions, the earlier which deified the formless, flowing, changing character of reality, and the later, symbolised by the Olympian gods, centering on the rational principle of form which transcends the stream of chaos.[39]

Secondly, there is the Christian ground-motive: 'creation, fall, and redemption through Jesus Christ in communion with the Holy Spirit'.[40] We need to spend some time on each element here, for Dooyeweerd believes that it is this motive which informs an authentic Christian philosophy.

As far as creation is concerned, over against the Greek form-matter dualism, the Christian speaks of the will of God as the origin of all things. God is the source of all meaning, the origin of the laws and ordinances in creation as well as of every created thing subject to these laws.[41] Creation finds its point of unity in man and woman, above all in the human heart. With our hearts set upon God, our lives are to be lived in self-surrender, to God and to others. We were also created to be lords of creation: the "powers and potentials which God had *enclosed* within creation were to be *disclosed* by man in his service of love to God and neighbour."[42] This could only happen, however, insofar as the 'central command of love' was obeyed: the command to love God and our neighbour.[43] With the coming of sin, the human heart turned away from God and fixed on something within the created world. What was relative was thereby made absolute, and our relationships with God, with others and with creation were hideously corrupted.[44] Moreover, the effects of sin extend far beyond humanity. The whole of creation has been distorted: "the disruption of the fall permeated all temporal aspects of meaning of cosmic reality."[45] Humankind has wreaked havoc in God's world, bringing widespread disharmony. Be that as it may, sin has not destroyed the fundamental cosmic law-order itself. For example, the laws of logic and the laws of physics still stand.

> "Neither the structures of the various aspects of reality, nor the structures which determine the nature of individual creatures, nor the divine principles which regulate human action, are altered by the Fall."[46]

Turning to redemption, Dooyeweerd says that at the centre of the Gospel lies the claim that the Word of God has become flesh and has made possible the renewal of humankind and creation. In him, the image of God is restored and our true relationship with the created order recovered.[47] In him, the human heart has been redirected towards God; he is the one who has acknowledged perfectly the sovereignty of God and obeyed the divine will. In a telling passage, Dooyeweerd writes:

"the *totality of meaning* of our whole temporal cosmos is to
be found in Christ with respect to His human nature, as the
root of the reborn human race. In Him the *heart*, out of
which are the issues of life, confesses the Sovereignty of God,
the Creator, over everything created. In Christ the heart
bows under the lex (in its central religious unity and in its
temporal diversity, which originates in the Creator's holy
will), as the *universal boundary* (*which cannot be transgressed*) between the *being* of God and the *meaning* of his
creation."[48]

Where does common grace fit into this scheme of things? Most
importantly, common grace sustains the structural laws of
creation in the wake of sin.

"In our temporal cosmos God's Common Grace reveals itself,
as Kuyper brought to light so emphatically, in the
preservation of the cosmic world-order.   Owing to this
preserving grace the framework of the temporal refraction of
meaning remains intact............It is all due to God's common
grace in Christ that there are still means left in the temporal
world to resist the destructive forces of elements that have
got loose; that there are still means to combat disease, to
check psychic maladies, to practise logical thinking, to save
cultural development from going down into savage barbarism,
to develop language, to preserve the possibility of social
intercourse, to withstand injustice, and so on."[49]

Moreover, common grace upholds the whole of humankind,
so that "traces of the light of God's power, goodness, truth,
righteousness, and beauty still shine even in cultures directed
towards apostasy."[50] Further, through common grace God gives
specific people certain skills and abilities to maintain human
culture, even when he himself is rejected or ignored.[51] Further
still, Dooyeweerd believes that common grace is rooted in Christ.
In an effort to integrate creation and redemption more effectively
than Kuyper, Dooyeweerd urges that common grace be
understood only in the light of special or saving grace. Any
dualism between special and common grace is to be shunned,
for outside of Christ "there is no Divine grace, no 'common
grace' either, but only the manifestation of God's wrath on
account of sin."[52] The effects of common grace "are the fruits of
Christ's work, even before his appearance on the earth. From
the very beginning God has viewed his fallen creation in the
light of the Redeemer."[53] In another place, the same point is
made very forcefully:

"Apart from Christ [common grace] does not become a
blessing, but a judgement on humanity. Consequently every

dualism in the conception of the relation between gratia communis and gratia specialis, in the sense that the former has an independent meaning with respect to the latter, is essentially a relapse into the scholastic schema of nature and grace. It is even a greater set-back than the Thomistic-Aristotelian conception, which at least conceived of 'nature' as a 'praeambula gratiae'."[54]

Common grace does not therefore undermine the antithesis. Just the opposite. Common grace can only be understood in the light of the antithesis for it is conferred on the world precisely because of sin. In any case, for Dooyeweerd, the antithesis cannot be affected by common grace for the former operates at the level of the heart, the 'supra-temporal' root of human existence. Common grace protects only the temporal order from the ravages of sin.

As Dooyeweerd sees it, this Christian ground-motive is not simply a proposition arrived at by theological enquiry and put forward as a matter for theoretical debate. It rather refers to the underlying presupposition of all authentic theology and of all genuine knowledge, for it concerns not simply our intellect but our heart. It is a *religious* ground-motive, the "supra-theological starting-point of all really biblical Christian thought, the key to the knowledge of God and of ourselves."[55] We can only discover it and confess it as true as we are enlightened, together with fellow believers, by the Holy Spirit.[56] Hence there is a crucial difference between seeing this motive as the ground of our religious existence and viewing it as an object of theological study. In theology, we are working logically; our logical faculty gets to work on the facts and phenomena which arise from our faith as Christians. Theology can and should reflect upon, for example, the doctrine of God, the nature of Christ, the Person and work of the Holy Spirit. But the basal motive of holy Scripture cannot be treated in this way; it can only be received humbly in faith.[57]

Later, we shall question whether this is an adequate way of understanding the task of theology. For the present, brief mention should be made of Dooyeweerd's other two ground-motives. The third is the 'scholastic' motive of 'nature and grace'. Introduced by Aquinas, who attempted a synthesis of the form-matter motive with Christian thought, it led to a dualism between natural reality on the one hand, composed of form and matter, and supernatural grace on the other.[58] Fourth and lastly, there is the 'humanistic' ground-motive, with its two poles of 'nature' and 'freedom', characteristic of the Enlightenment. Here, men and women are viewed as autonomous individuals striving for their own freedom, struggling against the apparent inflexibility of the determined, natural world of cause and effect.[59] Like the first, the third and fourth motives are in the last resort apostate, and should never be confused with the Christian ground-motive which alone undergirds a truly God-centred culture.

(4) Art

A glance back at Dooyeweerd's list of modal spheres reveals that the aesthetic aspect lies between the economic and juridical spheres, and that its nuclear moment is 'harmony (*harmonie*)'. It is harmony which qualifies art and provides it with its most basic norm.[60] Harmony is said to connote unity-in-multiplicity (a numerical or mathematical anticipation) and *mēden agan* (nothing to excess) simplicity (an economic retrocipation).[61] This latter analogy — aesthetic economy — reminds us of the need for a measure of restraint in art:

> "The aesthetically *superfluous*, the 'piling it on', the 'overdoing it', ought to be warded off in harmonic sobriety or economy if the harmony is to remain intact.......the aesthetic modality of meaning is not possible without economic retrocipation."[62]

> "[Aesthetic economy] requires the artist to abstain from ostentation, burlesque, and precocity in the style; it demands clear simplicity in the aesthetic content, frugality, manifesting itself in a careful selection of the means of expression."[63]

According to Dooyeweerd, it was 'classicist aesthetics' — in Descartes, Le Bossu and Boileau-Despréaux — which recovered these mathematical, logical and economical analogies in art.[64] Dooyeweerd also stresses the importance in art of the symbolic, lingual elements. The aesthetic mode points back to the linguistic sphere because the artist expresses his aesthetic conception in colour, sound, words and pictures. "The aesthetic harmony of a natural object, or of a complex of natural objects, is necessarily a *signified* meaning."[65] The historical retrocipation of the aesthetic aspect is seen in the phenomenon of artistic style. For example, "classicism is nothing but a typical style giving aesthetical expression to the prevailing spirit of a particular period of western culture."[66]

While granting these correspondences between the aesthetic and other law-spheres, Dooyeweerd also wants to safeguard the sovereignty of the aesthetic. The aesthetic is not primarily about feeling or emotion, nor about scientific accuracy and precision.[67] Nor must the aesthetic be allowed to swallow up other aspects of meaning, as if it had some supreme access to truth. In this respect, Dooyeweerd attacks the 'aesthetic irrationalism' of the 'Sturm und Drang' movement, the early Romantics' 'feeling-philosophy', Schiller's 'aesthetic Humanism', and (somewhat unfairly) Immanuel Kant.[68]

Unfortunately Dooyeweerd is anything but clear about just what it is that makes the aesthetic aspect unique. He only seems able to describe harmony in terms of analogies with other spheres. Considerably more attention, however, is given to art itself, even if only one particular type of art. In the context of a discussion of individuality structures which are 'normatively qualified', that is, characterised by a normative object-function,[69] he analyses at extraordinary length an ancient marble statue of Hermes and Dionysus by the Greek sculptor Praxiteles.[70] I can only give a broad outline of his discussion here.

Marble, he begins, is one variability-type (or pheno-type) of the primary-type 'sculptural art work'. The last subject-function of this statue is found in the physical aspect. Yet, as a work of art, we must qualify it not physically but as an aesthetic object: the aesthetic object-function is its guiding/leading structural function. It seems to have no function in the biotic modality — the artist has worked with inorganic material — and this might at first appear to contradict Dooyeweerd's belief that an object-function is founded in all its substrate functions. But biological factors clearly play a part in our perception of the sculpture, and moreover, in this case, the statue is an image of two living bodies which are themselves qualified by the biotic function.[71]

Even though the sculptor probably used a model, the statue is not a mere copy of a particular human body.[72] If we try to see it as a primitive attempt at a photographic report, its power will be lost to us, for we have eliminated the 'forming' activity of the artist which is an essential factor in the production of any work of art.[73] Rather, as the artist observed the living model, he formed an image of the Hermes figure in which the aesthetic function played a leading role, that is, in which the main concern was with beauty and harmony.

> "The artist.........visualised his Hermes as a product of his aesthetic fantasy in the body of his living model. He was concerned essentially with the individual, aesthetically qualified total structure of his conception, to which he must give expression also in the visual sensory form of the sculpture."[74]

The resulting sculpture is a reproduction of this imagined Hermes in the mind of Praxiteles, "an image or copy of the visionary sensory shape, originally born in the productive fantasy of the artist."[75] Another name for this 'productive fantasy' is 'imagination', that faculty which "in a restrictive sense is also to be observed in animal psychical life, at least in that of the higher organised animals."[76] The imagination produces 'phantasms' or 'fancied thing-structures' which are of "merely *intentional* objectivity, entirely apart from the sensory objectivity of real things."[77] In the mind of the artist "the productive imagination has *projected* the sensory image of his Hermes as a merely *intentional* visionary object."[78] The final artefact is a physical representation of an imagined mental phantasm. Here Dooyeweerd appears to be drawing on the language of medieval philosophy (and possibly modern phenomenology); a 'phantasm' denotes the content or object of an act of consciousness, considered quite apart from any extra-mental reality. He seems to be claiming that the statue should be understood primarily as a reproduction of an idea which exists only in the imagination of the artist.

Faced with this analysis, we might be tempted to respond that being a sculptor must be a good deal easier than being a Christian philosopher! Even a devotee of Dooyeweerd would have to admit that he borders here on unintelligibility. Nevertheless, if I understand him aright, he seems to be trying to steer a middle course between two extremes: on the one hand, the view that an artist is merely attempting a reproduction of some external object or event, and on the other, the view that an artist is concerned chiefly with giving vent to some inner feeling or disposition. Art arises from an artist's encounter with an objective reality, out of which he tries to encapsulate in a mental idea or image the inner beauty and harmony of that reality, and present this in the form of a painting, sculpture, or whatever.

In any case, Dooyeweerd does not leave Praxiteles there. With painstaking care, and all his passion for logical niceties, he scrutinises the statue's individuality structure. As with all things qualified by a normative object-function, the leading function (the aesthetic) rests on a 'foundational function'. The individuality of the sculpture points back to an earlier function which enables us to distinguish it from physical objects in general. What is this foundational function? It cannot be located, so Dooyeweerd argues, in the physical aspect:

"The physico-chemical aspect of the marble Hermes can no more be considered as the *typical foundational function* of

the [work of art], because, even in its internal physico-
chemical function within the work of art, the marble continues
to be a bare *material* for the aesthetic expression."[79]

To put it more simply, there is nothing inherent in the marble
which implies it will be made into a statue. Dooyeweerd
concludes that the foundational function of Praxiteles' sculpture
is found in the historical law-sphere. That is to say, it came
into being through that controlled shaping and forming of
material which is characteristic of all culture. Its foundational
function, as with all works of art, is the *historical* function.[80]

Finally, Dooyeweerd considers the marble itself, and notes
that the individuality structure of the stone, its character as
inorganic material, is not set aside: "the material, however much
moulded by the artist, continues to be marble, and.........the
actual qualifying function of the latter is still physico-chemical
in nature."[81] Indeed, in the case of a sculpture, the medium
must not be seen as an enemy of the artist. When used by a
true master, its latent possibilities are opened up in such a way
that its natural properties actually contribute to the beauty
and quality of the finished product.[82]

(5) Summary and Comments

We have seen in this chapter that Dooyeweerd's vast philosophical vision is sustained by a number of crucial convictions.
Philosophy is the supreme and over-arching discipline whose
study is the structure of creation. There is an absolute
discontinuity between Christian and non-Christian philosophy:
to believe in some kind of unbiased, autonomous reason is
completely misguided. Dooyeweerd would like us to see his
own philosophy as directed by the Christian 'ground-motive' —
creation, fall and redemption through Christ. Central to
Dooyeweerd's project is the recognition that all reality belongs
to God as Sovereign, and that creation is characterised by a
magnificent law-order, ordained by the will of God, and upheld
through common grace. The structures of creation Dooyeweerd
explicates in two ways. First, he locates and sets out
systematically the various ways in which things in the world
exist or events occur — his theory of modal spheres. Here he is
at pains to highlight at one and the same time the plurality of
the world and its essential unity under God, the distinctiveness
of the spheres and their interrelatedness, sphere sovereignty
and sphere universality. Second, he analyses individual entities
or phenomena within creation, classifying them into various

groups — his theory of individuality structures. Culture is interpreted as the activity whereby the latent potential of creation is actualised in obedience to God's cultural mandate. No culture is religiously neutral; all specific cultures take their cue from deep-rooted religious ground-motives.

In all this, the principal traits of Kuyper's theology are plainly visible. For all its daunting complexity, Dooyeweerd's system is essentially augmented Kuyper, albeit refined, sharpened, and at times modified. If Kuyper could have read the *New Critique* — perhaps it is required reading in heaven, but I doubt it — he would no doubt have been stunned by its schematic intricacy, but would certainly have seen much of himself in its pages.

We have already glanced at Dooyeweerd's theological assumptions in connection with his exposition of the 'biblical ground-motive'; I shall delay detailed discussion of these until a later point. But here it is worth making a comment on the place of theology in his system. Dooyeweerd's eagerness to preserve the 'religious' character of the biblical ground-motive means that it is granted a strange kind of immunity to theological criticism. Theology, we recall, is a theoretical discipline devoted to reflecting on the contents of the Church's creeds and confessions. The biblical motive is to be *assumed* in Christian theology, it cannot be deduced or scrutinised theologically, for it is *religious* in nature, a deep, pre-theoretical current flowing beneath all authentic Christian thought and endeavour, and all genuine Christian philosophy. This, I submit, assumes far too wide a separation between intellect and religious conviction. It may well be that there is some kind of religious ground-motive (the basic assumption or assumptions of Scripture), yet if we are ever to give content to this — perhaps to ensure that we really are being motivated properly as Christians — then the intellect, and thus theology, is bound to have a part to play. The point becomes especially pertinent when applied to Dooyeweerd himself. For his own understanding of the ground-motive which allegedly runs through the Bible and supports all truly Christian philosophy is hardly self-evident. Indeed, it would have benefited from much more rigorous theological analysis. Even though the terms Dooyeweerd uses — 'creation', 'fall', 'redemption' — might gain wide consent, the significance which Dooyeweerd attaches to them will be unlikely to command universal agreement, not even amongst Calvinists! And might not a sharp disagreement at the theoretical level indicate disparity at a supra-theoretical or 'religious' level? I shall argue below that Dooyeweerd is, in fact, working with doctrines of God and creation which are not as

securely based in Scripture as he claims. My point here is simply
that, by cutting theology so ruthlessly down to size, some of his
own supposedly biblical tenets are protected from the kind of
close, critical assessment which they need. Vincent Brümmer
graciously remarks that "Dooyeweerd's views on the character
of theology are not the best part of his philosophy".[83]
As far as art is concerned, Dooyeweerd treads a middle path
between seeing it as self-expression on the one hand and
imitation on the other. The artist perceives an external reality
with an eye to its beauty and harmony, and by means of his
imagination, forms a mental image of what he intends to
communicate, which is then embodied in a work of art. Beauty
or harmony is the key-stone of the aesthetic mode. As such, it
is not just a quality to which art aspires, but a dimension of
creation, a distinct mode of being in its own right. Here again,
Dooyeweerd comes close to Kuyper. But the ghost of Plato has
been well and truly exorcised; there is no suggestion in
Dooyeweerd that beauty is some sort of timeless, other-worldly
universal.
I remarked at the beginning of this chapter that many have
fallen under Dooyeweerd's spell, both here and abroad. To
complete our survey of Dutch Neo-Calvinism, we now turn the
spotlight on two recent disciples of Dooyeweerd who have
believed that his system (at least in outline) offers a particularly
promising foundation for a Christian theory of art.

Notes

1. (Henceforth *NCTT*) 3 Vols., trans. D. H. Freeman and W. S. Young,
   Philadelphia: Presbyterian and Reformed Publishing Co., 1969. In
   Dutch: *De Wijsbegeerte der Wetsidee*.
2. Cf. C. T. McIntyre, *loc. cit.*, pp. 179ff.
3. "Kuyper's Wetenschapsleer," *Philosophia Reformata*, IV (1939), pp.
   193-232. Cf. *NCTT*, I, p. 523; Cornelius Veenhof, *In Kuyper's Lijn*,
   Goes: Oosterbaan & Le-Cointre, 1939.
4. In his mature thought, while recognising his debt to Calvin (*NCTT*,
   I, pp. 516ff.; II, pp. 152, 161; III, pp. 480, 504, 509f., 519ff., 533ff.),
   Dooyeweerd rejects the term 'Calvinistic' as for his philosophy,
   preferring instead 'Christian philosophy'. *NCTT*, I, pp. 524f.
5. *NCTT*, I, pp. 4ff.; 545-566.
6. *Ibid.*, p. 8. Archimedes was reputed to have said: 'Give me a fixed
   point and I will move the earth.'
7. *NCTT*, I, p. v. Cf. also *NCTT*, I, pp. 8, 12, 16; II, pp. 298ff.; *In the
   Twilight of Western Thought* (henceforth *ITWT*), Nutley, New Jersey:
   Craig Press, 1960, pp. 173-195; "Kuyper's Wetenschapsleer," pp.
   228f.; *Transcendental Problems of Philosophical Thought*, Grand
   Rapids, Michigan: Eerdmans, 1948, p. 67.
8. *ITWT*, pp. 1-60; *NCTT*, I, pp. 86ff.; pp. 123f.

⁹ *NCTT*, I, 12ff.

¹⁰ Cf. Veenhof, *op. cit.*, pp. 32ff.

¹¹ From *Vernieuwing en bezinning* (1963), as translated by L. Kalsbeek, *Contours of a Christian Philosophy. An Introduction to Herman Dooyeweerd's Thought*, Toronto: Wedge Publishing Foundation, 1975, p. 46.

¹² *NCTT*, I, p. viii.

¹³ From "*Van Peursen's critische vragen bij* A New Critique," as translated by Kalsbeek, *op. cit.*, pp. 59f. Cp. Dooyeweerd, "De Verhouding tussen Wijsbegeerte en Theologie en de Strijd der Faculteiten" *Philosophia Reformata*, XXIII (1958), p. 50.

¹⁴ *ITWT*, pp. 113-172.

¹⁵ *Ibid.*, pp. 13ff.

¹⁶ *NCTT*, I, pp. 3ff.; II, pp. 3-32. The created order does not *have* meaning, but rather *is* meaning: "it will not do to conceive of created reality as merely the bearer of meaning, as *possessing* meaning..........Such a conception remains founded in an Idea of the 'being of what is', which is incompatible with the radically Christian confession of the absolute sovereignty of God.......If created things are only *the bearers of meaning*, they themselves must have another mode of being different from that of the dependent creaturely existence referring beyond and above itself". *Ibid.*, pp. 30f.

¹⁷ *NCTT*, I, p. 99. Dooyeweerd quotes Calvin favourably: "Deus legibus solutus est, sed non exlex". *Ibid.*, p. 93. He claims that he chose the term *Wetsidee* because he was struck by the way in which many philosophical systems took their cue from the idea of a divine order in the world. *Ibid.*, pp. 93f. The 'boundary' spoken of here is not a spatial or physical boundary. Still less is it a boundary for God. *NCTT*, I, p. 99 n. 1; 100. William Masselink believes that Dooyeweerd here comes perilously close to deism ("New Views of Common Grace in the Light of Historic Reformed Theology," *The Calvin Forum*, 20 (1954), pp. 194-204), but Dooyeweerd can be defended on the grounds that he is making an ontological rather than a cosmological point: that God's being is utterly distinct from and in no way dependent on the being of creation. Cf. Ronald H. Nash, *Dooyeweerd and the Amsterdam Philosophy*, Grand Rapids, Michigan: Zondervan, 1962, pp. 40-46.

¹⁸ *NCTT*, II, Part 1, *passim*.

¹⁹ *Ibid.*, p. 50.

²⁰ *NCTT*, I, pp. 3, 24.

²¹ In his later works, Dooyeweerd calls the psychic sphere the 'sensitive' sphere. Cf. Kalsbeek, op. cit., p. 101. In the first (Dutch) edition of *De Wijsbegeerte der Wetsidee*, Dooyeweerd held that there were fourteen spheres.

²² *NCTT*, I, pp. 3ff.

²³ *NCTT*, II, pp. 51ff.

²⁴ *Ibid.*, pp. 298-319.

²⁵ *NCTT*, II, pp. 36ff.

²⁶ *NCTT*, I, p. 102. Cp. I, pp. 101ff; II, pp. 74ff.; III, pp. 662f., 692f. In his later writings Dooyeweerd prefers the phrase 'mutual irreducibil-

ity' of the spheres, reserving the term 'sphere sovereignty' for social relationships.

27 *Roots of Western Culture*, pp. 44f.

28 Dooyeweerd also uses the terms 'guiding' (or 'directing') to describe the qualifying function. *NCTT*, II, pp. 184f.

29 *Ibid.*, pp. 75f.; 163-180. Dooyeweerd sometimes (confusingly) uses 'analogy' to refer to 'retrocipation' as opposed to 'anticipation'; we use it here in his wider sense to refer to both retrocipations and anticipations.

30 *Ibid.*, pp. 237ff.

31 This is the main theme of Volume III of *NCTT*.

32 *NCTT*, III, pp. 83ff. He also uses the term 'primary-type' as synonymous with 'geno-type'. *Ibid.* p. 93. In certain cases further 'sub-types' can be distinguished. *Ibid.*, p. 94.

33 *NCTT*, II, ch. III *passim*.

34 *Ibid.*, pp. 183ff.

35 *Ibid.*, p. 203; *Roots of Western Culture*, ch. 4.

36 *Roots of Western Culture*, p. 65.

37 *Ibid.*, pp. 64f.

38 *NCTT*, I, pp. 94ff.

39 *Roots of Western Culture*, pp. 15-28.

40 *Ibid.*, pp. 12, 28-39. *NCTT*, I, p. 173.

41 *Roots of Western Culture*, pp 28f.

42 *Ibid.*, p. 30.

43 *NCTT*, I, p. 60; *Roots of Western Culture*, p. 30.

44 *Roots of Western Culture*, p. 33ff.; *NCTT*, I, p. 175.

45 *NCTT*, I, p. 100.

46 *Vernieuwing en bezinning*, as translated by Kalsbeek, *op. cit.*, p. 65.

47 *NCTT*, I, p. 99, 175; III, p. 71.

48 *NCTT*, I, p. 99.

49 *NCTT*, II, pp. 33ff.

50 *Roots of Western Culture*, p. 37.

51 *Ibid.*, p. 38.

52 *NCTT*, III, p. 525. "Particular grace," Dooyeweerd claims, "is the real root and foundation of common grace." *Ibid.*, p. 507.

53 *Ibid.*, p. 35.

54 *Ibid.*, p. 309. Cp. *NCTT*, I, p. 523; *Roots of Western Culture*, p. 38.

55 *ITWT*, p. 136.

56 *NCTT*, I, p. 61; II, p. 302; "De Verhouding," p. 4.

57 *ITWT*, p. 146.

58 *Roots of Western Culture*, pp. 115-147.

59 *Ibid.*, pp. 148ff.

60 *NCTT*, II, p. 128. Dooyeweerd concedes that although the 'primary principles' of art remain invariable, some aesthetic norms will vary from age to age.

61 *Ibid.*, pp. 128, 347.

62 *Ibid.*, p. 128.

63 *Ibid.*, p. 347.

64 *Ibid.* Aesthetics, when subsumed under Descartes' rationalism, spoke not so much of art as the imitation of nature, but of art as the imit-

ation of the ideal or the essential: the reflection of the form, order and underlying harmony in things and events in the world. Cf. Monroe C. Beardsley, *Aesthetics from Classical Greece to the Present*, Alabama: University of Alabama Press, 1966, pp. 140-165.

[65] *NCTT*, II, p. 139.

[66] *Ibid.*, p. 345.

[67] *NCTT*, I, p. 251; II, pp. 346f.

[68] *NCTT*, I, pp. 462f.

[69] *NCTT*, III, pp. 109ff. Not all works of art, he observes, display the structure of ordinary objects. Music, poetry and drama can only be objectified in scores and books. They are *symbolically qualified*; they can only "*signify* the aesthetic structure of a work of art in an objective way [but] cannot *actualise* it." *Ibid.*, p. 110. In short, they need a performance. Objectified works of art (scores and books) are of a 'secondary typical' character — they belong to the category of 'secondary radical types' — since they only belong in a structural subject-object relation. *Ibid.*

[70] *Ibid.*, pp. 110-128. Praxiteles (c. 375-330 B. C.) was the most eminent Athenian sculptor of the fourth century B. C. and worked mainly in bronze and marble.

[71] *Ibid.*, pp. 111f. Dooyeweerd recognises that this does not explain sculptures of a more 'abstract' nature, but he does not elaborate on this point.

[72] *Ibid.*, p. 113. Dooyeweerd distinguishes the relation between the statue and the original human bodies from what he calls the '*natural Abbild-relation*'. In *NCTT*, II, pp. 375ff., he explains the latter relation as that between the 'original objective perceptual image' in perception and its 'representation in sensory objectivity'; for example, the relation between a thing and its inverted image on the retina of the eye. The language here is obscure, but the main point seems to be that this statue must never be seen as an attempt at a direct imitation or copy of what the artist perceived.

[73] *NCTT*, III, p. 114.

[74] *Ibid.*, p. 113.

[75] *Ibid.*, p. 114.

[76] *Ibid.*, p. 115.

[77] *NCTT*, II, p. 425.

[78] *NCTT*, III, p. 115.

[79] *Ibid.*, p. 120.

[80] *Ibid.*, p. 122. Dooyeweerd believes that a parallel account can be given of music and literature (p. 123).

[81] *Ibid.*, p. 123.

[82] *Ibid.*, p. 125ff.

[83] *Op. cit.*, p. 244.

4. Rookmaaker and Seerveld: Art, Beauty and Allusiveness

"Why should you spend your life evangelising? I have done twenty-five years thinking, relating Biblical principles to art. You should be willing to do the same in your areas of life and work."

Hans Rookmaaker, to a student audience in Oxford

In 1971, so impressed was Malcolm Muggeridge with a new book entitled *Modern Art and the Death of a Culture* that he made it his *Observer* Book of the Year.[1] He was not alone in his enthusiasm. No other work from the pen of a Dutch Neo-Calvinist has ever reached such a wide readership as that remarkable study of the major currents of twentieth-century art. Yet few would have known that it was Dooyeweerd who had the most decisive influence on its author, Hans Rookmaaker (1922-1977). Rookmaaker first encountered Dooyeweerd's philosophy during the second World War, and it had a lasting impression on him, deeply affecting the way he tackled his own speciality, the history of art. His appointment to the chair of Art History at the Free University of Amsterdam in 1965 could not have been more appropriate.

On the other side of the Atlantic, Calvin Seerveld, of the Institute for Christian Studies in Toronto, has recently been exploring some of the implications of Dooyeweerd's work for the world of the arts.[2] Much in demand as a speaker, with a colourful, flamboyant literary style, Seerveld has been mainly active in the sphere of philosophical aesthetics, but his comments on specific works of art are invariably stimulating and perceptive.

As we shall see, Rookmaaker and Seerveld share much in common. Both acknowledge their debt to Dooyeweerd and see themselves as travelling further along the routes which he opened up.[3] Both are eminently qualified in their own fields. Neither claim to be expert theologians. They show a sound grasp of the main lines of Neo-Calvinist philosophy but doctrinal issues are rarely raised at length or in any great depth. Like Dooyeweerd, a theological matrix tends to be assumed rather than expounded or defended. But they also part company with each other on some key issues; indeed, we can learn more from the areas of disagreement than the areas of affinity.

(1) Dooyeweerd's Legacy

Anyone coming to Rookmaaker or Seerveld after Dooyeweerd will soon find themselves in familiar territory. All the Dooyeweerdian leitmotives are present. Seerveld argues that theology's task is to be

> "engaged in scientifically studying and servicing the pivotal confessional aspect of revelation and reality, not...... interrelating the meanings of the sciences and arts.........In line with the vision of Kuyper and Dooyeweerd, I understand the role of philosophy to be the architectural and janitorial service to all other sciences, that which points up the coherent, interdependent oneness of the many different forms of thoughtful activity, assists in their technical repairs, and constantly focuses their particular attentions upon the pre-theoretical Truth conditioning all their investigations."[4]

Christian philosophy is founded on the conviction that creation is a rich and marvellously ordered whole, replete with laws and ordinances instituted by God. The following passage from Rookmaaker is typical:

> "No human activity can take place outside the appropriate structural laws, whose presence in creation provide man with a norm for all his undertakings.................We cannot live and work without them. They give meaning to all our activities, whether we are simply feeding animals or boiling water."[5]

Seerveld follows the same tack. Taking his cue from Calvin's description of creation as the *theatrum Dei*, he claims that Christian cosmology is built on the notion of the world as a 'Cosmonomic Theatre' under the direction of the sovereign God. Creation is a "gracious handiwork in which all aspects of reality are equally pregnant with meaning." And within creation, there are "various, mutually irreducible...........relative structurations which order all things, events, acts" and which apply to all temporal reality.[6] In this context Rookmaaker adds an important rider:

> "We should not see these laws as a deterministic system which compels us to do certain things. That is why I prefer the term 'norm' to describe them........Our relation to them is not one of compulsion, but rather of love and freedom........

They are at one and the same time a gift, and a guideline to enable us to live effectively. God 'commands' us to love and be free (Galatians 5:1); and although the word 'command' for many connotes restriction, God's words are not meant to be a prison, but just the opposite."[7]

In addition, Rookmaaker appropriates Dooyeweerd's distinction between normative and non-normative spheres: "God did not give specific laws concerning the arts, nor for any other cultural element. These things belong to human 'possibilities': God created them, and made and structured man in such a way that he could discover these possibilities, and gave man the freedom and the task to realise and fulfil them."[8]

Sin is also understood by Rookmaaker and Seerveld along the lines of Dooyeweerd. By usurping God as Lord, we have enslaved ourselves and lost touch with the core of reality. Here Rookmaaker offers what was probably his most original contribution to Neo-Calvinism, his illuminating account in *Modern Art and the Death of a Culture* of the dehumanisation of our age as reflected in contemporary visual art. For Rookmaaker, the tragedy today is that for so many the world has lost meaning altogether. The creature has been worshipped instead of the Creator, and the structures of the cosmos, intended as vehicles of freedom, have become a source of frustration:

"Separated from the Lawgiver, law becomes a deadly tyrant. The norm, the law intended to lead to life, can.......become a harsh demand, whereby man in the end is dehumanised into a thing 'under the law'."[9]

This strong awareness of the seriousness of sin leads both Rookmaaker and Seerveld to adopt Dooyeweerd's notion of the antithesis between saved and unsaved.[10] And yet, following Dooyeweerd, we are warned against its misuse. Rookmaaker, for instance, writes:

"There *is* a deep difference between Christians and non-Christians, but we must not look for it in the wrong place. The difference lies ultimately in man's basic attitude, his hope, and his understanding of his task. But when it comes to any specific activity, the Christian may be foolish and sinful and the unbeliever wise and right."[11]

What of common grace? Seerveld is happy to speak of it as God's preservation of the ordinances of the created world, and of sin affecting only our response to these structures rather than the structures themselves.[12] Rookmaaker prefers not to use the term, "unless we call it grace that God has not yet removed the unbeliever from this world, as not yet belonging here." But he still believes that God upholds the cosmos in all its structural diversity and that this is what makes human culture possible.[13]

In their treatment of culture, again, both owe much to Dooyeweerd. Culture, Rookmaaker says, "means nothing more, and nothing less, than the building of a civilisation within the structures, laws and norms given by God". Or again, it is "the creation of life's forms, customs, and institutions, as well as our utilisation of nature and its resources."[14] For Seerveld, culture is "the cultivation of creation by humankind, the formative development in history of creaturely life tended by human creatures".[15] For both Seerveld and Rookmaaker, culture is not an option for a few but an obligation for all, grounded in the cultural mandate of Genesis 1. The Church lives under a command to be active in every zone of cultural life in order that God's spoiled world might be restored and renewed.[16] Such a renewal can only begin with the re-creation of humanity through Jesus Christ. So Rookmaaker asserts that

> "Christ came to redeem us in order that we might be human, in the full sense of that word. To be new people means that we can begin to act in our full, free, human capacity, in all facets of our lives...............to be a Christian means that one has humanity, the freedom to work in God's creation".[17]

Only through Christ can we be properly related to the created order, for all things were brought into being through him.[18] Only when we are in Christ do the norms of creation cease to be a burden and our relation to them becomes "not one of compulsion but rather of love and freedom."[19] Freedom in Christ and obedience to the norms of creation can thus never be set off against each other. For Rookmaaker and Seerveld alike, Christ does not curb our freedom but actualises it so that we are enabled to obey God's structural laws.

(2) Rookmaaker and Art

Despite the common allegiance to Dooyeweerd's broad philosophical vision, Rookmaaker and Seerveld diverge in a number of respects when speaking directly of the arts. Rookmaaker is the most faithful to Dooyeweerd. For him, beauty holds pride of place. The nuclear moment of the aesthetic sphere is 'beautiful harmony (*schone harmonie*)'.[20] Beauty is a formal quality, seen in the coherent arrangement and inter-relationship of parts within a whole. It is thus closely linked with unity-in-multiplicity. In art, beauty is displayed in the formal structure of the subject-matter. It can also be seen in the internal composition of the work of art itself:

> "Beauty is expressed in line, colour, shape and form, rhythm and sound, rhyme and the relationship of words and composition, unity and diversity. It is through these very things that beauty is realised: it is not found abstractly in them."[21]

Like Kuyper and Dooyeweerd, Rookmaaker maintains that it should be the main goal of the artist "to make something beautiful (as well as useful), just as God made the world beautiful and said, 'It is good.'"[22]

From this vantage point, Rookmaaker highlights the various aesthetic analogies in other law-spheres. In art, ideally we should see 'prevention of excess (*wering van exces*)' or *mēden agan* (economic retrocipation); social harmony (social retrocipation); balance between feeling and words (symbolical retrocipation); the phenomenon of 'style' (historical retrocipation); the principle of identity and contradiction (logical retrocipation); emotional power (psychical retrocipation); art which has 'soul-life (*bezielde*)'; aesthetic movement and rhythm (kinematic retrocipation); 'polyphony (*lijnenspel*)' (spatial retrocipation); and 'unity-in-multiplicity (*eenheid in de menigvuldigheid*)' (numerical retrocipation). We should also find a predominance of one theme over another (juridical anticipation); the portrayal of the love of our neighbour (moral anticipation); and a general faith-orientation towards God determined by the artist's heart (an anticipation of the faith aspect).[23] Notwithstanding his marked stress on harmony and unity-in-multiplicity, there are hints in Rookmaaker, particularly in *Modern Art and the Death of a Culture*, that there is more to beauty than harmonious form. There he claims that neither beautiful form nor a beautiful medium will of itself guarantee beautiful art. The same applies to beautiful subject-matter: in Grünewald's picture of the Temptation of St. Anthony and Roger van der Weyden's 'Last Judgement' we see a profound beauty, but in each case the subject-matter is ugly, even demonic.[24] We would be foolish to stake very much on a few sentences, but there seem to be unmistakable signs that Rookmaaker wanted to widen and deepen the concept of beauty he inherited from Dooyeweerd.

But there is no doubt that Rookmaaker's account of the creative process follows Dooyeweerd's pattern:

"The artist forms his conception (*conceptie*). This conception is objectivised on the basis of a (psychical) fantasy-image (*fantasiebeeld geobjectiveerd*). So we have an intentional (this means only in the 'spirit' of the artist, not yet actually existing) aesthetically qualified objective structure. This objective fantasy-image has to be actualised and objectivised by the artist in historical-cultural formation."[25]

More distinctive of Rookmaaker is his emphasis on artistic inspiration. Inspiration, he claims, involves a heightened awareness of the aesthetic norms, especially beauty.[26] It comes about through the work of the Holy Spirit: "God's Spirit is needed to produce what is truly beautiful or positive......... [Inspiration] comes because God thinks a certain thing necessary for his creation, for the benefit of men, women, children, and animals".[27] Art without the Spirit tends to lack purpose and direction because creation's norms are not being honoured.[28] However, inspiration is not restricted to believers; to suggest otherwise wrongly implies that the Spirit can only operate among professing Christians.[29] On the same theme, he reminds us that it is just as possible to be inspired by the forces of evil as by the Holy Spirit.[30]

We recall Dooyeweerd's double stress on the uniqueness and interrelatedness of each aspect of reality. Both are applied to art by Rookmaaker. On the one hand, he insists that art possesses a certain independence. It does not need an evangelical message tagged on to it to qualify for divine approval. Art 'needs no justification'; it requires no defense for its existence in terms of some end or purpose it might fulfil. The aesthetic aspect is, after all, a distinct mode of reality in its own right. Art's justification is "its being a God-given possibility.........Art has its own meaning. A work of art can stand in the art gallery and just be cherished for its own sake."[31] On the other hand, art is not an isolated activity, unrelated to creation as a whole.

"Just as a tree, being more than the totality of its functions, nevertheless *has* functions, so art is not just there to be art, but is bound by a thousand ties to reality. Nothing is simply autonomous. A tree, a human being, a work of art — all are part of that wonderful fabric which we call reality; no thread can be missing without impoverishing the whole."[32]

These ties with reality should be understood in a double sense. Somewhat vaguely, Rookmaaker says that "art deals *with* reality — it is *about* fear, hope, joy, love, our surroundings, the things we love or hate." It deals with thoughts, objects, people, which we encounter daily. He also says that "art is used *in* reality."

For instance, "Music, rhetoric, poetry make up a large part of our social functions and religious activities; and architecture, furniture and textile design, interior decoration, painting and illustration provide the setting for our movements and actions."[33]

As we might expect, Rookmaaker is emphatic that the artist is constrained by certain God-given, objective norms. He must be sensitive to the properties of his medium so that they can serve his overall objective; for instance, a painter uses bright colours for joyful subjects.[34] An artist must seek to follow the principles which apply to all culture, principles summarised, so Rookmaaker believes, in Philippians 4:8 (truth, honour, justice, etc.).[35] Most important of all, he should respect that irreducible dimension of beauty. And yet, despite this stress on fidelity to external norms, Rookmaaker is equally emphatic that the artist possesses a genuine freedom. He cannot afford to be a prisoner of a past style, or a slave of present current fashions, or be too anxious about the future significance of his work.[36]

As far as 'Christian art' is concerned, this can never be defined as art which deals with biblical subjects, or art which has come from the pen or brush of a Christian believer. Many portrayals of biblical themes are artistically incompetent and much art produced by Christians is anything but exemplary. The crux of Christian art, so Rookmaaker believes, lies at a profounder level, in a Christian vision of the world under the Lordship of God. Christian art is art "in line with the God-given structures of art, [with] a loving and free view on reality". It is "art which is inspired and in which norms are posited under the direction of the Christian faith, proceeding from a religious attitude aiming towards God and Christ."[37]

(3) Seerveld and Art

There is much in Rookmaaker which Seerveld endorses: the rejection of superficial concepts of Christian art; the twin emphasis on the independence and relatedness of art; his stress on respecting an artistic medium; the importance of interpreting art in its social setting. Nevertheless, in two important areas Seerveld finds himself parting company with Rookmaaker (and indeed with the whole Kuyperian line).

Seerveld's first target of attack is the dogma of beauty. Beauty, he protests, is not the kernel of art nor of the aesthetic aspect. Still less is it some kind of universal towards which art should aspire. Christian aestheticians are sorely mistaken in giving it such a prominent place.[38] First, it is misleading to ground beauty in God's glory, like Kuyper. Glory is not some kind of static divine quality; it speaks of God's grace in action, supremely in the 'unlovely form' of Jesus Christ. The key to art is to be found by examining *creaturely* reality, not some supposed perfection of God.[39] Secondly, to make beauty the key to art runs the risk of countenancing a sub-Christian metaphysics. In particular, Seerveld is scathing about what he sees as Kuyper's merger of Christianity and Platonism. Rookmaaker and Dooyeweerd are also sternly rebuked; the notion of 'beautiful harmony' "is an unexamined and undeveloped presupposition, replete with Greek overtones."[40] Thirdly, Seerveld observes that Dooyeweerd and Rookmaaker can only describe beauty by means of analogies with other modal aspects, leaving its distinctiveness in question. "Dooyeweerd none too carefully emphasises the requirement of unity-in-multiplicity......and *mēden agan* simplicity.......and one is left thinking that those analogical functions are not sufficient pointers for what might be peculiarly 'aesthetic'".[41] Fourthly, to speak of beauty as the true goal of art fails to do justice to the physical character of an artist's task. Art is mainly about wrestling with material reality, not striving after a spiritual ideal. "Beauty is intellectually refined, spiritual; art is generally a physical, always a sensuous, craft-made object."[42] Fifthly, to over-stress the place of artistic beauty runs the risk of reducing art to a means towards some higher end and losing sight of its inherent value.

> "The curse of this Beauty upon art is evident when it presses art into its service as a lower rung on the divine ladder ....Thus art under the aegis of Beauty can be good only insofar as it denies its nature, and metamorphosed serves as some kind of lowdown step toward something truly worthwhile."[43]

Nevertheless, Seerveld does not wish to jettison beauty altogether. He has no quarrel with the claim that certain things can and should be described as beautiful and that they thereby witness to the goodness and glory of God. What he rejects is beauty understood as the decisive feature of art, and as the quality which sets the aesthetic apart from other modes of reality.[44]

Seerveld's second bête noire in Kuyperianism is the notion of inspiration. We have seen that both Kuyper and Rookmaaker make use of the concept in different ways. Seerveld's anxiety is that to suggest an intimate link between God's Spirit and the artist both threatens the uniqueness of God's creativity and

ıs deifying human creativity. Art is a human activity through
ıd through, so Seerveld insists.   Except for our inspired
:riptures, he declares, "literature and art is wholly human,
..ɔt a whit divine."[45] Furthermore, the traditional theory of
artistic inspiration is in danger of exalting the professional
artist into some kind of superstar, far above ordinary mortals.
This quickly results in the downgrading of artists who receive
no public recognition but who are nevertheless carrying out
their work in a way which honours God.[46]

If beauty is to be dethroned, what is to be put in its place at
the centre of art? Seerveld's answer is 'allusiveness'. It is
allusiveness which distinguishes prose from poetry, photographic
duplication from a photographic portrait: "Peculiar to art is a
parable character, a metaphorical intensity, an elusive play in
its artifactual presentation of meanings apprehended."[47]
Accordingly art can be defined as "the symbolical objectification
of certain meaning realities, subject to the law of *allusiveness*."[48]

> "To posit that symbolic objectification must be law-abiding
> allusive is to affirm that it must be heightened by a playful,
> suggestion-rich ambiguity, its internal thematic convergence
> and consistency must make aesthetic sense by bearing a
> characteristically oblique, metaphorical constituency."[49]

This allusive quality is not just a feature peculiar to art but a
dimension of created reality, a modal sphere in its own right.
Seerveld believes that there is an allusive aspect to our daily
lives, a 'dimension of nuance' which needs to be nourished and
nurtured.   Far from being only a concern of those who are
artistically expert, it is incumbent on us all to develop
aesthetically rich lives.[50] Unfortunately, Seerveld is anything
but clear when he tries to give an account of what this
allusiveness looks like in everyday life. He mentions such things
as surprises, practical jokes, playfulness, the ability to be
humoured and to be merry, to imagine things, but it is hard to
see what makes all these activities particularly 'allusive'.[51]

Seerveld speaks much more fully than Rookmaaker about
the way in which an artist goes about his task. The
primary material with which the artist works, Seerveld
maintains, need not be an emotion or some kind of psychological
state. Such is the mistake of all 'subjectivistic' theories of art:
in over-reacting to the idea that art is there to duplicate the
external world, the inner world of the artist himself becomes
pre-eminent. In fact, the range of starting-points for the artist
is much wider: he may begin with a model, a question, an
issue, an historical event, a memory, etc. In any case, whatever

the artist chooses, he gives it

> "a searching stare; he stops, looks and listens to it, at it, not
> past and through it as one does practically every day, and
> not 'against' it as scientists do when they turn things into
> theoretical *Gegenstände*, but the artist focuses all his
> symbolically intending attention upon that primary object
> and lets its multiple meanings, connoting detailed properties
> and apprehended import stir him to give it a name, to identify
> it symbolically, to finally stop the associating play of his
> pregnant, absorbed memory upon all that is richly presented
> and implied and finally, to express, virtually (not actually)
> reproduce by a metaphorical finishing process the meaning
> he has uncovered. That meaning then is explicated in lines,
> shapes and colours, sounds and rhythms, words, thoughts
> and actions informed symbolically."[52]

The first part of this rather convoluted passage is concerned
with a particular kind of attentiveness to an object, peculiar to
the artist, in which different meanings of that object are
suggested to him. This is where the imagination comes into
play. Seerveld rejects two leading theories of the imagination.
The first holds that the imagination does nothing more than
express deep emotional impulses, attitudes and desires; this
makes art a kind of fantasy or illusion with no cognitive content
at all. The second, associated with the Romantics, elevates the
imagination to the point where it seen as the supreme key to
ultimate reality. The first wrongly suggests that scientific,
denotative statements are the only legitimate type of meaningful
assertion (improperly excluding art as a means of knowledge)
and the second considerably overestimates the power of the
imagination.[53] Seerveld picks up Dooyeweerd's notion of
intuition as the starting-point for his own account of the
imagination. Dooyeweerd claimed there was a trans-modal level
of human consciousness which, ever present, makes all human
knowing possible and bridges the gap between the analytic
function and the field of investigation which it confronts. This
deep layer of consciousness Dooyeweerd called 'intuition'.[54]
Seerveld is prepared to say that when we use our imagination
we are acting on some such bed of pre-theoretical intuition. An
artist looks at things neither scientifically, nor as he would in
naive experience, but instead

> "holds himself still in attention toward the originally perceived
> given and works at apprehending it in a certain facet which
> eclipses yet collocates all the other modal complexities of the
> object. A person who is imaginatively busy tries to live into
> a given object's multiple meanings, peripheral nuances and

tributary connections, and catch all these meanings symbolically together.........as they present themselves through one special aspect of the object."[55]

This kind of apprehension Seerveld calls 'Hineinlebenshaltung', a "peculiar structuration of human consciousness which permits a man's aesthetic, that is, symbolising ability singularly to dominate his action toward reality."[56]

We can discern two further key factors in Seerveld's account of artistic creativity. First, unlike Dooyeweerd, he disapproves of any theory which centres on some kind of mental image or 'phantasm', which holds that "there be purely eidetic objects which are aesthetically qualified, rounded off 'aesthetic Ideas' which need only objective sensory representation."[57] The artist's medium — paint, sound, marble — is not merely a vehicle for the conveying of an aesthetic idea; its very nature radically affects the artist's conception as he sets about his work. Second, Seerveld argues that a work of art is only truly complete when it is performed or heard or seen by others. A symphony which is only written is not strictly speaking finished; it needs to be performed in front of others on a specific occasion before it can legitimately be considered as art.[58]

Let me try to summarise as best as I can Seerveld's account of the artist in action. Firstly, Seerveld seems to be saying that an artist perceives an object (whatever this may be) in such a way that he does not analyse it, nor use it as a means to some end, but lets it suggest many and varied meanings to him. By means of his imagination, which brings his aesthetic sensitivity to the fore, he allows the given reality to be allusive, suggestive. Secondly, the artist then ceases this imaginative apprehension and embodies metaphorically, in a work of art, the meaning which he has encountered. Thirdly, as he sets about his task, the artist will find that his chosen medium will affect and modify his initial vision; his material is not simply some kind of neutral channel through which a fixed idea is transmitted. Fourthly, the object which emerges — the script, the score, the poem, the choreographer's directions or whatever — can only properly be described as a work of art when it is understood and appreciated as such by others.

If works of art are objects of appreciation by others, how are we to understand the *way* in which they communicate? Here we see Seerveld trying to do justice both to the uniqueness and the inter-relatedness of the aesthetic dimension of reality. On the one hand, a work of art does not normally make a direct or literal statement. We cannot reduce Picasso's 'Guernica' to some clearly identifiable 'message', or flatten a poem down to prose without loss of content. Literal statements are characteristic of the lingual aspect of reality, not the aesthetic. Art involves 'symbolical objectification.' It communicates symbolically, indirectly, 'allusively'. Symbolic actions, events, conditions, never aim for clarity, because they operate through suggestion.[59] On the other hand, art is quite capable of presenting us with sound, discernible knowledge. "Art is not vague because it is not analytically precise, and it is not confused because it is not articulated clearly in some language with dictionary references."[60] Seerveld reinforces the point in his article "The Relation of the Arts to the Presentation of Truth," where he says that the imaginative character of art consists "not in being 'fictional' but in presenting whatever reality is fascinating the artist..........*symbolically*". The fact that art works are produced in colours, notes, gestures does not indicate that they are void of cognitive content.[61]

Like Rookmaaker, Seerveld eschews the idea that Christian artists or biblical subject-matter guarantee Christian art.[62] Christian art is art with a specific 'slant' to it, what Seerveld calls 'the surd of sin and joy'. It unmasks sin for what it is, exposing the evil and misery of the world, yet at the same time reveals the grace of God. To neglect either of these elements will lead either to sentimentality (as in much so-called 'Christian' art), or simply to empty despair. The greatest art combines both. Citing many examples - including works by Dürer, Holbein, Rembrandt, Cowper and Rouault - Seerveld claims that art of this calibre displays "awe at the terribleness of sin......and the soft play of forgiveness", "the hurt and the laughter", "sorrow under sin in the world and joy at the presence of the Comforter".[63]

(4) Summary

In this chapter, we have encountered two twentieth-century scholars who have endeavoured to carry the leading ideas of Dutch Neo-Calvinism into the arena of the arts. Rookmaaker stands closest to Dooyeweerd. For Rookmaaker, it is beauty which qualifies the aesthetic aspect and art; Seerveld makes a clean break with this tradition, substituting the concept of 'allusiveness'. Rookmaaker revives the ancient concept of artistic inspiration; Seerveld denounces it. Rookmaaker adopts Dooyeweerd's notion of art as the externalisation of a mental idea or image; Seerveld rejects it.

Both men begin to develop arguments which will prove important for us later. For example, although both endorse

Dooyeweerd's broad frame of reference, they seem keen to balance his rather austere emphasis on obeying God-given laws with the insight that these laws have been provided by God to enable true freedom, not inhibit it. Both stress the double-sided nature of art, its irreducibility and its unbreakable connections with other aspects of reality. Seerveld defends art against the charge that it transports us into a world of fantasy, bereft of contact with the real. And, along with Rookmaaker, he urges that art can grant us genuine knowledge, albeit of a distinctive kind.

Notes

1. (Henceforth *MADC*), London: IVP, 1970.
2. Principal among his works are *A Turnabout in Aesthetics to Understanding* (henceforth *TAU*), Toronto: Wedge Publishing Foundation, 1974; *A Christian Critique of Art and Literature* (henceforth *CCAL*), Toronto: Association for the Advancement of Christian Scholarship, 1977; and *Rainbows for the Fallen World* (henceforth *RFW*), Toronto: Tuppence Press, 1980.
3. Cf. Linette Martin, *Hans Rookmaaker*, London: Hodder & Stoughton, 1979, pp. 82, 125, 143f.; Seerveld, *CCAL*, pp. 19, 22ff., 40; *TAU*, p. 21; *RFW*, p. 197.
4. *CCAL*, p. 19.
5. *The Creative Gift* (henceforth *CG*), Leicester: IVP, 1981, pp. 56f. Cp. *MADC*, pp. 224f.
6. *CCAL.*, p. 22; *RFW*, p. 107.
7. *RFW*, 57.
8. *MADC*, p. 235.
9. *CG*, p. 59. Cp. *RFW*, p. 28.
10. *CG*, pp. 25f. Cp. *CCAL*, pp. 25ff.
11. *CG*, pp. 25f.
12. *CCAL*, p. 25.
13. *CG*, pp. 24ff.
14. *Ibid.*, pp. 73, 40.
15. *RFW*, p. 179.
16. *Ibid.*, pp. 24,177-182; *CCAL*, pp. 15-28. Cp. *CG*, pp. 26f.; 41ff.
17. *Art Needs No Justification* (henceforth *ANNJ*), Leicester: IVP, 1978, p. 24.
18. *CG*, p. 56. Cp. Seerveld, *CCAL*, p. 23.
19. *CG*, p. 57. Cp. Seerveld: "God's commands are always blessings when followed. They become hard and hurt only when disobeyed." *RFW*, p. 25.
20. "Ontwerp ener Aesthetica op grondslag der Wijsbegeerte der Wetsidee," *Philosophia Reformata*, 11, 3 (1946), p. 142.
21. *MADC*, p. 242.
22. *CG*, p. 111. For Rookmaaker, beauty is not restricted to works of art. *MADC*, pp. 241f.; *Kunst en Amusement*, Kampen: Kok, 1962, p. 135.
23. "Ontwerp ener Aesthetica," pp. 143ff.

[24] *MADC.*, p. 234. "A horrible thought can never be beautiful, for a lie is not truth; but truth is beautiful, when shown in its depth and fullness." *Ibid.*, pp. 233f. Cp. "Modern Art and Gnosticism," *Zeitschrift für Aesthetik und allgemeine Kunstwissenschaft*, 18 (1973), pp. 171ff.

[25] "Ontwerp ener Aesthetica," p. 159.

[26] *Ibid.*, p. 160.

[27] *CG*, p. 68.

[28] *Ibid.*, p. 69.

[29] *Ibid.*, p. 68; "Ontwerp ener Aesthetica," p. 164.

[30] *CG*, p. 70.

[31] *ANNJ*, p. 40. Cp. pp. 34, 39ff.; *MADC*, pp. 229ff.; *CG*, p. 112.

[32] *CG*, p. 112. Cp. *Art and the Public Today*, p. 49.

[33] It is Rookmaaker's conviction that much modern art is essentially 'gnostic' - that is, it has become alienated from creation, and from the reality of God ("Modern Art and Gnosticism," pp. 167ff.).

[34] *MADC*, p. 235.

[35] *Ibid.*, pp. 236ff. Cp. *Kunst en Amusement*, pp. 103-139.

[36] *CG*, pp. 70f.

[37] *MADC*, p. 228; "Ontwerp ener Aesthetica," p. 164.

[38] *Ibid.*, pp. 32-35; *RFW*, pp. 116-125. Seerveld cites (among others) Clyde Kilby's *Christianity and Aesthetics*, Downers Grove: IVP, 1961 and Frank Gaebelein, "The Aesthetic Problem: Some Evangelical Answers," *Christianity Today*, 12 (30 August 1968), pp. 4-6. He also notes with disdain Karl Barth's discussion of the 'beauty of God'. *RFW*, p. 44. (Cf. Karl Barth, *Church Dogmatics*, II:1, ed. G. W. Bromiley and T. F. Torrance, Edinburgh: T. & T. Clark, 1957, pp. 650ff.)

[39] *CCAL*, p. 32; *RFW*, p. 124, n. 10.

[40] *RFW*, p. 122.

[41] *Ibid.*, pp. 122ff.

[42] *CCAL*, p. 35.

[43] *Ibid.*

[44] *RFW*, pp. 124f.

[45] *CCAL*, p. 37.

[46] *RFW*, pp. 26f.

[47] *Ibid.*, p. 27.

[48] *RFW*, p. 132.

[49] *CCAL*, p. 45. Seerveld recognises that this notion of allusiveness is not an *exhaustive* explanation of every art work. A piece of art also needs, for example, internal order and integration to make its effect. *RFW*, p. 129.

[50] *RFW*, pp. 129ff.; ch. 2, *passim*. Cp. *CCAL*, pp. 74f.

[51] Cf. Nicholas Wolterstorff's review of Calvin Seerveld's *Rainbows for the Fallen World*, in *Third Way*, 5, 7 (June 1982), p. 23.

[52] *CCAL*, p. 43.

[53] *Ibid.*, pp. 61-73. Seerveld blames Dooyeweerd for reducing all human knowing either to theoretical knowledge or pre-theoretical naive experience, allowing for no third possibility. *NCTT*, II, p. 482.

[54] *NCTT*, II, pp. 473ff.

[55] *CCAL*, p. 70.
[56] *Ibid.*, p. 71.
[57] *Ibid.*, p. 77.
[58] *Ibid.*, pp. 79f.
[59] Thus Seerveld can speak of the aesthetic sphere as the 'symbolical'. *Ibid.*, p. 74.
[60] *RFW*, p. 79.
[61] In *Truth and Reality*, Festschrift for H. G. Stoker, Braamfontein: De Jong, 1971, pp. 161-175.
[62] *CCAL*, pp. 46ff.; *RFW*, pp. 63ff.
[63] *CCAL*, pp. 52-59. Seerveld is also convinced that much art, including Christian art, takes itself far too seriously. Cf. "Comic Relief to Christian Art," *Christianity Today*, 12 (1 March 1968), pp. 10ff.

5. Calvinism, Christ and Art

Having completed our survey of five prominent Dutch Neo-Calvinists, and seen something of the interplay between their theology and their approach to art, it is time to offer some evaluative comments.

Only the most grudging critic would refuse to acknowledge that the movement deserves considerable respect. Three particularly impressive features of this theology stand out. First, there is its consistency. The Dutchmen are driven by an unshakable belief in the order, coherence and interconnectedness of the world, and an incessant desire to offer a cogent theoretical account of this God-given unity. Whatever the drawbacks of this approach — the tendency to overlook irregularities is the most obvious — the unified picture of reality which is offered will be greeted with warm approval by those committed to a similar quest for an all-embracing world-view. Second, there is the sheer scope and breadth of their interests. Many theologians have waxed eloquent about the need for a comprehensive theology of culture while in practice ignoring vast areas of cultural life. By contrast, the Neo-Calvinists venture into virtually every field. And when it comes to art, questions too often left to the élite circle of professional aestheticians are tackled fearlessly, even by non-specialists like Kuyper and Dooyeweerd. Third, there is a healthy determination to expose philosophical preconceptions in every academic credo, every political programme, every discipline of thought and enquiry. Their repeated insistence that no human activity is value-free may at times be overplayed, but there is surely much to be learned here, especially when we consider how easily in post-Enlightenment culture we have been bewitched by the fantasies of 'pure objectivity' and 'pure rationality'.

Compared to Tillich, the Dutchmen are obviously rooted much more firmly in the soil of Protestant orthodoxy. To those of a more conservative frame of mind, who find Tillich's modified Idealism hard to swallow, the Neo-Calvinists will likely come as a welcome contrast. Methodologically they also follow a more traditional pattern. When tackling an issue in culture, they take their cue from what they see as the bedrock of biblical doctrine. In the case of art, the movement is always *from* doctrine *to* a philosophy of art. They would be deeply suspicious of Tillich's method of correlation and would frown upon the idea that the arts might themselves influence theological procedure.

Bearing these points in mind, in this chapter, two major questions need to be addressed. First, is Dutch Neo-Calvinism — as it appears in the writers we have examined — as solidly grounded in biblical presuppositions as its proponents claim? And second, are the philosophies of art which the Neo-Calvinists advocate as distinctively shaped by the Christian faith as they would wish? I shall begin by looking closely at the theology which undergirds Neo-Calvinism, trying to bring to light the controlling doctrines, and then, in the light of that, go on to offer some comments on the various interpretations of art which have emerged from our study.

(1) God's Law, Grace and Culture

God's Law and God's Love

We begin with the doctrine of God. Here, I believe, is the lynch-pin of the whole Dutch Neo-Calvinist system. Once we grasp what is being assumed about the nature and character of God, virtually everything else in Neo-Calvinism falls into place. Two closely related elements need to be highlighted: first, a pronounced emphasis on the inviolable *will* of God; and second, an inclination to conceive God first and foremost as the *Lawgiver*. These are fused together most forcibly in the oft-repeated affirmation of God's sovereignty. Divine sovereignty, for the Neo-Calvinist, is essentially the absolute power of God's will enacted in the establishment and enforcement of law. We are not permitted to speak of grace at the heart of God or any kind of grace at work in creation before the fall.

Thus the tendency is for God's love to be treated as little more than a potential quality or attitude which operates only among the chosen and fortunate few. This is thrown into sharp relief in the Calvinists' adoption of the traditional federal Calvinist distinction between the covenant of works (made with all humankind) and the covenant of grace (made with the elect) — a distinction assumed most notably by Kuyper and Bavinck.[1] The covenant of works was established with Adam, guaranteeing eternal life for all humanity on condition that he obeyed the laws of nature (the laws of God). When this covenant was broken, a new covenant of grace was rendered necessary. This manifests the love of God and is restricted to the elect. It finds its climax in the life, death and resurrection of Jesus Christ. The logical consequence of this scheme, spelt out very clearly in Bavinck, is that all are related to God as recipients of his law, but only some as objects of his love. Doubtless, this scheme has a certain logic and attractive elegance. But it seriously undermines the unity of God's purposes, the oneness of the divine covenant of grace.[2] Furthermore, the covenant of works is not a true covenant in the sense of an unconditional pledge, but a legal agreement dependent on the fulfilment of certain conditions on Adam's part for its continuation. Kuyper is quite clear about this. "The fact is that there is a stark contrast in Holy Scripture between the covenant of grace (*Verbond der genade*) which is based on *faith*, and the covenant of works (*Verbond der werken*) which is based on *human action*."[3] Bavinck follows suit. According to him there are 'two entirely different covenants,' one belonging to the realm of law and the other to the realm of grace. Prior to the fall, he says, "the rule was: through works to eternal life. Now, after the fall, in the covenant of grace, the eternal life comes first, and out of that life good works follow as the fruit of faith."[4] Christ's saving work thus becomes the means of fulfilling the divine demands set out in the covenant of works. The demands of God's law set the stage for his work of redemption.[5] The net effect of interpreting God's primal relationship with Adam in terms of law is to construe God's essential attribute as justice, and his love towards creation (and humankind) as something which he exercises only if he so wills.

Law, Creation and Redemption

This type of doctrine of God will be familiar to virtually any student of scholastic Calvinism, and has been subject to severe criticism from a number of quarters in recent times.[6] What gives the Kuyperian theology its characteristic hue is the way in which the doctrine is wedded so firmly to a distinctive picture of creation as a beautifully ordered system, impregnated with divinely given laws. Kuyper invites us to see the world chiefly in terms of unchanging structures which express God's unalterable will. Bavinck follows a very similar path, and Dooyeweerd's philosophy is shot through from beginning to end by what Vincent Brümmer calls a 'nomological ontology', a theory of creation dominated by the notion of law.[7] Indeed, surely it is this, whatever Dooyeweerd may claim, which *de facto* constitutes the main thrust of his 'biblical ground-motive'. As Bernard Zylstra puts it succinctly, "In my view, the most important premise of this [i.e. Dooyeweerd's] philosophy lies in its assumption that reality is created by God whose will is the sovereign and redeeming law for reality."[8] Similar emphases, though much less marked, can be seen in Rookmaaker and Seerveld.

This combination of an austerely law-centred doctrine of God with a law-dominated doctrine of creation prompts two critical remarks. First, such a massive stress on the rationality and stability of creation obscures what the natural sciences have been bringing to our attention so vividly in recent years, that the universe is characterised by a subtle interplay between spontaneity and regularity, freedom and necessity. The picture of the world offered by the Neo-Calvinists has (despite Dooyeweerd's notion of an 'opening process') a curiously rigid and Newtonian feel about it, leaving little room for the recognition that creation has its own history, or for the constant creative activity of God, which, alongside a proper emphasis on the order and inherent intelligibility of the cosmos, has generally been accepted as an axiom of mainstream Christian theology. This is a point I shall try to expand later; it has profound implications for the arts, and for the concept of beauty.

Second, more seriously, the overall trend in the Neo-Calvinists is for their theory of structural laws to form the matrix within which redemption is interpreted. Kuyper tells us that "while that Royal Child of Bethlehem protected sphere-sovereignty with his shield, he did not create it. It was there from of old. It was embedded in the creation order, in the plan for human life."[9] And as we have seen, Bavinck echoes Kuyper when he writes: "Grace is something other and higher than nature, but it nevertheless joins up with nature, does not destroy it but restores it rather. *Grace........[flows] on in the river-bed which has been dug out in the natural relationships of the human race.*"[10] Turning to Dooyeweerd, we read that "In Christ the heart bows under the lex (in its central religious unity and in its temporal diversity, which originates in the Creator's holy will), as the *universal boundary* (*which cannot be transgressed*) between the *being* of God and the *meaning* of his creation."[11] Notwithstanding the laudable attempt to hold grace and nature together, there is an acute danger here that the inner meaning of creation will be sought apart from Jesus Christ, and that a theology of redemption will all too easily sanction a sub-Christian theology of creation. W. J. Aalders reminds us that we cannot read the "law of God *for* the cosmos (his purpose) simply by examining the law *of* the cosmos".[12] To be fair, the Neo-Calvinists frequently tell us that grace and redemption fulfil the purposes of creation, but invariably 'creation' has already been defined

in advance outside Christ according to some theory of universal
law. Kuyper may have had every intention of placing his account
of common grace under the corrective influence of the doctrine
of special grace,[13] yet the general drive of his theology points in
the opposite direction. Bavinck, when speaking of the expansion
of the structures of creation under God's providence as Creator,
states that "The gospel honours fully this development, today
as in the days of the apostles. It allows freedom and places no
obstacles in the path of such development."[14] Grace flows on
the river-bed of nature. It is not hard to see how Kuyperianism
has been used to fuel the South African *apartheid* regime: grace
does not abrogate nature (racial distinction) but fulfils and
perfects it. John de Gruchy, writing from within that turbulent
political context, observes: "The fundamental theological problem
with Kuyper's doctrine is that it assumes a relationship between
nature and grace, derived from the Synod of Dort and not Calvin,
in which nature and creation, not grace and reconciliation, are
determinant."[15] It is also not surprising to find Karl Barth
attacking the Kuyperians during the rise of Nazism for their
incipient but dominant 'natural theology'.[16] Even Vincent
Brümmer criticises his erstwhile teacher for leaving no room
for the notion of creation through God's Logos: "Since
[Dooyeweerd] starts from the law but fails to account for its
execution through the creative *Logos*........[he] fails to recognize
the reality of *creation* as something different from legislation."[17]
Brümmer goes on to remark: "Dooyeweerd does not realise that
if the basic theme of the Christian faith were really to determine
the content of his cosmonomic Idea, it would would force him to
reject the 'nomological' ontology implied in this cosmonomic
Idea."[18] Few comments on Dooyeweerd have been so perceptive.

A more promising way of integrating God's creative and
redemptive activity would be to recover two cardinal
affirmations. The first is that the very heart of God's nature,
shown supremely in the communion between the incarnate Son
and his Father, is self-giving love. There can be no separation
between God's will and his love, for his will is always his will to
love; all that he wills is an expression of his love. Love is no
mere divine 'attribute'. As John Zizioulas expresses it: "Love is
not an emanation or 'property' of the substance of God.....but is
constitutive of His substance......Thus love ceases to be the
qualifying — i.e. secondary — property of being and becomes
the supreme ontological predicate. Love as God's mode of
existence 'hypostasises' God, *constitutes* His being."[19] Clearly,
such an assertion can only be made if we take with the utmost
seriousness the epistemological significance of the incarnation,

and, consequently, the trinitarian ontology of God. The second affirmation is that there is an intrinsic connection between the humanity of Christ and the created order as a whole. For if in Christ we see the one 'through whom' and 'for whom' all things were created, and if we see also in him the Son of God coming as part of his creation to renew and re-establish this world, then any understanding of God's original and final purposes for creation must ultimately focus on the crucified and risen man Jesus Christ. Quite what this might mean for the arts we have yet to discover. The point to note here is that the Neo-Calvinists in effect deny this link between Christ's humanity and creation. A subtle Nestorianism vitiates their Christology, a tendency to hold apart the deity and humanity of Christ. Christ as man is related only to elect humanity. Accordingly, Christ is not head over creation as man, only as Son of God. Kuyper can write eloquently of Christ's universal Lordship — it is one of his favourite themes — but he distinguishes very carefully between Christ as Mediator of creation as the second Person of the Trinity, and Christ as Mediator of our salvation as Son of God *and man*.[20] With respect to his humanity, Christ is not Lord over the created world; only as the majestic and powerful Son of God can he be confessed as such. Compare Bavinck's very sharp distinction between Christ's kingship of grace and his kingship of power.[21] For Bavinck too, Christ, as man, is head only of the Church, as Mediator of the elect. He is head over the rest of humankind and creation as sovereign or King.[22] Dooyeweerd's stance is somewhat different: "As regards his human nature, Christ is the root of reborn creation, and as such the fullness of meaning, the creaturely Ground of the meaning of all temporal reality".[23] Sadly, however, Dooyeweerd fails to spell out sufficiently the implications of this insight. Taken as a whole, the shape of his programme bears the marks of traditional Kuyperian theology. The overriding tendency in Dutch Neo-Calvinism, therefore, is to limit the significance of the humanity of Christ to the salvation of the elect, and to lose sight of what it might reveal about God's attitude to, and plans for, the entire created order. We are left with the uneasy feeling that creation and redemption belong to two distinct spheres.

Christ and Common Grace

With these considerations in mind, what are we to make of the doctrine of common grace? In the Calvinist world, the issue has frequently engendered intense controversy. Some are convinced that the very future of Reformed theology depends on it. Others vehemently oppose it, denouncing it as a menace.[24] We cannot hope to survey the minefield of debate here in any great detail, but four comments are in order.

First, the categorisation of grace into 'common' and 'special' — which is only one instance of the chronic tendency of Western theology to schematise grace into different types ('concomitant/consequent', 'prevenient/subsequent', 'habitual/actual' etc.) — runs the serious risk of obscuring the unity of God's nature and the consistency of his intentions. This is even more so when some theologians make further demarcations between different kinds of common grace.[25]

To be more specific, second, this artificial differentiation of 'graces' arises because of an abstraction of grace from Christ, and thus from the inner being of God. In the majority of New Testament uses of the word 'grace', Christ is the basis and even the content of its meaning. In the Pauline corpus in particular, the concept refers supremely to the self-giving of God towards us in Jesus Christ, the personal, loving presence and action of God himself. The entire life, death and resurrection of Christ is a manifestation of divine grace in our midst.[26] And, if we are to take the incarnation seriously, we shall have to speak of grace as internal to the being of God. For the advent of Christ is the advent of the eternal Son of God, *homoousios* with the Father. Through Christ, in the Spirit, we are given to share in that relationship of love which the Son has enjoyed from all eternity with the Father. Grace, seen from this perspective, is grounded ultimately in the inner trinitarian life of God, in his being-as-love.

Grace, therefore, can only properly be understood relationally, personally, and, supremely, in trinitarian terms. As Timothy Dearborn rightly contends, an "adequate understanding of the Trinity is central to an adequate understanding of grace."[27] Grace is not merely an objective action, nor merely a subjective power. It is, first and foremost, the triune God's life in communion — it refers to what God *is* in the eternal self-giving love of Father, Son and Spirit; and second, it is God's reconstitution of humanity's life into communion with himself through the life of Jesus Christ and the indwelling of the Holy Spirit.

In Dutch Neo-Calvinism, the epistemological centrality of the incarnation has not been taken to heart, nor, it would seem, has trinitarian conceptuality. That God's very being is constituted by relatedness-in-love, by a communion of Persons-in-relation, is a truth long proclaimed by the ancient Catholic

Church. But it is doubtful whether it has been accorded sufficient importance by the Neo-Calvinists, who often appear to construe God as a kind of undifferentiated supreme Subject (despite paying lip-service to the doctrine of the Trinity). Grace is thus dissociated from the being of God as a triunity of love, and is effectively depersonalised. God is not inherently gracious; it is only after the fall that he begins to act in a gracious way, as a response to human sin. The depersonalisation of grace is seen nowhere more clearly than in the traditional Kuyperian doctrine of common grace. This 'grace' has nothing to do with God's love. It is viewed causally and impersonally in terms of the divine power or influence on humanity and the world at large. What needs to be asked is whether there is such a thing as divine power which is not at the same time an expression of divine, personal love.

Third, the most damaging effect of this failure to appreciate the unity of God's grace is to open up a dichotomy between the orders of creation and redemption (and between the eternal and the temporal).[28] Creation is first and foremost the product of God's omnipotence and wisdom, not his love. We recall Bavinck's assertion that 'the cause of the creation is simply and solely the free power of God'. Redemption, on the other hand, appears to be the work of God's unmerited love in response to sin. What is absent is a recognition that grace, as Derek Kidner puts it, "so far from being a mere answer to sin, is fundamental to creation itself."[29] To his credit, Kuyper makes a special effort to ground common grace in Christ, but he posits a very hard and fast line between common grace in creation and special grace in salvation, and when he speaks of common grace as earthly and temporary and of special grace as supernatural and eternal, he only weakens his case.[30] It is heartening to find Dooyeweerd rebuking Kuyper for the latter's dualism and urging that common grace be interpreted Christologically.[31] Yet there is too much in Dooyeweerd's system to indicate that he is working with the very dualism he detects in Kuyper, that he has not penetrated to the heart of the problem in Kuyper's doctrine of God. Moreover, Dooyeweerd seriously undermines his own position by confining common grace to the temporal world and special grace to the 'supra-temporal root' of humanity.

Fourth, the weaknesses of the common/special grace distinction become even more evident when we consider the supposed role of common grace in culture. Kuyper wants to maintain at one and the same time that there is a hiatus between regenerate and unregenerate *and* that even in the absence of true religion, God restrains sin and encourages righteousness. But it is very hard to hold both of these positions without discarding the common/special grace schema as traditionally formulated.[32] Furthermore, Kuyper argues that common grace is of enormous benefit to the Christian in holding back evil, allowing him to develop culturally etc., and yet also affirms that all good works performed by a believer are due to the special grace of God. From this it is hard to avoid the conclusion that the Christian functions in two realms: that of his earthly cultural pursuits and that of his salvation. Jacob Klapwijk perceptively highlights this ambivalence in Kuyper:

> "In part his work echoes the mystery of the born-again heart and the sigh of the weary pilgrim who longs for his eternal home. In part he is driven to work with an extraordinary vigour at the unfolding of God's creation in state, society and science.......At times he sees the creation mandate as a common human task in which Christian and non-Christian stand shoulder to shoulder. Then again he is sure that the great cultural mandate must start from the antithesis and must be translated into a programme of organised Christian action in all areas of life."[33]

Should we then discard the notion of 'common grace' altogether? Not necessarily, provided we can find different terminology, and provided we observe the distinction between the *ontological* and the *methodological*. In the order of being, it seems impossible to deny God's preservation of the structures of creation, his restraint of sin, the existence of a 'common terrain', ways of thinking common to all, and so on. What I have been arguing here, however, is that methodologically, it is theologically hazardous to build a theology of culture on any concept of grace which is sharply distinguished from God's redeeming work in Christ. In Part III we shall attempt to suggest a more acceptable way forward.

The Cultural Mandate

It is quite consonant with what we have found already that the Neo-Calvinists expound human destiny primarily in terms of *duty* and *obedience* to God. The human condition before the fall casts its shadow over all that follows. Elect and reprobate all stand under God's law, whether this is received through divine command, or through conscience, or through the structures of creation. This is the basic state of humankind. Bavinck writes:

> "man is........always and everywhere bound by laws not invented by man, but set forth by God as the rule for life.........there

are norms which stand above man. They form a unity among themselves and find their origin and continuation in the Creator and Lawgiver of the universe. To live in conformity to those norms in mind and heart, in thought and action, *this is what it means most basically to become conformed to the image of God's Son. And this is the ideal and goal of man.*"[34]

Not all the Neo-Calvinists put the matter as bluntly as Bavinck, but it is fair to say that he reflects the general tenor of their thinking. The upshot is that culture, which finds its origin in the cultural mandate delivered before the fall, is construed first and foremost as a legal requirement imposed on us by a law-giving God. The relevant imperative here is God's charge to be fruitful and multiply, fill the earth, subdue and have dominion over it (Gen. 1:28; 9:1). (Sometimes Gen. 2:15 is also added — God's command to Adam to till and keep the garden.) In Kuyper, due to the prominent place he gives to common grace, the significance of the cultural mandate is muted. But, as we have seen, it is crucial for Bavinck, Dooyeweerd, Rookmaaker and Seerveld. As traditionally interpreted, the mandate was an essential part of Adam being created 'under law' and thus an element of the covenant which needed to be kept if eternal life was to be secured. Now, after the fall, God in his common grace enables humankind to engage in the task of cultivating the earth and unfolding the potential goodness of creation, according to his requirements. And special grace is given to Christians to equip them to be transformers of culture, bringing the renewing influence of Christ to every sphere of life. Neither common grace nor special grace annuls the mandate. Quite the contrary; God's grace supports and fulfils it.

Such a theology of culture may have its merits, but it carries with it a cluster of interconnected problems. Firstly, the essence of humanity is defined in terms of obedience. The early chapters of Genesis are seen through the fixed grid of the dual-covenant schema, reinforced by a legalistic doctrine of God. Anthropology thus takes a legal turn from the outset. A close examination of Genesis 1-3, however, reveals rather a different picture. Obedience does play an important part in Adam's life before the fall, but the question is whether or not that is where the centre of gravity lies. It would seem more faithful to the text to see it as offering us a vision of humanity created not primarily for obedience but to be God's counterpart: man and woman were made as those with whom God could have communion.[35] This finds its focus in the concept of the 'image of God' (1:26f.), which is generally interpreted today as referring (at the very

least) to our relatedness to God, our standing as those to whom
God can speak and those who will listen to him.[36] In an eloquent
passage, Walther Eichrodt helpfully links Gen. 1:26f. with the
covenantal tradition of Israel:

> "What Israel, through God's self-communication in the
> covenant, had experienced as the fundamental character of
> the divine nature.........the Priestly writer now succeeds in
> bringing vividly to life as the determining force behind the
> process of creation ....the Creator is seen as a personal
> Thou who discloses himself for the purpose of fellowship with
> his noblest creature..........[Man] has a share in the personhood
> of God; and as a being capable of self-awareness and self-
> determination he is open to the divine address and capable
> of responsible conduct."[37]

Moreover, if we approach the opening chapters of Genesis
Christologically, we are bound to bring God's desire to 'bring
many sons to glory' back into the centre of the picture. His
ultimate purpose for each of us, glimpsed in Genesis but displayed in glorious splendour in Christ, is for us to enjoy a relationship of unending love with him. Human culture will thus be at
its best, its most fitting and God-honouring, when it is
undertaken not out a sense of being under some universal law
but out of an awareness of God's undeserved love for each of us.

Secondly, to put so much weight on capitulating to the
inherent laws of creation runs the risk of forgetting that the
orders of creation are in the first place expressions and
outworkings of divine grace. They are there for us to enjoy,
channels through which we can delight in the goodness of the
Creator. In creating all things out of nothing, and in conferring
upon the world its own appropriate rationality and order, God
is the same God of unconditional mercy which he has shown
himself to be in Christ. This is surely part of what it means to
take seriously the New Testament claim that all things were
made 'through' or 'in' Christ.[38] Rookmaaker and Seerveld seem
to grasp this point well. Rookmaaker speaks of Christ's
Lordship over creation as the 'model' for our relationship to it,
"a relationship of love and freedom". And he goes out of his
way to stress that "We should not see [creation's] laws as a
deterministic system which compels us to do certain
things......our relation to them is not one of compulsion, but
rather of love and freedom."[39] It is only regrettable that this
insight was not allowed to question more rigorously the theology
which he inherited.

Thirdly, for the Neo-Calvinist, the cultural mandate stands
primarily as a command to be obeyed, imposed — directly or

indirectly — on all men and women. Its first occurrence pre-dated the fall, and thus originally had nothing to do with grace, whether common or special. However, once again, a careful exegesis of Genesis 1:28 suggests something rather different. There the imperative to be fruitful and multiply, to fill the earth and subdue it and so forth, is presented in the form of a *blessing*, that is, a command which carries with it the power of fulfilment, or, better still, a gift which includes a demand. It is prefaced by the words: 'And God blessed them, saying.....' 1:28 needs to be seen in the light of 1:22. The earlier verse states that before the creation of man and woman, God blessed all the living creatures, saying: 'Be fruitful and multiply and fill the waters in the seas, and let birds multiply on the earth.' The words *l'mr* between the first two sentences of 1:22 imply that God's blessing is simultaneous with his saying 'Be fruitful.......' As Claus Westermann puts it: "There is one operation which is made effective by the pronouncement of the word."[40] The imperative is not simply directed, it confers something, it endows with power, with a potentiality *to be* fruitful. It is, to borrow J. L. Austin's term, a 'performative' pronouncement.[41] Gen. 1:28, addressed to man and woman, can be interpreted likewise. The same unity between blessing and action is intended.[42] It is not as if God pronounced a blessing and then subsequently gave a task to perform; the blessing itself gave power. As Von Rad remarks, "Man received from the hand of God........the blessing that empowers him to reproduce and multiply."[43] Indeed, elsewhere in the Old Testament fruitfulness and abundance are more often than not seen as both signs and effects of God's blessing.[44] Of course 1:28, unlike 1:22, includes God's command to have dominion over all creatures (echoing 1:26b) and to subdue the earth. But there is no compelling reason why the later command should not also be described in terms of divine blessing.[45] Likewise in 9:1, where a 'cultural mandate' is given to Noah, and where the first sentence repeats 1:28 word for word, the context is that of blessing. Similarly, 2:15 (God's injunction to till and keep the garden) is best understood not as an additional command imposed on his newly made creature, but as a further exposition of what it means to be made in the image of God.[46]

Furthermore, as Westermann has made clear, blessing in the Old Testament came to mean not simply an act of bestowing, a magical transfer of power, but a manifestation of divine activity, a sign of God's active presence.[47] In sum, although we may not be able to go as far as Douglas Bax when he states that Gen. 1:28 is "not an ethical command..........not a commandment"[48] (for clearly there is a type of command here), we can say that if we are to interpret culture in the light of blessing then it is best construed primarily as a gift rather than a demand; a task perhaps, but one which God enables us to perform.

I am not saying that the Neo-Calvinists have no concept of God equipping us for culture. All of them claim that God enables us to fulfil our cultural duties, by means of common grace (directed to all) and special grace (for the elect only). Indeed, Kuyper's theory of artistic inspiration rests on this very truth. And Seerveld stands out as one who is especially eager to hold the ideas of blessing and command together. Nevertheless, even Seerveld still adheres to the common/special grace distinction so that he fails to follow through his shrewd comments on the cultural mandate. And, as I have tried to show, in all the Neo-Calvinists, common grace is essentially an impersonal power, having little or nothing to do with God's love, so that culture tends to be seen as essentially the means by which God's legal demands are met, rather than as a gift for us to enjoy and a means through which he develops and brings to fruition the world he loves. And although the Dutchmen tell us repeatedly that special grace motivates the Christian into active cultural engagement, there needs to be greater stress on culture as an obligation of love, something which arises out of God's unconditional commitment to us and to the created order. Once again, everything here hinges on whether we see self-giving love as belonging to the inner being of God, or only as one of a number of equally important attributes, one of many possible ways in which he can relate to the world.

This last point can be brought to a head if we approach the issue of the cultural mandate Christologically. In the New Testament, we are told that Christ is the one through whom all things were created, who sustains the world in being, who carries all things forward towards their ultimate goal. And we are told that this is the one who has come as man, in an act of sheer grace, to re-order and renew creation. Part of what this means is that our humanity, in him, has been restored to its proper relationship with the created order. Through the Spirit we are now invited into communion with the risen Son so that we can discover that relationship with creation which God longs for each of us, so that we can realise authentically our calling as agents of culture, so that we can share in God's work of bringing creation to its intended end. Clearly, many questions are being begged here; in Part III we shall explore this theme further. But if we are on the right track, it is clear that culture, seen from this perspective, is from beginning to end a gift and that there is little need to speak of 'common' and 'special' grace, only of that love which ceaselessly moves out from the heart of God to redeem that which he has made.

(2) Art and Beauty

Turning now to the Neo-Calvinists' treatment of art, I believe two main issues deserve attention.

Art and Objectivity

First, even a cursory glance at the writings of the Dutch Neo-Calvinists reveals at every turn their belief in what we might call the objectivity of value. Beauty, moral goodness and truth are not human inventions, nor merely the expressions of inner preferences, but are built into the very fabric of the created world, and (especially for Kuyper and Bavinck) are rooted in God himself. Thus, beauty — the most distinctive quality which makes art worthy of praise — is not relative to individual taste or cultural inclination; it is something given, something to which the artist must be faithful. This provides the Dutchmen with what they see as a secure foundation on which aesthetic judgements can be based. Even Seerveld, though he discards beauty in favour of 'allusiveness', still wants to stress its embeddedness in the created order.

This approach will be welcomed by those who hold that values are grounded in an order external to ourselves and that there are means of assessing art which transcend individual likes and dislikes. Indeed, it will come as a breath of fresh air in an intellectual climate where even the suggestion that an artist is bound by norms beyond himself is repeatedly met with disdain. In the Dutchmen, there is no sniff of the perilous subjectivism of Tillich, nor the preoccupation with the artist's inner psychological life which has plagued so much recent philosophy of art.

Beauty: the Key to Art?

Now to the second and most striking feature of their account of art (with the exception of Seerveld): the concentration on beauty. The claim here is not simply that beauty is something which merits approval in art. It is that beauty should be the overriding concern of the artist. Moreover, the quest for beauty — for harmony, proportion, balance, unity-in-multiplicity — is more characteristic of art than any other human activity, so the Neo-Calvinists aver, and is therefore that which distinguishes it from other forms of creativity.

The notion of beauty as unity-in-multiplicity (or some similar notion) has had a long and distinguished heritage.[49] The Pythagoreans believed that beauty was essentially the quality of perfect proportion and order. For the Greeks, *kalon* denoted a total state of soundness, health, wholeness, whether in external appearance or internal disposition. Through Platonism the concept found its way into early Christian thought. Boethius argued that beauty was nothing more than *commensuratio partium*, and Augustine could write: "All bodily beauty consists in the proportion of the parts (*congruentia partium*), together with a certain agreeableness (*suavitas*) of colour".[50] Augustine's emphasis on unity, equality and proportion was taken up by many medieval writers: for example, by John Scotus Erigena in the thirteenth-century treatise *Summa Alexandri*, and in the writings of Hugh of St. Victor, Alexander of Hales, St. Bonaventura, and Robert Grosseteste. After the Renaissance, the same concept penetrated into the heart of Baroque and seventeenth-century aesthetics.[51]

Kuyper, Bavinck, Dooyeweerd and Rookmaaker patently stand in this broad tradition. For Kuyper, beauty in creation, which reflects the glory of God, is recognised primarily by the presence of harmony, symmetry, order, proportion etc. and carries with it a certain effulgence or radiance. The artist must not simply mirror natural beauty; he must fashion out of it a new beauty which excels that of fallen nature, and in so doing he will anticipate heaven and recall paradise lost. Bavinck follows his mentor: beauty in nature and art speaks of the glory of God and is seen "in the agreement between content and form, idea and appearance; in harmony, proportion, unity in differentiation, organisation".[52] Both Kuyper and Bavinck tilt strongly towards Platonism. Dooyeweerd and Rookmaaker follow the same basic trend, but shun Platonism and prefer to speak in terms of 'harmony' rather than beauty.

Such a strong focus on beauty in art may have its benefits, but it carries with it many drawbacks. In the first place, there are immense problems in claiming that what makes art distinctive is its aspiration towards beauty. For we need only think of objects which most people would call 'works of art' (even 'great works of art') which are anything but beautiful, at least not in the Neo-Calvinist sense. What are we to say about Goya's 'Bull Fight' or Stravinsky's 'Rite of Spring'? John Macquarrie asks:

"is *King Lear* beautiful? Or the demonic fantasies of Hierony-
mus Bosch? Or Picasso's *Guernica*........? These are all
indisputably great works of art, but if they have beauty, it is
a very different kind of beauty from that of the butterfly."[53]

Further, what are we to say about works which are explicitly
'Christian' (and generally acknowledged as masterpieces) but
which seem to lack the quality of beauty as traditionally
understood — Penderecki's *Passion of Luke* for example? Further
still, if beauty refers to 'unity-in-diversity' or suchlike, a good
case could be made for saying that the quest for beauty is no
stronger in art than it is in many other fields of human endeavour. In the natural sciences, for instance, the search for beauty
or elegance seems to occupy a significant place.[54] We would
readily concede that there is an aesthetic dimension to reality
distinguished by something akin to harmoniousness or unity-
in-multiplicity, but it is much more debatable to claim that it is
the attempt to emulate or embody this quality which makes art
unique. Emil Brunner comments: "Often art has been defined
as the production of the beautiful, and therefore the secret of
art has been identified with the secret of beauty. But the idea
of beauty seems inadequate to indicate the mystery of art."[55]

Second, an account of the arts dominated by beauty will often
tend to suggest that the chief benefit we gain from a work of
art is the contemplation of its formal structure, or the formal
structure of that which is represented. The Neo-Calvinists do
not actually draw this conclusion but the logic of their argument
moves in this direction. Such a view, sometimes referred to as
'formalism', and in recent times associated with writers such as
Clive Bell, has certainly not gained widespread support.[56] In
most works of art, form is only one part of what we value, and
in many cases may not be particularly crucial for enjoying the
art work at all. We have already noted the predominance of the
contemplative model (albeit of a different kind) in Tillich. In
Part III, I shall suggest that it would do us no harm to lay less
stress on contemplation and considerably more on action. At
this juncture, I am merely pointing out that although some
works of art are clearly designed for the contemplation of their
formal features, we have little warrant for asserting that this
is a necessary or qualifying feature of art.

Third, turning now to Kuyper and Bavinck, it is hazardous to
smuggle Platonism into a philosophy of art which claims fidelity
to a biblical vision of the world, as Seerveld correctly points
out. Neither the Old or New Testament has any interest in the
Greek ideal of beauty (*kalon*) as an other-worldly universal[57]
(though something faintly similar does appear in the wisdom

literature[58]). Paradoxically, the Platonism in Kuyper and Bavinck only undermines their repeated and proper affirmation that the created world contains order *within* itself. As Colin Gunton rightly observes, this tendency to abstract beauty from the arena of space and time has been very strong in our culture:

> "the Western tradition of aesthetics has been vitiated by a pervasive belief in the irrationality and formlessness of matter. The outcome is often that beauty comes to be ascribed to something lying beyond the material world itself, such as the rational forms of the platonic theory".[59]

Fourth, perhaps the greatest danger of being entranced by the traditional concept of beauty is that we fail to see how it might be modified and transfigured by distinctively Christian insights. Suppose we take beauty to be roughly equivalent to 'orderliness', could not the Christian understanding of God's ordering and re-ordering of creation convey to us something peculiarly profound about this orderliness, something which could not be discovered elsewhere? Might it not be that the pattern of the Christian narrative of creation, salvation and consummation displays a type of beauty which would, if not displace the conventional notion, at least lend it a new depth? Kuyper touched on this matter, but only just.

What, then, about Seerveld, the nonconformist in the Neo-Calvinist camp? For him, the prime concern of art is not (and should not be) with beauty, but with allusiveness. Unfortunately, as Seerveld expounds it, the concept of allusiveness is too vague and undefined (even allusive!) to be particularly helpful. It would require a good deal more elucidation before it could service a cogent philosophy of art. No doubt, Seerveld himself would be the first to admit this; much of his thought is still at an embryonic stage. Nevertheless, as will become clear, what he does say about allusiveness is extremely close to what I shall contend lies at the heart of art, namely metaphor.

(3) Summary and Comments

It is time to sum up and see where our study of the Dutch Neo-Calvinists has led us. Although not ignoring their substantial strengths, I have tried to indicate where I believe the key areas of weakness to lie. Above all, I have been concerned to show that the Neo-Calvinist concept of God is insufficiently shaped by the self-disclosure of the Trinity in the history of Jesus

Christ. God is portrayed fundamentally as the powerful Law-giver, whose absolute and sovereign will is enacted in the establishment of precepts which we are summoned to obey; his love is a secondary attribute, reserved for the elect. I have endeavoured to contrast this with what I take to be the core of the New Testament witness, namely that in the life, death and resurrection of Christ, we witness God's innermost nature as ecstatic, self-giving love. God's will is thus the expression of his triune being, of that eternal love which ceaselessly flows within the Godhead and which has been opened out and poured forth for us supremely in Jesus Christ.

I have tried to show that to portray God along Neo-Calvinist lines issues in a series of unacceptable consequences. Sharp antitheses arise — between humanity's state prior to the fall (under law) and after the fall (under grace), a general calling and a special calling, the covenant of works and the covenant of grace — all of which impair the constancy of God's character. Moreover, in the Dutch system, God's demands logically precede his grace; Adam's standing before the fall sets the scene for all that follows. Grace, in whatever form it appears, is introduced to meet the requirements of God's law. The doctrine of common grace only compounds the problems. Common grace, especially in Kuyper and Bavinck, becomes little more than God's power in creation, detached from his purposes of love. We noted Dooyeweerd's attempt to wrestle free from Kuyper's common grace theory but concluded that his theology was still too deeply coloured by the tenets of scholastic Calvinism. I also argued that a stress on the innate orderliness of the world has so dominated the picture that redemption tends to be interpreted very largely in the light of creation's inherent structures, seen apart from Christ.

In short, running through Dutch Neo-Calvinism there appears to be a tendency towards a dualism between creation and redemption, a dualism which cannot be avoided unless some of the basic doctrinal axioms of Calvinism are relinquished and a fresh grasp of the divine-human Lordship of Christ over the created world is recovered.

We also observed the Neo-Calvinists' propensity to speak of our calling principally in terms of obedience to divine law (humanity's condition prior to the fall) rather than in terms of being invited to share in the life and purposes of the triune God. Culture centres around the concept of obedience. In contrast, I suggested that a more satisfactory approach would view cultural involvement chiefly as a gift rather than a legal requirement and that a more thorough-going Christological perspective would greatly assist us.

Turning to art, we found that the Neo-Calvinists' theory of beauty had the merit of providing an objective basis for evaluating art. Yet making beauty the qualifying feature of art carries with it a number of drawbacks. It can take us unhelpfully close to Platonism, it over-emphasises the importance of form in art, and it fails to do justice to great art which lacks harmoniousness. Further, we suggested that the concept of beauty employed by the Neo-Calvinists could well benefit from being modified by the distinctive notions of order inherent in the shape of the Gospel story.

Is there, then, a better way forward?

Notes
[1] In the Netherlands, *Foederaltheologie* was proposed by Gomarus, Trelcatius, Ravensperger, Cloppenburg, but above all by Johannes Cocceius (1603-1669) who taught at Franeker and Leyden. It found its way into the Netherlands through the English Puritans. Cf. David A. Weir, *The Origins of the Federal Theology in Sixteenth-Century Reformation Thought*, Oxford: Clarendon Press, 1990. Dooyeweerd and his followers do not make much of the covenant of works/covenant of grace distinction, but there is nothing in the Dooyeweerdian theology which would question it.
[2] In his study of covenant, William J. Dumbrell writes: "there can only be one divine covenant..........the chain of connection....[moves] from creation to Noah, leads us from Noah to Abraham, from Abraham to Sinai, to David, to the Jeremaic new covenant and thence to Jesus its fulfiller." *Covenant and Creation*, Exeter: Paternoster Press, 1984, p. 42. Ironically this insight lay at the very heart of Calvin's theology. Cf. Holmes Rolston III, "Responsible Man in Reformed Theology: Calvin versus the Westminster Confession," *Scottish Journal of Theology*, 23 (1970), p. 141.
[3] *DGG*, I, p. 163.
[4] *RF*, p. 272. The root confusion here is that between a covenant and a contract. Cf. James B. Torrance, "Covenant or Contract? A Study of the Theological Background of Worship in Seventeenth-Century Scotland," *Scottish Journal of Theology*, 23 (1970), pp. 51-76; "The Covenant Concept in Scottish Theology and Politics and its Legacy," *Scottish Journal of Theology*, 34 (1981), pp. 225-243.
[5] In at least one passage Kuyper describes the covenant of works as an eternal relation between God and his creature. Cf. e.g. *Dictaten Dogmatiek*, IV, Kampen: Kok, 2nd ed., 1910, pp. 38ff.
[6] The penetrating analysis by Eberhard Jüngel of the growth of misleading views of God's power and omnipotence is particularly relevant in this connection. *God as the Mystery of the World*, Grand Rapids, Michigan: Eerdmans, 1983, especially pp. 3-42, 299-396. Cf. also James B. Torrance, "The Incarnation and Limited Atonement," *Scottish Bulletin of Evangelical Theology*, 2 (1984), pp. 32-

40. Colin Gunton remarks that "the tendency to see God as primarily power and only secondarily as love or self-giving is very deep-seated in our tradition". *Enlightenment and Alienation*, Basingstoke: Marshall Morgan and Scott, 1985, p. 65.

[7] *Transcendental Criticism and Christian Philosophy*, Franeker: T. Wever, 1961, p. 247.

[8] "Introduction," in Kalsbeek, *op. cit.*, p. 31. H. G. Stoker uses the term 'nomologism' to describe Dooyeweerd's thought. *De Nieuwere Wysbegeerte aan de Vrije Universiteit*, Potchefstroom: "Die Westedrukkery", 1933, pp. 50f.

[9] As quoted and translated by Spykman, *loc. cit.*, p. 183.

[10] *RF*, p. 277. My italics.

[11] *NCTT*, I, p. 99.

[12] "Calvinisme en Wijsbegeerte," *Nieuwe Theologische Stüdien*, XVI (1933), p. 246. Cp. Douglas Bax's comments about the tendency of the Dutch Reformed Church in South Africa to argue from what *is* to what *ought to be*, in "The Bible and Apartheid," in *Apartheid is a Heresy*, ed. John de Gruchy and Charles Villa-Vicencio, Guildford: Lutterworth, 1983, p. 116.

[13] Even here, however, Kuyper is ambiguous. Cf. A. Van Ruler, *Kuyper's Idee Eener Christelijke Cultuur*, Nijkerk: G. F. Callenbach, no date, p. 68.

[14] As quoted and translated by Spykman, *loc. cit.*, p. 181.

[15] *Bonhoeffer and South Africa*, p. 109. Cp. *The Church Struggle in South Africa*, pp. 201ff. We should add that some Dooyeweerdians (e.g. Stuart Fowler) have gone to great lengths to distance their theology from the cruder forms of 'orders of creation' theology.

[16] *Op. cit.*, pp. 173f. It must be stressed, however, that Kuyperian theology was a good deal more refined than the German *Ordnungstheologie*.

[17] Brümmer, *op. cit.*, p. 184.

[18] *Ibid.*, p. 247.

[19] *Being as Communion*, Crestwood, New York: St Vladimir's Seminary Press, 1985, p. 46.

[20] *DGG*, III, pp. 646-653.

[21] See above, p. 92.

[22] *RF*, pp. 267, 333f., 283, 384.

[23] *NCTT*, II, p. 32.

[24] Cf. Cornelius Van Til, *op. cit.*, pp. 23-33; William Masselink, *General Revelation and Common Grace*, Grand Rapids, Michigan: Eerdmans, 1953, pp. 187-262.

[25] Cf. e.g. H. Hoeksema, *The Protestant Reformed Churches in America*, Grand Rapids, Michigan: First Protestant Reformed Church, 1936, p. 322; Kuiper, *op. cit.*, pp. 179f.

[26] Cf. J. M. Myers, *Grace and Torah*, Philadelphia: Fortress Press, 1975; T. F. Torrance, *The Doctrine of Grace in the Apostolic Fathers*, Edinburgh: Oliver & Boyd, 1948; Timothy A. Dearborn, "The Trinitarian Nature of Grace," PhD Thesis, University of Aberdeen, 1988, pp. 9ff.

[27] Dearborn, *op. cit.*, p. 8.

[28] Cf. Jacob Klapwijk, "Rationality in the Dutch Neo-Calvinist Tradition," in *Rationality in the Calvinian Tradition*, eds. Hendrik Hart, Johan van der Hoeven and Nicholas Wolterstorff, Lanham and London: University Press of America, 1983, p. 106.

[29] Derek Kidner, *Genesis*, London: Tyndale, 1967, p. 38.

[30] Cf. Henry Van Til, *The Calvinistic Concept of Culture*, Philadelphia: Presbyterian and Reformed Publishing Co., 1974, p. 134.

[31] *NCTT*, I, pp. 523ff.; *Roots of Western Culture*, p. 38.

[32] Significantly, in the United States, this tension in Kuyper has led to the spawning of two divergent schools of thought. Cf. Bratt, *loc. cit.*, pp. 145ff. It is also interesting to note that Kuyper's appeal to the antithesis peaked in the first half of his career when the need for a distinctively Calvinist approach was at its strongest; the idea of common grace came to the fore in his later years.

[33] *Loc. cit.*, p. 101.

[34] As quoted and translated by Spykman, *loc. cit.*, pp. 181f. My italics.

[35] Cf. T. C. Vriezen, *An Outline of Old Testament Theology*, Oxford: Blackwell, 1958, p. 200: "God is known as the God who concerns Himself with the human world and has communion with man."

[36] Cf. Douglas John Hall, *Imaging God: Dominion as Stewardship*, Grand Rapids, Michigan: Eerdmans, 1986, especially pp. 98ff.; Claus Westermann, *Genesis 1-11*, trans. J. J. Scullon, London: SPCK, 1984, pp. 147-158; F. Horst, "Face to Face. The Biblical Doctrine of the Image of God," *Interpretation*, 4 (1950), pp. 230f.; Vriezen, *op. cit.*, pp. 145-147; Walther Eichrodt, *Theology of the Old Testament*, II, London: SCM, 1967, pp. 125-127.

[37] *Op. cit.*, p. 126.

[38] Col. 1:16; Heb. 1:2, Jn. 1:3.

[39] *CG*, pp. 56, 57.

[40] *Op. cit.*, p. 138.

[41] Cf. Anthony Thiselton, "The Supposed Power of Words in the Biblical Writings," *Journal of Theological Studies*, 25 (1974), pp. 293f.

[42] The only structural difference between vss. 22 and 28 is that in the former the blessing is introduced with *l'mr*, in the latter with *wy'mr lhm*. In v. 28, God is speaking to both man and woman.

[43] *Das erste Buch Mose*, Göttingen: Vandenhoeck & Ruprecht, 1964, p. 47.

[44] E.g. Pss. 128:3, 107:38; Dt. 30:16. Cf. A. Murtonen, "The Use and Meaning of the Words lᵉbarek and bᵉrakah in the Old Testament," *Vetus Testamentum*, 9 (1959), p. 166; H. Mowvley, "The Concept and Content of 'Blessing' in the Old Testament," *The Bible Translator*, 26 (1965), p. 78.

[45] Cf. C. Westermann, *Creation*, London: SPCK, 1974, pp. 50ff.

[46] Westermann, *Genesis* 1-11, p. 220.

[47] *Blessing in the Bible and the Life of the Church*, Philadelphia: Fortress Press, 1968.

[48] *Loc. cit.*, p. 116.

[49] Wladyslaw Tatarkiewicz, "The Great Theory of Beauty and Its Decline," *Journal of Aesthetics and Art Criticism*, 31 (1972), pp. 165-180.

[50] *City of God*, XXII, xix.

[51] The break-up of the 'great theory' has been well charted by Jerome Stolnitz, "'Beauty': Some Stages in the History of an Idea," *Journal of the History of Ideas*, 22, 2 (1961), pp. 185-204.

[52] "VSS," p. 276.

[53] *In Search of Humanity*, London: SCM, 1982, p. 193.

[54] Cf. Paul Davies, *God and the New Physics*, London, Toronto and Melbourne: Dent, 1983, pp. 220f.

[55] *Christianity and Civilisation*, 2, London: Nisbet, 1949, p. 73.

[56] Cf. Clive Bell, *Art*, London: Chatto and Windus, 1947. Bell argued that it is 'significant form' in a work of art, and not that which it represents, which triggers 'aesthetic emotion'.

[57] "There is no reference to the *kalon* in the Platonic and Hellenistic sense [in the Old Testament]. The problem of the beautiful is outwith the range of biblical thinking, for these facts apply to the NT as well......*kalon* does not occur at all as an aesthetic quantity". Georg Bertram, "*καλος*" in *Theological Dictionary of the New Testament*, III, ed. Gerhard Kittel, Grand Rapids, Michigan: Eerdmans, 1965, pp. 543f. In the majority of cases in the LXX, *καλος, καλον* mean 'morally good', often occurring alongside *αγαθος* and *χρηστος* as a translation of *ṭwb*. The closest we get to the Greek idea of beauty is in the 'P' narrative of Genesis. In the LXX, Gen. 1:31 (which sums up the verdicts of 1:4, 10, 12, 18, 21, 25) is translated *και ειδεν ὁ Θεος τα παντα, ὁρα ἐποιησε, και ιδου καλα λιαν*. In this context, *ṭwb* has the sense of successful accomplishment, i.e. 'well done'. Cf. I. Höver-Johag, "*ṭwb ṭwb yṭb*" in *Theological Dictionary of the Old Testament*, V, ed. G. J. Botterweck and H. Ringgren, Grand Rapids, Michigan: Eerdmans, 1986, p. 317. The oft-quoted words of I Chron. 16:29, sometimes translated 'in the beauty of holiness', have little to do with the Greek aesthetic concept of *kalon*. Cf. P. R. Ackroyd, "Some Notes on the Psalms," *Journal of Theological Studies*, 17 (1966), p. 394.

[58] E.g. Wisdom 13:7; Eccles. 3:11. Bertram shows how these inter-testamental ideas, spurred on by the Hellenistic concept of beauty as intrinsic to deity, led to a strong tradition in the early Church which emphasised the beauty of Christ (despite Isaiah 53). *Loc. cit.*, pp. 553ff.

[59] "Creation and Re-Creation: An Exploration of Some Themes in Aesthetics and Theology," *Modern Theology*, 2, 1 (1985), p. 7.

Part III

Towards a Theology
of the Arts

1. Introduction

The conclusion to which we have been drawn is that although both Tillich and the Dutch Neo-Calvinists show a commendable concern to integrate theology and the philosophy of art, it is questionable whether they espouse a theology adequate to establish and sustain this integration. In the case of Tillich, this was due in large part to the fact that the axioms on which his system was constructed could not do sufficient justice to the particularities of history and especially the person and history of Jesus Christ. Christology tended to be overmastered by the general scheme in which it was set. In the case of the Calvinists, a law-dominated doctrine of creation led to a legalistic understanding of humankind and culture, and to a philosophy of art with an exaggerated stress on beauty. In the last resort, their main weakness appeared to be a lack of Christological determination in their doctrine of God.

Theologically, therefore, the direction in which we have been moving has been gradually closer to Christology. In this the final part of the book, I want to enquire as to what kind of philosophy of art might emerge if we take our bearings from a more rigorous concentration on the incarnation, crucifixion and resurrection of the Son of God, thus responding to the challenge implicit in Dietrich Bonhoeffer's claim that "the more exclusively we acknowledge Christ as Lord, the more the wide range of his dominion will be revealed to us."[1] I am not of course recommending that theology should begin *and end* with Christology. That will become very evident as we proceed. Nor do I want to maintain that this is the only legitimate way ahead for a cogent theological account of the arts. Still less am I suggesting that adopting this strategy will instantly untangle the vast range of problems which have attended enquiry into the nature of the arts. And I am acutely aware that this approach requires a good deal more defence, qualification and expansion than space here permits. But I do believe that to pursue our topic from this angle will mark out some especially fruitful paths for a theological view of the arts, paths which have been insufficiently explored to date. Most of all, I hope to show that to travel along these paths will more adequately illuminate the way people actually practise and enjoy the arts than either of the two traditions examined so far.

Notes
[1] As quoted in L. Rasmussen, *Dietrich Bonhoeffer: Reality and Resistance*, Nashville: Abingdon Press, 1972, p. 28.

2. Christ, Creation and Creativity

"Hands that flung stars into space
To cruel nails surrendered."

Graham Kendrick

As our point of entry, I should like to address a theme which we touched upon earlier in connection with the Dutch Calvinists, but which we observed was insufficiently developed by them: Christ as the Mediator of creation. The concept appears in a number of places in the New Testament (e.g. 1 Cor. 8:6; Col. 1:15-20; Eph. 1:3-14; Jn. 1:3) and, it seems, was part of the very earliest Christian confession.[1] Yet what are these passages, which have occasioned the most heated controversy in the past, actually telling us? What are we affirming if we say that the one who made 'peace by the blood of the cross' is also the one 'through whom' and 'for whom' all things were created? For some, the idea of Christ as the Mediator of creation is 'merely a metaphor', and therefore instantly falls under suspicion as being incapable of saying anything true or false about the character or nature of God, Christ, or the world as they are in themselves. Such an approach to metaphor is now largely discredited, as we shall see in the next chapter. It tends to go hand in hand with empiricist assumptions about language; for instance, that only clear and distinct literal statements can convey the truth about things as they really are — a view which, to say the least, is highly questionable. Others adopt a subtler position, maintaining that when verses like Col. 1:15-16 affirm that all things were created 'in, through and for Christ' who is 'the image of the invisible God, the first-born of all creation', they do indeed convey truth about Christ and God, but not that Christ was present with God in the beginning, nor that he is a pre-existent hypostasis or divine being, but only that he embodies, expresses and defines "that power of God which is the manifestation of God in and to his creation."[2] Without space to argue a full case, I can only register that I find such views less than convincing, and suspect that they have more to do with a general dislike of ontology and talk about God's inner nature than the exegesis of particular verses.[3] At any rate, my main purpose here is to demonstrate that the metaphor of Christ as the agent, sustainer and goal of creation has in fact considerable potential to illuminate both the acts and the eternal being of God as triune, and, by extension, the nature of the created world. I shall attempt to do so by drawing out five interrelated motifs implicit in the metaphor. It is my hope that, taken together, these motifs will furnish us with a useful framework with which we can go on to approach the concept of human creativity.

(1) Christ and the Cosmos

Creation out of nothing

We begin with the affirmation, reiterated in recent years by many theologians, that God's creation 'out of nothing' is best understood as an act of gracious love. God 'went beyond' himself, renouncing isolation, solitude and independence. He was compelled by nothing beyond himself, only by the love at the heart of his being which is supremely revealed to us in the life, passion and resurrection of Christ. Creation out of nothing is accordingly not to be seen as an act of arbitrary power but as an expression of the ceaseless self-giving love within God. So Ephesians 1:3-14 describes God's electing purpose of love as his will to unite all things in Christ, and since God's election precedes creation, his electing intention is not only the ground of his activity within creation, but is also, by implication, the ground of the act of creation itself. This also seems to be the underlying logic of Col. 1:16, Heb. 1:2, Jn. 1:3 and Rom. 4:17.[4] The disclosure of God's love in Christ is, as Emil Brunner writes, "the revelation of the purpose of His creation, and this purpose of creation is the reason why he posits a creation. The love of God is the *causa finalis* of the Creation. In Jesus Christ this ideal reason for the creation is revealed."[5]

Taking the matter a stage further, if the one who suffered the shame of humiliation and crucifixion is also the one 'through whom' all things came to be, then the act of creation *ex nihilo* can be construed as an act of suffering or sacrificial love, or at the very least, an act which lays God open to the possibility of suffering. In creating a reality distinct from himself and allowing it a measure of genuine freedom, God risks exposing himself to the pain and rejection it can bring. The divine love takes the risk of getting no return for its expense. The vulnerability of

the stable at Bethlehem and the ignominious death of an alleged
criminal is the selfsame vulnerability at the heart of the Creator.
So Robin Barbour writes:

> "only the Creator can create His own creatureliness, and
> only He who has done this can be seen to be at the deepest
> level the Creator; for the only truly creative and sovereign
> act visible to man is the act of self-abnegation in love —
> nothing else represents unconquerable power. Something of
> that insight, as it seems to me, lies behind the New Testament
> assertion that it is Christ crucified and exalted through whom
> all things are made."[6]

Creation and Covenant

Our second motif concerns God's continuing relationship with
that which he has made. In the letter to the Colossians, Christ
is described not only as the first-born of all creation (πρωτοτοκος
πασης κτισεως) (1:15) and the head (κεφαλη) of all rule and
authority (2:10), but also as the one in whom all things 'hold
together (συνεστηκεν)' (1:17). As Moule paraphrases it, "the
universe owes its coherence to him."[7] This betokens God's
continual commitment and loyalty to creation. The unsparing
and unremitting love which took Jesus to the cross for
humankind is none other than the love which maintains and
sustains the created order. In Ruth Etchell's words, "God is
[not] to be understood as having 'made something' and then
wondered what to do with it; rather........from the first the
creative purpose was one of profound and secure relationship,
to be felicitous and glorious."[8] This suggests a strong link
between the concepts of creation and covenant; creation is not a
mere prelude to grace, as with the Dutch Neo-Calvinists.[9] Jürgen
Moltmann rightly comments that the "history of God's
relationship to the world begins with creation itself and not
just the fall of man."[10]

Nevertheless, God's loyalty is a respectful loyalty. He gives
his world a measure of independence and autonomy, allowing
it 'room' to be itself. For his love achieves its ends by respecting
the 'otherness of the other'. This should make us wary of
attempts to interpret the New Testament 'cosmic Christ'
passages as suggesting a 'sacramental universe', impregnated
with divine causes, as if Christ could in some sense be 'read off'
the face of nature. A more judicious approach to Biblical
language about the relation between Christ and creation should
properly remind us that God's love for creation entails him
honouring its integrity as something distinct from himself. The

created world may indeed be regarded as the arena for Christ's ceaseless activity, but this does not alter its finite, contingent createdness: its deepest secret lies outside its own reality. Indeed, as is often pointed out, a proper stress on the contingency of the created order has proved crucial to the momentum of contemporary science. Moreover, to speak of this divine repect in terms of God's 'self-limitation', as some are keen to do, is arguably unnecessary and potentially misleading. It may be appropriate to use such language in certain contexts, but God's refusal to violate the created order is better construed as an expression of his unswerving faithfulness to it, not as a sign of a retreat into some kind of self-imposed impotence.

Order and Disorder

Third, we come to the twin themes of order and disorder. It has normally been a central assumption of mainstream Christian theology (and a tacit one of modern natural science) that the universe possesses a latent order and rationality of its own, even though such order may exist in many different forms at different levels. This is itself a witness to the divine goodness: the Creator has endowed his creation with structure and form, to be elicited, studied, explored and enjoyed. Yet we need to set this alongside what we have just said about the significant measure of freedom which God has granted his world. Faithfulness to Christian tradition and to natural science will make us wary of understanding the world's order in too frozen and static a sense, something which many theologians of recent years have been arguing with almost wearisome persistence. God, we are told, is *semper Creator*, always creating. Advances in the physical sciences make it increasingly clear that the universe exhibits a subtle balance and interplay between law and circumstance, pattern and process, being and becoming.[11] The cosmos constantly astonishes and surprises us through its interaction of randomness and regularity. It may carry with it an assurance of its own development, yet it would be wrong to claim that the precise nature of that development is, so to speak, built into the system. Indeed, Prigogine and Stengers go as far as to claim: "We see now that there is a more subtle form of reality involving both time and eternity."[12] In more measured tones, John Polkinghorne writes:

> "However much the fundamental physicist may wish to frame his understanding in terms of being, the scientist who is describing the processes of the world must also take account of the role of becoming.......It is one of the great discoveries of

this century that the universe itself has a history and partakes of becoming."[13]

Hence an undue emphasis on the permanence and stability of creation, such as we found in the Neo-Calvinists, needs to be resisted. As Daniel Hardy and David Ford put it, "a rigid, over-ordered and over-ordering God is far too impoverished to be responsible for a universe such as ours."[14] A more Christological orientation helps us here too. Indeed, to speak of Christ as the 'Word' draws on both the Stoic notion of the *logos* — the rational principle embedded in creation — and the Hebrew *dābār* — the creative, active Word of God. Or again, in Heb. 1:3, Christ is described as 'upholding the universe by his word of power'. 'Upholding' (φερων) could be understood in the sense of 'maintaining in existence' but a more likely rendering would be 'governing', 'being responsible for'.[15] F. F. Bruce glosses it: "Christ upholds the universe not like Atlas supporting a dead weight on his shoulders, but as One who carries all things forward on their appointed course."[16] There is not only a holding in being but also a dynamic purposeful activity which propels the world towards its goal. With this in mind, Hardy and Ford suggest that we should talk not only of order and disorder in the world but also of 'non-order': that unpredictable, creative, spontaneous element in creation and in human life which reaches its apogee in Jesus Christ.[17]

But what then of disorder? The subject is of course vast and complex, and fraught with difficulties, theological and philosophical. But the view which probably presents the fewest problems is that which conceives disorder as the incomprehensible consequence of the precarious freedom which God has granted to creation — manifest in the non-human world as well as in sinful humanity. It arises when order becomes distorted and warped, and when 'non-order' becomes destructive rather than creative. At its most sinister, it counterfeits order (can we ever forget that it was in the name of law and order that Jesus was crucified?), but it is hardly less damaging when it masquerades as non-order (an obsession with spontaneity in worship would be a good example). Whatever form it assumes, it is this twisted, corrupt dimension of creation which God has unmasked and laid hold of in the incarnation and humiliation of his Son. This brings us to our fourth motif.

The Transformation of Disorder

Even when Paul writes about the 'futility' of creation in Romans 8, he never loses sight of its glorious future (vss. 18-21, 24f.), anticipated by the resurrection of Christ. It is of course all too easy to succumb to a facile and simplistic picture of the future of the universe. To view the cosmos as proceeding in one smooth, continuous crescendo towards eternal perfection is palpably naive; the physicist today reminds us that the world, in temporal terms at least, is heading for a fairly bleak future. Nevertheless, a number of specifically theological points can and should still be made with regard to the hope which awaits creation. First of all, there needs to be a proper grasp of the extent of this hope, that it is a hope for the entire cosmos, not simply for humanity. To restrict the scope of salvation to humankind is effectively to abandon belief in the God of Scripture, the God who is committed to redeeming that which he has created. We are involved in a common history with the physical world and cannot entertain our own redemption in isolation from it. More than that, it is surely inadequate to see God's redemption of creation as a mere appendix to the Gospel, as if he had no interest in the non-human for its own sake but only in so far as it contributed to the welfare of men and women. In Col. 1:20, the blood of the cross is juxtaposed with the reconciliation of 'all things (τα παντα)', and in Eph. 1, we are told that God's purpose as revealed in Christ is to unite 'all things (τα παντα)' in Christ (v. 10). Similarly, in Heb. 1:2, Christ is described as the 'heir of all things (κληρονομον παντων)'.[18] We have often wrongly assumed

> "the contribution of nature to the enactment of the gospel not to be to the *stage* of the theatre but to the scenery, the backcloth................nature has been relegated to the beautiful, valuable but essentially passive and inert role of providing an introduction, backdrop and setting for the supremely *human* drama."[19]

Another glance at Romans 8 is instructive at this point, for there the implications of Christ's Lordship in the life of the Christian are drawn out in parallel with those of his Lordship over the created order. The two are bound together by the one redemptive purpose at work in both Christians and creation — from suffering to glory, as evidenced by 'hope' (vss. 20, 24) and waiting 'with eager longing for the revealing of the sons of God' (v. 19). John Gibbs properly insists that the descriptions of God's redemptive work in creation "are not mere reflections of the inner working of redemption in the 'heirs,' but descriptions of a reality alongside the reality of the Christian's freedom, even in suffering, for glory."[20] The Lord who is working in the lives of Christians is the same Lord who is at work gaining victory over death, life, angels, principalities and all else in creation which sets itself against him (vss. 38-39). Gibbs concludes:

> "[The] relationship between Creator and creature cannot be squeezed through the bottleneck of justification by faith, for the latter is neither the beginning nor the end of God's ways. Redemption includes the creation not merely for man's sake, but because the cosmic totality itself, as the *gloriae dei theatrum*.........was created to glorify God."[21]

Second, the redemption of creation entails transformation. The Creator Son comes as man, enters the depths of cosmic chaos which sin has wrought. He takes on himself the full force of the Father's judgement: the Judge is judged in our place (Barth), absorbing the impact of evil and disorder. On the third day, the destruction and distortion are transfigured and redirected. In Christ, all that is ugly and subversive in the cosmos has been purified, beautified and fulfilled. Therein lies the promise for the transformation of all things. Like our bodies, which will be changed in resurrection from physical to spiritual bodies while still remaining bodies, creation will be remade by the God who promises never to let it go. Third, the *way* in which this transformation has been set in motion in Christ displays yet again that respectful love which marks all God's dealings with his world. At the cross, God meets evil not with brute or arbitrary might, but by the power of self-giving love, by submitting to the forces that hold creation in thrall and then breaking their grip. It is this power which will transform the cosmos. Fourth, the goal of transformation is clearly best thought of as re-creation, rather than 'a return to Eden', to what 'once was', a *status quo ante*. The entire universe is summoned by the Spirit to a new future, a destiny not given 'in the beginning', a destiny centred — as the book of Revelation reminds us so clearly — on the one who says 'Behold, I make all things new'.

The Humanity of Christ and Creation

And so to the fifth of our main motifs. In the wide sweep of God's creative and re-creative work we have been sketching above, we must not lose sight of the colossal significance of the humanity of Christ. The remaking of creation is something which has been accomplished *in* the humanity assumed by the Son of God. In Christ, creation has been healed and redirected towards the Father. In this vein, T. F. Torrance speaks of the incarnation of the Son of God as

"the deep ontological intersection of the patterns of our world
by the divine order of love — that is, the intersection of
patterns that have somehow gone wrong and have become
twisted in disorder — in order to inject into them a reordering
at a deeper level. Hereby the disturbance and violence and
lawlessness of our world are transfixed and taken in command
in such a way that they are made........to serve the ultimate
triumph of the love of God over all."[22]

So in Jesus' temptations in the wilderness, his humanity is not
simply the instrument through which the divine encounters
evil; rather the battle with the demonic is fought out *within*
our physical humanity taken on by him, and it is Jesus' own
refusal to submit to the demonic — made possible by the Spirit
— which enables him to to wage war against all the evil he
meets in his subsequent ministry. In the cross and resurrection,
again, the divine victory over evil is a victory as much human
as it is divine. The resurrection of the crucified humanity of
Christ is itself the embryonic promise for the entire physical
cosmos. In him all things have already been made new, and in
him the destiny of creation has been set forth. Thus to speak of
Christ as the 'end' of creation (in the manner of e.g. Rev. 3:14)
is not merely to speak of his supremacy or of his decisiveness in
bringing creation to completion, it is also to say that in his very
Person, as the risen and ascended God-Man, he embodies and
constitutes the *telos* of created reality.[23]

As we noted above, it is just this close association between
the humanity of Christ and the created order which the Dutch
Neo-Calvinists never properly appreciated. For them, we recall,
Christ was Mediator of Creation only *as God*. Even apart from
the evidence of the Gospels, there is much elsewhere in the
New Testament which suggests otherwise. In Hebrews 1 and 2,
we find a 'high' theology of Christ as ruling Lord (he has put
everything under his feet (1:2 — 2:9)), set alongside an equally
uncompromising stress on his humanity (he partook of our
nature (2:14, 18), suffered (2:11, 18; 5:7f.), was tempted (2:17f.,
4:15), and tasted death (2:9, 14)). The one who has put all
things under his feet is none other than the one who has borne
the full weight of the world's evil as man. In Phil. 2, Paul's
stirring affirmation of Christ's rule as Lord over creation cannot
be divorced from what he has to say about Christ as man
assuming the form of a servant and obeying God even to the
point of death.[24] Or again, in Rev. 4, a typical Old Testament
vision of creation is painted for us — the rainbow signifying the
covenant of order in creation, the angelic council, etc. — and it
is followed in chapter 5 by a vision of the Lamb of Isaiah 53, 'as

though it had been slain' (v. 6). It is *this Lamb* who is Lord of all (vss. 12-14). Christ is Lord of creation not simply as God, but also in his full humanity.

(2) Human Creativity in Christ

Secretaries of God's Praise

What, then, are we to say about our own place within this design? We begin by recalling the frequent declaration of the Psalmists that creation, in a myriad of ways, is endlessly praising its Creator. In all its colour, movement, subtlety, richness, diversity and splendour, it brings glory to God: 'The heavens are telling the glory of God; and the firmament proclaims his handiwork.' (Ps. 19:1) Our calling, I would suggest, is to articulate and extend that praise in ever fresh ways, to be 'priests of creation'. In humankind, creation finds a voice; to use George Herbert's word, each of us is invited to be a 'secretary' of praise. Through the human creature, the inarticulate (though never silent) creation becomes articulate. As Douglas John Hall puts it, "In this creature the speaking God, *Deus loquens*, locates a counterpart within the *saeculum*, a speaking animal. Here the creation gathers itself and addresses the One whose glorious Word brought it into being, word answering Word."[25]

Yet this priestly task needs to be linked closely, I would suggest, with Christology. To open up this horizon, let me highlight five interrelated themes. First of all, in Jesus Christ we see from the side of God a movement of divine grace and condescension, in which God assumes to himself our fallen human nature, identifies with us in our alienation and disobedience, both to deliver an unconditional pledge of love from his very heart, and at the same time to reject all that conflicts with his holy will. Second, in Jesus Christ, we see from the side of humanity a perfect life of loving obedience to his Father. Jesus Christ constitutes the true and exemplary human response to the Father's will. Humanity as God intends it to be is thus not to be found by conjuring up an ideal from out of the blue, nor by trying to imagine some pre-fall era. It is given in the obedient humanity of the incarnate Son. Third, through this two-fold movement, and by virtue of his resurrection and exaltation, we can say that in Christ our broken and distorted humanity has been re-established in its proper orientation toward the Creator. Fourth, through the Holy Spirit, we are invited to share in the renewed humanity of Christ, to be taken through him into the life of the triune God, and thus to discover our true destiny as his sons and daughters. Authentic humanity is thus not something which we possess so much as something we grow into through the Spirit.[26] Fifth, to be drawn in the Spirit through Christ into God's own life will inevitably carry with it an obligation towards the created order, to bring creation to praise its Maker. A 'high' Christology, such as we have been expounding, moves inescapably in this direction. Growth in our relationship with Christ brings with it growth and maturity in our relationship with the physical world, the world which has been made and redeemed through him.

The advantages of viewing creativity from this Christological angle will, I hope, become clearer as we proceed. But at this stage it is worth pointing out how fruitful it can be in tackling one of the most crucial problems which any theologian of culture faces, that of reconciling human creativity and God's sovereignty. How can we give an account of divine authority that does not negate but establishes our free creative activity? Or, to turn the question around, how can we speak of authentic human creativity without usurping divine authority? The Dutch Neo-Calvinists, we saw, passionately believed that both poles needed to be affirmed. Yet in most cases they were tied to a theology in which God's power rather than his love was pre-eminent, and in which the idea of obedience dominated their view of what it is to be human. Thus, despite their best intentions, they exposed themselves to the oft-repeated charge that orthodox Christianity suppresses rather than encourages human freedom. It is all too easy to respond by proposing that the essence of creativity is autonomous self-expression and self-assertion, and abandon the notion of obedience to any external agency or norm. Such a theory, of course, has had its advocates, but it is surely far removed from the heart of the Christian tradition.

As long as the problem is handled by trying to find some uneasy alliance between God's power and our freedom, we are unlikely to get very far. The discussion inevitably runs into abstractions and delicate metaphysical balancing acts. However, tackling the matter from the point of view of the humanity of Jesus Christ gives us rather a different picture, quickly taking us into the realm of personal relationships. We can begin by recognising that in the humanity of Christ, our humanity has been incorporated into the divine life by the Son of God, set free by the Spirit from its debilitating self-obsession, from its self-will and its evasions of the truth, liberated to respond to the Father's love and his will, and freed to respond appropriately to the created world. Therein lies the very foundation and source of authentic freedom and authentic creativity. Our freedom is not akin to a possession which we bargain over with God, but is something which can only be given and sustained by his triune life. To try and gain freedom through autonomous self-direction can only be self-defeating, for it is precisely this closed circle of self-centredness which needs to be broken. But to claim that obedience is a matter of bowing before a divine tyrant is equally mistaken; God operates not by imposing demands externally, but by coming in Jesus Christ to stand beside us and take responsibility for those demands, and by inviting us through the Spirit to share in the realisation of his Father's purposes for the world. To respond to that invitation is not have our free creativity undercut or lessened, it is to have it established, affirmed and fulfilled.

Discovering, Respecting, Developing, Redeeming, Together

I am suggesting, then — albeit in a very compressed outline — that human creativity is supremely about sharing through the Spirit in the creative purpose of the Father as he draws all things to himself through his Son. In this light, various aspects of our creative interaction with the world under God become apparent, some of which we can outline very briefly here, even at the risk of superficiality. There will be *discovery* and *respect* — arising out of the conviction that God has endowed his world with an inherent order, and that our role is to allow the different levels of reality to define and express their rationality through our engagement with them. It is the antithesis of love to dominate and manipulate, but of the essence of love to find order in its object and act faithfully in accordance with it. In Eberhard Jüngel's words, "In love there is no having which does not arise out of surrender."[27] This respect, of course, is not the same as a grudging subservience. The structures of the created world are God's gifts of grace to be enjoyed; they are channels which enable true creativity, not primarily restrictions to obstruct us. Moreover, respect is not the same as absolute passivity. There needs to be an interaction with creation, a *development*, a bringing forth of new forms of order out of what we are given at the hand of the Creator. And there will be a *redeeming of disorder*, mirroring God's redeeming work in Christ, a renewal of that which has been spoiled, a re-ordering of what is distorted. This redeeming activity will entail a penetration of the disorder of the world — human and non-human, just as the Son of God penetrated our twisted and warped existence. It will also entail judgement: an unmasking of disorder, a denunciation of that which disfigures the world, as at Golgotha. There will also be transformation, the forging of a new order out of the ugliness of disorder, as in Christ's resurrection. Alan Lewis, speaking of the slain lamb of Revelation 5, writes:

> "those who serve him and own his lordship, must surely in his name penetrate into the world of decay and suffering as healers of its brokenness and celebrators of its coming wholeness, declaring and demonstrating that the God who raised the slain lamb will raise with him everything that is wounded and bruised, to newness of life."[28]

Finally, creativity will need to be set in a *corporate* context, for the inner logic of the Gospel compels us to affirm that self-fulfilment is discovered only in relationship. In the humanity assumed by his Son, the Father has released our humanity from its crippling self-concern in such a way that a new corporate humanity has been made possible, one which is bound together with that same self-forgetful love which binds Father and Son. It is in such relatedness-in-love that we discover our true humanity. In Ray Anderson's words, "Because humanity is originally and essentially co-humanity, the fundamental affirmation of human existence is surely one of relatedness."[29] Human creativity, by extension, is intrinsically corporate. In this connection, we might note that it is no accident that Colossians 1 declares in the same breath that Christ is the first-born of all creation *and* that he is 'head of the body, the Church' (v. 18).[30] I am not maintaining that the Spirit has abandoned all outside the confines of the Church, that no creativity beyond ecclesiastical quarters can ever glorify God. I am only emphasising that God's ultimate purpose for humanity is to call together a community, whose life will reflect his own 'being as communion', as Father, Son and Spirit,[31] and in which human creativity should find its most potent expression.

(3) Concluding Comments

In this chapter, I have endeavoured to present in very brief terms a view of creation and humankind which pays special attention to the New Testament's witness to the divine-human Lordship of Christ over creation. A number of key doctrinal points have emerged, two of which need to be highlighted here. First, it is clear that we should be very cautious about drawing too sharp a demarcation between God's creative and redemptive activity, or between his 'sustaining' activity and his 'renewing' activity, between providence and salvation. There is no question of identifying the two (for this will almost certainly lead to some kind of historicism and a trivialisation of evil), yet to drive a wedge between them (the tendency of the Neo-Calvinists) blinds us to the fact that creation and redemption find their source and unity in the love which is internal to the triune God.

Second, and implicit in the last point, our discussion would indicate that the Church's confession of the Trinity should occupy a prominent place in the theology of culture. The God who calls us to cultivate the earth is not an impersonal Monad of absolute singularity, but the triune God who *is* love in his very heart. His very being is relational; he is ecstatic love, love that always goes out to the other. His relation to the creation is thus not to be described in terms of logical necessity (as in pantheism or monism) or naked omnipotence (the tendency of the Calvinist tradition), but in terms of personal commitment and faithfulness. This in turn will affect the way in which we perceive human culture. A responsible developing of the earth depends on refusing to see creation outside its relation to the divine love. Moreover, the Son has taken flesh and, as it were, offered creation back to the Father in his own humanity, and now through the Holy Spirit invites us to share in the task of bringing creation to praise and magnify the Father in and through him.

Furthermore, a proper grasp of the doctrine of the Trinity reminds us of the irreducible 'relatedness' of humanity. Implicit in all I have tried to say is that the core of being human is to be correctly related — whether to God, others, or the natural order. To be authentically free is to be in an appropriate relationship with what lies beyond our individuality, with what is other than ourselves. In the last resort this freedom can only be received as a gift, as we share in the humanity of Christ, the one in whom our own humanity has been freed and properly related to the Father and to the created order. This can be usefully amplified by reference to the notion of the 'image of God'. As Douglas John Hall has recently observed, it is ironic that the very concept which should remind us of our relatedness has been so often used to endorse an aggressive individualism.[32] Engrained in Western theology is a tendency to see the uniqueness of humanity in terms of a quality which makes human beings distinct from, and superior to, the rest of creation — our rationality, freedom, volition, or whatever. This leads quickly to a denigration of non-human creation and loses sight of that physical nature which we share with the non-human

order. In line with an increasing number of scholars, Hall
develops instead a relational concept of the *imago Dei*, centering
his thought on Jesus Christ, himself described in the New
Testament as the 'image of God'.[33] Hall pleads for a rediscovery
of an 'ontology of communion' rooted in the biblical conviction
that being as such is relational. Through Christ we discover
our true humanity by being appropriately related in a three-
fold way: to God, to each other, and to the non-human world.
And all three forms of relation, Hall contends, should reflect
the self-giving love focused in the history of Jesus Christ. Hall's
argument may have its weak points, but his main contention is
thoroughly in line with all we have been proposing.

By now, the reader who tends to get impatient with doctrinal
talk will be getting decidedly restless. Cosmic assertions and
wide-ranging claims about human creativity have been made
with very little in the way of particular application. It is time
to be more specific and narrow our attention to the arts.

Notes

1   This is certainly true if we take 1 Cor. 8:6 and Phil. 2:6-11 as pre-
    Pauline and Colossians and Ephesians as from Paul's own hand.
    Cf. C. F. D Moule, *The Epistles of Paul the Apostle to the Colossians
    and to Philemon*, Cambridge: Cambridge University Press, 1962,
    pp. 13f., 60ff.; Markus Barth, *Ephesians 1-3*, Garden City, New
    York: Doubleday, 1974, pp. 36-50. It was probably a conviction
    about the final Lordship of Christ which led to the assertion of
    Christ's activity in the creation of the world. Cf. R. S. Barbour,
    "Creation, Wisdom and Christ," in *Creation, Christ and Culture*, ed.
    Richard W. A. McKinney, Edinburgh: T. & T. Clark, 1976, pp. 30ff.
2   James D. G. Dunn, *Christology in the Making*, London: SCM, 1980,
    p. 194.
3   For alternative approaches, cf. Adrio König, *The Eclipse of Christ
    in Eschatology: Towards a Christ-Centred Approach*, Grand Rapids,
    Michigan: Eerdmans; London: Marshall, Morgan & Scott, 1989; Peter
    T. O'Brien, *Word Bible Commentary: Colossians, Philemon*, Waco,
    Texas: Word Books, 1982, pp. 42ff.; G. Kittel, "*εικων*," *Theological
    Dictionary of the New Testament*, II, ed. Gerhard Kittel, Grand
    Rapids, Michigan: Eerdmans, 1973, p. 395.
4   Col. 1:16: all things (*τα παντα*) were created 'through' or 'in' Christ
    (*εν αυτω*) — best understood in an instrumental sense, i.e. 'by
    means of Christ.' Moule, *op. cit.*, p. 65. In Heb. 1:2, Christ is spoken
    of as the one through whom (*δι' ου*) God created the world. *τους
    αιωνας* (vs. 2) is best translated 'the world' rather than 'the ages'.
    "The whole created universe of space and time is meant". F. F.
    Bruce, *The Epistle to the Hebrews*, Grand Rapids, Michigan:
    Eerdmans, 1977, p. 4. In Jn. 1:3, we are told that all things were
    made through the Word 'and without him was not anything made
    that was made.' (An important part of the background here is

undoubtedly the Old Testament and inter-testamental wisdom tradition, particularly as found in Prov. 8:22ff., Wis. 7:15-8:1, 9:1f., 9. Barbour, *loc. cit.*, pp. 22-42.) Cp. Rom. 4:17 which unites the call of Abraham, the resurrection of the dead and creation out of nothing, all in the setting of a vigorous exposition of the justifying grace of God.

5   *The Christian Doctrine of Creation and Redemption*, 2, London: Lutterworth Press, 1952, p. 13. Cp. Karl Barth: "Creation is grace......God does not grudge the existence of the reality, distinct from Himself; He does not grudge it its own reality, nature and freedom". *Dogmatics in Outline*, trans G. T. Thompson, London: SCM, 1966, p. 54.

6   *Loc. cit.*, p. 36. The theme is movingly amplified in W. H. Vanstone, *Love's Endeavour, Love's Expense*, London: Darton, Longman and Todd, 1977, pp. 62f.

7   *Op. cit.*, p. 67. Cp. 1 Cor. 8:6. Wisdom literature is again relevant here; cf. e.g. Wis. 1:7, 7:24, 18:10; Ecclesiasticus 24:5f.

8   *A Model of Making: Literary Criticism and its Theology*, Basingstoke: Marshall, Morgan and Scott, 1983, p. 50. Cp. John Gibbs, writing of Phil. 2:6-11: "If the form of man and the form of the servant are taken up into glory, the implication is that God's redemptive purpose will not let creation go, but treasures it and holds it fast through Jesus the Lord". *Creation and Redemption*, Leiden: E. J. Brill, 1971, p. 88.

9   We have to concede that apart from passing references in Jeremiah 33:19, 25, the Bible does not explicitly speak of God's relationship with creation in terms of covenant. But this does not invalidate the theological inference we are making from the concept of Christ as the revealer of God's intentions for creation. Cf. W. J. Dumbrell, *Covenant and Creation*, Exeter: Paternoster, 1984. For Karl Barth, creation is the 'external basis for the covenant', and the covenant the 'internal basis of creation'. (*Church Dogmatics*, III:1, ed. G. W. Bromiley and T. F. Torrance, Edinburgh: T. & T. Clark, 1958, pp. 94ff.)

10   "Creation and Redemption," in McKinney, *op. cit.*, p. 122.

11   Paul Davies, *The Accidental Universe*, Cambridge: Cambridge University Press, 1982, p. 130; John Polkinghorne, *Science and Creation*, London: SPCK, 1988, pp. 22ff.

12   I. Prigogine and I. Stengers, *Order out of Chaos*, London: Heinemann, 1985, p. xxx.

13   *Op. cit.*, p. 39.

14   *Jubilate: Theology in Praise*, London: Darton, Longman and Todd, 1984, p. 119.

15   *Ibid.*, pp. 96-99

16   Jean Héring, *The Epistle to the Hebrews*, London: Epworth Press, 1970, p. 5.

17   *Op. cit.*, p. 6. Significantly, there is evidence that φερων carries with it the connotation of motherly care for the creature of God in need. O. Michel, *Der Brief an die HebrUaer*, Kritisch-exegetischer Kommentar, 1975, p. 100.

[18] The 'nature miracles' of Jesus can usefully be seen from this angle. The Pauline theology of the 'powers' is also relevant here — the ἀρχαι and δυναμεις (e.g. 1 Cor. 15:24; Rom. 8:38; Col. 2:10), the κυριοτητες (Col. 1:16; Eph. 1:21), the στοιχεια (Gal. 4:3, 9; Col. 2:8, 20) etc. Although the exact interpretation of these phrases remains a matter of intense debate, for our purposes, two important things need to be said. First, the 'powers' exercise an influence not simply within the realm of human affairs but throughout the cosmos; second, they have been robbed of ultimate significance by being 'disarmed' by Christ on the cross (Col. 2:15). Cf. H. C. Macgregor, "Principalities and Powers: the Cosmic Background of Paul's Thought," *New Testament Studies*, I (1954-55), pp. 17-28; George B. Caird, *Principalities and Powers*; Oxford: Clarendon Press, 1956, pp. 68ff.

[19] Alan E. Lewis, *Theatre of the Gospel*, Edinburgh: Handsel Press, 1984, p. 6.

[20] *Op. cit.*, p. 34.

[21] *Ibid.*, p. 144. Even more pointedly, John Baker asserts that "nature [in the Old Testament] is not to be evaluated simply in terms of man's needs and interests; and to think that it is, is merely a mark of folly. God created the greater part of the world for its own sake". As quoted in Peacocke, *Creation and the World of Science*, Oxford: Clarendon Press, 1979, p. 85.

[22] *The Ground and Grammar of Theology*, Belfast: Christian Journals, 1980, p. 133.

[23] König, *op. cit.*, pp. 25ff;

[24] It is probable that Paul, in writing of Christ's Lordship, had in mind the whole created world (Ragnar Leivestad, *Christ the Conqueror*, London: SPCK, 1954, pp. 113f.; Gerald F. Hawthorne, *Word Bible Commentary: Philippians*, Waco, Texas: Word Books, 1983, p. 93); it is faintly possible that he means only the angelic powers. In any case, Paul is clearly moving beyond the realm of humanity. Cf. Gibbs, *op. cit.*, pp. 75ff.

[25] *Op. cit.*, p. 204.

[26] For a fuller treatments of this theme, cf. James B. Torrance, "The Vicarious Humanity of Christ," in *The Incarnation*, ed. Thomas F. Torrance, pp. 127-145; T. E. Pollard, *Fullness of Humanity: Christ's Humanity and Ours*, Sheffield: Almond Press, 1982, ch. V.

[27] *God as the Mystery of the World*, trans. Darrell L. Guder, Edinburgh: T. & T. Clark, 1983, p. 320.

[28] *Op. cit.*, p. 31.

[29] *On Being Human: Essays in Theological Anthropology*, Grand Rapids, Michigan: Eerdmans, 1982, p. 168.

[30] Some commentators insist that the reference to the Church here is an interpolation; the 'body', it is said, originally referred to the cosmos in the earliest version of the hymn. However, along with stylistic considerations which suggest otherwise, there is no compelling evidence to suggest that 'body' ever denoted the cosmos. Cf. O'Brien, *op. cit.*, pp. 48ff.

[31] John Zizioulas, *Being as Communion*, Crestwood, New York: St Vladimir's Seminary Press, 1985.

[32] *Op. cit., passim.*
[33] Col. 1:15; 1 Cor. 11:7; II Cor. 3:18, 4:4; Heb. 1:3.

3. The Alienation of Art

"......the vocabulary of art, artists and aesthetics appears
obsolete today because a great dimension of human life and
experience is presently catastrophically threatened."

Peter Fuller

It is always hazardous to generalise about so complex a matter
as the place of the arts in any given society. Nevertheless, it
would be hard to deny that among the more dominant features
of Western European culture (and to a certain extent those
cultures directly influenced by Western Europe) is a cast of
mind which tends to alienate and isolate the arts from other
spheres of human activity. The notion of the artist as an
essentially solitary figure with little responsibility to his
community; the concept of 'art for art's sake'; the widespread
belief that there are no universal criteria for assessing the
worth or quality of art; the commonplace assumption that the
arts, though perhaps entertaining for those who can afford to
enjoy them, have little (if anything) to do with the public world
of demonstrable fact — all these, I submit, are signs of an attitude
which treats the experience of art as somehow profoundly
discontinuous with the rest of our experience. The attitude is
well exposed (even if in an exaggerated way) by Peter Fuller in
his essay *Aesthetics After Modernism*.[1] In contrast to a healthy
society, claims Fuller, in which no neat boundary divides art
from life, in the West the 'aesthetic dimension' has been
gradually expunged from everyday concerns, progressively
emasculated by technological and economic structures. From
the Renaissance onwards, "men and women were compelled to
shift uneasily between an emotional participation in the world,
and the pose that they were outside a system they could observe
objectively."[2] The division of labour in the eighteenth and
nineteenth centuries severed the creative relationship between
imagination and intellect, heart and hand. Art kept its distance
from craft; the lofty Romantic poet from the common artificer.
This is the legacy we have inherited today. In the 1980's, Fuller
sees signs of hope on the horizon — a revival in the crafts, a
return to representational carving and modelling in sculpture,
to still life and landscapes in painting — yet he is ambivalent
about the future. We have lost our roots in a shared symbolic

order. Significantly, Fuller ends with a biblical allusion: "Art, I believe: help thou mine unbelief."[3]

It is against this background of the marginalisation of art in contemporary thought that I shall attempt to extend the theology of the preceding chapter. This, I believe, is a better way of proceeding than trying to explicate a theology of art in a cultural vacuum. In this chapter we shall paint in very broad brush-strokes some influential currents of philosophical thought which have contributed to modern attitudes to the arts. The next chapter will seek to appraise these lines of thinking from an explicitly theological angle.

(1) Kant and his Predecessors

As anybody working in the area will know, modern philosophy of art is a tapestry of many colours. At the same time, there are a few strong threads which hold its theoretical fabric together. And there can be little doubt that one man is more responsible than any other for putting those threads firmly in place, the philosopher standing at the apex of the Enlightenment, Immanuel Kant (1704-84). I am not, of course, suggesting that Kant has been slavishly followed by every aesthetician since, nor that we can brush over the diversity of art-theory since Kant. Least of all do I want to imply that all our current problems in the philosophy of art can be traced back to Kant himself. My contention is simply that it was Kant more than anyone else who synthesised and consolidated the thought of his time in a way which encapsulates most of the key assumptions about art which we take for granted today. For this reason, we must take him very seriously.

Before tackling Kant, however, it is worth glancing at some of his forebears. We can begin with the rationalists. For the seventeenth-century rationalist philosopher, to find a respectable place for art was anything but easy. Aesthetic pleasure seemed too intimately tied up with sensual pleasure, and the senses were generally regarded as unreliable for getting at the truth of things. As is well known, for René Descartes (1596-1650), truth was to be discovered through careful deduction from clear and distinct ideas. Despite his own love of the arts, he sharply contrasted the data of the 'senses and imagination' with the concepts of things as they are in themselves, and spoke disdainfully of "the fluctuating testimony of the senses" and the "misleading judgement that proceeds from the blundering constructions of imagination".[4] Nonetheless, Descartes attempted to show that some aesthetic experience was dependent on innate ideas and thus could at least partly measure up to his stringent criteria of clarity, distinctness and mathematical rigour. Some of his followers took matters further. A. G. Baumgarten distinguished between the clear, abstract discourse of the sciences and the confused, though more or less clear, discourse of art, but still went as far as elaborating a 'science' of aesthetics founded on strictly rationalist principles.[5]

The empiricists of the seventeenth and eighteenth centuries accounted for art not by turning to in-built ideas but directly to sensual stimulation, to the experience of pleasure and pain. Much attention was focused on how aesthetic pleasure arose, especially on that special capacity to discern and enjoy beauty — the faculty of 'taste'. For Francis Hutcheson, a beautiful object excites in us both the idea of beauty and a distinctive type of pleasure. This is due to our 'internal sense' of beauty, the "power of receiving ideas of beauty from all objects in which there is uniformity amidst variety".[6] It is worth noting that although Hutcheson can speak of beauty in this way, he employs an epistemology in which the connection between sense-data and the world beyond the experiencing self is very loose.[7] For the empiricists, beauty becomes increasingly associated with particular sensations. According to David Hume (1711-1776), we are aware of 'impressions' (in sense experience), and less vivid 'ideas' (in memory, imagination, dreams). Beauty is not an *a priori* concept, but an idea which arises from a series of impressions. It is "such an order and construction of parts, as either by the *primary constitution* of our nature, by *custom*, or by *caprice*, is fitted to give a pleasure and satisfaction to the soul...........Pleasure and pain, therefore, are not only necessary attendants of beauty and deformity, but constitute their very essence".[8]   Elsewhere he writes: "tastes and colours, and all other sensible qualities, be *not in the bodies, but merely in the senses*. The case is the same with beauty".[9]

Along with this tendency to weaken the ties between beauty and reality external to the self, we also find in empiricist philosophy a marked tendency to drive a wedge between aesthetic experience and knowledge. John Locke (1632-1704) is a case in point. Locke was convinced that all non-literal, figurative language should be banned when talking about the objects of knowledge. "Since wit and fancy find easier entertainment in the world than dry truth and real knowledge, figurative speeches and allusion in language will hardly be admitted as an imperfection or abuse of it". But, Locke continues: "if we would speak of things as they are, we must allow that all the art of rhetoric, besides order and clearness; all the artificial and figurative application of words eloquence hath invented.......where truth and knowledge are concerned, cannot but be thought a great fault".[10]   Locke reinforces the point through his famous contrast between the faculties of 'wit' and 'judgement': wit freely combines the images of sense-perception for no special purpose other than to give us pleasure, judgement carefully separates and distinguishes them to avoid error. Only the latter is concerned with truth. Wit and judgement lead away from each other, one towards entertainment, the other towards knowledge.[11] In a similar way, Hume proposed a disjunction between 'reason' and 'taste': "the former conveys the knowledge of truth and falsehood: the latter gives the sentiment of beauty and deformity, vice and virtue. Reason, being cool and detached, is no motive to action.........Taste, as it gives pleasure or pain, and thereby constitutes happiness or misery, becomes a motive to action".[12] It comes as no surprise to find that during this period art was increasingly thought of as something that existed only to give a very unique kind of pleasure, quite apart from any claim to inform or convey truth.

Clearly, the rationalists and empiricists differ in many respects, but when it comes to the philosophy of art, it is their common ground which should claim our attention. As Gilbert and Kuhn rightly remark, "the esthetic creed of the new 'inner sense' school inspired by Locke never seriously differed from the upholders of reason."[13] All assume that we are immediately aware only of the content of our own consciousness: all implicitly adopt Descartes' turn towards the thinking self as the way to achieve certainty.   All are highly dubious about the ability of the senses to establish contact with the world beyond the knowing mind — for rationalist and empiricist alike it is the active reason which affords us access to truth. Hence the rationalists make strenuous efforts to give art Cartesian credibility in terms of rational ideas, and, we might add, the empiricists, though claiming that the 'inner sense' for beauty is non-intellectual, end up speaking about it in markedly intellectual terms.[14] Overall, a yawning gulf opens up between art and knowledge, the former relegated to second-class status.

Kant was well acquainted with these developments. And, as in so much else, he brought things impressively to a head. In Kant's view, most aesthetic judgements are simply reports of pleasure and pain — 'judgements of sense'. But some are appraisals of beauty — 'judgements of taste'. It is these which Kant spends most time examining. Unlike the empiricists, Kant distances aesthetic pleasure from sense-experience by distinguishing between 'sensation (*Empfindung*)' and 'feeling (*Gefühl*)'. The former is an objective representation of sense, whereas feeling is inherently subjective. When we look at a green meadow, we 'sense' its greenness, but only 'feel' aesthetic pleasure. The judgement of taste is therefore one "whose determining ground can be *no other than subjective*".[15] With this goes Kant's strong conviction that judgements of taste must be sharply distinguished from cognitive judgements even though they might bear a formal resemblance to each other. In the case of a cognitive judgement such as 'This is blue', we apply a concept ('blue') to an object we perceive. But an aesthetic judgement does not apply a concept to an object. Because the beautiful evokes a satisfaction apart from concepts, a judgement of taste is not a claim to knowledge. A judgement of taste is quite 'disinterested'; that is, it is indifferent to the real existence or utility of the object.[16] A judgement of taste is emancipated from scientific or moral considerations as to type, end or purpose. It is not determined by any needs or wants of ours concerning the object. For Kant, the enjoyment of beauty takes place in a separate sphere from knowledge and moral experience.

Does this mean that judgements of taste are merely arbitrary or idiosyncratic? No. Kant wants to affirm that they carry with them a claim to universality. That is, if we say of something 'This is beautiful', we are implicitly saying that all others should agree with our judgement. But how can we hold this without confusing judgements of taste with claims to knowledge? Kant's solution is to say that the experience of beauty depends on an interaction between two faculties of the mind which are common to all people. All knowing takes place by virtue of the underlying harmony between the imagination (which gathers together the manifold of sense-intuition) and the understanding (which unifies these representations under concepts). In aesthetic experience, these cognitive faculties engage in 'free play'. They are idling, so to speak; they are not bound to any concepts or any particular sensations. And this results in a feeling of pleasure — the experience of beauty. Because this feeling depends on the interplay between cognitive faculties which we all possess, judgements of taste, although grounded in human subjectivity, are not merely relative to an individual subject. They bear a claim to universal validity.[17]

And what is it that gives rise to this aesthetic experience? Kant answers: the 'form of purposiveness' of an object. He is careful not to say 'a purpose' because this would be to apply a concept to the aesthetic object and turn the judgement of taste into a conceptual judgement. A judgement of taste does not add to our stock of knowledge about the world; it is not a claim to knowledge; it never asserts that there *is* purpose and order in the world. According to Kant, art manifests the world in such a way that we view it *as if* there were order in it, but only 'as if'. What gives us satisfaction is "the mere form of the purposiveness in the representation by which an object is *given* to us, so far as we are conscious of it".[18]

Set out in so cursory a way, there might seem nothing very striking about Kant's proposals. In fact, his approach has wide-ranging significance and has proved influential. In order to see this, let us expand and clarify what he says under seven closely related points.

(2) The Enlightenment Legacy

The first point to note is the way in which Kant, when speaking of aesthetic experience, gravitates away from the physical world beyond the mind towards the inner mental experience of the individual. The tendency to abstract aesthetic experience from physical reality has antecedents far back in ancient Greek thought, particularly in the Platonic and Neo-Platonic traditions. As we have already indicated, it came to be very much part of seventeenth and eighteenth-century aesthetic theory. After Kant, it appears in a striking way in the aesthetics of G. W. F. Hegel (1770-1831). For Hegel, through art, humanity projects itself out of the conscious stream of worldly life in which it would otherwise be totally immersed. Art depends on man's need to "strip the external world of its inflexible foreignness and to enjoy in the shape of things only an external realisation of himself."[19] Yet art carries with it a great drawback — its dependence on the external and material world. Art can only represent the infinite spirit in a form foreign to that spirit. It is in philosophical thought that spirit finds its truly immaterial medium of expression. Thus Hegel believed that art reaches its highest form in poetry, because poetic verse comes closest to pure thinking.

In modern aesthetics, this shift away from the material has taken a myriad of forms, by no means all as intellectualist as in Kant or Hegel. One of the most prominent is a neo-Romantic focus on inner emotional dispositions, where the main task of art is seen as 'expressing feelings'. Another is the theory we met in Dooyeweerd; that an object of art is the externalisation of an inner vision or idea in the mind or imagination of the artist. But whatever form it takes, remarkably persistent in

Western aesthetics has been the tendency to subordinate the sensuous and material to the spiritual and immaterial.

Second, Kant's aesthetics all too easily generates a divorce of art from action. His concept of 'disinterestedness' bears this out. At root, we see here an adaptation of Descartes' model of the knowing self, gazing impassively on its object. The term 'disinterestedness' goes back to the Earl of Shaftesbury (1671-1713) who introduced it to counter what he saw as the egoism of seventeenth-century empiricism. In time, as Jerome Stolnitz has shown, it began to be applied to what we now call the 'fine' arts (in opposition to 'useful' arts), i.e. those arts which serve no end beyond themselves but are to be enjoyed purely for their own sake. Like a Cartesian object, such art is to be studied with detachment and precision, with 'disinterested' delight.[20] The notion of disinterestedness has attracted many advocates since Kant. In the philosophy of art, the idea has been pursued and developed rigorously by writers such as Arthur Schopenhauer, Edward Bullough and Roman Ingarden. If we are to treat a work of art *as art*, it is urged, we should be scrupulously careful never to regard it as a means to an end. We must fix our attention on the work itself. Today, even a brief survey of what our society commonly calls 'works of art' would very likely reveal that the majority were intended, by producer or distributor, for some form of disinterested contemplation. In his book, *Art in Action*, Nicholas Wolterstorff goes as far as to say that in the West, "No matter what the art, in each case the action that you and I tend to regard as intended is a species of.........*perceptual contemplation*". He continues: "Virtually every statement concerning the purposes of the arts which comes from the hands of aestheticians, our art theorists, our critics, makes this assumption."[21] Yet it is easy to forget how comparatively modern and Western such an idea is. As André Malraux observes:

> "So vital is the part played by the art museum in our approach to works of art today that we find it difficult to realise that no museums exist, none has ever existed, in lands where the civilisation of Modern Europe is, or was, unknown; and that, even amongst us, they have existed for barely two hundred years.......we forget that they have imposed on the spectator a wholly new attitude towards the work of art. For they have tended to estrange the works they bring together from their original functions and to transform even their portraits into 'pictures'."[22]

Third, as is well known, Kant's epistemology commits him to the view that form and order are essentially created and imposed on the plurality of the world by the human mind, not discovered. We should not be misled by the word 'disinterested'. The crucial factor in the experience of beauty is the 'form of purposiveness' and by definition 'form' is something given by the subject's mind: "the understanding is itself the source of the law of nature, and so of its formal unity".[23] Aesthetic pleasure is derived from those powers which enable *us* to arrange the plurality of sense-data, not from the apprehension of order beyond ourselves: in an aesthetic judgement, says Kant, "nothing in the object is signified, but [only] a feeling in the subject as it is affected by the representation."[24] In this respect too, Kant has been remarkably influential. Highly prominent since his day has been the view that art triumphs by working the wonders of the human mind upon the formlessness of the world, not by interacting with an order already given to hand. It is the same line of thinking which led the Romantics to see a work of art as a bulwark against chaos, a stay against confusion. As Roger Lundin observes, art "becomes the place in which inert nature and chaotic history are brought to life by the unifying imagination. The ability of the imagination to impart beauty to objects creates a restful place for man.........in an otherwise hostile world."[25] Taken to its extreme, the distancing of art from natural form inevitably leads to a collapse of form in the work of art itself, a phenomenon brilliantly charted in much of the visual art of this century in Erich Kähler's *The Disintegration of Form in the Arts*.[26]

Fourth, one of the most obvious outcomes of the Kantian approach is to isolate a work of art from the particularities of everyday life and affairs. For Kant, an aesthetic object has a finality in itself which must not be subsumed under external categories. Mary Warnock paraphrases Kant thus: "We do not identify the object as a member of a certain class of objects when we judge it aesthetically. We do not classify it as having certain characteristics or falling under certain scientific laws. *Our perception, as it were, stops at the appearance of the thing, and it is within that limit that we discover its finality.*"[27] Hence Kant's stress on the formal character of judgements of taste. "In painting, sculpture, and in all the formative arts," he tells us, "the *delineation* is the essential thing; and here it is not what gratifies in sensation but what pleases by means of its form that is fundamental for taste."[28] Subsequent philosophy of art, although not always showing such a marked interest in the structural features of art, has largely followed suit with respect to Kant's denigration of the representing or referring capabilities of art. Once again, we should not forget how Western this disjunction of art from the contingencies of history is, nor how recent. Speaking of persistent claims for the absolute autonomy of art, M. H. Abrams comments that for many of us,

> "such assertions........seem to be patent truths, confirmed by our ordinary experience of works of art. The historical facts, however, should give us pause. For some two thousand years of theoretical concern with these matters, it occurred to no thinker to claim that a human artifact is to be contemplated disinterestedly, for its own sake, as its own end and for its internal values, without reference to things, human beings, purposes, or effects outside its sufficient and autonomous self."[29]

The American composer Roger Sessions reminds us that

> "Listening to music, as distinct from reproducing it, is the product of a very late stage in musical sophistication, and it might with reason be maintained that the listener has existed as such only for about three hundred and fifty years. The composers of the Middle Ages and the Renaissance composed their music for church services and for secular occasions.......Or else they composed it for amateurs.....whose relationship with it was that of the performer responding to it through active participation in its production".[30]

Curt Sachs extends the same point:

> "The growth of musical forms that we observe in Europe from the seventeenth century on seems to be connected with the growing separation of music from social life and extramusical claims. Contents, sizes, and forms underwent an obvious change when music became self-contained, to be listened to in public concert halls and opera houses by audiences wholly devoted to its artful elaboration."[31]

In aesthetic theory, the theme of the 'self-containedness' of art has been driven home in various ways in the last two hundred years. Kant's aesthetics quickly spawned the idea of 'art for art's sake' — the view that art is answerable only to itself and must never be judged according to the degree of correspondence it has to phenomena beyond itself, such as a moral order, the artist's intentions, the circumstances of its production, and so on.[32] Considerations of social and psychological context are strictly barred from consideration. Indeed, the very attempt at external allusion in art is seen by some as detrimental. George Steiner pinpoints the French poet and theorist Stéphane Mallarmé as a key figure in this respect. For Mallarmé, the erasure of external reference brought a glorious liberation:

"Enfranchised from the servitude of representation, purged of the lies, imprecisions and utilitarian dross which this servitude has brought it, the 'word-world' can, via poetry and the poetics of thought in philosophy, resume its magic, its formal and categorical infinity.......Neither the poem nor the metaphysical system is made of 'ideas', of verbalised external data. They are made of words. Paintings are, insisted Degas, made of pigments and internally relational spaces. Music is made up of conventionally organised sounds. *It signifies only itself.*"[33]

In the very early days of cinema, Kant's ideas were applied to that medium by the German psychologist Hugo Munsterberg in a book which was to hold sway for some fifty years as the most thorough study of its kind. He boldly asserted that "The work of art shows us the things and events perfectly complete in themselves, freed from all connections which lead beyond their own limits, that is, in perfect isolation".[34] Recent examples of the same attitude can be seen in some of the more influential theories of literary criticism. One of the best known of modern literary critics, Northrop Frye, has insisted that questions of fact or truth in literature must be subordinated to the primary aim of producing a structure of words for its own sake: "what entertains is prior to what instructs, or, as we may say, the reality-principle is subordinate to the pleasure-principle."[35] More extreme positions have been advanced by movements such as deconstructionism, where language actually becomes constitutive of reality. Karsteen Harries claims that the poet directs our attention away from reality towards that 'world' which the work of art opens up.[36] In a different field, the ablest and most influential Marxist art critic this century, Clement Greenberg, claims in his essay on 'The New Sculpture', that "The avant-garde poet or artist tries in effect to imitate God by creating something valid solely on its own terms, in the way nature itself is valid....something *given*, increate, independent of meanings, similars or originals."[37] In an exhibition catalogue of recent 'minimal' art, visitors were boldly told that "Today's real art makes no direct appeal to the emotions, nor is it involved in uplift, but instead offers itself in the form of the *simple, irreducible, irrefutable object.*"[38]

Closely related to this, fifth, in Kant we find a hardening of the distinction between aesthetic experience and knowledge which he inherited from his predecessors. Very significant here is the way in which Kant contracted the bounds of epistemological legitimacy. Colin Gunton comments:

"Set up is an a priori criterion of cognitive rectitude which by
excluding aesthetic judgements entirely from the realm of
the objectively knowable opens a breach between different
kinds of judgement about the world. What begins as a
distinction becomes an epistemological and ontological
chasm."[39]

Accordingly, we are left with a picture all too common today: it
is the natural sciences which are thought to grant us publicly
verifiable truth — Locke's 'dry truth and real knowledge' —
while the arts are concerned with matters of private taste, with
little or no bearing on the way things actually are beyond
ourselves. With this goes an inclination to divide language
rigidly into two types: factual statements which are fitted to
convey objective truths, and 'metaphor' or 'symbolic' language
which can only express what is lodged within the human psyche.
We might note that hidden behind the current debate about
funding the arts in Britain there often lurks a tacit belief that
the arts are highly suspect as bearers of knowledge and thus
need a Herculean effort to justify public financial support.

Sixth, it is clearly hard for Kant to provide a convincing
account of the universal validity of aesthetic judgements, despite
his intention to avoid relativism. The universality of judgements
of taste is grounded only in the universality of the subjective
conditions for judging objects, and it is not evident that we can
ever ascertain whether the subjective conditions necessary for
an authentic experience of beauty are actually operative. Not
surprisingly, Kant says little about aesthetic disputes and how
they might be resolved. He may succeed in demonstrating that
aesthetic judgements are not direct, straightforward conceptual
judgements, but he gives us no substantial help in seeing how
they can ever be more than simply idiosyncratic, entirely relative
to the person who makes them. If aesthetic statements have
no cognitive relation to states of affairs beyond the person who
utters them, then the vortex of relativism — at least in some
form — appears inescapable. In the world of the arts today, we
are certainly not strangers to this situation. To seek even
minimal objective standards in the arts is a courageous
undertaking, and even when attempted, frequently invites
charges of obscurantism and dogmatism. Richard Bernstein
remarks that if we follow Kant's aesthetics, "we are easily led
down the path to relativism. And this is what did happen after
Kant — so much so that today it is extraordinarily difficult to
retrieve any idea of taste or aesthetic judgement that is more
than the expression of personal preferences."[40] The attitude is
summed up well by the painter Whistler who remarked about

art that "You shouldn't say it is not good. You should say you do not like it; and then, you know, you're perfectly safe."

Seventh, the Kantian tradition in the philosophy of art is undoubtedly affected by Kant's turn towards the solitary thinking self as the locus of the plenitude of being and truth — what Roger Scruton calls 'first-person certainty'.[41] (In this regard, the influence of Descartes never left Kant. As Lundin observes, Kantian aesthetics, as developed by Romantic formalism in the late eighteenth and early nineteenth centuries, is "Cartesianism set in large type or painted on a very broad canvas."[42]) It would be easy to exaggerate the extent to which 'first person certainty' has coloured attitudes to the arts today, but it is far from absent. The psychologist Paul Vitz, in his penetrating book *Psychology as Religion*, notes how easily the word 'creative' can cloak a narcissist self-indulgence: "Today in the secular world creativity is simply a gift from the self *to* the self, it has degenerated into a synonym for any form of personal pleasure without reference to others."[43] Accordingly, conventions and traditions are all too often regarded as something from which to wrestle free rather than as potential sources of benefit. Here Clement Greenberg can be quoted again; he said of the 'New Sculpture' that it has "almost no historical associations whatsoever — at least not with our own civilisation's past — which endows it with a virginity that compels the artist's boldness and invites him to tell everything without fear of censorship by tradition."[44] (The reference to 'virginity' is significant: 'pure' art is unspoiled by the past.) It hardly needs pointing out that for the artist today, the pressure to produce something instantly distinguishable from all that has gone before can assume a ferocious strength. Moreover, it is relatively rare to hear today about an artist's obligations to his society. The image of the artist as the lone Bohemian — misunderstood, eccentric and unconventional, omnipotent in mind, careless of matter, oblivious of his audience, faithful only to his own inner creative urge — may be a caricature, but it is doubtful whether the content it enshrines is extinct. Peter Fuller comments:

> "Fine artists have been granted every freedom except the only one without which the others count as nothing: *the freedom to act socially*. It is only a mild exaggeration to say that no-one wants Fine Artists, except Fine Artists, and that neither they nor anyone else have the slightest idea of what they should be doing, or for whom they should be doing it ....It is possible to say that a major infringement of the freedom of the artist at the moment is his lack of genuine social function".[45]

In a recent perceptive article in *The Times*, Janet Daley remarked that in Britain, under governments of all complexions, it seems that "alienation is, as it were, part of the professional brief," that "the only artistic productions which can be respected are those which reject, either explicitly or implicitly, their own society". But, she continues: "if they consistently repudiate their own society, in whatever political hands or historical mood it finds itself, then that is evidence not so much of the irretrievable evil of society as of the demoralisation of the arts." If this trend continues, "There will be no place any longer for an art that affirms, that contributes to a society's sense of its own worth."[46]

(3) An Alternative Way Forward?

At this point, let me reinforce what I said earlier about the significance of Kant himself. I am not claiming that Kant was the sole and direct cause of the alienation of art which is so characteristic of our time. I am not unaware of the extent to which he differed from some of his immediate successors — for example, the Romantics, who saw in art the key to unlock all truth — nor of the fact that Kant would have been horrified by what some others have made of his aesthetics. I am also conscious that a fuller overview of attitudes to the arts in the West today would have to take account of a complex web of socio-political factors, not to mention many other strands in the philosophy of art prior to and subsequent to Kant. My contention is simply that, even acknowledging a fair degree of generalisation, Kant's work on aesthetic experience encapsulates a characteristic frame of mind which sums up, and to a significant extent has affected, a very large proportion of modern thinking and writing about the arts.

It would of course be foolish to ignore Kant's strengths. In a way that only a philosopher of his stature could achieve, he offered an ingenious way of evading relativism while at the same time refusing to speak of aesthetic judgements as direct statements of fact. He sought to outline a coherent account of aesthetic experience which would preserve its distinctiveness and autonomy in an age when it lay under considerable philosophical suspicion. As is so often said, we cannot turn the clock back and pretend that Kant had never lived. Neither the challenges he tackled nor the way in which he tackled them can be ignored. Nonetheless, I think there are reasons to believe that the disadvantages of his approach outweigh the benefits.

The fact that his epistemology has been shown to be so wanting in other areas should itself give us pause for thought.[47] The overall logic of his aesthetics, I would submit, is one which leads towards alienation — of art from knowledge, of art from action, of artist from the physical world, of artist from fellow artist, of artist from society. Of course, Kant had no intention of isolating the aesthetic category completely, but his guiding principles inevitably move in this kind of direction. Therefore, while we may not be able to bypass Kant, I believe there are ways of moving through him and beyond him. Moreover, in doing so, we need to ask whether the kind of theology we were outlining in chapter 2 (pp. 169-185) might, if carefully appropriated, be our most valuable resource. I hope to show that the tools implicit in that theology will help us lay the foundations for a richer philosophy of art, more faithful to the way in which the majority of artists have seen their task, and more faithful to the way we enjoy and value the arts. To prepare the way, we can glance briefly at two writers who, with no theological axe to grind, have sought to open up fresh routes which lead to very different conclusions from Kant.

Few have been so critical of Kantian and post-Kantian aesthetics as Hans-Georg Gadamer (1900-) in his massive study *Truth and Method*.[48] In the first part of this work, Gadamer's main concern is to question the deep-seated assumption in our culture that the appreciation of art and beauty has nothing to do with knowledge and truth. He launches a sustained attack on what he calls 'the subjectivisation of aesthetics' since Kant, in particular the notion of 'disinterested', 'aesthetic consciousness' — that an individual subject contemplates an aesthetic object and in so doing enjoys the immediacy of pure sensuous form. Gadamer insists that we do not react merely to the form of a work of art as opposed to its content; rather we respond to it as something which mediates meaning as a unity. Moreover, the experience of art leads not simply to self-awareness but to genuine knowledge. Art, to pick up Anthony Thiselton's paraphrase of Gadamer, "is not merely a matter of subjective consciousness, but of ontological disclosure."[49] In this disclosure, *we* are questioned — our self-understanding is revealed, illuminated and challenged. Searching for a model to illustrate this, Gadamer alights on the phenomenon of a game.[50] Like a game, the work of art is a dynamic reality which grasps and envelops us, drawing us into its life and world. The game has its own essence (*Wesen*) independent of the consciousness of those who play. We do not control the game; rather, we find ourselves caught up in it. "The structure of the play absorbs the player into itself, and thus takes from him the burden of the initiative".[51] Gadamer argues that the same applies to a work of art. Thus he effectively turns on its head the Kantian stress on *our* imposition of form and meaning. In addition, Gadamer is committed to laying great stress on the act of enjoying and interpreting art: a work of art is strictly speaking only art when it is experienced as such by someone. There is no play without players: we are not playing if we are detached and disinterested spectators. Likewise, the work of art is not a self-contained and self-enclosed object which stands in front of a spectator or listener waiting to be contemplated. Just as Gadamer calls attention to the buoyancy, the to-and-fro movement which belongs to play, so he does the same in the case of art. There is a dynamic interaction or transaction between the work of art and the spectator. "The work of art has its true being in the fact that it becomes an experience changing the person who experiences it."[52] The meaning of a work of art is not simply 'there' to be discovered, it comes to realisation only as the work is encountered.

Gadamer also believes that the Kantian alienation of aesthetic consciousness is part of a more widespread alienation, that of historical consciousness. We must find a way to win back a horizon that includes both art and history together, that does not leave art floating in an ethereal 'aesthetic' realm.[53] The timelessness of Kantianism is thus countered by Gadamer's plea that we appreciate the positive role of corporate tradition as an essential element in interpreting art. We need to overcome our 'prejudice against prejudice' — our innate suspicion of the inherited assumptions and conventions of the past.[54] Indeed, Gadamer argues that it is only through an encounter with prejudices and prejudgements which are alien to us that we will ever have our own prejudices tested and judged. Hence when we interpret a work of art, the historical distance between us and the art work need not alienate us from it; it can actually facilitate better understanding by calling into question our deeply ingrained (and often damaging) assumptions.

Gadamer, we should note, is often grouped with a cluster of scholars — such as Richard Rorty, Jürgen Habermas, Hannah Arendt, Richard Bernstein — who in their different ways have challenged the dominant conceptions of human rationality inherited from the Enlightenment and have sought to move beyond the traditional extremes of objectivism and relativism in all fields of human experience and enquiry. Bernstein believes that today we are witnessing the playing out of what Rorty calls the 'Cartesian-Lockean-Kantian tradition'.[55] This may or may not be so. But there is no doubt that very similar concerns are evident in the work of the scientist Michael Polanyi (1892-1976). We shall have much to say about Polanyi's treatment of art at a later stage. Here we only need draw attention to some features of his epistemology which are especially pertinent to our theme. If Gadamer and others are correct in their contention that the arts can provide cognitive apprehension of the objectively real, then clearly a wider conception of knowledge than Kant's is required. This is where Polanyi is of considerable help. Polanyi sees all human knowing as a fully self-involving ('participatory') activity, which employs all our faculties — sense, mind and reason. Through our senses, we engage actively with that which lies beyond ourselves. (This assumes, of course, that the world beyond the self is the kind of reality which can be known.) However, Polanyi stresses that no knowledge is final and complete, since every human act of knowing presupposes a range of 'tacit' awareness which can never be exhaustively specified. Everything we do employs tacit ('subsidiary') awareness as a means to achieving a more, yet never completely, explicit ('focal') awareness. Thus no proposition about the world is ever completely adequate to the world; all statements are corrigible and revisable. But to say that is not to claim they are necessarily false. Because all knowing involves both personal commitment and risk, total uncertainty is as much a fiction as total certainty. The opposition between objectivism and relativism falsely assumes that the only two viable options are absolute indubitability and absolute doubt. Polanyi urges that all knowing is a form of faith moving towards understanding. With this goes a very different attitude to the senses than the dominant tradition of the Enlightenment. Rather than assuming that the senses are inherently passive and untrustworthy, needing to be compensated for by the active mind (a view which undermines our continuity with the world), Polanyi argues that through our senses we relate actively to — or, to use his word, 'indwell' — the world, not in such a way as to give us complete certainty but nevertheless to grant us cognitive access to what is objectively real. Significantly, the concept of 'indwelling' was borrowed from Wilhelm Dilthey (1833-1911) who used it to explain how different understanding in the humanities is from understanding in the natural sciences. Polanyi uses it to speak of *all* human knowing, thus pointing to a unity of knowledge never grasped by Dilthey and his contemporaries. It is quite inappropriate to divide our experience into the certain (which we can know) and the doubtful — the former pertaining to the sciences, the latter to everything else. This, says Polanyi, overlooks many legitimate types of non-scientific knowing (for example, knowledge of other people) and also seriously misrepresents scientific enquiry and discovery. Even granting the diversity of types of knowledge, all human knowledge, in its basic shape at least, displays the same pattern: the focusing and integrating of subsidiary awareness by a human agent. Crucial for Polanyi also is his belief that knowing the world is intrinsically a corporate activity. His is a thoroughly communal epistemology. Like Gadamer, Polanyi is convinced that without a community, without other people (living and dead), without a common language, shared traditions and common authorities, there simply can be no knowledge.[56]

We have mentioned Gadamer and Polanyi here not because of their immediate relevance to theology, and certainly not because they are without any weaknesses, but principally because they point to a more promising way of understanding the arts than that offered by the tradition we have studied in this chapter. As we now draw on the resources of theology to offer a critique of that tradition, the importance of their insights will become increasingly apparent.

Notes

[1] New York: Writers and Readers Publishing Cooperative, 1983.

[2] *Ibid.*, p. 19.

[3] *Ibid.*, p. 40.

[4] 'Principles of Philosophy,' in *The Philosophical Works of Descartes*, trans. Haldane and Ross, Vol. 1, Cambridge: Cambridge University Press, 1973, pp. 249ff.

[5] *Reflections on Poetry*, trans. K. Aschenbrenner and W. B. Holther, Berkeley: University of South California Press, 1954, especially pars. 13, 16, 41.

[6] *An Enquiry into the Original of Our Ideas of Beauty and Virtue*, London, 1726, sec. 6, p. 82.

[7] *Ibid.*, pp. 14f.

[8] *A Treatise of Human Nature*, ed. Ernest Mossner, Harmondsworth: Penguin, 1969, II, part I, Sect. VIII, p. 350.

[9] 'The Sceptic,' as quoted in Israel Knox, *The Aesthetic Theories of Kant, Hegel and Schopenhauer*, New York: Columbia University Press, 1936, p. 20.

[10] *Essay Concerning Human Understanding*, ed. A. C. Fraser, Oxford, 1894, II, ix, 2.

[11] *Ibid.*

[12] *Enquiries Concerning the Human Understanding and Concerning the Principles of Morals*, ed. L. A. Selby-Bigge, London: Oxford University Press, 1972, par. 246, p. 294.

[13] K. E. Gilbert and H. Kuhn, *A History of Esthetics*, New York: Dover, 1972, p. 234.

[14] As Gilbert and Kuhn show, specifically intellectual elements creep

into the empiricists' account of the 'inner sense' of beauty — an affinity for proportion, balance etc., a susceptibility to intellectual training, and (in some writers) the inclusion of the faculty of judgement. *Ibid.*, pp. 247f.

15 *Critique of Judgement*, trans. J. H. Bernard, 2nd ed., New York and London: Hafner, 1968, p. 37.

16 *Ibid.*, pp. 38ff.

17 *Ibid.*, pp. 48ff.

18 *Ibid.*, p. 56.

19 *Aesthetics*, London: Oxford University Press, 1975, p. 31.

20 "On the Origins of 'Aesthetic Disinterestedness,'" *Journal of Aesthetics and Art Criticism*, 20 (1961), pp. 131-143. M. H. Abrams traces the notion further back to Neo-Platonised Christian thought. "Kant and the Theology of Art," *Notre Dame English Journal*, 13 (1981), pp. 75-106.

21 Grand Rapids, Michigan: Eerdmans, 1980, p. 10.

22 *Voices of Silence*, trans. Stuart Gilbert, St. Albans: Paladin, 1974, pp. 13f.

23 *Critique of Pure Reason*, trans. N. Kemp Smith, Edinburgh, 1929, p. 127.

24 *Critique of Judgement*, p. 38. The term 'disinterested' only refers to our lack of interest in an object's function, utility or perfection.

25 "Our Hermeneutical Inheritance," in Roger Lundin, Anthon C. Thiselton, Clarence Walhout, eds., *The Responsibility of Hermeneutics*, Grand Rapids, Michigan: Eerdmans, 1985, p. 13.

26 George Braziller, 1968.

27 *Imagination*, London and Boston: Faber and Faber, 1976, p. 47. My italics.

28 *Critique of Judgement*, p. 61. Kant does not say that representational elements in a work of art are completely irrelevant aesthetically, but he does hold that the *principal* element in aesthetic experience is the apprehension of form. Cf. Donald Crawford, *Kant's Aesthetic Theory*, London and Wisconsin: University of Wisconsin Press, 1974, pp. 117f.

29 *Loc. cit.*, p. 76.

30 *The Musical Experience of Composer, Performer, Listener*, as quoted in Wolterstorff, *op. cit.*, p. 25.

31 *The Wellsprings of Music*, New York: Da Capo, 1977, p. 124.

32 Cf. Monroe Beardsley, *Aesthetics from Classical Greece to the Present*, Alabama: University of Alabama Press, 1977, pp. 175ff., pp. 284-290. The "sources of what came to be called 'art for art's sake' are mostly there in the Kantian system, though they no doubt had to be somewhat exaggerated and oversimplified" (p. 286).

33 *Real Presences*, London: Faber and Faber, 1989, p. 98. My italics.

34 *The Photoplay: A Psychological Study*, New York: D. Appleton, 1916, p. 64. Cf. Ian Jarvie, *Philosophy of the Film*, New York and London: Routledge & Kegan Paul, 1987, pp. 69-95.

35 *Anatomy of Criticism: Four Essays*, Princeton: Princeton University Press, 1957, p. 75.

36 "The Many Uses of Metaphor," in Sheldon Sacks, ed., *On Metaphor*,

Chicago: Chicago University Press, 1979, pp. 171f.

[37] *The Collected Essays and Criticism: Volume I: Perceptions and Judgements, 1939-1944*, Chicago and London: Chicago University Press, 1968, p. 8

[38] As quoted in Fuller, *Aesthetics After Modernism*, p. 32. My italics.

[39] "Creation and Re-Creation: An exploration of Some Themes in Aesthetics and Theology," *Modern Theology*, 2, no. 1 (1985), p. 4.

[40] *Beyond Objectivism and Relativism: Science, Hermeneutics, and Praxis*, Oxford: Blackwell, 1983, p. 120.

[41] *From Descartes to Wittgenstein: A Short History of Modern Philosophy*, New York: Harper and Row, 1982, p. 284.

[42] *Loc. cit.*, p. 9.

[43] *Psychology as Religion: The Cult of Self-Worship*, Grand Rapids, Michigan: Eerdmans, 1977, p. 61.

[44] *Op. cit.*, p. 318.

[45] *Beyond the Crisis in Art*, London: Writers and Readers Publishing Cooperative, 1980, pp. 45f. My italics.

[46] "Making an Art of Subversion," *The Times*, August 23, 1989, p. 10.

[47] Cf. e.g. Anthony Quinton, *The Nature of Things*, London: Routledge and Kegan Paul, 1973; Arthur Peacocke, *Intimations of Reality*, Notre Dame: University of Notre Dame Press, 1984; Brian Hebblethwaite, *The Ocean of Truth*, Cambridge: Cambridge University Press, 1988; Colin Gunton, *Enlightenment and Alienation: An Essay Towards a Trinitarian Theology*, Basingstoke: Marshall Morgan & Scott, 1985; Alasdair McIntyre, *After Virtue. A Study in Moral Theory*, London: Duckworth, 1981.

[48] London: Sheed and Ward, 1975, pp. 39-90.

[49] Anthony C. Thiselton, *The Two Horizons: New Testament Hermeneutics and Philosophical Description with Special Reference to Heidegger, Bultmann, Gadamer and Wittgenstein*, Exeter: Paternoster Press, 1980, p. 296.

[50] *Op. cit.*, pp. 91ff.

[51] *Ibid.*, p. 94.

[52] *Ibid.*, p. 92.

[53] *Ibid.*, pp. 108ff.

[54] *Ibid.*, pp. 245ff.

[55] Cf. Bernstein, *op. cit.*, *passim*.

[56] *Personal Knowledge*, London: Routledge and Kegan Paul, 1973, particularly pp. 49-65, 249-268; *The Tacit Dimension*, London: Routledge & Kegan Paul, 1966, *passim*.

4. Artistry in Christ

"Love.........achieves its creativity by being perceptive."

Oliver O'Donovan

In the last chapter, I tried to elucidate some of the philosophical assumptions which have encouraged the modern tendency to conceive art as intrinsically independent of other dimensions of human experience. It is now time to offer some extended comments on what we have uncovered, drawing on the theological insights opened up in chapter 2 of this Part. To structure the discussion, I shall use the seven features of Kant's aesthetics we have just examined.

(1) Art and the Physical

A faithfulness to the biblical tradition suggests that we are not disembodied spirits or intellects but unities of spirit and matter inhabiting a physical world with which we are intimately bound up and have a large measure of continuity, and that part of what it means to be human is to interact thoroughly with this physical reality. The non-human world need not be seen in terms of 'inflexible foreignness' (Hegel). By assuming and redeeming the material world in Christ, God has confirmed it as a proper, meaningful environment for us to enjoy, explore and develop. Moreover, if this is so, our senses can be regarded as the means through which we actively indwell and engage with the physical order, not as passive channels of unreliable information.

I can see no compelling reason why the arts should not be approached from this perspective, or, to be more specific, why we should construe art as constantly moving us beyond this material world to some 'higher' realm, or see the heart of an artist's work as giving outward expression to inner, non-material realities, as if the 'real' work was carried out in the sanctuary of the self, and the piece of art merely served to externalise and convey this interior experience. I am not suggesting that art can be explained entirely in physical terms, nor that mental activity has no place in artistic creation, nor that artists are never blessed with inner visions of great clarity. But, against the Enlightenment tradition, I would argue for a recovery of a deeper sense of our embeddedness in creation, and of the physicality of artistic creation; the rootedness of art in substance, in the human body, in stone, pigment, in the twanging of gut, the blowing of air on reeds. Wolterstorff stresses that a devaluation of the physical just because of its being physical "flies in the face of God's affirmation of His creation. The sheer physicality or materiality of something is never a legitimate ground for assigning to it a lower value in our lives."[1]   The artist should not "despise the creation in which he finds himself. He will not see it as something from which to be liberated.......... he will see the world as a storehouse of materials out of which he can select so as to make his work. He will think of those materials more as something whose potential are to be realised than as something constricting the scope of his own self-expression."[2] Wolterstorff speaks of the 'Duchamp' attitude — the abhorrence of materials; the 'Cage' attitude — the total subservience to materials; and the 'Croce' attitude — seeing materials as no more than the bearers of a message.[3] By way of contrast, he urges that "the fundamental fact about the artist is that he or she is a worker in stone, in bronze, in clay, in paint, in acid and plates, in sounds and instruments, in states of affairs."[4] Similar comments come from the Roman Catholic theologian John Dixon.[5]   We have been captivated, Dixon believes, by the view that a work of art is merely a means for the communication of some non-physical entity. Dixon proposes that we see art as essentially a 'constructive' rather than a symbolic or expressive activity. The work of art, he insists, "is fundamentally a structure........before anything else it is a thing, an object. It is therefore inseparable from the material of which it is a part. It is generated out of a very specific piece of specific material."[6] Along the same lines, the composer Igor Stravinsky writes:

> "The very act of putting my work on paper, of, as we say, kneading the dough, is for me inseparable from the pleasure of creation. So far as I am concerned, I cannot separate the spiritual effort from the psychological and physical effort; they confront me on the same level and do not present a hierarchy. The word *artist* which, as it is most generally understood today, bestows on its bearer the highest intellectual prestige, the privilege of being accepted as a pure mind — this pretentious term is in my view entirely incompatible with the role of the *homo faber*".[7]

If we take this kind of comment to heart, we might well be led to ask whether visual categories have been too pervasive in modern philosophy of art (as they have undoubtedly been in philosophies of perception[8]). We hinted at this in the course of our discussion of Tillich's art-philosophy, which tended to be dominated by analysing the experience of being grasped by ultimate reality through a painting.[9] It is not that there is anything intrinsically problematic about this in itself. The problems arise when we treat visual apprehension as in some sense paradigmatic for all art. And one of the chief problems, as far as the work of the artist is concerned, is that it will tend to reinforce a sense of *distance* between the artist and his world, rather than a sense of physical continuity and engagement with his environment. (It will also encourage, we might add, the notion that the ideal attitude to adopt before an art work is one of detached contemplation.) It is noteworthy that Polanyi's fruitful notion of 'indwelling' centres on touch, not sight. Perhaps one of the main contributions of a modern theological philosophy of art will be to challenge the frequent assumption that our primary appeal ought to be to the visual arts.

(2) Art and Action

We observed that Kant's concept of 'disinterestedness' was at root a product of the Cartesian model of knowledge — the self impassively surveying its object — transferred to the aesthetic realm. Clearly, this carries with it an implicit divorce of art from action, for the aesthetic attitude is essentially intellectual and timeless. But there seems no reason why this should not be open to the searching criticism which Christian anthropology brings to any model of the person which stresses intellectual abstraction at the expense of practical engagement. To return to Wolterstorff, the core of his thesis in *Art in Action* is that works of art are first and foremost instruments and objects of action, inextricably part of the fabric of human purpose, through which we carry out our intentions with respect to the world, our fellows, and ourselves. Our society's institution of 'high' or 'fine' art makes us focus exclusively on the work of art itself, encouraging us to contemplate it and regard it for its own sake. Although 'perceptual contemplation' is *one* of the uses to which some art can legitimately be put, to insist on it as the *sine qua non* of art is unhelpfully restrictive. Art plays an enormous variety of roles in human life — evoking emotion, expressing grief, praising, celebrating, etc. "Works of art equip us for action. And the range of actions for which they equip us is very nearly as broad as the range of human action itself. The purposes of art are the purposes of life......any aesthetic which neglects the enormous *diversity* of actions in which art plays a role, in fact and by intent, is bound to yield distortion and inscrutability."[10] In this connection, Wolterstorff comments that the anthropologist will be only too keen to remind us of the inseparability of art and action in many other cultures — for example, in the dances and songs of the Balinese, the small clay figures made by Mexicans to accompany the dead in their after-life, the paintings of cave-dwellers scratched in stone to ensure success in hunting.

To recover a proper sense of the link between art and action clearly chimes in well with Polanyi's concept of participatory knowing, his refusal to construe knowledge in terms of detached intellectual reflection. And in the same circle of ideas lies Gadamer's stress on the active, 'performative' aspect of the arts: he too is highly critical of any attempt to abstract art from its social and historical context, and rightly associates the growth of the modern museum with the kind of disinterested 'aesthetic consciousness' propounded by Kant.[11]

In adopting this line, I am aware that the point can easily be overplayed, leading to a purely 'functionalist' or 'productivist' approach to art, according to which we assign value to an art work only if and when it can be put to some immediate use. Such a view has enjoyed significant support in recent times in Britain, ironically from both extremes of political right and left,[12] and follows hard on the heels of the attempt to free art from all issues of objective value. Yet it must falter, for otherwise we would be unable to make any distinction between, say, a Rubens nude and a tabloid page-three photograph. Questions of artistic worth and excellence cannot be reduced to questions about utility, commercial or otherwise. To say that works of art are primarily instruments and objects of action is not to say that *no* attention should ever be paid to what they are in themselves, it is only to say that we cannot abstract them from their context in human action if they are to be interpreted aright and enjoyed to the full.

(3) Discovering Order and Redeeming Disorder

Discovery and Respect

In contrast to the weight Kant puts on the contribution of the mind in bringing form to a world which we experience as a plurality, I have argued that the Christian faith presents us with a vision of created existence possessing its own latent orderliness and meaning, and that a crucial part of human creativity is to be attentive to that inherent order, to discover it and to bring it to light. A theological account of human creativity will need to question the ancient suspicion of the goodness of physical creation, the tendency to deny the intrinsic meaningfulness of configurations of matter. As Oliver O'Donovan puts it: "How can creativity function with its eyes closed upon the universe? For man does not encounter reality as an undifferentiated raw material upon which he may impose any shape that pleases him". Love, he continues, "achieves its creativity by being perceptive."[13] Artistic examples of such 'love' are not hard to find. We need only think of Van Gogh's landscapes and interiors, Dürer's meticulous drawings of the human body, Bach's exploration of the properties of the harmonic series. We might call to mind S. T. Coleridge's comments on Wordsworth's *Lyrical Ballads*: they serve the purpose of "awakening the mind's attention from the lethargy of custom and directing it to the loveliness and the wonders of the world before us".[14] The painter likewise can detect in the sky or sea, colours we only begin to notice when our attention is drawn to them; the novelist awakens us to human traits and qualities often bypassed in day to day life. So John Macquarrie speaks of art as "something like revelation. What is revealed has been there all the time, but it has gone unnoticed in our humdrum everyday experience. It needs the sensitivity of the artist to bring it to light, so that we notice things for the first time."[15]

Hand in hand with discovery, we said earlier, goes respect. One very obvious way in which this affects the artist concerns the way he deals with his medium: paints, notes, marble or whatever. A serious artist will endeavour to know and honour his material, to show it a courtesy. Dorothy Sayers insisted that the business of the artist "is not to escape from his material medium or bully it, but to serve it; but to serve it he must love it. If he does so, he will realise that its service is perfect freedom."[16] W. H. Auden said that in order to become a good poet, you must like "hanging around words listening to what they say."[17] In Wolterstorff's view, the artist must learn

"that he can only go so far in imposing his will upon [his material]. Or to put it from the other side, he learns that his material will be receptive only to certain aims on his part. Others it will permanently frustrate. And to others it will yield only with enormous reluctance."[18]

In the field of music, the American composer and conductor Leonard Bernstein, through a comparison with the deep and surface structure of language, has recently argued that at a profound level all music is grounded in that set of vibrations which in varying degrees accompanies any tone sung or played — the harmonic series. Any attempt to wrestle free entirely from this universal phenomenon, he believes, is in the last resort self-defeating.[19] Along somewhat different but related lines, the musicologist Deryck Cooke has sought to demonstrate that certain melodic, harmonic and rhythmic forms have been persistently connected with certain emotions and moods and that by no means all such associations are conventional.[20] We could also point to the impressive body of psychological data gathered by Osgood and others supporting the validity of 'synesthesia': stimulation in one sense modality producing a sensation in another. The extent of cross-cultural agreement on this is significantly large.[21] Needless to say, controversy rages around these issues. But we would be hard pressed to demonstrate conclusively that music evokes a response in us *solely* on the basis of social and cultural influences and that universal physical factors have no part to play at all.

These issues have recently been brought to the fore vividly in Peter Fuller's remarkable book *Theoria: Art, and the Absence of Grace*. From the mid-nineteenth century onwards, Fuller avers, the study of nature "risked descent into the darkling plain of utter meaninglessness..........That 'disassociation of sensibility' which was so to trouble T. S. Eliot in the following century was everywhere apparent; the world seemed to have lost its enchantment and to have become *mundane*."[22] Fuller bemoans the subsequent 'collapse of the idea of art as a channel of grace'. He looks back to the tradition embodied in Ruskin's *theoria* — a moral response to beauty rooted in the awareness of natural form — and cites evidence suggesting that in our 'post-modern age' science is "rediscovering the aesthetic and spiritual meanings of nature".[23] Fuller's discussion of the sculpture of Jacob Epstein, Henri Gaudier-Brzeska, Eric Gill and Henry Moore is especially illuminating. Far from trying to sweep away Victorianism, Fuller insists that these sculptors were celebrating natural organic form against the backdrop of an increasingly technocratic and machine-dominated culture. Their stress on abstraction does not represent a move away from objective order but an attempt to rediscover it in a profounder way.[24] Whether or not we share Fuller's enthusiasm for Ruskin's notion of a 'natural theology without God', and whether or not he gives sufficient weight to the artist's creativity, his call for an aesthetic grounded in natural structure is noteworthy, especially since it implicitly questions so many of the trends in contemporary aesthetics.

What Place for Creativity?

At this point the champion of the Enlightenment begins to protest, and understandably so. Are we not here committing ourselves to a total passivity and subservience to the given order of creation, and thus returning to a simplistic 'heteronomy'? Are we not heading for some form of 'imitation' theory of art? Does not the kind of model we have been developing effectively deny artistic freedom?

The anxiety behind this kind of objection must be felt. There can be no sneaking behind Kant to a pre-Enlightenment innocence. There simply has to be imposition of some kind in all our commerce with reality; that much is beyond question. At the same time, our general reflections above on freedom and creativity in relation to God will have their counterparts in the sphere of artistic creativity. It is clearly not a matter of a stark choice between complete submissiveness and total imposition. To clarify this, five comments are in order.

First, as I have already argued, if we regard the orderliness of creation chiefly as gift, it will not be seen as a cramping constraint, a strait-jacket to which we yield grudgingly, but rather as a framework provided and sustained by the covenant love of God, as something which is given to stimulate rather than restrict authentic creativity.

Second, the concern for artistic freedom is proper and justifiable, but it is highly dubious to construe the essence of such freedom as escaping objective order. Genuine freedom is not constituted by the absence of limits, or by multiplying the number of possibilities open to us; it is realised only in *relation* to real possibilities, by acting in accordance with the way things are. Again, some fascinating words of Stravinsky are worth quoting.

"I have the seven notes of the scale and its chromatic intervals at my disposal......strong and weak accents are within my reach, and......in all these I possess solid and concrete elements which offer me a field of experience just as vast as the upsetting and dizzy infinitude that had just frightened me ....What delivers me from the anguish into which an unrestricted freedom plunges me is the fact that I am always able to turn immediately to the concrete things that are here in question........Whatever diminishes constraint diminishes strength."[25]

Not all composers would be content with Stravinsky's estimation of the Western chromatic scale. But that is beside the point. What we should notice is his implicit conviction that to be free as a composer does not entail breaking away from that which is given to hand. In more theological terms, artistic freedom consists in being properly related through Christ to that world which was brought into being and is sustained 'through him'. To be so related will not constitute an infringement of our freedom but the realisation of it, a restoration of God's original intention for us.

Third, to recommend that an artist operates with respect for the orderliness of the world does not commit us to a 'reproductive' or 'copy' theory of art. For art involves an interaction with the created order, not merely bowing down before it. As I said before, creativity encompasses not only discovery and respect, but also development. For the artist simply to mirror what he perceives will never be adequate; new connections and novel meanings need to be established through developing what is given to hand. A composer, for example, does more than discover and respect; he combines sounds in novel ways, explores fresh melodic lines, juxtaposes rhythms and harmonies to create new musical meanings.

Moreover, fourth, a respect for objective order need not undercut an artist's 'redemptive' responsibility, to fashion a new order out of disorder, whether in the human or non-human realms. The very fact that artists frequently describe their work in terms of a struggle with their chosen medium, of the intractibility and recalcitrance of their material (inanimate or animate), can bespeak an encounter with the chaotic, destructive dimension of created existence, and a desire to re-order it for good. As Gunton puts it, artistic creation

> "must necessarily take the form of a re-creation, of a re-ordering of that which is out of place as well as an ordering of material given to hand and mind...........something new is made in such a way that there is also a making up of that which is lacking, a reintegration of the unity of things........by creating [the artist] helps to re-create what is subject to disorder."[26]

To speak of the redemptive possibilities of art is of course hazardous, lest we detract from the supremacy of the redemption wrought in Christ, and lest we suggest that Christ's redemption is no more than an aesthetic re-ordering of material reality (when it is clearly much more than that). Nevertheless, God's redemption in Christ clearly has an aesthetic dimension to it, and there would seem no good reason to deny that we can share in this dimension of divine activity through artistic endeavour. We can now indicate some of the implications of this.

I suggested above that responsible creativity involves a penetration of disorder. So too for the artist. David Harned writes: "The man of letters must follow where the man from Nazareth led, through all the twists and crannies and depths of the finite".[27] The artist cannot pass lightly over the disorder of the creation without being guilty of colossal self-deception and becoming utterly irrelevant to the needs of a broken and torn world. Many Christian theories of art falter by implying that disorder in a work of art is a mark of discredit. Here the sting of Tillich's attack on 'beautifying naturalism' should be felt, as should these comments of Flannery O'Connor:

> "The sorry religious novel comes about when the writer supposes that because of his belief, he is somehow dispensed from the obligation to penetrate concrete reality. He will think that the eyes of the Church or of the Bible or of his particular theology have already done the seeing for him, and that his business is to arrange this essential vision into satisfying patterns, getting himself as little dirty as possible in the process".[28]

To the Church's shame, much so-called 'Christian' art has degenerated into an inoffensive and superficial *Kitsch* which turns a blind eye to the pain of the world. The American psychologist William James once visited a supposedly idyllic Christian resort in Chautauqua, New York, and afterwards spoke of "the atrocious harmlessness of all things" and of how he longed for the outside world with all its "heights and depths, the precipices and steep ideals, the gleams of the awful and the infinite".[29] Arguably, church music in Britain today could well do with a few more 'gleams of the awful and the infinite' if it is to reflect faithfully the condescension of the Son of God to be one with us.

We also indicated above that redemption entails judgement. Part of this judgement will be in the form of a protest against disorder. Of course, the theme of protest has been a recurrent one in much twentieth-century art. We cannot issue a blanket dismissal of all such protest as anti-Gospel, especially since God in his Son has declared a 'No' against all evil.[30] Yet, having said that, protest, as Tillich saw so clearly, cannot be divorced from affirmation. All cries of anger and indignation can only issue from some more ultimate conviction. Disorder is recognised as such only because of some prior conviction about what is orderly. The distorted portraits of Francis Bacon affect us and horrify us only because we recognise them as brutally fragmented pictures of human beings. To describe modern art as 'meaningless' is thus crude and innacurate. As Hans Küng observes, contemporary art is "certainly complex and problematic, but not meaningless: it was never meaningless."[31] All art to some extent exhibits a dialectic between negation and affirmation — a protest against things as we find them in the name of some intuition of what they are meant to be or could be. This is powerfully captured by Albert Camus in *The Rebel*:

> "Art is the activity that exalts and denies simultaneously. 'No artist tolerates reality,' says Nietzsche. That is true, but no artist can get along without reality. Artistic creation is a demand for unity and a rejection of the world. But it rejects the world on account of what it lacks and in the name of what it sometimes is."[32]

Put in theological terms, a 'No' of protest in art may well echo God's rejection of all that corrupts his world, but it will never be sufficient on its own. The Christian confession is that God's 'No' yields its true meaning only in the light of his 'Yes', his unconditional love towards creation, a 'Yes' which has found its supreme enactment in the resurrection of Christ from the dead.

In the resurrection too we are reminded that redemption not only achieves the exposure and rejection of evil, but the transformation of that which has been distorted, a renewal of what is disordered.[33]   On this score, Christian theories of art which begin and end with the incarnation are seen to be woefully inadequate.   Speaking of some strands of modern literary criticism, Leland Ryken remarks:

> "Contrary to the statements of literary theorists who are obsessed with the Incarnation, Christ came to redeem and transform human life, not simply to affirm what he saw. As with Christian writers, so too with Christian critics: their calling is to wrest beauty and meaning from a fallen world and to help others to do so."[34]

If this is so, shallow theories of artistic 'realism' also need to be questioned. All too often, the promotion of realism in art hides a cynicism about any ultimate good or purpose in the world. A film replete with violence is sometimes praised simply because it is 'true to reality' — that is, it holds before our eyes the violent character of contemporary society. Apart from the false implication that a work of art can actually reach a state where it only portrays and never interprets reality,[35] there is also the questionable suggestion that art has no other responsibility than to present 'life as it is lived today'. What is surely required here is careful attention to the many different senses and levels of realism in art, not least the level of religious commitment. Whatever else 'Christian art' is, it will be art which takes for its final 'realistic' reference-point the raising of the crucified Son of God from the dead. Such art will inevitably resound with an inner joy, even though it may only be a joy won through despair. These words of Hardy and Ford could well apply to the Christian artist: "The resurrection of the crucified Jesus Christ is [the] logic at the heart of Christianity.......If this is basic reality then all existence can be thought through in the light of it. *True realism will take account of this first, and live from it.*"[36] As examples of this art in our own day, we might include Olivier Messiaen's 'L'Ascension', Duke Ellington's 'Come Sunday', the early works of Graham Sutherland, and the tender portraits of Georges Rouault.

Finally, fifth, insofar as fresh order is wrought out of disorder, there will be an anticipation of the final goal of creation. Kuyper and Bavinck glimpsed something of substantial importance here. Thus Hans Küng can write that "[Art's] particular service to man consists in symbolising.......how man and society might be ....[It is].....a provisional manifestation and reflection of a future consummation."[37] Or, to quote another Roman Catholic,

> "[Art] proceeds from the longing for that perfect existence which is not yet, but which man, despite all disappointments, thinks must come to be when the existent has reached its full truth and reality has been subordinated to actual entities..........Thus art projects in advance something that does not yet exist."[38]

To sum this section up, I am contending that although a certain receptivity needs to take precedence in artistic creativity, it does not follow that the vocation of the artist should consist in mirroring the reality he encounters. True artistic creativity will be more a matter of an intensive but appropriate engagement with the world in which we are set, in which there is not only discovery and respect, but also a concern to develop and (in some cases) redeem what is given to hand.

(4) Art for Art's Sake?

We observed Kant's insistence on art's internal finality and resultant isolation from concrete particularity, and noted something of how influential this kind of theory has been. The fact that such an attitude to the arts is anything but universal, we suggested, should give us pause for thought. Moreover, we should now add that even in Western European culture, the belief that art cannot refer beyond itself if it is to retain its character as art, simply lacks cogency. Art can, in fact, illuminate (or obscure) reality in ways that can be assessed and appraised, and it can do so without converting into something other than art. So Robin Skelton in his book *Poetic Truth* claims that poetry is quite capable of conveying "to the sensitive reader a remarkably precise picture of the situation of man with regard to his apprehensions of time, history, evolution, language, and the world 'outside' him."[39] Similarly, in his recent study of theology and literature, T. R. Wright sternly criticises the fashionable retreat from talking about reference in some strands of modern criticism. He comments: "it may bring methodological purity to literary criticism to say that it is concerned solely with the process of reading literature and not with the 'meaning' of literary works themselves. But it is an impotent purity that undermines the importance of literature as a means of expressing the 'truth' about the real world."[40] Or, to take another example, it is generally agreed that certain types of music in worship are more appropriate for some services than others, and more fitting at certain points in a service than at others. It would be curious in the extreme to claim that such music has ceased to be art (or necessarily lost artistic excellence) simply because it is being employed to refer beyond its own immediacy. Of course, quite *how* works of art 'refer' is a massive, complex and highly elusive matter. Attacks on crude theories of artistic referral (and on propagandist art) are often quite justified. But *that* a work of art can direct our attention to states of affairs beyond itself (and beyond the consciousness of the artist), and that it can reflect (with varying degrees of potency) values which transcend cultural preference, *without thereby losing its distinctiveness as art*, seems *de facto* undeniable. By the same token, when interpreting art works, the refusal to date or historicise them lest such location distort some putative purity of aesthetic apprehension appears singularly misguided. Language, style, structure and content are all grounded in historical particularity. It would be foolish to claim, for example, that an appreciation of the social struggles which form the background to William Blake's work will somehow inhibit an appropriate response to his poetry, or that it drastically diminishes our understanding of Shostakovitch's symphonies if we fail to make every effort to abstract them from the turbulent political matrix in which they were composed. Considerations of context do not, of course, provide an exhaustive explanation of an art work, and the dangers of over-estimating authorial context (and intent) are well known. Art works possess a measure of independence from their artists. What I am questioning is the assumption that our understanding of art increases in direct proportion to the degree in which we can exclude consideration of specific, historical reference and circumstance.[41]

(5) Art and Knowledge

Clearly, the drift of our argument to this point challenges the sharp dualism between knowledge and the arts so deeply rooted in Enlightenment thought. To his credit, Kant shunned the Romantics' extravagant claim that the key to all knowledge and all morality lies with the arts. He also rightly saw that art has a real measure of autonomy, that it is qualitatively different from our day to day commerce with the world. Aesthetic awareness — whether occasioned by a great painting or a beautiful sunset — cannot be 'explained away' or 'reduced' to some other mode of experience. In all this we concur with Kant. Nevertheless, the way in which he insists on such a sharp distinction between cognition and aesthetic perception creates, I believe, more problems than it solves. Frank Lentricchia observes that Kant's

> "intention of isolating the distinctive character of the aesthetic experience was admirable, but his analysis resulted in mere isolation. By barring that experience from the phenomenal world while allowing art's fictional world entertainment value, he became the philosophical father of an enervating aesthetics which ultimately subverts what it would celebrate".[42]

Whatever the subtleties of Kant, he employs an epistemology far too narrow to do justice to the depth and power of aesthetic experience, not least our encounter with the arts. As Polanyi has seen so well, it is oppressively restrictive to say that we know something only when we have a completely clear and indubitable conceptual grasp of it, and equally misleading to claim that art affords no cognitive contact with reality. The autonomy of art will best be safeguarded, I believe, not by wrenching it apart from knowledge, nor by equating it with conceptual or moral knowledge, but by see it as a distinctive, particular, but quite genuine means of knowing the world. In the next chapter, we shall have more to say on this matter.

But the way ahead is indicated by Gunton:

> "the artist, craftsman or performer does discover and create
> a kind of meaning — aesthetic meaning, which has close
> links with other kinds of meaning, since it can be discussed
> theoretically, and becomes the object of moral and intellectual
> appraisal, even though it may not justifiably be reduced to
> these overlapping forms."[43]

(6) Evaluating Art

If art can provide us with authentic knowledge of what is real
beyond the individual human self, and if we are committed to a
vision of the way the world is under God, then we are inevitably
driven towards the conclusion that there are norms pertaining
to the arts which are not wholly relative to our own theoretical
frameworks, paradigms, forms of life or whatever. However, it
would be an understatement to say that eliciting and applying
artistic norms is fraught with difficulties. The complications
are legion. It is not simply that tastes differ. The very criteria
thought to be relevant for assessing art may vary enormously
between (and within) different cultural groups. Even to outline
a strategy for formulating such criteria would require a book in
itself. Here I make only three brief points. First, it makes good
sense to follow the distinction made by Wolterstorff between
aesthetic excellence and artistic excellence.[44] Artistic excellence
is measured by how effectively a work of art serves the purpose
for which it was made or distributed or performed. Aesthetic
excellence is measured by how effectively it serves the purpose
of contemplation for aesthetic delight, and may thus belong to
things which are not works of art — for example, a well-built
skyscraper. It follows that a work of art may have artistic
excellence without having aesthetic excellence, simply because
it was not made for aesthetic contemplation. At the same time,
just because something has not been produced with the main
intention of giving delight on contemplation — a hymn, for
example — this does not mean that aesthetic merits are
irrelevant to its quality. A hymn will serve its purpose of
bringing glory to God much more effectively if it is aesthetically
good. As far as aesthetic excellence is concerned, we might well
want to adopt Wolterstorff's suggestion that there are three
main types: unity (coherence, completeness), internal richness
(a variety of significantly different parts), and 'fittingness-
intensity' (a particular, distinctive character).[45] Our second

comment concerns the theological evaluation of art. Needless to
say, the Church has hardly covered itself with glory in this
respect. Aesthetic excellence has frequently been disregarded
in the name of a stifling orthodoxy. Far too often, church
buildings have been torn down, books burned, paintings defaced,
without a glimpse at their possible aesthetic merit. At the
same time, we cannot wrap art up in a cocoon and protect it
from judgements which move beyond the purely aesthetic. If a
work of art is capable of disturbing and unsettling us,
illuminating our daily lives, changing our perception of the
world, provoking us into a different course of action, then moral
appraisal cannot be discounted. In George Steiner's words,
"We cannot touch on the experiencing of art in our personal
and communal lives without touching, simultaneously, on moral
issues of the most compelling and perplexing order."[46]   Of
course, something similar must be said of the theological
dimension. Above, we have already hinted implicitly at some
theological norms for art. In some cases, a theological
assessment of the 'world-view' latent in a work of art might be
appropriate. To quote Wolterstorff again, works of art "are not
simply the oozings of subconscious impulses; they are the result
of beliefs and goals on the part of the artist." There is 'a world
behind the work of art',

> "that complex of the artist's beliefs and goals, convictions
> and concerns, which play a role in accounting for the existence
> and character of the work. The beliefs in question may
> range all the way from relatively trivial and passing
> convictions to the artist's world-and-life view, his or her
> *Weltanschauung*; the goals, all the way from minor transitory
> aims to an ultimate concern."[47]

Wolterstorff rightly adds that although a work of art may be
"an expression of the world behind it", it "by no means always
fully *reveals* the world behind it."[48]   Third and last, perhaps
the difficult process of making judgements about art can be
most fruitfully illuminated by reflecting on the character of
divine judgement. God's judgement is ultimately aimed towards
re-creation, not destruction. Likewise, I would submit, artistic
judgement should rarely, if ever, be a matter of writing off, of
blatant rejection. There may be occasions when wholesale
dismissal is the order of the day — when a work of art is
patently perverse and anti-Christian — but such instances are
uncommon. A better strategy is indicated by Ruth Etchells:
"Judging is discerning truly what is good and what is bad, and
then putting it right."[49]

(7) Beyond the First Person

In the course of a penetrating critique of Kant, John Macmurray claims that any philosophy "which takes its stand on the primacy of thought, which defines the Self as Thinker, is committed formally to an extreme logical individualism."[50] In contrast to this, we were earlier reminding ourselves that the Christian Gospel presents us with a picture of human existence as intrinsically relational, that we find our true being only in relationship, when we receive from, and give to, others. The passion for self-determination is the pursuit of the illusion of self-defined rather than relationally defined being, and thus can only be regarded as the pursuit of unreality.

The ramifications of this for the philosophy of art are immense. Here we have space only to adumbrate a few. First, a theory of art which is sensitive to the relatedness of human existence will be keen to view works of art as ineluctably acts of communication. Of course, an artist may say he makes things 'only for himself' or 'only because he has to'. A poet can write verse for himself alone, a composer can write a score for no other ear, and so on. But in the history of art, these are exceptions. Instead of being a gift 'from the self to the self' (Paul Vitz's phrase), we would arguably do better to regard an art work as a medium of personal exchange, in Steiner's suggestive phrase, a 'trial of encounter'.[51]   For Steiner, the "meaning, the existential modes of art, music and literature are functional within the experience of our meeting with the other. All aesthetics, all critical and hermeneutic discourse, is an attempt to clarify the paradox and opaqueness of that meeting as well as its felicities."[52]

In view of this, it is not surprising that some artists have spoken of their finished work as only a beginning. "A work of art," says Naum Gabo, "restricted to what the artist has put into it, is only part of itself. It only attains full stature with what people and time make of it."[53]   Gadamer made the same point through his analogy of a work of art with a game: "The work of art has its true being in the fact that it becomes an experience changing the person who experiences it."[54]   Art, we might say, is inherently dialogical. Indeed, Richard Bernstein believes that for Gadamer, "what is most distinctive about our being-in-the-world is that we are dialogical beings."[55]

Closely related to this, second, it would not be inappropriate to plea for greater attention to be given to an artist's responsibility to his society. If it is true, as I have indicated, that art carries ethical and cognitive dimensions, then questions

of an artist's obligation to a given community simply cannot be
side-stepped, (nor, by implication, can issues of constraint and
censorship). Part of this obligation will be a sensitivity to the
shared values and assumptions of his social setting (insofar as
there *are* shared values and assumptions). An artist's very
vocabulary depends on communities of interest, on established
precedents and particular conventions of appraisal. These cannot
be ignored, even if they are to be modified and in part rejected.
Albert Camus — hardly a champion of the Christian cause —
remarks: "One of the greatest temptations of the artist is to
believe himself solitary, and in truth he hears this shouted at
him, with a certain base delight. But this is not true. His very
vocation......is to open the prisons and give voice to the sorrows
and joys of all."[56] C. S. Lewis writes with characteristic bite:

> "In the highest aesthetic circles one now hears nothing about
> the artist's duty to us. It is all about our duty to him. He
> owes us nothing; we owe him 'recognition', even though he
> has never paid the slightest attention to our tastes, interests,
> or habits.........When an artist is in the strict sense working,
> he of course takes into account the existing tastes, interests
> and capacity of his audience. These, no less than the
> language, the marble, the paint, are part of his raw material;
> to be used, tamed, sublimated, not ignored or defied. Haughty
> indifference to them is not genius; it is laziness and in-
> competence."[57]

Despite Lewis' strictures, however, 'recognition' surely needs to
work both ways. Governments which are inclined to be cynical
about subsidising the arts would do well to recall that in most
communities, in practice, the arts are very much more than an
optional luxury, whatever the institution of 'high art' might
suggest. If we believe that the flourishing of the arts can
contribute to the health of society, and that the accessibility of
a wide range of art is beneficial, then there are going to be
occasions when we are bound to speak of a community's
responsibility to, and support of, its artists, whatever the precise
form such support takes.

Third, we will be suspicious of sanctifying originality as the
supreme artistic virtue, and will seek to rehabilitate a sense of
the importance of tradition. The proclivity of the Enlightenment
is to cut off the artist (and the interpreter) from the past, and
thus from abundant reservoirs of insight and truth. John Cage's
outrageous pronouncement puts the point in an extreme form:
"we will certainly listen to this other music — this totally
determined music of Beethoven, or whatever, but we'll never
again take it seriously".[58] Of course, financial pressure can

have a key part to play here. Lack of funds leads some artists to aim for instant satisfaction (and thus gain immediate popular support), but it can lead others into an obsession with innovation, matched in the art-critics by a celebration of new techniques, media and materials simply because they are new. As Christopher Butler shrewdly observes in his study of the avant-garde, "The art which we recognise as avant-garde may.......lull us into accepting sheer novelty of experience without, immediately at least, raising questions of value. In a consumer society the serious and the trivial alike profit by being new".[59] An infatuation with originality not only makes us immune to anything in the past which might criticise and challenge us; it is also self-defeating. For in artistic creativity, originality without tradition stagnates just as quickly as tradition without originality. Some would argue that the history of the avant-garde itself bears this out. Steiner rightly argues that art can develop only

> "via reflection of and on preceding art, where 'reflection' signifies both a 'mirroring', however drastic the perceptual dislocation, and a 're-thinking'. It is through this internalised 're-production' of and amendment to previous representations that an artist will articulate what might appear to have been even the most spontaneous, the most realistic of his sightings."[60]

Back in 1919, T. S. Eliot explored this theme with singular insight in his essay, "Tradition and the Individual Talent."[61] He notes the tendency of the critic to "insist, when we praise a poet, upon those aspects of his work in which he least resembles anyone else. In these aspects or parts of his work we pretend to find what is individual, what is the peculiar essence of the man."[62] (An interesting parallel is the New Testament critic who will only accept as authentic those teachings of Jesus which can be shown to have no parallel in contemporary or Old Testament literature.) Yet, speaking of the creative writer, Eliot continues, "we shall often find that not only the best, but the most individual parts of his work may be those in which the dead poets, his ancestors, assert their immortality most vigorously."[63] Eliot argues for a strenuous engagement with tradition, for an 'historical sense' in the writer which involves "a perception, not only of the pastness of the past, but of its presence" and which "compels a man to write not merely with his own generation in his bones, but with a feeling that the whole of the literature of Europe from Homer and within it the whole of the literature of his own country has a simultaneous existence and composes a simultaneous order."[64] In Polanyi's terms, to be creative, a writer must indwell his tradition thoroughly. And far from making an artist forgetful of his own particular context, the effect is just the opposite. As Gadamer saw clearly, the artist becomes more keenly aware of his own historical conditionedness, including those prejudices which distort his understanding of the world. Thus Eliot claims that it is a proper 'historical sense' "which makes a writer most acutely conscious of his place in time, of his own contemporaneity."[65] The implications of this for the interpreter of art are equally significant. The interpretation of art is now seen not as an attempt to transcend tradition, but rather as an engagement with tradition; the interpreter does not stand outside his own context but seeks to understand the past in the present; and this encounter with the past is not simply a process whereby we understand the past, but is at the same time a continual process of self-discovery as our own preconceptions are constantly modified and revised.

Fourth, it is clear that the arts will flower best in the context of what Richard Bernstein calls a 'dialogical community', in which conversation, undistorted communication, and communal judgement inform our commerce with the world.[66] For Fuller, good art "can only be realised when a creative individual encounters a living tradition with deep tendrils in communal life."[67] Needless to say, it would be naive in the extreme to imagine that we live in a society which shares one symbolic system reflecting a single comprehensive outlook on reality. Fuller recognises (and laments) that such a living tradition simply does not exist in our culture. More optimistically, Bernstein believes that "shared understandings and experience, intersubjective practices, a sense of affinity, solidarity, and those tacit affective ties that bind individuals together into a community must already exist." We need "to seize upon those experiences and struggles in which there are still the glimmerings of solidarity [so that] the promise of dialogical communities ....can prevail."[68]

Bernstein may well be right. But this is where the Christian artist can and should recall that he is first and foremost a member of another community, one which has access to resources that can only be received (not seized) and which impart to it a genuinely 'dialogical' character. The Church is summoned to be a provisional embodiment within the finite world of a type of human existence that truly mirrors the being-in-relatedness of God, a society in which, to use Fuller's words, we are granted 'the freedom to act socially'. It is little use bemoaning the atrocious failures of the Church if we do not at the same time recognise its high cultural calling, not least in the arena of the arts. To be sure, the Church's contribution to the arts in modern times has been anything but laudable. But why should this blind us to the immense possibilities of the future? And, I would add, if the Church *is* to play a significant part in the renewal of art in the years to come, perhaps this will happen not chiefly through a few highly trained performers — which can so easily plough into a new individualism — but through the emergence of new forms of ecclesial corporate art, in which the unique relationships generated and sustained by the Holy Spirit are allowed to affect the very character of artistic creativity itself.

(8) Beauty and Inspiration Revisited

Before we close the chapter, let us to return to two themes touched upon in Part II — beauty and inspiration. Towards the end of Part II, I concluded for various reasons that it is unhelpful to think of art being qualified by the aspiration towards beauty. We need to add here that it would still seem quite proper to speak of beauty as a *desirable* feature in art. If we adopt a very broad understanding of beauty — as the quality of harm-oniousness, unity-in-multiplicity or suchlike — this would still merit approval in a work of art, in that it reflects the God-given diverse unity of creation. (It would correspond to two of Wolter-storff's marks of aesthetic excellence listed above, namely unity and internal richness.[69]) But we need to go further than this, by re-opening a question posed in Part II: might not the creation and redemption of the world in Christ yield a richer and deeper concept of beauty than many traditional philosophical theories presuppose? Beauty, I mentioned earlier, has all too often been abstracted from time and temporal movement, and turned into a static, timeless quality. Suppose, however, we refuse to divorce it from the transformation of the disorder of creation in the history of Jesus Christ. Suppose we begin there. Does this not open up a more dynamic, and more theological paradigm of beauty? Karl Barth writes: "*God's beauty* embraces death as well as life, fear as well as joy, what we might call the ugly as well as what we might call the beautiful. It reveals itself and wills to be known on the road from one to the other, *in the turning from the self-humiliation of God for the benefit of man to the exaltation of man by God and to God.*"[70] In a not dissimilar way, Hans Urs von Balthasar urges that we see God's creation out of nothing and his saving economy as together the exemplar of true beauty. He asks: "should we not.......consider this art of

God's to be precisely the transcendent archetype of all worldly and human beauty?"[71]   Here some perceptive words of John Dixon are worth pondering very carefully, written in the context of a discussion of art:

> "No Christian who takes his work and his faith seriously can go on acting as though the order of the world is one thing and the act of redemption is an act like all others, of relevance only to the individual who might take note of it."[72]

We are back to one of the cardinal issues raised in our study of the Dutch Calvinists: do we interpret the order of creation purely on its own terms or against the horizon of the divine redemption enacted in Jesus Christ? I am contending here that the most fruitful model of beauty for the artist will be found not by attempting to distil some formal principle from the contingent processes of the created world, but by directing our attention first of all to the redeeming economy of God which culminates in Jesus Christ. This, I submit, would equip us with a concept of beauty much more distinctively Christian than the somewhat pale Platonic notions which are so often offered in theological discussions of art.

Again, the tendency to appeal chiefly to visual models in the philosophy of art has done little to help. Would it not be more frutiful to turn our attention to an art in which motion and the succession of phenomena in time is intrinsic to the apprehension of meaning? Victor Zuckerkandl, in his study entitled *Sound and Symbol*, proposes that music has a unique role to play in our understanding of the physical world, a role which the visual arts are incapable of playing. Early in his book, he remarks that the world

> "in which we usually live, the world of everyday existence......is a world of visible things. Into it we integrate the impressions of the other senses; our speech, our actions, our thinking, are largely formed and oriented upon its pattern......We integrate even the audible into the frame of the visible — with one exception: music.....Music does not integrate itself into the world of the eye."[73]

For Zuckerkandl, the consequence of this is that music gives us a distinctive insight into the nature of spatio-temporal reality. The greatness of music does not, as is so often thought, lie in its capacity to release us from the bounds of materiality. "The moment music become the voice of the 'other' world, musical experiences can no longer challenge our concept of reality".[74] But how does it challenge our concept of reality? Among other things, Zuckerkandl argues that music presents us with an order not abstracted from time but actually inherent *within* time — "the unprecedented spectacle of an order in what is wholly flux".[75] Therefore, "The old prejudice in favour of being, rest, changelessness, which had the whole wieght of our symbols on its side, is discredited: a completely new symbol world opens, in which we discover genuine, immediate symbols of becoming, of motion, of change."[76] In other words, music calls into question the ancient tendency to treat order and beauty as essentially a-temporal, expressible only in that which is enduring, fixed and immutable.[77] This clearly has close links with our own theological reflections on beauty. Whatever we make of the details of his case, if Zuckerkandl's basic contention here is correct, it would imply that a consideration of the ontology of music could usefully occupy a central place in any future theological re-appraisal of the concept of beauty.

From beauty we turn to inspiration. This concept too has had a long history. At the risk of over-simplification, up until the nineteenth century, two complementary ideas prevailed, both rooted in the classical period: first, the idea of alienation — that an inspired artist is transported into ecstasy, he is 'not in his right mind'; and second, the idea that inspiration involves an external power falling upon and working through the artist. The Romantics of the early nineteenth century adopted the first of these, but tended to see the artist not so much as being directed by an outside force as by an unconscious sub-rational spirit upwelling involuntarily from within, the same spirit which is ever active in nature. This bestowed on the artist a priestly and prophetic dignity. He became the Aeolian wind-harp played by nature, in Goethe's words, 'God's annointed'.[78]

How do we assess these notions? To be more specific, what is the connection between the work of the Holy Spirit and artistic creation? At the outset, we would be foolish to deny that the Spirit can be operative and effective in artists who have no Christian allegiance. To claim otherwise would be theologically unsupportable and makes little sense of the history of art. But what more can we say? Tentatively, I would like to suggest that the most helpful tool here is the concept of *responsiveness*.[79] Once again, let us take our bearings from Christ himself. There is a long and distinguished tradition of theology which lays great stress on the action of the Holy Spirit in the renewal of our humanity in Christ, without thereby denying of the incarnation.[80] We could express this in terms of responsiveness. In Christ, the incarnate Son, through the operation of the Spirit, our self-centred humanity has been made responsive — to the

Father, to others and to our created environment. It has been freed — which is to say it has been enabled to relate and respond appropriately to reality. In Christ, our personhood has been reconstituted in its true relatedness. It is the work of the Spirit in us to bring about (albeit provisionally) what he has already accomplished in the Son. In the artist, by extension, the Spirit will make possible that free, purposeful interaction with the Creator, with one another and the world around us that I have been trying to sketch above. He is the Spirit of dynamic interplay, of that mutual giving and receiving which is integral to the artist's work. To be inspired, accordingly, is first and foremost to be responsive. As John Taylor points out in his celebrated book *The Go-Between God*, we commonly speak about the Spirit as the source of power. "But in fact he enables us not by making us supernaturally strong but by opening our eyes. The Holy Spirit is that power which opens eyes that are closed, hearts that are unaware and minds that shrink from too much reality."[81]

On this account, inspiration will not be regarded as a wholly passive affair, as traditional theories often tend to suggest. The artist is not simply a tool in the hands of some irresistible force, nor is he one who effortlessly receives divinely authenticated visions from above and then simply lets them flow out through paint or stone or whatever. (Very few artists speak about what they do in these terms — even though they might wish it happened like this! Mozart may have been an exception, but he is an exception in most respects.) Rather, it is better to speak about the Spirit initiating, enabling and sustaining a process of interaction, spurring the artist into a profound engagement with his subject, artistic medium, fellow artists, society, or whatever. This, we hardly need say, is an immensely costly business, not least because our vision of reality is so clouded and distorted. Even artists who have been most conscious of being 'inspired' know only too well that they cannot escape hard struggle, the sweat of physical and mental exertion. Inspiration does not do away with the need for strenuous, painstaking and often frustrating effort. Quite the contrary, it is in just this kind of toil that the Spirit is probably most active.

In this model, moreover, inspiration will not be seen as inhibiting artistic freedom but actualising it. 'Where the Spirit of the Lord is, there is freedom' (2 Cor. 3:17). I have already spoken about freedom as arising from being appropriately related to a given reality beyond ourselves. This is achieved through the work of the Spirit, the Lord and Giver of Life. The ancient theory of inspiration as a divine 'take over' which pulls us into a super-human ecstasy is thoroughly misleading, for this would mean the end of our freedom. We would become less human, less ourselves. The Spirit is the one who draws alongside us, making us not less human but more human, not less free but more free. His work in us is to open us up to things as they really are, yet without disrupting our nature as limited, finite and contingent creatures. Therein lies our authentic 'ecstasy' (*ek-stasis*), our being-drawn-out-of-ourselves, our outgoingness. Similarly, the Romantic picture of inspiration — the immanent cosmic spirit surging up through the artist — is equally in danger of threatening our freedom. The Holy Spirit is first of all a divine Person, the Other, and his otherness is the very guarantee of our own freedom. We can only be set free by the infinite Other, who is not bound to the finite creation, who is not tied to and conditioned by the disorder which has infected the finite world. Inspiration, I would submit, is best thought of not as being in tune with an immanent cosmic spirit, but as being caught up in a movement originating in an infinite God who has created all things out of nothing and has willed to free his creation from all that enslaves it.

Finally, we need to add that art we choose to call 'inspired' will inevitably possess something of an eschatological quality, a theme we have mentioned a number of times in passing already. In the New Testament, the Holy Spirit is the foretaste of the new age, the age of the resurrection. Art which truly bears the imprint of the Spirit will thus not so much hark back to an imagined paradise, as anticipate within space and time, provisionally but substantially, the final transfiguration of the cosmos.

(9) Summary

In this chapter, I have endeavoured to show that there are resources latent in incarnational trinitarian theology which provide substantial help in developing a philosophy of art which eschews the Enlightenment's alienation of art but which takes the challenges of the Enlightenment seriously. Art, I have argued, is an engagement with the physical world involving our senses as much as our non-physical faculties. Not all art, I have urged, is intended for contemplation; works of art should be seen primarily as instruments and objects of action, and the purposes for which they are produced are many and various. The inherent order of the world is to be discovered, respected and developed, and disorder redeemed. Art is quite able to disclose truth beyond itself and beyond the inner life of the artist, in a manner which is amenable to evaluation. I have suggested that it is a valid, though distinctive, means of cognitive access to the world. I have also found myself questioning the primacy of the artist's subjectivity on which so much philosophy of art has come to depend, urging that the richest sources of artistic creativity are to be found not so much within the interior recesses of the artist's soul, as in his dynamic interaction with the created world, society, fellow artists both past and present, and (for the Christian) fellow believers and the supreme Artist who fashioned all things out of nothing through his Son. Lastly, I pointed very briefly to some ways in which the traditional concepts of beauty and inspiration might usefully be rehabilitated.

Notes

1 *Op. cit.*, p. 69.
2 *Ibid.*, p. 70.
3 The Dadaist Marcel Duchamp once displayed a commercially produced urinal in a museum: what counts here is the *gesture*, not the object with which the gesture is made. In John Cage's piece *4-33* (in which a pianist sits in silence at a piano for four minutes and thirty-three seconds), there is no 'mastering' of sound, only a submission to sounds which happen to arise. For Benedetto Croce (1866-1952), the external artefact serves only to facilitate the sharing of an idea in the artist's mind. The real work goes on in the mind of the artist.
4 *Ibid.*, p. 91.
5 *Nature and Grace in Art*, Chapel Hill: University of North Carolina Press, 1964.
6 *Ibid.*, p. 45.
7 *Poetics of Music in the Form of Six Lessons*, trans. Arthur Knodel and Ingolf Dahl, Cambridge, Massachusetts: Harvard University Press, 1947, p. 51.
8 On this, cf. Gunton, *Enlightenment and Alienation*, p. 33ff.
9 See above, pp. 70f.
10 *Op. cit.*, p. 5.
11 *Op. cit.*, p. 78.
12 Cf. Fuller, *Theoria: Art, and the Absence of Grace*, London: Chatto and Windus, 1988, pp. 211ff.
13 *Resurrection and Moral Order*, Leicester: IVP; Grand Rapids, Michigan: Eerdmans, 1986, pp. 25f.
14 *Biographia Literaria*, II, Princeton: Princeton University Press, 1983, p. 7.
15 *Op. cit*, p. 195.
16 *The Mind of the Maker*, London: Methuen, 1941, p. 53.
17 Quoted in Richard Ellmann and Charles Feidelson, eds., *The Modern*

Tradition, New York: Oxford University Press, 1965, p. 209.

18 *Op. cit.*, p. 92.

19 *The Unanswered Question. Six Talks at Harvard*, Cambridge, Massachusetts and London: Harvard University Press, 1976, pp. 422ff.

20 *The Language of Music*, London, New York and Toronto: Oxford University Press, 1959.

21 C. E. Osgood, "Cross-Cultural Generality of Visual-Verbal Synesthetic Tendencies," in *Semantic Differential Technique*, ed. J. G. Snider and C. E. Osgood, Chicago: Aldine, 1969, pp. 561-584.

22 p. 225.

23 *Ibid.*, 234.

24 *Ibid.*, 188ff.

25 *Op. cit.*, pp. 64f.

26 *Loc. cit.*, pp. 11, 12.

27 David Baily Harned, *Theology and the Arts*, Philadelphia: Westminster Press, 1966, p. 127.

28 *Mystery and Manners: Occasional Prose*, ed. S. and R. Fitzgerald, London: Faber and Faber, 1972, p. 176.

29 As quoted in William Edgar, *Taking Note of Music*, London: SPCK, 1986, p. 18.

30 Cf. Ruth Etchells, *Unafraid to Be*, London: IVP, 1969; Hans R. Rookmaaker, *Modern Art and the Death of a Culture*, London: IVP, 1970; John Wilson, *One of the Richest Gifts*, Edinburgh: Handsel Press, 1981, pp. 25-40; Hans Küng, *Art and the Question of Meaning*, London: SCM, 1980, *passim*.

31 *Op. cit.*, p. 20. Cp. Roger Hazelton, *A Theological Approach to Art*, Nashville and New York: Abingdon Press, 1967, p. 29.

32 Trans. Anthony Bower, Harmondsworth: Penguin Books, 1971, p. 219.

33 A particularly interesting example of this 'transformative' art, though from a non-Christian setting, is the Australian landscape painting of Lloyd Rees, Sidney Nolan, Arthur Boyd and others. These painters had to come to terms with an environment which was largely bleak and hostile, a desolate wilderness. And yet, as Peter Fuller observes, they managed to forge *out of this very ugliness* an impressive beauty. *Theoria*, pp. 218ff.

34 *Triumphs of the Imagination*, Downers Grove, Illinois: IVP, 1979, p. 244.

35 James Joyce may claim to be a 'realistic' novelist, but "his method is simply a way of controlling, of ordering, of giving a shape and a significance to the immense panorama of futility and anarchy which is contemporary history." Colin Wilson, *The Strength to Dream: Literature and the Imagination*, London: Abacus, 1976, p. 14.

36 *Op. cit.*, p. 73. My italics. Cf. T. R. Wright's excellent discussion of 'realism' in literature in *Theology and Literature*, Oxford: Blackwell, 1988, pp. 110-128.

37 *Op. cit.*, p. 51.

38 R. Guardini, as quoted and translated by Hans Küng, *ibid.*, pp. 51f.

39 Robin Skelton, *Poetic Truth*, London: Heinemann, 1978, p. 127.

40 *Op. cit.*, p. 32.

41 Those who want to argue that Christian doctrine is essentially a self-referring system will do little to advance their case by hasty appeals to the arts. Quite apart from the attendant theological hazards, this does little justice to the potential referentiality of art. T. R. Wright, the literary critic, remarks: "Recent 'post liberal' theories fed by developments in anthropology and linguistics have tried to [see] doctrines as 'merely' language, self-contained systems by which the Christian community constitutes its world. They appeal to literature as another example of a self-enclosed semiotic system. But to deny all referential function to these systems is........an extremely dangerous move to make." *Ibid.*, p. 22.

42 *After the New Criticism*, Chicago: University of Chicago Press, 1980, p. 41.

43 *Loc. cit.*, p. 13.

44 *Op. cit.*, pp. 156ff.

45 *Ibid.*, pp. 163ff. Cp. Gotshalk's 'harmony', 'balance', 'rhythm', and 'development'. D. W. Gotshalk, *Art and the Social Order*, New York: Dover, 1962, pp. 108-114.

46 *Op. cit.*, p. 144

47 *Op. cit.*, pp. 88f.

48 *Ibid.*, p. 89.

49 "God and Our Books," in Tim Dean and David Porter, eds., *Art in Question*, Basingstoke: Marshall Morgan and Scott, 1987, p. 67. For a fuller attempt to describe Christian literary criticism, cf. Leland Ryken, *Triumphs of the Imagination*, Downers Grove, Illinois: IVP, 1979, ch. 5.

50 *The Self as Agent*, London: Faber and Faber, 1969, p. 71.

51 *Op. cit.*, p. 137.

52 *Ibid.*, p. 138.

53 Quoted in E. Robinson, *The Language of Mystery*, London: SCM, 1987, p. 36.

54 *Op. cit.*, p. 92.

55 *Op. cit.*, p. 224.

56 Albert Camus, *The Myth of Sisyphus*, Harmondsworth: Penguin Books, 1975, pp.191f.

57 *Screwtape Proposes a Toast and Other Pieces*, London: Fontana, 1965, pp. 118f.

58 Quoted by Richard Kostelanetz, *John Cage*, Harmondsworth: Penguin Books, 1974, p. 11.

59 *After the Wake: An Essay on the Contemporary Avant-Garde*, Oxford: Oxford University Press, 1980, pp. 125f.

60 *Op. cit.*, p. 17.

61 In *Selected Essays*, London: Faber & Faber, 1932, pp. 13-22.

62 *Ibid.*, p. 14.

63 *Ibid.*

64 *Ibid.*

65 *Ibid.*

66 *Op. cit.*, pp. 223ff.

67 *Aesthetics After Modernism*, pp. 36f.

68 *Ibid.*, pp. 226, 228.

[69] See above, p. 218.

[70] *Op. cit.*, p. 665. My italics.

[71] *The Glory of the Lord. A Theological Aesthetics.* I, *Seeing the Form*, trans. E. Leiva-Merikakis, ed. Joseph Fessio and John Riches, Edinburgh: T. &. T. Clark, 1982, p. 70.

[72] *Op cit.*, p. 78.

[73] *Sound and Symbol*, London: Routledge & Kegan Paul, 1956, pp. 3f.

[74] *Ibid.*, pp. 363f.

[75] *Ibid.*, p. 241.

[76] *Ibid.*, p. 262.

[77] *Ibid.*, pp. 241f. Cf. Colin Gunton's lucid discussion of the theological implications of Zuckerkandl's ontology of music in *Yesterday and Today: A Study of Continuities in Christology*, London: Darton, Longman and Todd, 1983, pp. 119ff.

[78] *Goethe's Literary Essays*, ed. J. E. Spingarn, New York: Harcourt, Brace & Co., 1921, p. 12. In the later stages of the Romantic movement, the artist becomes a more Promethean figure, the rival of nature and God rather than their servant.

[79] Here I am indebted to Tom Smail's discussion in *The Giving Gift*, London, Sydney, Auckland, Toronto: Hodder & Stoughton, 1988, pp. 170ff.

[80] On this, cf. T. F. Torrance, *Theology in Reconstruction*, London: SCM, 1965, chs. 13 and 14; Tom Smail, *Reflected Glory*, London: Hodder & Stoughton, 1975; Alan Spence, "Inspiration and Incarnation: John Owen and the Coherence of Christology," *King's Theological Review*, XII (1989), pp. 52-55.

[81] London: SCM, 1972, p. 19

5. Art and Metaphor

"The poet.....brings the whole soul of man into activity......He diffuses a tone, and spirit of unity, that blends and (as it were) *fuses*, each into each, by that synthetic and magical power, to which we have exclusively appropriated the name imagination. This power........reveals itself in the balance or reconciliation of opposite or discordant qualities".

S. T. Coleridge

It could well be objected that our discussion so far, in this part of the book at any rate, has assumed that there is widespread agreement about the meaning of the word 'art', that we are dealing with a concept with clear and widely accepted semantic boundaries. Needless to say, the matter is far more complex. Contemporary philosophers are on the whole not inclined to attempt a definition of art.[1] Theologians are no less wary,[2] and frequently raise more problems than they solve. Any very tight definition of art is probably bound to falter, for almost inevitably we exclude instances of what we normally describe as works of art. But we need, I think, some idea of why we would choose to refer to a particular object as a work of art. While acknowledging the myriad of difficulties which crowd in at this point, I would like to offer an understanding of the concept of art which I hope is in large measure faithful to the way the word 'art' is employed (where such a word exists). First, it makes good sense to describe a work of art as a human artefact — i.e. it must have been produced by a human being. Second, I would propose that art is distinguishable from other forms of communication in that it functions metaphorically. The first point is, I hope, virtually self-evident. If we do speak of creation as the 'art' of God, we do so recognising that this is an extension of the normal use of the word. Some have claimed that a piece of driftwood can be called a 'sculpture'. But it is unlikely that we would do this unless it had in some way been set apart, used and regarded as such, and this is to introduce a human formative element — it is to 'make something' of it. The second point — that art's distinctive mode of functioning is metaphorical — is a tentative hypothesis which I shall seek to expand in the rest of this chapter. Space allows only the skeleton of an argument. But at the very least I hope to show that the notion has much to commend it. There is a close parallel between nearly every major philosophy of art and the principal theories of metaphor; many of the hotly contested issues in art-philosophy are clarified when viewed as debates about the shape and function of metaphor; to see art as operating metaphorically helps us understand how art can claim cognitive content; and, most importantly, there are signs that this approach could be highly fruitful when exploring the theological dimensions of art.

(1) Polanyi and Metaphor

The subject of metaphor has received an enormous amount of attention in recent years, not least in discussions of religious language. The flood of literature shows no signs of abating. Few contributions to the subject, however, are so lucid as Janet Martin Soskice's work *Metaphor and Religious Language*,[3] and it is to her that we turn for our definition of metaphor. A metaphor, she says, is that figure of speech whereby we speak about one thing in terms which are seen to be suggestive of another.[4] Soskice deals deftly with metaphor in philosophy, science and theology, but she confines her treatment to linguistic usage. To help us extend her observations into the field of the arts, we can turn again to Polanyi, whose few reflections on art are both provocative and persuasive.[5]

We recall Polanyi's distinction between subsidiary and focal awareness. When hammering a nail into a block of wood, I am focally aware of driving in the nail but only subsidiarily aware of the feelings in my hand and palm as I hold the nail. I rely on the feelings in my hand in order to perform the task, but I am not aware of them focally. All knowing, Polanyi contends, proceeds according to this pattern. When something is known, subsidiary elements are integrated to a focal target. The relation between the subsidiaries and the focal target Polanyi calls a 'from-to' relation. We know the subsidiaries only insofar as they direct our attention away *from* them *to* the focal target. This relationship is irreversible. This is where it differs from the process of deduction. Deduction connects two focal items and we can move back and forward logically between premise and conclusion. Integration makes subsidiaries *bear on* a focus. We rely on the subsidiaries and attend to the focal target. To be aware of something subsidiarily is not to be aware of it in itself but only as a clue or instrument pointing beyond itself. If we focus our attention on the subsidiaries (e.g. if we attend to the

printed words of a book rather than what they communicate)
then the semantic relationship breaks down.[6] Consequently,
the subsidiaries are by their very nature never fully specifiable.
It is not simply that we can never trace and enumerate all the
relevant factors in our knowledge of an object, it is that the
attempt to do so would deprive them of their meaning. To pick
up a Polanyian catch-phrase, 'we know more than we can tell.'
We can only 'live in' or 'indwell' the subsidiaries; we cannot
exhaustively specify them.[7] Further, it should be clear from
this that only a *person* can achieve and sustain a meaningful
integration: a machine cannot attend to a focal target by means
of subsidiary awareness. The from-to relation "lasts only so
long as a person, the knower, sustains the integration."[8] Human
knowing therefore involves three elements: subsidiary
particulars, the focal target, and the knower who links the
subsidiaries to the focal target.

On this basis, Polanyi goes on to distinguish three types of
integration: indication, symbol, and metaphor. First, there is
indication. When we use a word to designate something, the
word 'bears on' its object. We are subsidiarily aware of the
word and focally aware of that to which it refers. Further, the
word is not of any intrinsic interest to us, but the focal object is
of intrinsic interest.

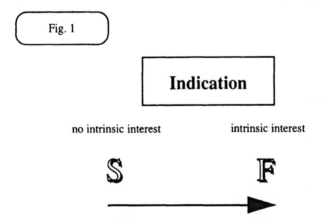

This is a 'self-centred' integration: made *from* the self as centre
to the object of integration. This Polanyi calls *indication*.
Second, there is *symbol*. Here, the subsidiary clues do not
function merely as indicators directing us to something else.

Instead, they are of intrinsic interest. When, for example, we see the Union Jack, very often our own memories, sense of pride in our country, and so on, become embodied in that piece of cloth. The subsidiary clues are more important than the focal object — the flag. That *to* which we attend — the flag itself — is of little or no intrinsic interest. Furthermore, as we look at the flag, we are picked up by the symbol, we become involved, we participate in it, we surrender ourselves to it — it 'carries us away'. The flag gathers together our inchoate experiences so that they are *embodied* in the flag.[9]

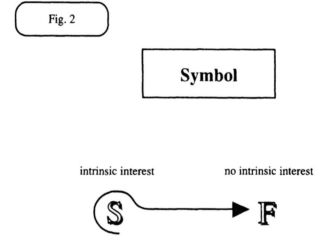

Indication and symbolisation are thus inverse to each other with respect to the location of intrinsic interest. Moreover, whilst indication is 'self-centred' — it moves away from the self as centre — symbolisation is self-*giving*. That is,

> "the symbol, as an object of our focal awareness, is not merely established by an integration of subsidiary clues directed *from* the self to a focal object; it is also established by surrendering the diffuse memories and experiences of the self *into* this object, thus giving them a visible embodiment."[10]

Third, there is *metaphor*. The same basic process is at work in both symbol and metaphor. But there is an important difference. Polanyi employs the distinction between the 'tenor' and 'vehicle' of a metaphor — in the metaphor 'Juliet is the sun', the tenor is 'Juliet' and the vehicle 'the sun'. In a metaphor, *both* 'tenor' and 'vehicle' of a metaphor are of intrinsic interest, both are interesting and significant in themselves. The intelligibility of the metaphor 'Juliet is the sun' depends on us regarding both Juliet and the sun as intrinsically significant.

But another level of explanation needs to be added. We enjoy the metaphor through our imaginative capacity to integrate two disparate elements into a single novel meaning. If we allow ourselves to become focally aware of the subsidiaries, the metaphor is in danger of collapsing, and its power lost. If however we enjoy the metaphor as a fusion of unlike elements, we are 'carried away' by it, it takes us into its life. The subsidiaries — the inchoate experiences of our own lives which are related to the two parts of the metaphor — are brought together and related to each other in novel ways, and it is this which gives a metaphor its force. We are embodied in the metaphor; we surrender ourselves to it.[11]

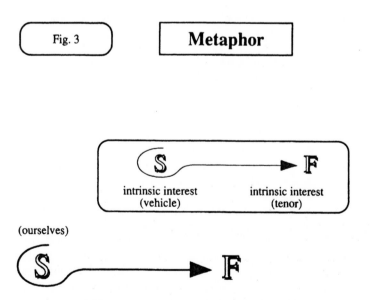

Fig. 3

Metaphor

intrinsic interest
(vehicle)

intrinsic interest
(tenor)

(ourselves)

Some comments are needed at this stage by way of clarification and qualification. Firstly, Polanyi's understanding of metaphor is an example of what is sometimes termed an 'interactive' theory.[12] Meaning is conveyed through the interaction of tenor and vehicle, and between the associations which tenor and vehicle call to mind (what Max Black calls 'associated commonplaces'). For Polanyi, the impact of a metaphor results from the interplay between tenor and vehicle as they draw on the subsidiaries of our diverse experience.[13]

Secondly, Polanyi effectively endorses a claim made with increasing force by a number of recent writers: that a metaphor is intrinsically irreducible, that it cannot be paraphrased in literal statement without loss of content. The meaning of a metaphor is grasped only through an imaginative integration of tenor and vehicle. To try to explain a metaphor by 'flattening it out' into prose would be to turn metaphor into indication, and thus dispossess it of its power. What it says cannot be said in any other way without at least some deprivation of meaning. This is so even of the simplest metaphor: 'he is a tiger' must communicate more than 'he is ferocious', otherwise 'tiger' would be synonymous with 'ferocious'. A metaphor seems to add something to our understanding which cannot be wholly accounted for in literal terms. Hence, the phrase 'merely a metaphor' is unhelpful, for it suggests that a metaphor is no more than a rhetorical technique to be discarded at will, "a sort of happy trick with words.............a grace or ornament or *added* power of language, not its constitutive form."[14] As Soskice observes, "The interesting thing about metaphor, or at least about some metaphors, is that they are used not to redescribe but to disclose for the first time. The metaphor has to be used because something new is being talked about."[15] On the other hand, to claim that a metaphor is irreducible is not thereby to say that it cannot be elaborated, clarified, and its content assessed. If a metaphor resisted all attempts to elucidate and evaluate its content — either by means of further metaphors, or by means of literal speech — we would be forced to conclude that it lacked significance.

Thirdly, for Polanyi it is clear that metaphors are quite capable of being vehicles of cognitive content, means by which we gain epistemic access to the world. His views are confirmed by much contemporary work on metaphor, not least in the natural sciences, where it has been shown that metaphors are indispensable not only to scientific enquiry but also to the expression of scientific truth. In Richard Boyd's words, metaphor is one of many devices "to accomplish the task of the accommodation of language to the causal structure of the world".[16] The implication is that by introducing a metaphor we shall often find that the way in which we are already using language is significantly altered; a metaphor can reflect back upon, and modify, the area of discourse from which it takes its terms. Thus, for instance, to describe God as 'personal' is to use a metaphor to speak of the triune God, but it is also to have our ordinary use of the word 'person' and all that is associated with it filled with fresh content in the light of the communion of the Trinity. In this way, metaphor can become a means through which our language is rendered more faithful to reality.

Fourthly, Polanyi would have little time for the 'emotivist' theory of metaphor, which holds that metaphors can have no genuine cognitive content but by losing cognitive import they gain emotional import. It is in fact very hard to give a non-cognitive account of this 'emotional import', for what is it if not a response to some cognitive aspects of the world? At root, the problem here is the assumption that the more something affects us emotionally, the more it loses its power to tell the truth. Polanyi's whole approach to human knowing undermines this sharp bifurcation between emotional participation and the grasp of truth. And so, although he makes no attempt to downplay the emotional potential of metaphor, he never claims that metaphors are incapable of doing any more than conveying emotion. Because a metaphor provokes intense emotional involvement, it is not thereby excluded from the halls of truth.

Fifthly, a further advantage of Polanyi is that he avoids construing a metaphor as possessing both a literal meaning and a metaphorical meaning. Some have argued that the power of a metaphor arises out of an interaction between these two putative meanings.[17] But such a view rests on a confusion between what a speaker says and what he intends through his utterance. In most utterances, metaphors included, a speaker has *one* intended meaning, which can be grasped in the context of utterance. Polanyi has seen that we are focally aware of one meaning even if there is more than one network of subsidiaries. There may of course be a dual (or multiple) *construal* of a metaphor, but this is usually seen as a failing of the metaphor, not a normative feature of it.

Sixthly, implicit in the Polanyian account is the important truth that metaphors cannot be isolated from their personal context — the speaker's or writer's intention, shared beliefs, assumptions etc.[18] A metaphor is not simply a calculus of word meanings; it gains its force within a life-setting appropriate to it. A metaphor is only a metaphor because someone, a speaker or hearer (ideally both) regards it as such. Otherwise, we could never distinguish metaphor from nonsense. For Polanyi, meaning is a function not so much of words and sentences but of the person or persons who utter them and of those who receive them.

Seventh, we need to add a minor qualification to Polanyi. Granted that a metaphor comprises two basic elements, tenor and vehicle, it may well have more than one vehicle. Black's 'associated commonplaces' need not be limited to two in number: a metaphor may draw on two *or more* sets of subsidiaries. Polanyi's account leaves open this possibility without speaking explicitly of it.

(2) Polanyi and Works of Art

In normal usage, of course, the word 'metaphor' applies to a figure of speech. But Polanyi believes that we can apply the concept beyond the sphere of language to art. Limiting himself to what he calls the 'representative' arts,[19] he develops his argument by employing I. A. Richards' terms, 'frame' and 'story'. The frame of an art work consists of those outward features of it which enable us to recognise it as a work of art. In the case of a poem, its frame comprises its rhythm, expressive sounds, grammatical constructions, etc. It is because of these subsidiary elements that we can distinguish it from prose. They set the poem apart from everyday life: we do not, after all, normally speak in poetic verse. Similarly, in a play there are subsidiary signs which tell us that we are witnessing a play and not a real-life drama, clues which detach it from the ordinary world of daily affairs — a darkened theatre, a stage, the way in which transitions in space and time are elided, and so on.[20] So when a murder is acted on stage we do not normally leap out of our seat to rescue the victim. By the same token, the frame of a work of art also has the effect of giving the work of art a measure of independence from its creator. We do not have to share in the personal feelings, memories etc. of the artist to enjoy a poem.[21] Knowledge of Rembrandt's personal circumstances may enrich our enjoyment of his self-portraits, but such knowledge is not required to initiate that pleasure in the first place.

In addition to the frame, there is another major subsidiary to take into account — broadly speaking, its representative element, what Polanyi calls its 'prose' content, or 'story'.[22] This story is logically incompatible with the frame: there is something unnatural and contradictory about frame and story being

brought together. Yet our imagination fuses these two elements
(of which we are subsidiarily aware) so that we can enjoy the
meaning of the art work, in just the same way as we fuse tenor
and vehicle in a metaphor. This relationship between frame
and story, Polanyi continues, is not one of 'bearing on' or
symbolisation, but one of embodiment. The frame and the
story embody each other, they speak in one voice as the
subsidiaries of the poem's meaning. Moreover, the work of art
draws from the great store of the diffuse inchoate experience of
our ordinary life, so that our existence (the cluster of subsidiaries
which relate to the work of art) is embodied in the work of art.
We surrender ourselves to it, just as we surrender ourselves to
a metaphor.[23] This clearly corresponds to Gadamer's thesis
that we are drawn into a work of art in the same way that we
are drawn into a game.

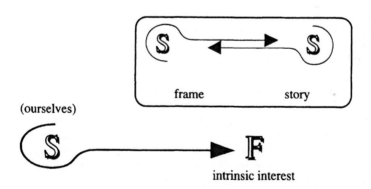

And, we might add, if the work of art actually contains many
metaphors within itself (for example, in a play of Shakespeare)
the experience will be all the richer, for the imagination will be
compelled to make integrations at more than one level.

This might have some cogency for poetry and drama, but what about other forms of representative art? With regard to painting, Polanyi develops an intriguing extension of his theory, building on the work of M. H. Pirenne.[24] When we look at a painting, we have a subsidiary awareness of the flat, two-dimensional canvas.[25] If we look at an ordinary perspectival picture from an angle, we do not see it as distorted because of our subsidiary awareness of the flat canvas. But we are also subsidiarily aware of the representative aspect of the painting; it represents (to varying degrees) realities we ordinarily encounter in daily life. The important thing to note about the flatness of the canvas with brush strokes on it and the three-dimensional depth represented is that they are logically contradictory. Yet when we look at the painting, these two elements are imaginatively fused so that we experience the meaning of the whole.[26] Polanyi compares his view with some observations of Ernst Gombrich. If we move very close to a painting and examine it only inches from the canvas, we see only a meaningless array of brush strokes and paint blobs. As we back off, there comes a point when we discern it as a painting. According to Gombrich, we can see *either* the canvas plus blobs of paint *or* a painting, but not both at the same time: "We cannot have it both ways".[27] But, as Polanyi observes, this is only true if we mean that we cannot have a focal awareness of both simultaneously. It is more accurate to say that when we view and enjoy the painting from a distance, we have a subsidiary awareness of the brush strokes on a flat canvas, a subsidiary awareness of that which is represented, and these subsidiary elements are unified by the imagination in order that we can apprehend their joint meaning. In a real sense, then, we can and do have it both ways.[28]

A refinement to Polanyi's discussion needs to be injected at this point to clear up a possible confusion. There is an important distinction between, on the one hand, the internal structure of a work of art — its 'line', 'harmony', 'balance' etc., and on the other, its 'frame' in Polanyi's sense — those outward factors which enable us to identify it as a work of art. In the case of a painting, its frame comprises its flat two-dimensional canvas, the brush strokes, the wooden frame in which it is set, the gallery in which it is hung, etc. Its form would be what artists often call its 'composition'. Of course, the internal structure of a work of art may also possess an artificiality, and might therefore contribute to our recognition of it as an art work. This would be the case in many poems. Nonetheless, the basic point still holds — that form and frame should not be confused.

Polanyi confines himself largely to the representative arts. But how would his ideas pertain to non-representative art? We can perhaps focus the matter best by considering what is usually thought to be the most abstract of the arts, namely music.[29] We can begin with Leonard Bernstein's courageous attempt to elaborate a philosophy of music through a comparison with poetry, employing Noam Chomsky's theory of transformational grammar.[30] Bernstein argues that music achieves its effect by means of a multitude of metaphors, each involving the merging together of mutually contradictory elements, whether harmonic, melodic or rhythmic. Meaning in music is "generated by a stream of metaphors".[31] He supports his case with a vast array of illustrations. Among the structural metaphors he mentions are antithesis (juxtaposition of contrasting phrases), alliteration (repetition of notes or groups of notes in successive phrases, yet sufficiently modified to produce a violation of expectation), and chiasmus (phrases set against each other in the form ABBA). These are all 'metaphorical' devices involving the conjunction of disparate elements. Moreover, music, says Bernstein, is *essentially* metaphorical. There is no such thing as a 'prose' version of music: "music already exists in the poetic sense." It is a "totally *metaphorical* language."[32]

Bernstein's account of linguistic metaphor never achieves great sophistication, but his theory of the way meaning is created in music through metaphor is formidable and to a large extent convincing. However, even if we accept this account of the *internal* structure of music as metaphorical, how might we interpret 'frame' and 'story' in music, and wherein lies their their incompatibility? It is not hard to identify the subsidiary components with constitute the 'frame' of a piece of music: it is written as a score, performed over a specific period of time, played by musicians, perhaps on a stage, and so forth. But what can we say about its 'representational' aspect? There is a type of music — 'programme' music — which is designed to 'tell a story', to convey or reflect some kind of narrative. And there are songs, settings of words with references of varying degree of specificity. But what of music which has no words or programme attached? What could 'reference' possibly mean here?

The commonest drawback of theories of musical reference is that they are too narrow in scope. The best-known relate musical meaning to the emotional life. It has been claimed that music 'expresses' emotions or emotional states (even though these emotions may not have been what the composer felt at the time of composing), and it evokes corresponding emotion in the hearer. Music's 'story' is the content of our emotional life. It is essentially this view which underlies Deryck Cooke's famous book *The Language of Music*. Cooke seeks to demonstrate that a musical lexicon can be devised which assigns emotive meaning to basic terms of musical vocabulary. In Western music since 1400, he points to numerous correlations between emotions and particular patterns of melodies, rhythms and harmonies which have been used to convey these emotions. Such evidence, Cooke believes, suggests that music is a means of communicating moods and feelings.[33] The wealth of material Cooke amasses to support his theory is impressive. However, the thesis which he builds from the evidence is open to three decisive objections. First, he sees a piece of music as being related in a certain way to an experience which can be fully characterised without reference to the music itself. He tends to regard music purely as a tool, the function of which is to arouse in the listener the experience the composer wishes him to feel. Second, as I have already indicated, and as the music theorist Eduard Hanslick stressed long ago, emotion is essentially relational — emotions require objects. Fear is fear of something or someone, anger is anger directed against something or someone, and so on.[34] It is hard to understand quite how a piece of music can convey an emotion or emotions. Third, Cooke leaves little room for cultural conditioning, for differences in reaction to music between different ethnic groups. Ethnomusicologists have been only too keen to point out the flaws in Cooke's approach.[35]

Leaving aside the first and third objections, aestheticians like Susanne Langer have sought to meet the second by modifying Cooke's line. Langer wants to speak of an analogy of dynamic structure between emotion and music, and argues that music conveys not the content of specific feelings but the *form* of feelings.[36] For her, music is an example of 'presentational' symbolism. A presentational symbol does not symbolise by means of fixed units of meaning as in the case of language or discursive symbolism. The elements of a presentational symbol are understood only through the meaning of the whole symbol as its elements interrelate with each other. A presentational symbol is a dynamic instrument of discovery and clarification rather than a purveyor of static references; it does not so much assert as articulate.[37] A piece of music, Langer believes, is a non-linguistic presentational symbol. It symbolises human feelings, not by ostensive denotation, but through possessing the same temporal structure as some segment or segments of emotional life. The dynamic structure of a musical work and the form in which emotions are experienced can resemble each other in their patterns of motion and rest, tension and release, fulfilment, excitation, sudden change, etc. Music, and indeed all art, "is the creation of forms symbolic of human feeling."[38]

Langer rightly exposes the bankruptcy of a crude understanding of emotional representation and expression in music, and her theory is in many respects illuminating. But why should we limit the dynamic properties which music can reflect to the emotions? Might not music reflect the morphology of many other occurrences (which may or may not be linked with the emotions) — for example, physiological processes, the movements of natural phenomena. As Malcolm Budd rightly argues:

> "The ways in which emotions and feelings can develop have nothing distinctive about them that is not shared with the modes of development of the rising and setting of the sun, the mounting of a storm, the explosion of a volcano and countless other natural and artificial processes. Hence, even if musical works have structures congruent with the forms in which feelings can be realised these forms are not specific to feelings (and works of art)."[39]

A similar comment comes from Victor Zuckerkandl:

> "[Music] can be called the myth of the inner life, but not the myth of a soul or of the psyche in a broader sense; or if it is the myth of the soul, it is the myth of the world soul, the myth of the world's inner life".[40]

Perhaps then it is best to see Langer's theory as not so much as incorrect but too restrictive because she locates the significance of music in the inward life of the composer or listener. Would it not be more plausible to suggest that the 'story' or representational aspect of music is the temporal morphology of creation as we encounter it, that is, the structure of processes which we experience in time — both within and beyond ourselves. Indeed, music, as Gunton suggests, "is that which perhaps most expresses the life in movement of the creation, while other art forms are more directly linked to human feeling."[41] Such a supposition would need to be elaborated and defended with a greater thoroughness than is possible here. However, this widening of musical representation is in keeping with the theology of creation we have been advancing, which stresses the continuity between humankind and non-human creation. It is also consonant with the findings of psychologists concerning the connection between physical bodily processes and our response to music.[42]

If our broad conjecture is correct, then we can see how the 'story' in a piece of music is logically incompatible with its 'frame' in the way that Polanyi argues for the representative arts. A piece of music is clearly 'set apart' in performance: it has an artificiality which is incongruent with the givenness of the movements of creation. The paradox of music is that it is 'organised time', an artificially created order which is nevertheless recognisably related to the dynamics of the created world. When we listen to a piece of music, we are subsidiarily aware of these logically incommensurable elements, yet they are fused and integrated by our imagination in such a way that we come to appreciate the music as 'meaningful'. Taking this a step further, if we make the frame or the story an object of focal attention, we will destroy the possibility of apprehending the meaning. To concentrate on, for example, the sweat on the pianist's brow, the conductor's gesticulations, will hardly contribute to musical appreciation; nor will an exclusive preoccupation with a sonata's formal structure. Similarly, to attempt a focal awareness of music's 'story' is equally unhelpful. Very often because a person is moved by a piece of music, he or she will return to it frequently in order to recover that emotional state or feeling. The attempt is nearly always unsuccessful; the original emotions rarely return. The emotional pattern (part of its 'story') has wrongly been made the object of focal awareness. We have ceased to be carried into the work of art as a whole. From this perspective we can now appreciate better the key weakness of Deryck Cooke's thesis. As Budd puts it, "[Cooke's theory] implies that there is an experience which a musical work produces in the listener but which in principle he could undergo even if he were unfamiliar with the work".[43] We need to resist this "heresy of the separable experience".[44] Music yields an experience which cannot be detached from the experience of listening to the music. This, of course, is just what Polanyi is saying; an art work must be enjoyed as a unity of frame and story.

We can mention two further examples of non-representational art. In the case of architecture, the 'story' is again perhaps best described as the morphology of creation, but, unlike music, without any necessary link to time. Perhaps we can be no more specific than Geoffrey Scott when he says that in our experience of architecture,

> "[there is] a felt relation between ponderable things, an adjust-
> ment to one another of evident forces, a grouping of material
> bodies subject *like ourselves* to certain elementary laws.
> Weight and resistance, burden and effort, weakness and
> power, are elements in our own experience, and inseparable
> in that experience from feelings of ease, exultation, or
> distress."[45]

At any rate, it is clear that there is a logical discrepancy between this representative aspect or 'story' of architecture and the fact that the building is clearly an artificial, human creation, and, to a certain extent, is 'set apart' for our enjoyment. It is our ability to fuse these incompatible components which enables us to appreciate a piece of architecture as a work of art. As far as abstract painting is concerned, it is even harder to gain a purchase on what the 'story' might be. But clearly, even here such a painting can evoke or draw on something we have perceived or known or felt. In *Personal Knowledge*, Polanyi makes a comparison between the apprehension of order by the scientist and by a person enjoying an abstract painting.[46] In the context of this discussion, he says of such a painting that however abstract, "it will echo some experience, and would be as meaningless to someone lacking any such experience, as arithmetic would be to a person living in a gaseous universe."[47] Such abstract forms, whatever their precise relationship to the experience of forms in creation, logically conflict with the fact that the painting is set in a frame, exhibited, hung on a wall, and so on. Once again there is an imaginative combination of these contradictory factors which enables us to apprehend the meaning of the painting.

We have wandered far from theology. In a very sketchy way, my purpose has been to show that to interpret art essentially as extended metaphor has at least a fair measure of plausibility, that it is worthy of further exploration. Admittedly, there are a number of perplexities in Polanyi's account, many loose ends and some apparent inconsistencies. But his central thrust — that art (and metaphor) involve the imaginative fusion of incompatible subsidiaries toward a focal target — has much to commend it, not least because it presupposes a theory of knowledge which is not beset with the more problematic features of the legacy of the Enlightenment.

(3) Metaphor and a Christian Theology of Art

It should be clear by now that I am seeking to propose a cognitive understanding of art — that is, one which sees art as capable of affording genuine knowledge of reality beyond the confines of human self-consciousness, and therefore as in principle open to clarification, elucidation and assessment. Polanyi's work, I believe, is especially useful in this respect, for he resists the temptation to divide experience into the absolutely certain (and therefore knowable) on one side and the dubious or 'not really true' (and unknowable) on the other. A work of art can be faithful or unfaithful to what lies beyond itself. It may not deal in the currency of direct, literal statement, but, like a metaphor, through its conjunction of contradictory subsidiary experience, it is able to depict reality beyond itself and beyond the self-awareness of the artist. Alongside this, however, we need to remember that it is not so much an art work which depicts reality, but an art work as employed and used by a person or group of persons. In the case of metaphor, "It is the fact that it is not strictly words which refer but speakers using words, which makes metaphor possible, and enables us to speak about one things in terms which are seen to be suggestive of another."[48] Likewise, we are bound to say that it is not strictly works of art which refer but people (or groups of people) who refer when they create, use and enjoy works of art in various contexts. This lends weight to our repeated stress on the dialogical nature of art.

Now we need to indicate at least some of the theological ramifications of this metaphor-centred, cognitive view of art.

The Irreducibility of Art

A Christian painter recently wrote that "once the pressure is there to make a painting 'message-orientated' there is a strong tendency to undervalue or ignore the reality of a painting as a painting."[49] It is all too easy to castigate totalitarian regimes for their repressive attitudes to the arts, and forget that some Christians have scored no better by insisting that beyond the confines of the liturgy, only a kind of artistic evangelical propaganda could ever qualify for divine approval. And in worship, especially in the Protestant West, the representative arts are frequently seen as a kind of ornament, a decorative substitute for what can be plainly stated, a colourful wrapping to attract people's attention, dispensable when the 'real' truth appears elsewhere in the service (usually in the sermon).

Such a view implies that works of art are essentially dressed-up statements, no more than thinly disguised or second-rate assertions.[50] But, even in the case of works with a strong representative element, we simply cannot reduce art to literal statement without simultaneously robbing it of content. Art seems capable of generating meanings which cannot be attained in any other way. When Robert Schumann was asked to explain a difficult étude he had just performed, he sat down and played it a second time. Its meaning could only be grasped in performance, by a personal, imaginative fusion of frame and story. Likewise, George Steiner claims that the most profound interpretation of a work of art is its performance.[51] We should never find ourselves saying to an artist: 'what you are *really* saying is......' When the 'meaning' of a poem has been restated in another person's prose, the 'meaning' has already been lost. T. R. Wright speaks for nearly all literary critics when he claims that "The whole point of reading literature.......... is that it says something about life which cannot be said in any other way."[52] Whatever meaning is disclosed in a piece of art is given in and with the work itself, not as an ingredient to be distilled out, but as a total impact which claims our attention and involvement. The Churches would be foolish to forget this. In the mission and witness of the Church, the arts will be no mere decorative luxury; as any experienced Christian communicator will know, the outsider will frequently be grasped by the truth of the gospel more profoundly if it is embodied in artistic form than if it is couched in straightforward prose.

This is an extension of the point we made earlier about the irreducibility of metaphor. A metaphor is not simply an embellishment, or a covert assertion, or an expendable substitute for what can be stated plainly. It cannot be squeezed down to a literal statement without losing at least some of its force. So it is with art, which, we have suggested, is essentially a complex and extended form of metaphorical communication. To adapt Soskice's words, the interesting thing about works of art, or at least about some works of art, is that they are used not to redescribe but to disclose for the first time.

Emotivism

Parallel to emotivist theories of metaphor are emotivist theories of art, according to which art's main function is to release and provoke emotional dispositions. C. K. Ogden and I. A. Richards sought to work out for poetry a theory of 'emotive meaning' in which issues of truth and reference beyond our emotional experience had no place.[53] Yet such attempts are exposed to just the same kind of criticisms as emotivist theories of metaphor. They are symptomatic of the common tendency to divorce emotional commitment from matters of truth and falsity. Much suspicion of the arts by the Churches has undoubtedly been engendered by the fear that the arts are essentially about the expression of emotion rather than the more serious business of truth-telling. The advantage of Polanyi's approach to art is that he is prepared to acknowledge the immense emotional impact of much art — and provide an account of why it should carry such power — while at the same time refusing to detach art from realities exterior to human emotion.[54]

Evaluating Art

The complex and arduous task of evaluating art is also illuminated by viewing a work of art as a complex metaphorical system. We limit ourselves here to three brief comments. First, we have said that to claim that a metaphor is irreducible to literal statement is not to assert that it resists all attempts to explicate its content and assess it, either through the use of further metaphors, or by means of literal speech. The same will hold for art. If a work of art could not be elucidated and evaluated in any form at all, we could only presume that it lacked significance. Nevertheless, second, we have to be especially careful not to attempt to distil the 'message' or 'story' of a work of art without first approaching it as integration of frame and story, even when words are attached. Sadly, some Christian art-criticism has been quick to adjudicate on the supposed 'meaning' of a piece of art when the work in question has not actually been seen or heard or read. Third, by the same token, we cannot afford to restrict our evaluation of art to its 'frame' — its performance, its 'setting', its technique, etc. It makes little sense, for instance, to recommend that a film which portrays satanic practices in detail should be free from all censorship on the grounds that the photography is masterly.

Art and Illusion

The fear that art is at base a sophisticated form of trickery or deception has led many Christians to be intensely distrustful of it. David Hume's words come to mind: "Poets themselves, tho' liars by profession, always endeavour to give an air of truth to their fictions".[55] To take the arts too seriously will mean we shall be sucked into dangerous fantasy, so some claim. Works of art are inclined to conjure up such an attractive world that we begin to believe it to be the real world; it becomes the frame of reference for the interpretation of the rest of our experience. In Wolterstorff's words, we begin to

> "prize the world of a work of art for its falsehood in various respects to what we believe actuality to be like. We want for a while to burrow into a world significantly different from our actual world. We want for a while to escape the drudgery and the pain, the boredom, perplexity, and disorder of real life."[56]

That this has happened with some forms of art — by intention or default — is incontestable. And an exaggerated emphasis on the autonomy of art will certainly not help matters. But is there really something inherent in the nature of art which makes illusion inevitable? In fact, it has rarely been the primary intention of art to make us believe things which are not the case. Polanyi helps us to see that illusion does not belong to the heart of art, not even representative art. If we see a play in which a suicide is enacted, we are not deceived into thinking there has been a genuine death on stage, because of the subsidiary clues involved in any theatrical production which form its frame. Similarly a representative painting is not normally intended to be an illusion.[57] If it was, it would have to convince the viewer that the objects represented were there in factual reality. Not only would there have to be a point-for-point likeness, but our subsidiary awareness of the canvas would have to disappear altogether. But this is virtually impossible to achieve in practice, and even when paintings have come close to it, the results are not usually considered to be works of art. Representation is not the same as imitation. As Roger Scruton reminds us, representation depends on recognising the distinction between subject and medium. "Merely to *mistake* a painting for its subject is to misunderstand it".[58]

Of course, artists do frequently encourage us to *envisage* or *imagine* a world distinct from the actual world. Wolterstorff calls this 'world projection', and believes it to be the most pervasive and important of the actions performed by an artist. Whether Wolterstorff is right or not, such 'projection' is far from uncommon. Fictional literature or drama are the most obvious examples, where the artist bids us consider states of affairs distinct from any that we know (or perhaps believe could ever occur). And yet, in so doing, he does not *assert* that such a state of affairs is actual, he only invites us to consider such a state of affairs. Speaking about cinema, Ian Jarvie observes:

> "When we have experienced many movies and have become familiar with their conventions, their depiction of typical streets and interiors, their way of showing how people behave, the stars they use again and again, the manner in which space and time transitions are elided, we build up a rough and ready map of the world on film, one we can talk of, retrieve, describe, and refer to in the course of discussing matters in the real world. But, like Alice, however familiar or curious that world gets, we do not lose track of the benchmark of the real world to which we actually belong."[59]

Though a piece of art may indeed engross us, 'carry us away', take us into something bigger than ourselves, fusing our inchoate experience, this experience need not be identical with the experience of illusion. There is nothing in art *per se* which draws us irrevocably away from the world of everyday affairs. Moreover, even in the case of fiction, as Wolterstorff rightly observes, *"by way of* fictionally projecting his distinct world the fictioneer may make a claim, true or false as the case may be, about our actual world."[60] That is, the composed, projected world of an artist bears the potential of showing us something of the actual world. In Renaissance pictures of the nativity, Christ is often portrayed as being born in a West European village. By presenting it in this way, the artists reminded their contemporaries of the ordinariness, the down-to-earth character of the incarnation. This can be linked to a comment we made earlier about the power of a metaphor to modify or deepen the meaning of the area of discourse on which it draws.[61] A work of art, even if fictional, may lead us to change our attitude to the states of affairs with which it deals and which inform our day to day lives. This is not a case of confusing the imagined world with the real world, but of having our experience of the everyday world enriched and illuminated by the imagined world. In the course of an article on Polanyi's theory of art, Robert E. Innis writes that works of art "can present a focus upon states of affairs and possibilities of experience that *light up crucial components of human being-in-the-world.*" He continues: "Fiction, for example ....functions as a bearer of insight and revealer of truths that otherwise, in their felt qualities, would remain hidden."[62]

Properly speaking, then — and this surely applies to the best and most enduring 'fantasy' art — we are taken out of ourselves *in order* that we may return to a deeper appreciation of the reality in which we have our ordinary existence. As Richard Palmer puts it, paraphrasing Gadamer: "When we see a great work of art and enter its world, we do not leave home so much as 'come home'."[63]

Notes

[1] For a survey of attempts, cf. Wladyslaw Tatarkiewicz, "What is Art? The Problem of Definition Today," *British Journal of Aesthetics*, 11 (1971), pp. 134-153.

[2] E.g. Walter Nathan in his substantial work on the Church's role in the arts, rightly claims that we "lack an adequate theology of Christian art for our time" (*Art and the Message of the Church*, Philadelphia: Westminster Press, 1961, p. 123) but nowhere does he define art or distinguish it from other forms of creativity. Similarly Harned (*op. cit.*) provides a helpful critique of different theologies of art, but fails to tell us what it is about an object which makes us

call it a 'work of art'. Küng raises the question of definition (*op. cit.*, p. 10) but declines to address it at length.

3 Oxford: Clarendon Press, 1985.

4 *Ibid.*, p. 15. It does not have to take a particular syntactic form, nor does it have to possess a particular grammatical structure (pp. 18ff.).

5 Cf. Michael Polanyi and Harry Prosch, *Meaning*, Chicago: University of Chicago Press, 1975, chs. 4 and 5. I have been told that Polanyi was not entirely happy with all that was printed under his name in *Meaning*. But it is the content of the argument which matters, not the originator. Moreover, if we restrict ourselves to the fourth and fifth chapters, what is said about metaphor concurs very well with the epistemology expounded in Polanyi's main works.

6 Polanyi wants to use the word 'semantic' to cover all meanings artificially created by man, but to exclude those meanings achieved through perception or by our productive skills. *Meaning* , p. 74.

7 *Ibid.*, p.61.

8 *Ibid.*, p. 38. The distinction between subsidiary and focal awareness is not to be confused with that between unconscious and conscious awareness. Focal awareness is always conscious but subsidiary awareness "can exist at any level of consciousness". *Meaning*, p. 39.

9 *Ibid.*, pp. 71ff.

10 *Ibid.*, p. 75.

11 *Ibid.*, pp. 78f.

12 Cf. Max Black, "Metaphor," in *Models and Metaphors*, Ithaca: Cornell University Press, 1962, pp. 25-47; "More about Metaphor," in *Metaphor and Thought*, ed. Andrew Ortony, Cambridge: Cambridge University Press, 1979, pp. 19-43.

13 We should note that Polanyi's theory marks a significant advance on Black's approach to 'interaction'. Black seems to believe that a metaphor must have two distinct 'subjects' — 'primary' and 'secondary' ("Metaphor," p. 93), and tends to understand 'subject' as equivalent to 'thing'. But this is not the structure of all metaphors. Many metaphors have terms which do not refer to some object — e.g. the metaphor 'sad sky'. Polanyi's account fully allows for this kind of possibility. Tenor and vehicle are not to be confused with Black's 'subjects', and are not necessarily terms in the metaphorical utterance. (E.g. in the metaphor 'that rat's tricked me again', the tenor (the person who has deceived me) is not actually mentioned.) Furthermore, in his later article on metaphor, Black seems to suggest that it is only the the secondary subject which brings with it associated commonplaces. This runs the risk of reducing a metaphor to a comparison. Polanyi's account allows for the full interaction of the subsidiaries of *both* tenor and vehicle.

14 I. A. Richards, *The Philosophy of Rhetoric*, Oxford: Oxford University Press, 1936, p. 90.

15 *Ibid.*, p. 89. Cf. Paul Ricoeur, *The Rule of Metaphor. Multidisciplinary Studies of the Creation of Meaning in Language*, trans. R. Czerny and others, Toronto and Buffalo: University of Toronto Press, 1977.

16 "Metaphor and Theory Change: What is "Metaphor" a Metaphor

for?" in A. Ortony, ed., *Metaphor and Thought*, Cambridge: Cambridge University Press, p. 358. Cp. Soskice, *op. cit.*, chs. VI and VII.

[17] E.g. Ricoeur *op. cit.*, pp. 216ff.

[18] Cf. Soskice, *op. cit.*, pp. 35ff.

[19] *Meaning*, p. 83.

[20] *Ibid.*, pp. 82ff.

[21] *Ibid.*, pp. 84f.

[22] *Ibid.*, p. 82. The story can be auditory, visual, verbal or non-verbal.

[23] This is parallel to Heidegger's notion of the 'gathering power' of art. Cf. "The Origin of the Work of Art," in *Poetry, Language, and Thought*, trans. A. Hofstadter, New York: Harper & Row, 1971, pp. 15-87. Works of art, Heidegger claims, 'collect' reality into a single eloquent presence.

[24] *Meaning*, pp. 88-92; "What is a Painting?," *The American Scholar*, 39 (1969-70), pp. 655-669. Cp. M. H. Pirenne, *Optics, Painting and Photography*, Cambridge: Cambridge University Press, 1970, ch. 8.

[25] This is confirmed by an examination of Andrea Pozzo's painting on the vault of the church of St. Ignazio in Rome. A distortion occurs when the ceiling is viewed from any position other than that of the centre of the aisle, because the perspectival design is not counteracted by a subsidiary awareness of a two-dimensional surface. "What is a Painting?," pp. 655ff.; *Meaning*, pp. 90f.

[26] Polanyi here takes issue with Arnheim's thesis (Rudolf Arnheim, *Art and Visual Perception*, Berkeley: University of California Press, 1954) that there is a fusion of complementary features. For Polanyi there is a fusion of *contradictory* features. "What is a Painting?," p. 662.

[27] *Art and Illusion*, London: Phaidon Press, 1972, p. 237.

[28] *Meaning*, pp. 90ff.

[29] For the sake of clarity, we are excluding from the discussion music that accompanies words, and what Franz Liszt called 'programme' music (music connected with some kind of narrative). In a number of places Polanyi tantalisingly touches on music (e.g. "What is a painting?," p. 665; *Personal Knowledge*, pp. 58, 193-195, 196, 199, 200, 319, 345) but does not expand his remarks at any length.

[30] *Op. cit., passim.*

[31] *Ibid.*, p. 131.

[32] *Ibid.*, pp. 128, 139.

[33] *Op. cit., passim*, but especially pp. 32f.

[34] Eduard Hanslick, *The Beautiful in Music*, Indianapolis: Bobbs-Merrill Educational Publishing, 1957, pp. 21ff.

[35] John Blacking, *How Musical is Man?*, Seattle and London: University of Washington Press, 1973, pp. 58ff.

[36] *Feeling and Form*, London: Routledge & Kegan Paul, 1953.

[37] *Philosophy in a New Key*, Cambridge, Massachusetts: Harvard University Press, 1957, ch. IV.

[38] *Feeling and Form*, p. 40.

[39] *Music and the Emotions*, London, Boston, Melbourne and Henley: Routledge & Kegan Paul, 1985, p. 114.

[40] *Man the Musician*, Princeton: Princeton University Press, 1973, pp. 153f.

[41] *Loc. cit.*, p. 14.

[42] Cf. above, p. 210.

[43] *Op. cit.*, p. 123.

[44] *Ibid.*, p. 125.

[45] *The Architecture of Humanism*, 2nd ed., Garden City, New York: Doubleday, 1954, p. 95.

[46] pp. 193ff.

[47] *Ibid.*, p. 194.

[48] Soskice, *op. cit.*, p. 136.

[49] Peter Smith, "Making Paintings," in Tim Dean and David Porter, eds., *op. cit.*, p. 11.

[50] See the classification of poetical statements as 'pseudo-statements' by I. A. Richards in *Science and Poetry*, London: Kegan Paul, Trench, Trubner & Co., 1926, pp. 55ff.

[51] *Op. cit.*, pp. 16ff.

[52] *Op. cit.*, p. 4.

[53] *The Meaning of Meaning*, London: Kegan Paul, 1936.

[54] For critiques of the emotivist theory of art, cf. Allen Tate, *Reason in Madness*, New York: Putnams, 1941, and John Hospers, *Meaning and Truth in the Arts*, Chapel Hill, North Carolina: University of North Carolina Press, 1970.

[55] *A Treatise of Human Nature*, I, part III, Sect. X.

[56] *Op. cit.*, p. 147. Cf. J. R. Tolkien's comments on 'escapism' in Percy Lubbock, *The Craft of Fiction*, New York: Viking Press, 1957, pp. 45ff. Kierkegaard's notion of the 'aesthetic' attitude comes to mind here. "The flight into imagined possibilities, into fantasy, is the essence of what Kierkegaard calls the 'aesthetic' attitude to life. It is a way of keeping life at a distance, a result of not being willing to acknowledge the claims which life makes upon us." G. Pattison, "Søren Kierkegaard and Imagination," *Theology*, 87 (1984), p. 10.

[57] An exception would be the Pozzo painting mentioned above, p. 254.

[58] *The Aesthetic Understanding*, Manchester: Carcanet Press, 1983, p. 62.

[59] *Op. cit.*, p. 39.

[60] *Op. cit.*, p. 125.

[61] Cf. above, pp. 238f.

[62] "Art, Symbol and Consciousness: A Polanyi Gloss on Susanne Langer and Nelson Goodman," in *Philosophical Quarterly*, 17 (1977), p. 472. My italics.

[63] Richard E. Palmer, *Hermeneutics. Interpretation Theory in Schleiermacher, Dilthey, Heidegger, and Gadamer*, Evanston: Northwestern University Press, 1969, p. 168. T. S. Eliot said that the function of literature consists in "imposing a credible order upon ordinary reality......thereby eliciting some perception of an order *in* reality." *On Poetry and Poets*, New York: Farrar, Strauss and Cudahy, 1957, p. 94.

6. Conclusion

Let us retrace our steps. In Part I, we turned the spotlight on the work of Paul Tillich, and saw that throughout his intellectual development, the connection between his art-theory and theology was very close, and the influence mutual. His account of art hinged on the concept of expression — the disclosure of ultimate reality in and through finite form. Illuminating and shrewd as Tillich's discussion of art was, we found ourselves questioning whether his ontology — despite his intentions — was adequately shaped by the saving economy of God in Christ, and thus whether his philosophy of art was sufficiently marked by distinctively Christian insights. Little in the way of non-symbolic criteria of value in art were in evidence. For all his strengths, Tillich appeared to be governed chiefly by the idiosyncratic requirements of his philosophical method.

In Part II, we surveyed some key members of the Dutch Neo-Calvinist tradition, a movement emanating from that redoubtable colossus, Abraham Kuyper. Assuming a more traditional Christian ontology and epistemology, they avoided many of the problems which beset Tillich's approach. However, a profound dichotomy between the spheres of creation and redemption seemed to pervade their thinking, together with an insufficient grasp of the significance of the humanity of Christ. Their doctrine of God needed a stronger Christological focus and greater emphasis on the trinitarian ontology of God: God was conceived primarily as the Law-giver, and only secondarily as the one who gives himself in love. The created world was construed as a system of fixed laws and structures; redemption tended to be seen in this light, apart from Christ. Our basic standing before God was portrayed in terms of duty and obedience, and culture in the light of a divine 'cultural mandate'. In response, we argued that humanity was created first and foremost for communion-in-love with God, that the cultural mandate is best perceived as a gift, and the fulfilment of the mandate as something which God himself enables and sustains. We found that the Neo-Calvinists' philosophy of art was dominated by the notion of beauty (understood as harmony, order, proportion, etc.). It was urged that pinpointing beauty as the qualifying kernel of art was unhelpful, and that if a concept of beauty was to be employed in a Christian philosophy of art, it would need to reflect more closely the dynamic of God's renewal of creation in Christ.

This led us to ask what kind of account of art might emerge from a theology more systematically centred on God's unique interaction with space and time in the history of Jesus Christ. In Part III, I tried to draw out the implications of affirming that the love revealed in the incarnate Son is internal to the being of God and motivates all divine activity in creation and redemption. On this model, God is the one who has his being in communion, and whose every act is part of his yearning towards ever more actualised relationship and mutuality. Human creativity, at its highest, will be a corporate participation in the vicarious humanity of Christ through the Spirit, which enables, gathers up and focuses the praise of creation, directing it towards the Father. We argued that art is not essentially projectionist — a matter of imposing on the world something which has its source in the mind or emotions of the artist. To counter the excessive emphasis — so beloved of the Enlightenment — on the movement *from* the artist outward *to* the world, we sought to recover a sense of the priority of reception over imposition. An attentiveness and fidelity to what is beyond ourselves, I proposed, should take precedence over a desire to mould the world according to our own wishes. But I have also tried to show that art is no slavish copying or reproducing of what is given to hand — the artist not only discovers and respects, but with due deference to the given order of things, his vocation is also to develop and redeem. Art, I submit, is best construed as a vehicle of interaction with the world: a work of art is an object or happening *through which* we engage with the physical world we inhabit, and *through which* we converse with those communities with whom we share our lives.

The all too common alienation of art today is, then, not only unfortunate; it rests on a misconception of the nature of art. Art has potential to help us grow in our grasp and understanding of the world we inhabit. The assumption that only literal statement can convey truth, and that anything else is either merely decorative or can only reflect the inward dispositions of the individual, needs challenging. The experience of art is a mode of knowing the world, certainly different from conceptual and moral knowledge, but by no means inferior to them. Polanyi's account of art as elaborated metaphor, I have tried to indicate, provides us with a fruitful way of illuminating this cognitive character of art. Consequently, the Church need feel no shame in employing the arts as media of theological truth. Although nothing should be allowed to usurp the more obviously direct avenues of communication, we should not be trapped by popular assumptions about art which fail to measure up to the way art actually operates. The belief that the arts are always aimed at creating illusion, or that they can express nothing more than emotional states, or that they can never be anything more than ornamental — all these are regrettable mis-understandings which can only impoverish the Church's life and mission.

In drawing to a close, I am all too aware that I have frequently dealt in generalities, and that many arguments have been left open-ended. Much more needs to be said, for example, about the distinctive contribution of the arts in the outreach of the Church, about how artistic communication relates to conceptual communication, about how we might go about assessing particular works of art theologically. But my main aim has not been to offer an all-encompassing philosophy of art, nor a comprehensive strategy for the Church's use of the arts, still less a theological check-list for the art-critic. My primary purpose in this part of the book has been to open up paths along which others might usefully travel.

At the very least, I hope that this book will have shown that the arts supply the theologian with an immensely rich and fruitful field to explore. Indeed, I hope it will be clear that this is a sphere which theology simply cannot afford to ignore, especially if we are to be faithful to a God whom we confess as the Creator and Sustainer of all things. The fact that so few theologians have seen fit to journey into this area can only be a cause for regret. A greater willingness to do so could well pave the way for a reintegration of dimensions of our lives which have been disastrously torn apart in modern times. It would also lead to a deeper thankfulness to God for providing us with such a glorious gift as artistic creativity to voice creation's praise.

Bibliography

(1) Paul Tillich

(a) Books and Articles by Tillich

"Art and Ultimate Reality," *Cross Currents*, 10 (Winter 1960), pp. 2-14

Dynamics of Faith, London: Allen & Unwin, 1957

"Existentialist Aspects of Modern Art", in *Christianity and the Existentialists*, ed. Carl Michalson, New York: Charles Scribner's Sons, 1956, pp. 128-147

Gesammelte Werke, ed. Renate Albrecht, Stuttgart: Evangelisches Verlagswerk, I, 1959; II, 1962; IX, 1967

"Honesty and Consecration," in *Protestant Church Buildings and Equipment*, 13, 3 (September 1965), pp. 15-17

"I'll always Remember........One Moment of Beauty," *Parade*, (25 September 1955), pp. 1-2

Morality and Beyond, New York: Harper and Row, 1963

My Travel Diary:1936, London: SCM, 1970

On the Boundary, London: Collins, 1967

"Religion and Secular Culture," *The Journal of Religion*, 26, 2 (April 1946), pp. 78-86

Systematic Theology, London: Nisbet, 1, 1953; 2, 1964; 3, 1963

The Courage to Be, London: Nisbet, 1952

The Interpretation of History, trans. N. A. Rasetzki and Elsa L. Talmey, New York and London: Charles Scribner's Sons, 1936

"The Meaning and Justification of Religious Symbols," in *Religious Experience and Truth*, ed. S. Hook, New York: New York University Press, 1961, pp. 301-321

"Theology and Symbolism," in *Religious Symbolism*, ed. F. Ernest Johnson, New York: Harper & Bros., 1955, pp. 107-116

"Theology, Architecture and Art," *Church Management*, 33, 1 (1956), pp. 55-56

Theology of Culture, ed. Robert C. Kimball, New York: Oxford University Press, 1959

The Protestant Era, London: Nisbet, 1951

The Religious Situation, trans. H. Richard Niebuhr, London: Thames and Hudson, 1956

"The Self-Understanding of Man in Contemporary Thought," The Lowell Lectures delivered at King's Chapel, Boston, 1958, unpublished

The System of Sciences according to Objects and Methods, trans. Paul Wiebe, London and Toronto: Associated University Press, 1981

"The Word of God," in *Language: An Enquiry into its Meaning and Function*, ed. Ruth N. Anshen, New York: Harper Bros., 1957, pp. 122-123

The World Situation, Philadelphia: Fortress Press, 1965

What is Religion?, ed. James Luther Adams, New York: Harper & Row, 1969

(b) Secondary Works

Adams, James Luther, *Paul Tillich's Philosophy of Culture, Science and Religion*, New York: Harper & Row, 1965
——"What Kind of Religion has a Place in Higher Education?," *Journal of Bible and Religion*, 13 (1945), pp. 185-192
Bird, Michael S., "Cinema and the Sacred: An Application of Paul Tillich's Theory of Art to the Film in the Aesthetic Apprehension of the Holy," PhD Thesis, University of Iowa, 1975
Bulman, Raymond F., *A Blueprint for Humanity. Paul Tillich's Theology of Culture*, London and Toronto: Associated University Presses, 1981
Cardinal, Roger, *Expressionism*, London: Paladin, 1984
Clayton, John P., "Is Jesus Necessary for Christology?," in *Christ, Faith and History*, ed. S. W. Sykes and J. P. Clayton, Cambridge: Cambridge University Press, 1972, pp. 147-162
——*The Concept of Correlation: Paul Tillich and the Possibility of a Mediating Theology*, Berlin and New York: de Gruyter, 1980
Crary, S. T., "Idealistic Elements in Tillich's Thought," PhD Thesis, Yale University, 1955
Dillenberger, Jane and John, eds., *Paul Tillich on Art and Architecture*, Crossroad, 1987
Dixon, John, *Nature and Grace in Art*, Chapel Hill: University of North Carolina Press, 1964
Dube, Wolf-Dieter, *The Expressionists*, London: Thames and Hudson, 1972
Ferre, Nels, "Three Critical Issues in Tillich's Philosophical Theology," *Scottish Journal of Theology*, 10 (1957), pp. 223-258
Ford, Lewis S., "The Three Strands of Tillich's Theory of Religious Symbols," *The Journal of Religion*, 46 (1 January 1966), pp. 104-130
——"Tillich's One Non-Symbolic Statement: A Propos of a Recent Study by Rowe," *Journal of the American Academy of Religion*, 38, 2 (1970), pp. 176-182
Gabus, Jean-Paul, *Introduction à la Théologie de la Culture de Paul Tillich*, Paris: Presses Universitaires de France, 1969
Gerhardus, Maly and Dietfried, *Expressionism*, Oxford: Phaidon, 1979
Halsey, Brian, "Paul Tillich on Religion and Art," *Lexington Theological Quarterly*, 9 (1974), pp. 100-112
Hamilton, Kenneth, *The System and the Gospel: A Critique of Paul Tillich*, London: SCM, 1963
Heron, Alasdair I. C., *A Century of Protestant Theology*, Guildford and London: Lutterworth, 1980
Holmer, Paul L., "Paul Tillich and the Language about God," *Journal of Religious Thought*, 22, 1 (1 January, 1965-66), pp. 35-50
Kähler, Martin, *The So-called Historical Jesus and the Historic, Biblical Christ*, trans. and ed. Carl E. Braaten, Philadelphia:

Fortress Press, 1964

Kandinsky, W., *Über das Geistege in der Kunst*, München: R. Piper, 1912

Kegley, Charles, "Paul Tillich on the Philosophy of Art," *Journal of Aesthetics and Art Criticism*, 19 (1960), pp. 175-184

——(with Robert W. Bretall), ed., *The Theology of Paul Tillich*, London: Macmillan, 1956

Kelsey, David, *The Fabric of Paul Tillich's Theology*, New Haven: Yale University Press, 1967

Killen, R. A., *The Ontological Theology of Paul Tillich*, Kampen: Kok, 1956

Lynton, Norbert, *Concepts of Modern Art*, London: Penguin Books, 1974

McCollough, Thomas E., "The Ontology of Tillich and Biblical Personalism," *Scottish Journal of Theology*, 15 (1962), pp. 266-281

McDonald, H. D., "The Symbolic Theology of Paul Tillich," *Scottish Journal of Theology*, 17 (1964), pp. 414-430

McGrath, Alister, *The Making of Modern German Christology*, Oxford: Blackwell, 1986

Macquarrie, John, *20th Century Religious Thought*, London: SCM, 1971

Marc, Franz, *Briefe aus dem Feld*, Berlin: Helmut Rauschenbusch Verlag, 1948

Matthews, Thomas F., "Tillich on Religious Content in Modern Art," *College Art Journal*, 27 (1967), pp. 16-19

Mondin, Battista, *The Principle of Analogy in Protestant and Catholic Thought*, The Hague: Martinus Nijhof, 1963

Myers, Bernard, *Expressionism: A Generation in Revolt*, London: Thames and Hudson, 1963

Newport, John P., *Paul Tillich*, Waco, Texas: Word Books, 1984

Page, Ruth, "The Consistent Christology of Paul Tillich," *Scottish Journal of Theology*, 36 (1983), pp. 195-212

Palmer, Michael F., *Paul Tillich's Philosophy of Art*, Berlin and New York: de Gruyter, 1984

Pauck, Wilhelm and Marion, *Paul Tillich: His Life & Thought*, 1, London: Collins, 1977

Powell-Jones, Mark, *Impressionist Painting*, Oxford: Phaidon Press, 1979

Rowe, W. L., *Religious Symbols and God*, Chicago and London: University of Chicago Press, 1968

Scharlemann, R. P., "The Scope of Systematics: An Analysis of Tillich's Two Systems," in *Journal of Religion*, 48 (April 1968), pp. 136-149

——"Tillich's Method of Correlation: Two Proposed Revisions," *The Journal of Religion*, 46, 1, part 2 (January 1966), pp. 92-103

Selz, Peter, *German Expressionist Painting*, Berkeley & Los Angeles: University of California Press, 1957

Sommer, G. F., "The Significance of the Late Philosophy of Schelling for the Formation and Interpretation of the Thought of Paul Tillich," PhD Thesis, Duke University, 1961

Tavard, George, *Paul Tillich and the Christian Message*, New York:

Charles Scribner's Sons, 1962
Taylor, Mark Kline, *Paul Tillich: Theologian of the Boundaries,* London: Collins, 1987
Thatcher, Adrian, *The Ontology of Paul Tillich,* Oxford: Oxford University Press, 1978
Thiselton, Anthony C., "The Theology of Paul Tillich," *The Churchman,* 88, 2 (1974), pp. 86-107
Thomas, John Heywood, *Paul Tillich,* London: Kingsgate Press, 1965
——"The Problem of Defining a Theology of Culture," in *Creation, Christ and Culture,* ed. Richard W. A. McKinney, Edinburgh: T. & T. Clark, 1976, pp. 272-281
Thompson, Ian E., *Being and Meaning. Paul Tillich's Theory of Meaning, Truth and Logic,* Edinburgh: Edinburgh University Press, 1981
Troeltsch, Ernst, *Der Historismus und seine Überwindung,* Berlin: Rolf Heise, 1924
Weisbaker, Dimis Taylor, "The Place of Aesthetics in the Theology of Paul Tillich," PhD Thesis, Emory University, 1971
Whitford, Frank, *Expressionism,* London, New York, Sydney and Toronto: Hamlyn, 1970

(2) Calvinism

Aalders, W. J., "Calvinisme en Wijsbegeerte," *Nieuwe Theologische Stüdien,* XVI (1933), pp. 236-249
Bavinck, Herman, *Beginselen der Psychologie,* Kampen: Kok, 1897
——*Calvin and the Reformation,* New York: Revell, 1909
——*De Algemeene Genade,* Grand Rapids, Michigan: Eerdmans, no date
——*De Offerande des Lofs,* 'S-Gravenhage: Verschoor, 1903
——*De Overwinning der Ziel,* Kampen: Kok, 1916
——*Gereformeerde Dogmatiek,* 4 Vols., 2nd ed., Kampen: Bos, 1908
——*Handleiding bij het Onderwijs in den Christelijken Godsdienst,* Kampen: Kok, 1913
——*Kennis en Leven,* Kampen: Kok, 1922
——*Our Reasonable Faith,* Grand Rapids, Michigan: Eerdmans, 1956
——*Paedagogische Beginselen,* Kampen: Kok, 1904
——*The Philosophy of Revelation,* New York: Longmans, Green and Co., 1909
——*Verzamelde Opstellen,* Kampen: Kok, 1921
Bax, Douglas, "The Bible and Apartheid," in *Apartheid is a Heresy,* ed. John De Gruchy and Charles Villa-Vicencio, Guildford: Lutterworth, 1983, pp. 112-143
Berkouwer, G. C., *A Half Century of Theology,* Grand Rapids, Michigan: Eerdmans, 1977
Bratt, James D., *Dutch Calvinism in Modern America: A History of a Conservative Subculture,* Grand Rapids, Michigan: Eerdmans, 1984
——"The Dutch Schools," in D. F. Wells, ed., *Reformed Theology in*

America, Grand Rapids, Michigan: Eerdmans, 1985, pp. 135-152

Brümmer, Vincent, *Transcendental Criticism and Christian Philosophy*, Franeker: T. Wever, 1961

Daane, James, *A Theology of Grace*, Grand Rapids, Michigan: Eerdmans, 1954

De Gruchy, John W., *Bonhoeffer and South Africa*, Grand Rapids, Michigan: Eerdmans, 1984

——*The Church Struggle in South Africa*, London: Collins, 1986

Dooyeweerd, Herman, *A New Critique of Theoretical Thought*, 3 Vols., trans. D. H. Freeman and W. S. Young, Philadelphia: Presbyterian and Reformed Publishing Co., 1969

——"De Verhouding tussen Wijsbegeerte en Theologie en de Strijd der Faculteiten," *Philosophia Reformata*, XXIII (1958), pp. 1-22, 49-84

——*In the Twilight of Western Thought*, Nutley, New Jersey: Craig Press, 1960

——"Kuyper's Wetenschapsleer," *Philosophia Reformata*, IV (1939), pp. 193-232

——*Roots of Western Culture*, Toronto: Wedge Publishing Foundation, 1979

——*Transcendental Problems of Philosophical Thought*, Grand Rapids, Michigan: Eerdmans, 1948

Durand, Jaap, "Church and State in South Africa: Karl Barth vs. Abraham Kuyper," in *On Reading Karl Barth in South Africa*, ed. Charles Villa-Vicencio, Grand Rapids, Michigan: Eerdmans, 1988, pp. 121-137

Hart, Hendrik, (with Johann Van Der Hoeven and Nicholas Wolterstorff), *Rationality in the Calvinian Tradition*, Lanham and London: University Press of America, 1983

Hodge, A. A., *Outlines of Theology*, London and New York: Nelson and Sons, 1891

Hodge, Charles, *Systematic Theology*, II, Grand Rapids, Michigan: Eerdmans, 1940

Hoeksema, Herman, *The Protestant Reformed Churches in America*, Grand Rapids, Michigan: First Protestant Reformed Church, 1936

Jellema, Dirk, "Abraham Kuyper's Attack on Liberalism," *Review of Politics*, 19, (Oct. 1957), pp. 472-485

Kalsbeek, L., *Contours of a Christian Philosophy. An Introduction to Herman Dooyeweerd's Thought*, Toronto: Wedge Publishing Foundation, 1975

Kruithof, B., "The Relation of Christianity and Culture in the Teaching of Herman Bavinck," PhD Thesis, Edinburgh University, 1955

Kuiper, Herman, *Calvin on Common Grace*, Grand Rapids, Michigan: Smitter Book Co., 1928

Kuyper, Abraham, *Calvinism*, London: Sovereign Grace Union, 1932

——*De Gemeene Gratie*, 3 Vols., Kampen: Kok, 4th ed., no date

——*De Vleeschwording des Woords*, Amsterdam: J. A. Wormser, 1887

——*Dictaten Dogmatiek*, 5 Vols., Kampen: Kok, 2nd ed., 1910

——*Encyclopaedia of Sacred Theology*, trans. Hendrik de Vries, London: Hodder & Stoughton, 1899

——*Het Calvinisme en de Kunst*, Amsterdam: J. A. Wormser, 1888
——*Het Werk den Heiligen Geest*, Amsterdam: J. A. Wormser, 1888
——*Pro Rege*, Kampen: Kok, I, 1911; II and III, 1912
McIntyre, C. T., "Herman Dooyeweerd in North America," in D. F. Wells, ed., *Reformed Theology in America*, Grand Rapids, Michigan: Eerdmans, 1985, pp. 172-185
Mare, W. Harold, "The Cultural Mandate and the New Testament Gospel Imperative," *Journal of the Evangelical Theological Society*, 16, no. 3 (Summer 1973), pp. 139-147
Martin, Linette, *Hans Rookmaaker*, London: Hodder & Stoughton, 1979
Masselink, William, *General Revelation and Common Grace*, Grand Rapids, Michigan: Eerdmans, 1953
——"New Views of Common Grace in the Light of Historic Reformed Theology," *The Calvin Forum*, 20 (1954), pp. 194-204
Moodie, T. Dunbar, *The Rise of Afrikanerdom*, Berkeley, Los Angeles, London: University of California Press, 1975
Murray, John, "Common Grace," *The Westminster Theological Journal*, 5, 1 (1942), pp. 1-28
Nash, Ronald H., *Dooyeweerd and the Amsterdam Philosophy*, Grand Rapids, Michigan: Zondervan, 1962
Ramsay, M. P., *Calvin and Art*, London: Moray Press, 1938
Redmond, Howard A., "The Sense for Beauty in Calvinism," PhD Thesis, University of Southern California, 1953
Rolston III, Holmes, *Calvin versus the Westminster Confession*, Richmond, Virgina: John Knox Press, 1972
——"Responsible Man in Reformed Theology: Calvin versus the Westminster Confession," *Scottish Journal of Theology*, 23 (1970), pp. 129-156
Rookmaaker, Hans R., *Art and the Public Today*, Huémoz-sur-Ollon, Switzerland: L'Abri Fellowship, 1969
——*Art Needs No Justification*, Leicester: IVP, 1974
——*Gaugin and 19th Century Art Theory*, Amsterdam: Swets & Zeitlinger, 1972
——*Jazz, Blues, Spirituals*, Wadeningen: Gebr. Zomer & Keunings Uitgeversmaatschappij, 1960
——*Kunst en Amusement*, Kampen: Kok, 1962
——"Modern Art and Gnosticism," *Zeitschrift für Aesthetik und allgemeine Kunstwissenschaft*, 18 (1973), pp. 162-174
——*Modern Art and the Death of a Culture*, London: IVP, 1970
——"Ontwerp ener Aesthetica op grondslag der Wijsbegeerte der Wetsidee," *Philosophia Reformata*, 11, 3 (1946), pp. 141-167; 12, 1 (1947), pp. 1-35
——*The Creative Gift*, Leicester: IVP, 1981
Roper, D. L., *The Christian Task in the Arts: Some Preliminary Considerations*, Wellington, New Zealand: Foundation for Christian Studies, 1979
——*Wanted: A New Song Unto the Lord*, Wellington, New Zealand: Foundation for Christian Studies, 1981
Schilder, Klaas, *Christ and Culture*, trans. G. van Rongen and W.

Helder, Winnipeg: Premier, 1977

Scholes, Percy, *The Puritans and Music*, London: Oxford University Press, 1934

Seerveld, Calvin, *A Christian Critique of Art and Literature*, Toronto: Association for the Advancement of Christian Scholarship, 1977

——"Art: Temptation to Sin or Testimony of Grace?," *Christianity Today*, 10 (3 December 1965), pp. 7-9

——*A Turnabout in Aesthetics to Understanding*, Toronto: Wedge Publishing Foundation, 1974

——"Comic Relief to Christian Art," *Christianity Today*, 12 (1 March 1968), pp. 10-12

——(with Paul Vitz) *Human Responses to Art*, Dordt, Iowa: Dordt College Press, 1983

——"Imaginativity," unpublished paper provided by the author, no date

——*Rainbows for the Fallen World*, Toronto: Tuppence Press, 1980

——"Relating Christianity to the Arts," *Christianity Today*, 24 (7 November 1980), pp. 48-49

——Review of Hans-Georg Gadamer's *Truth and Method*, in *Journal of Aesthetics and Art Criticism*, 36, no. 4 (1978), pp. 487-490

——Review of Nicholas Wolterstorff's *Art in Action*, in *Third Way*, 5, no. 7 (June 1982), pp. 23-24

——"The Christian and the Arts," *For the Time Being*, 3 (1975), pp. 14-17

——"The Relation of the Arts to the Presentation of Truth," *Truth and Reality*, Festschrift for H. G. Stoker, Braamfontein: De Jong, 1971, pp. 161-175

——"Towards a Cartographic Methodology for Art Historiography," in *Journal of Aesthetics and Art Criticism*, 39 (1980), pp. 143-154

Spier, J. M., *An Introduction to Christian Philosophy*, Nutley, New Jersey: Craig Press, 1954

Spykman, Gordon, "Sphere-sovereignty in Calvin and the Calvinist Tradition," in David Holwerda, ed., *Exploring the Heritage of John Calvin*, Grand Rapids, Michigan: Baker Book House, 1976, pp. 163-208

Stoker, H. G., *Die Nuwere Wysbegeerte aan die Vrije Universitait*, Potchefstroom: "Die Westedrukkery", 1933

——"The Possibility of a Calvinistic Philosophy," *The Evangelical Quarterly*, 7 (1935), pp. 17-23

The Articles of the Synod of Dort and the Rejection of Errors, London: Sovereign Grace Union, 1932

Torrance, James B., "Covenant or Contract? A Study of the Theological Background of Worship in Seventeenth-Century Scotland," *Scottish Journal of Theology*, 23 (1970), pp. 51-76

——"The Covenant Concept in Scottish Theology and Politics and its Legacy," *Scottish Journal of Theology*, 34 (1981), pp. 225-243

——"The Incarnation and Limited Atonement," *Scottish Bulletin of Evangelical Theology*, 2 (1984), pp. 32-40

Vanden Berg, Frank, *Abraham Kuyper*, St. Catherine's, Ontario: Paideia Press, 1978

Van der Kroef, J. M., "Abraham Kuyper and the Rise of Neo-Calvinism in the Netherlands," *Church History*, 17 (1948), pp. 316-334

Van Ruler, A., *Kuyper's Idee Eener Christelijke Cultuur,* Nijkerk: G. F. Callenbach, no date

Van Til, Cornelius, "Calvinism and Art," *The Presbyterian Guardian,* 17 (1948), pp. 272-274

——*Common Grace and the Gospel,* Philadelphia: Presbyterian and Reformed Publishing Co., 1972

Van Til, Henry, *The Calvinistic Concept of Culture,* Philadelphia: Presbyterian and Reformed Publishing Co., 1974

Veenhof, Cornelius, *In Kuyper's Lijn,* Goes: Oosterbaan & Le-Cointre, 1939

——*Souvereiniteit in Eigen Kring,* Goes: Oosterbaan & Le-Cointre, 1939

Weir, David A., *The Origins of the Federal Theology in Sixteenth-Century Reformation Thought,* Oxford: Clarendon Press, 1990

Wencelius, Leon, *L'aesthétique de Calvin,* Paris: Belles Lettres, 1938

Wells, David, ed. *Reformed Theology in America. A History of its Development,* Grand Rapids, Michigan: Eerdmans, 1985

Wolterstorff, Nicholas, Review of Calvin Seerveld's *Rainbows for the Fallen World,* in *Third Way,* 5, 7 (June 1982), pp. 22-23

Young, William, *Toward a Reformed Philosophy,* Grand Rapids: Piet Hein, 1952

(3) General

Abrams, M. H., "Kant and the Theology of Art," *Notre Dame English Journal,* 13 (1981), pp. 75-106

Ackroyd, P. R., "Some Notes on the Psalms," *Journal of Theological Studies,* 17 (1966), pp. 392-405

Anderson, Ray, *On Being Human: Essays in Theological Anthropology,* Grand Rapids, Michigan: Eerdmans, 1982

Arnheim, Rudolf, *Art and Visual Perception,* Berkeley: University of California Press, 1954

Barbour, R. S., "Creation, Wisdom and Christ," in *Creation, Christ and Culture,* ed. Richard W. A. McKinney, Edinburgh: T. & T. Clark, 1976, pp. 22-42

Barfield, Owen, *Poetic Diction,* London: Faber and Faber, 1928

Barrett, C. K., *The Gospel According to St John,* London: SPCK, 1978

——*The Epistle to the Romans,* London: Black, 1971

Barth, Karl, *Church Dogmatics,* ed. G. W. Bromiley and T. F. Torrance, Edinburgh: T. & T. Clark, I:2, 1956; II:1, 1957; III:1, 1958

——*Dogmatics in Outline,* trans. G. T. Thompson, London: SCM, 1966

——*Theology and Church,* trans. Louise Pettibone Smith, New York: Harper & Row, 1962

Barth, Markus, *Ephesians 1-3,* Garden City, New York: Doubleday, 1974

Baumgarten, A. G., *Reflections on Poetry,* trans. K. Aschenbrenner and W. B. Holther, Berkeley: University of South California Press, 1954

Beardsley, Monroe C., *Aesthetics from Classical Greece to the Present*, Alabama: University of Alabama Press, 1966

Bell, Clive, *Art*, London: Chatto and Windus, 1947

Berdyaev, Nicolas, *The Meaning of the Creative Act*, trans. D. Lowrie, London: Victor Gollancz, 1955

Berger, John, *Permanent Red*, London: Methuen, 1960

Bernstein, Leonard, *The Unanswered Question. Six Talks at Harvard*, Cambridge, Massachusetts and London: Harvard University Press, 1976

Bernstein, Richard, *Beyond Objectivism and Relativism: Science, Hermeneutics, and Praxis*, Oxford: Blackwell, 1983

Bertram, Georg, "καλος," *Theological Dictionary of the New Testament*, III, ed. Gerhard Kittel, Grand Rapids, Michigan: Eerdmans, 1965, pp. 536-556

Black, Max, "Metaphor," in *Models and Metaphors*, Ithaca: Cornell University Press, 1962, pp. 25-47

———"More about Metaphor," in *Metaphor and Thought*, ed. Andrew Ortony, Cambridge: Cambridge University Press, 1979, pp. 19-43

Blacking, John, *How Musical is Man?*, Seattle and London: University of Washington Press, 1973

Boyd, Richard, "Metaphor and Theory Change: What is 'Metaphor' a Metaphor for?" in A. Ortony, ed., *Metaphor and Thought*, Cambridge: Cambridge University Press, pp. 356-408

Bruce, F. F., *The Epistle to the Hebrews*, Grand Rapids, Michigan: Eerdmans, 1977

Brunner, Emil, *Christianity and Civilisation*, 2, London: Nisbet, 1949

———*The Christian Doctrine of Creation and Redemption*, 2, London: Lutterworth Press, 1952

Budd, Malcolm, *Music and the Emotions*, London, Boston, Melbourne and Henley: Routledge & Kegan Paul, 1985

Butler, Christopher, *After the Wake: An Essay on the Contemporary Avant-Garde*, Oxford: Oxford University Press, 1980

Caird, George B., *Principalities and Powers*, Oxford: Clarendon Press, 1956

———*The Language and Imagery of the Bible*, London: Duckworth, 1980

Camus, Albert, *The Myth of Sisyphus*, Harmondsworth: Penguin Books, 1975

———*The Rebel*, trans. Anthony Bower, Harmondsworth: Penguin Books, 1971

Cardinal, Roger, *German Romantics in Context*, London: Studio Vista, 1975

Chiari, Joseph, *The Aesthetics of Modernism*, London: Vision Press, 1970

Coleridge, Samuel Taylor, *Biographia Literaria*, II, Princeton: Princeton University Press, 1983.

Collingwood, R. G., *The Principles of Art*, Oxford: Clarendon Press, 1955

Cooke, Deryck, *The Language of Music*, London, New York and Toronto: Oxford University Press, 1959

Cranfield, C. E. B., *The Epistle to the Romans*, I, Edinburgh: T. & T.

Clark, 1975

Crawford, Donald, *Kant's Aesthetic Theory*, London and Wisconsin: University of Wisconsin Press, 1974

Croce, Benedetto, *Aesthetic as a Science of Expression and General Linguistic*, trans. Douglas Ainslie, London: Macmillan, 1922

Crossan, John Dominic, *The Dark Interval: Towards a Theology of Story*, Niles, Illinois: Argus Communications, 1975

Daley, Janet, "Making an Art of Subversion," *The Times*, August 23, 1989, p. 10

Davies, Paul, *God and the New Physics*, London, Toronto and Melbourne: Dent, 1983

——*The Accidental Universe*, Cambridge: Cambridge University Press, 1982

Dean, Tim and Porter, David, *Art in Question*, Basingstoke: Marshall Morgan and Scott, 1987

Dearborn, Timothy A., "The Trinitarian Nature of Grace," PhD Thesis, University of Aberdeen, 1988

Descartes, René, *The Philosophical Works of Descartes*, trans. Haldane and Ross, Vol. 1, Cambridge: Cambridge University Press, 1973,

Dickie, George, *Aesthetics: An Introduction*, Indianapolis: Bobbs-Merrill Educational Publishing, 1979

Dillistone, F. W., *The Power of Symbols*, London: SCM, 1986

Dixon, John W., *Art and the Theological Imagination*, New York: Seabury Press, 1978

Dumbrell, William J., *Covenant and Creation*, Exeter: Paternoster, 1984

Dunn, James D. G., *Christology in the Making*, London: SCM, 1980

Edgar, William, *Taking Note of Music*, London: SPCK, 1986

Eichrodt, Walther, *Theology of the Old Testament*, II, London: SCM, 1967

Eliot, T. S., *On Poetry and Poets*, New York: Farrar, Strauss and Cudahy, 1957

——"Tradition and the Individual Talent," in *Selected Essays*, London: Faber & Faber, 1932, pp. 13-22

Ellmann, Richard and Charles Feidelson, eds., *The Modern Tradition*, New York: Oxford University Press, 1965

Etchells, Ruth, *A Model of Making: Literary Criticism and its Theology*, Basingstoke: Marshall, Morgan and Scott, 1983

——"God and Our Books," in Tim Dean and David Porter, eds., *Art in Question*, Basingstoke: Marshall Morgan and Scott, 1987, pp. 52-68

——*Unafraid to Be*, London: IVP, 1969

Eversole, F. ed., *Christian Faith and the Contemporary Arts*, Nashville: Abingdon Press, 1962

Ferguson, Donald N, *Music as Metaphor*, Minneapolis: University of Minnesota Press, 1960

Firth, Raymond, "The Social Framework of Primitive Art," in *The Many Faces of Primitive Art*, ed. Douglas Fraser, Englewood Cliffs, New Jersey: Prentice-Hall, 1966, pp. 12-33

Fraser, Douglas, ed., *The Many Faces of Primitive Art*, Englewood

Cliffs, New Jersey: Prentice-Hall, 1966

Frye, Northrop, *Anatomy of Criticism: Four Essays*, Princeton: Princeton University Press, 1957

Fuller, Peter, *Aesthetics After Modernism*, New York: Writers and Readers Publishing Cooperative, 1983

——*Beyond the Crisis in Art*, London: Readers and Writers Co-operative, 1980

——*Images of God: The Consolations of Lost Illusions*, London: Hogarth Press, 1985

——*Theoria: Art, and the Absence of Grace*, London: Chatto and Windus, 1988

Furst, Lilian R., *Romanticism in Perspective*, London and Basingstoke: Macmillan, 1979

Gadamer, Hans-Georg, *Truth and Method*, New York: Seabury Press, 1975

Gaebelein, Frank, "The Aesthetic Problem: Some Evangelical Answers," *Christianity Today*, 12 (30 August 1968), pp. 4-6

Gaillie, W. B., "Art as an Essentially Contested Concept," *Philosophical Quarterly*, 6, no. 23 (1956), pp. 97-114

Gibbs, John, *Creation and Redemption*, Leiden: E. J. Brill, 1971

Gilbert, K. E. and Kuhn, H., *A History of Esthetics*, New York: Dover, 1972

Gilson, Étienne, *Painting and Reality*, Princeton, New Jersey: Princeton University Press, 1957

Gombrich, Ernst H., *Art and Illusion*, London: Phaidon Press, 1972

Gotshalk, D. W., *Art and the Social Order*, New York: Dover, 1962

Greenberg, Clement, *The Collected Essays and Criticism: Volume I: Perceptions and Judgements, 1939-1944*, Chicago and London: Chicago University Press, 1968

Griffiths, Richard, *Art, Pornography and Human Value*, Nottingham: Grove Books, 1975

——*Censorship and the Arts*, Nottingham: Grove Books, 1976

Gunton, Colin, "Creation and Re-Creation: An Exploration of Some Themes in Aesthetics and Theology," *Modern Theology*, 2, 1, (1985), pp. 1-19

——*Enlightenment and Alienation: An Essay Towards a Trinitarian Theology*, Basingstoke: Marshall Morgan & Scott, 1985

——*The Actuality of Atonement*, Edinburgh: T & T Clark, 1989

——*Yesterday and Today: A Study of Continuities in Christology*, London: Darton, Longman and Todd, 1983

Hall, Douglas John, *Imaging God: Dominion as Stewardship*, Grand Rapids, Michigan: Eerdmans, 1986

Hanslick, Eduard, *The Beautiful in Music*, Indianapolis: Bobbs-Merrill Educational Publishing, 1957

Hardy, Daniel and David Ford, *Jubilate: Theology in Praise*, Darton, Longman and Todd, 1984

Harned, David Baily, *Theology and the Arts*, Philadelphia: Westminster Press, 1966

Harries, Karsteen, "The Many Uses of Metaphor," in Sheldon Sacks, ed., *On Metaphor*, Chicago: Chicago University Press, 1979, pp.

165-172

Hawthorne, Gerald F., *Word Bible Commentary: Philippians*, Waco, Texas: Word Books, 1983

Hazelton, Roger, *A Theological Approach to Art*, Nashville and New York: Abingdon Press, 1967

Hebblethwaite, Brian, *The Ocean of Truth*, Cambridge: Cambridge University Press, 1988

Hegel, G. W. F., *Aesthetics*, London: Oxford University Press, 1975, p. 31

Heidegger, Martin, "The Origin of the Work of Art," in *Poetry, Language, and Thought*, trans. A. Hofstadter, New York: Harper & Row, 1971

Héring, Jean, *The Epistle to the Hebrews*, London: Epworth Press, 1970

Heyer, George S., *Signs of our Times*, Edinburgh: Handsel Press, 1980

Hofstadter, Albert and Kuhns, Richard., *Philosophies of Art and Beauty*, Chicago and London: University of Chicago Press, 1964

Horst, F., "Face to Face. The Biblical Doctrine of the Image of God," *Interpretation*, 4 (1950), pp. 259-270

Hospers, John, *Meaning and Truth in the Arts*, Chapel Hill, North Carolina: University of North Carolina Press, 1970

Höver-Johag, I., "*ṭwb ṭwb yṭb*" , in *Theological Dictionary of the Old Testament*, V, ed. G. J. Botterweck and Helmer Ringgren, Grand Rapids, Michigan: Eerdmans, 1986, pp. 26-317

Hume, David, *A Treatise of Human Nature*, ed. Ernest Mossner, Harmondsworth: Penguin, 1969

——*Enquiries Concerning the Human Understanding and Concerning the Principles of Morals*, ed. L. A. Selby-Bigge, London: Oxford University Press, 1972

Hutcheson, Francis, *An Enquiry into the Original of Our Ideas of Beauty and Virtue*, London, 1726

Innis, Robert E., "Art, Symbol and Consciousness: A Polanyi Gloss on Susanne Langer and Nelson Goodman," in *Philosophical Quarterly*, 17 (1977), pp. 455-476

Jarvie, Ian, *Philosophy of the Film*, New York and London: Routledge & Kegan Paul, 1987

Jüngel, Eberhard, *God as the Mystery of the World*, trans. Darrell L. Guder, Edinburgh: T. & T. Clark, 1983

Kähler, Erich, *The Disintegration of Form in the Arts*, George Braziller, 1968

Kant, Immanuel, *Critique of Judgement*, trans. J. H. Bernard, 2nd ed., New York and London: Hafner, 1968

——*Critique of Pure Reason*, trans. N. Kemp Smith, Edinburgh, 1929

Kidner, Derek, *Genesis*, London: Tyndale, 1967

Kilby, Clyde, *Christianity and Aesthetics*, Downers Grove: IVP, 1961

Kittel, G., "*εικων*," *Theological Dictionary of the New Testament*, II, ed. Gerhard Kittel, Grand Rapids, Michigan: Eerdmans, 1973, pp.

Knox, Israel, *The Aesthetic Theories of Kant, Hegel and Schopenhauer*, London: Thames and Hudson, 1958

König, Adrio, *The Eclipse of Christ in Eschatology: Towards a Christ-Centred Approach,* Grand Rapids, Michigan: Eerdmans; London: Marshall, Morgan & Scott, 1989

Kostelanetz, Richard, *John Cage,* Harmondsworth: Penguin Books, 1974

Küng, Hans, *Art and the Question of Meaning,* London: SCM, 1980

Langer, Susanne, *Feeling and Form,* London: Routledge & Kegan Paul, 195

———*Philosophy in a New Key,* Cambridge, Massachusetts: Harvard University Press, 1957

Leivestad, Ragnar, *Christ the Conqueror,* London: SPCK, 1954

Lentricchia, Frank, *After the New Criticism,* Chicago: University of Chicago Press, 1980

Lewis, Alan E., *Theatre of the Gospel,* Edinburgh: Handsel Press, 1984

Lewis, C. S., *An Experiment in Criticism,* Cambridge: Cambridge University Press, 1961

———*Screwtape Proposes a Toast and Other Pieces,* London: Fontana, 1965

Locke, John, *An Enquiry into the Original of Our Ideas of Beauty and Virtue,* London, 1726

-:*Essay Concerning Human Understanding,* ed. A. C. Fraser, 2 Vols., Oxford, 1894

Lundin, Roger, "Our Hermeneutical Inheritance," in Roger Lundin, Anthony C. Thiselton, Clarence Walhout, eds., *The Responsibility of Hermeneutics,* Grand Rapids, Michigan: Eerdmans, 1985, pp. 1-29

Lynton, Norbert, *Concepts of Modern Art,* London: Penguin Books, 1974

MacGregor, Geddes, *Aesthetic Experience in Religion,* London: Macmillan, 1947

Macgregor, H. C., "Principalities and Powers: the Cosmic Background of Paul's Thought," *New Testament Studies,* I (1954-55), pp. 17-28

McIntyre, Alasdair, *After Virtue. A Study in Moral Theory,* London: Duckworth, 1981.

McKinney, Richard W. A., ed., *Creation, Christ and Culture,* Edinburgh: T. & T. Clark, 1976

MacLaughlin, Terence, *Music and Communication,* London: Faber and Faber, 1970

Macmurray, John, *The Self as Agent,* London: Faber and Faber, 1957

Macquarrie, John, *In Search of Humanity,* London: SCM, 1982

Malraux, André, *Voices of Silence,* trans. Stuart Gilbert, St. Albans: Paladin, 1974

Maritain, Jacques, *Creative Intuition in Art and Poetry,* Princeton: Princeton University Press, 1977

May, Stephen C. A., "The Communication of Truth in Story with Special Reference to C. S. Lewis," PhD Thesis, University of Aberdeen, 1985

Meyer, Leonard B., *Emotion and Meaning in Music,* London and Chicago: University of Chicago Press, 1956

Michel, O., *Der Brief an die Hebräer*, Kritisch-exegetischer Kommentar, Gottingen: Vandenhoeck & Ruprecht, 1975

Moltmann, Jürgen, "Creation and Redemption," in *Creation, Christ and Culture*, ed. Richard W. A. McKinney, Edinburgh: T. & T. Clark, 1976, pp. 119-134

Mothersill, Mary, *Beauty Restored*, Oxford: Clarendon Press, 1984

Moule, C. F. D., *The Epistles of Paul the Apostle to the Colossians and to Philemon*, Cambridge: Cambridge University Press, 1962

Mowvley, H., "The Concept and Content of 'Blessing' in the Old Testament," *The Bible Translator*, 16 (1965), pp. 74-80

Munsterberg, Hugo, *The Photoplay: A Psychological Study*, New York: D. Appleton, 1916

Murtonen, A., "The Use and Meaning of the words l'barek and b'rakah in the Old Testament," *Vetus Testamentum*, 9 (1959), pp. 74-80

Myers, J. M., *Grace and Torah*, Philadelphia: Fortress Press, 1975

Nathan, Walter L., *Art and the Message of the Church*, Philadelphia: Westminster Press, 1961

Nichols, Aidan, *The Art of God Incarnate: Theology and Image in the Christian Tradition*, London: Darton, Longman and Todd, 1980

Niebuhr, H. Richard, *Christ and Culture*, London: Faber and Faber, 1952

O'Brien, Peter T., *Word Bible Commentary: Colossians, Philemon*, Waco, Texas: Word Books, 1982

O'Connell, Robert J., *Art and the Christian Intelligence in St. Augustine*, Oxford: Blackwell, 1978

O'Connor, Flannery, *Mystery and Manners: Occasional Prose*, ed. S. and R. Fitzgerald, London: Faber and Faber, 1972

O'Donovan, Oliver, *Resurrection and Moral Order*, Leicester: IVP; Grand Rapids, Michigan: Eerdmans, 1986

Osborne, Harold, *Aesthetics and Art Theory*, London and Harlow: Longmans, Green and Co., 1968

——"Definition and Evaluation in Aesthetics," *Philosophical Quarterly*, 23 (1973), pp. 15-27

Osgood, C. E., "Cross-Cultural Generality of Visual-Verbal Synesthetic Tendencies," in *Semantic Differential Technique*, ed. J. G. Snider and C. E. Osgood, Chicago: Aldine, 1969, pp. 561-584

Palmer, Richard E., *Hermeneutics. Interpretation Theory in Schleiermacher, Dilthey, Heidegger, and Gadamer*, Evanston: Northwestern University Press, 1969

Pattison, G., "Søren Kierkegaard and Imagination," *Theology*, 87 (1984), pp. 6-12

Peacocke, Arthur, *Creation and the World of Science*, Oxford: Clarendon Press, 1979

——*Intimations of Reality*, Notre Dame: University of Notre Dame Press, 1984

Pirenne, M. H., *Optics, Painting and Photography*, Cambridge: Cambridge University Press, 1970

Polanyi, Michael and Prosch, Harry, *Meaning*, Chicago: University of Chicago Press, 1975

——*Personal Knowledge*, London: Routledge & Kegan Paul, 1973
——*The Tacit Dimension*, London: Routledge & Kegan Paul, 1967
——"What is a Painting?," *The American Scholar*, 39 (1969-70), pp. 655-669
Polkinghorne, John, *Science and Creation*, London: SPCK, 1988
Pollard, T. E., *Fullness of Humanity: Christ's Humanity and Ours*, Sheffield: Almond Press, 1982
Prigogine, I. and Stengers, I., *Order out of Chaos*, London: Heinemann, 1985
Quinton, Anthony, *The Nature of Things*, London: Routledge and Kegan Paul, 1973
Rabkin, Eric, *The Fantastic in Literature*, Princeton: Princeton University Press, 1976
Rasmussen, L., *Dietrich Bonhoeffer: Reality and Resistance*, Nashville: Abingdon Press, 1972
Read, Herbert, *The Meaning of Art*, London: Faber & Faber, 1968
Richards, I. A., *Science and Poetry*, London: Kegan Paul, Trench, Trubner & Co., 1926
——(with C. K. Ogden) *The Meaning of Meaning*, London: Kegan Paul, 1936
——*The Philosophy of Rhetoric*, Oxford: Oxford University Press, 1936
Ricoeur, Paul, *The Rule of Metaphor. Multidisciplinary Studies of the Creation of Meaning in Language*, trans. R. Czerny and others, Toronto and Buffalo: University of Toronto Press, 1977
Robinson, Edward, *The Language of Mystery*, London: SCM, 1987
Ryken, Leland, *Triumphs of the Imagination*, Downers Grove, Illinois: IVP, 1979
Sachs, Curt, *The Wellsprings of Music*, New York: Da Capo, 1977
Sanders, Jack T., *The New Testament Christological Hymns*, Cambridge: Cambridge University Press, 1971
Sayers, Dorothy L., *The Mind of the Maker*, London: Methuen, 1941
Sclafani, Richard J., "'Art', Wittgenstein, and Open-Textured Concepts," *Journal of Aesthetics and Art Criticism*, XXIX, 3 (1971), pp. 333-341
Scott, Drusilla, *Everyman Revived. The Common Sense of Michael Polanyi*, Lewes, Sussex: Book Guild, 1985
Scott, Geoffrey, *The Architecture of Humanism*, 2nd ed., Garden City, New York: Doubleday, 1954
Scruton, Roger, *Art and the Imagination*, London: Methuen, 1974
——*From Descartes to Wittgenstein: A Short History of Modern Philosophy*, New York: Harper and Row, 1982
——*The Aesthetic Understanding*, Manchester: Carcanet Press, 1983
Sheppard, Anne, *Aesthetics*, Oxford: Oxford University Press, 1987
Sherry, Patrick, "Creation and Re-creation: The Holy Spirit and the Ultimate Transformation of All Things," Unpublished paper delivered at the Society for the Study of Theology, 1990
Skelton, Robin, *Poetic Truth*, London: Heinemann, 1978
Smail, Tom, *Reflected Glory*, London: Hodder & Stoughton, 1975
——*The Giving Gift*, London, Sydney, Auckland, Toronto: Hodder & Stoughton, 1988

Smith, Peter, "Making Paintings," in Tim Dean and David Porter, eds., *Art in Question*, Basingstoke: Marshall Morgan and Scott, 1987, pp. 110-138

Soskice, Janet Martin, *Metaphor and Religious Language*, Oxford: Clarendon Press, 1985

Spence, Alan, "Inspiration and Incarnation: John Owen and the Coherence of Christology," *King's Theological Review*, XII (1989), pp. 52-55

Spingarn, J. E., ed., *Goethe's Literary Essays*, New York: Harcourt, Brace & Co., 1921

Stanford Reid, W. "A Reformed Approach to Christian Aesthetics," *Evangelical Quarterly*, 30 (1958/59), pp. 211-219

Steiner, George, *Real Presences*, London: Faber and Faber, 1989

Stolnitz, Jerome, *Aesthetics*, London and New York: Macmillan, 1965

——"'Beauty': Some Stages in the History of an Idea," *Journal of the History of Ideas*, 22, 2 (1961), pp. 185-204

——"On the Origins of 'Aesthetic Disinterestedness,'" *Journal of Aesthetics and Art Criticism*, 20 (1961), pp. 131-143

Stravinsky, Igor, *Poetics of Music in the Form of Six Lessons*, trans. Arthur Knodel and Ingolf Dahl, Cambridge, Massachusetts: Harvard University Press, 1947

Suh, Chul Won, *The Creator-Mediatorship of Jesus Christ*, Amsterdam: Rodopi, 1982

Tatarkiewicz, Wladyslaw, "The Great Theory of Beauty and Its Decline," *Journal of Aesthetics and Art Criticism*, 31 (1972), pp. 165-180

——"What is Art? The Problem of Definition Today," *British Journal of Aesthetics*, 11 (1971), pp. 134-153

Tate, Allen, *Reason in Madness*, New York: Putnams, 1941

Taylor, John V., *The Go-Between God*, London: SCM, 1972

Thiselton, Anthony C., "The Supposed Power of Words in the Biblical Writings," *Journal of Theological Studies*, 25 (1974), pp. 283-299

——*The Two Horizons: New Testament Hermeneutics and Philosophical Description with Special Reference to Heidegger, Bultmann, Gadamer and Wittgenstein*, Exeter: Paternoster Press, 1980

Torrance, James B., "The Vicarious Humanity of Christ," in *The Incarnation*, ed. Thomas F. Torrance, Edinburgh: Handsel Press, 1981, pp. 127-145

Torrance, Thomas F., *Divine and Contingent Order*, Oxford, New York, Toronto, Melbourne: Oxford University Press, 1981

——*Reality and Scientific Theology*, Edinburgh: Scottish Academic Press, 1985

——*The Doctrine of Grace in the Apostolic Fathers*, Edinburgh: Oliver & Boyd, 1948

——*The Ground and Grammar of Theology*, Belfast: Christian Journals, 1980

——ed., *The Incarnation*, Edinburgh: Handsel Press, 1981

——*Theological Science*, Oxford, London and New York: Oxford University Press, 1978

——*Theology in Reconciliation*, London: Geoffrey Chapman, 1975

——*Theology in Reconstruction*, London: SCM, 1965

Vanhoozer, Kevin J, "A Lamp in the Labyrinth: The Hermeneutics of 'Aesthetic' Theology," *Trinity Journal*, 8 (1987), pp. 25-56

Vanstone, W. H., *Love's Endeavour, Love's Expense*, London: Darton, Longman and Todd, 1977

Vitz, Paul, *Psychology as Religion: The Cult of Self-Worship*, Grand Rapids, Michigan: Eerdmans, 1977

von Balthasar, Hans Urs, *The Glory of the Lord. A Theological Aesthetics. I, Seeing the Form*, trans. E. Leiva-Merikakis, ed. Joseph Fessio and John Riches, Edinburgh: T. & T. Clark, 1982

von Rad, Gerhard, *Das erste Buch Mose*, Göttingen: Vandenhoeck & Ruprecht, 1964

Vriezen, T. C., *An Outline of Old Testament Theology*, Oxford: Blackwell, 1958

Warnock, Mary, *Imagination*, London and Boston: Faber and Faber, 1976

Westermann, Claus, *Blessing in the Bible and the Life of the Church*, Philadelphia: Fortress Press, 1968

——*Creation*, London: SPCK, 1974

——*Genesis 1-11*, trans. J. J. Scullon, SPCK: 1984

Wilson, Colin, *The Strength to Dream: Literature and the Imagination*, London: Abacus, 1976

Wilson, John, *One of the Richest Gifts*, Edinburgh: Handsel Press, 1981

Wingert, Paul S., *Primitive Art*, New York: Meridian Books, 1965

Wollheim, Richard, "Art and Illusion," *British Journal of Aesthetics*, III (1963), pp. 15-37

Wolterstorff, Nicholas, *Art in Action*, Grand Rapids, Michigan: Eerdmans, 1980

Worringer, Wilhelm, *Abstraction and Empathy*, trans. Michael Bullock, New York: International Universities Press, 1953

Wright, T. R., *Theology and Literature*, Oxford: Blackwell, 1988

Zizioulas, John, *Being as Communion*, Crestwood, New York: St Vladimir's Seminary Press, 1985

Zuckerkandl, Victor, *Man the Musician*, Princeton: Princeton University Press, 1973

——*Sound and Symbol*, London: Routledge & Kegan Paul, 1956

Index of Names

Index of Subjects

Lightning Source UK Ltd.
Milton Keynes UK
10 July 2010

156869UK00001B/25/P